OUTLAWED

A John Hope Franklin Center Book

The Cultures and Practice of Violence Series
SERIES EDITORS
Neil L. Whitehead, University of Wisconsin, Madison
Jo Ellen Fair, University of Wisconsin, Madison
Leigh Payne, University of Wisconsin, Madison

The study of violence has often focused on the political and economic conditions under which violence is generated, the suffering of victims, and the psychology of its interpersonal dynamics. Less familiar are the role of perpetrators, their motivations, and the social conditions under which they are able to operate. In the context of postcolonial state building and more latterly the collapse and implosion of society, community violence, state repression, and the phenomena of judicial inquiries in the aftermath of civil conflict, there is a need to better comprehend the role of those who actually do the work of violence—torturers, assassins, and terrorists—as much as the role of those who suffer its consequences.

When atrocity and murder take place, they feed the world of the iconic imagination that transcends reality and its rational articulation; but in doing so imagination can bring further violent realities into being. This series encourages authors who build on traditional disciplines and break out of their constraints and boundaries, incorporating media and performance studies and literary and cultural studies as much as anthropology, sociology, and history.

OUTLAWED

||||||||||| BETWEEN SECURITY AND RIGHTS IN A BOLIVIAN CITY ||||||||||||||||||

Daniel M. Goldstein

Duke University Press   Durham and London   2012

© 2012 Duke University Press
All rights reserved

Printed in the United States of America on acid-
free paper ♾

Designed by Heather Hensley

Typeset in Warnock Pro by Keystone Typesetting

Library of Congress Cataloging-in-Publication
Data appear on the last printed page of this book.

Frontispiece: Photo by the author

For Miguel

Contents

Acknowledgments

The writing of this book was made possible by the generous support of an ACLS Fellowship from the American Council of Learned Societies, 2010 11. During that time, my leave from my university responsibilities was supported by Rutgers University's Competitive Fellowship Leave policy, which allowed me to enjoy the full benefits of the ACLS award. The material contained herein is based on work supported by the National Science Foundation under Grant No. 0540702. Any opinions, findings, and conclusions or recommendations expressed in this material are those of the author and do not necessarily reflect the views of the National Science Foundation. Additional support was provided by a National Endowment for the Humanities Summer Stipend in 2010.

I am very appreciative of the intellectual, professional, and personal support I have received from my friends and colleagues in the Critical Interventions in Theory and Ethnography program in the Department of Anthropology at Rutgers University. The program has provided me with the intellectual space in which creative research, writing, and pedagogy can be practiced, and I am grateful for that. In particular, I thank my colleagues Angelique Haugerud, Dorothy Hodgson, David McDermott Hughes, Rocío Magaña, and Frances E. Mascia-Lees for their insightful feedback as I revised these chapters for publication. Ana Sverdlik and Natasha Bennett at Rutgers both assisted with data preparation and management. This work has also benefited from the critical readings of a number of colleagues in other departments and institutions, and through the conversations and interactions we have had about these ideas in conferences and other venues that they have organized. For their helpful contributions to this project, I thank Thomas Abercrombie, Robert Albro, Catherine Besteman, Jennifer Burrell, Andrew Canessa, Nicole Fabricant, Carol Greenhouse, Mark Goodale, Charles Hale, Susan Hirsch, Stuart Kirsch, Sian Lazar, Sally Engle Merry, Winifred Tate, Alejandro Velasco, and Leslie Vinjamuri. In addition, I am indebted to the anonymous reviewers for Duke University Press, who provided invaluable, constructive feedback on the first draft of this ethnography. I thank my friend Pamela Calla for her commitment to and help with the Bolivia international service learning program described in chapter 2, and Joanna Regulska and Stephen Reinert and his colleagues in the Rutgers Study Abroad office for their support of the program over the years. Thanks also to Valerie Millholland, Gisela Fosado, and the rest of their team at Duke University Press for their excellent work shepherding another book through to publication. And a special thank you to my cousin, Lisa Berg, for the use of her photos.

In Bolivia, I thank my colleagues in Acción Andina and in what I call the Center for Justice and Rights, both of which provided me with institutional homes while I conducted my research. In addition, the work on which this book is based could not have been completed without the collaboration of my Bolivian research team. For their help with research and with thinking through these various ideas, I wish to thank Rose Marie Achá, Eric Hinojosa, Ruth Ordoñez, Theo Roncken, and Ethel Saavedra. I extend my particular gratitude to my collaborator and compadre Guery Arteaga, who has participated in every phase of this project and to whom I am very grateful for his help and friendship. I thank Kathryn Ledebur of the Andean Information Network for being a constant source of reliable information, Lee Cridland of Volunteer Bolivia for help with the international service learning program, and Carlos and Anna Aliaga for their friendship.

A portion of chapter 1 of this book was first published in 2010 in the article "Toward a Critical Anthropology of Security," *Current Anthropology* 51 (4): 487–517; © 2010 by the University of Chicago Press. Another portion of this same chapter and a portion of chapter 6 appeared in 2007 in "Human Rights as Culprit, Human Rights as Victim: Rights and Security in the State of Exception," in *The Practice of Human Rights: Track-*

ing Law between the Global and the Local, edited by Mark Goodale and Sally Engle Merry, published by Cambridge University Press. I thank the publishers for permission to use this material in its present form. All translations from the Spanish cited in the text are my own, as is responsibility for any factual or analytical errors.

I am thankful to the people of Loma Pampa and the other barrios of Uspha Uspha for their willingness to collaborate on this research project and the other activities that spun off from it. In particular, I wish to express my thanks to don Miguel, doña Senobia, and their children, who from the outset opened their home and hearts to me and my family, and who have remained constant to this day. Without their support, friendship, and participation, this book could never have been written.

Finally, I extend my love and gratitude to my family, Claire, Ben, and Eli, who have endured my absences and accompanied me on my various explorations of Bolivia and anthropology. For their loving support, I am truly thankful.

1 | Security, Rights, and the Law in Evo's Bolivia

The law is like a snake: its bite is worse
for those who must go barefoot.
—LOCAL SAYING

On Sunday, January 25, 2009, Bolivians voted to approve a new constitution for the country. The Nueva Constitución Política del Estado (New Political Constitution of the State) was endorsed by 60 percent of the voting public, which President Evo Morales interpreted as a strong mandate for what had been his administration's signature objective since his election in December 2005. For Evo (as he is popularly known) and his supporters in the Movement toward Socialism (the Movimiento a Socialismo, or MAS), the new constitution represented the formal reversal of centuries of institutionalized oppression and discrimination against Bolivia's "original indigenous peasant" peoples, who compose the majority of the national population, and a significant step toward the goal of "refounding" the Bolivian "plurination" (Morales 2011).[1] For Evo's opponents, both in the Bolivian highlands and in the lowland *media luna* region,[2] the new constitution was another blow to their prestige and power in the nation, a frightening and unworkable tangle of articles that threatened to limit the size of individual landholdings, change the legal definition of property to allow for communal ownership of land, limit the autonomy of regional governments, and give the federal government more control over the nation's natural gas reserves.[3] Evo's political antagonists (including many observers in the United States) cited the constitution's allocation of increased power to the state as more evidence of the president's demagoguery; such critics frequently referred to the controversial president of Venezuela, Hugo Chávez, as an example of the extremes toward which Evo was tending.[4] Evo's supporters, viewing him as their ally and kinsman, pointed to the constitutional guarantee of rights for Bolivia's indigenous peoples as evidence of his progressive leadership and proof that, after centuries of discrimination and marginalization, there was now room for them in the national configuration.

Among its most important and controversial propositions, the new Bolivian constitution marked the formal recognition of *justicia comunitaria* (community justice) by the Bolivian state. According to the stipulations laid down in this document, "the nations and original indigenous peasant communities (las naciones y pueblos indígena originario campesinos) will exercise their jurisdictional functions through their authorities, and will apply their own principles, cultural values, norms and procedures" in implementing community justice (*Nueva Constitución Política del Estado* 2008, 45). Within their "indigenous jurisdictions," local authorities would have the right to resolve their own conflicts and disputes according to an indigenous legal tradition, which would apply to other members of those nations or communities.[5] Formal state law would exist parallel to this indigenous justice, but the constitution prescribed that the state had the obligation to "promote and reinforce" original indigenous peasant justice, and to make itself available to indigenous authorities should they desire the intervention of state judicial instruments (*Nueva Constitución Política del Estado* 2008, 45).

The formal recognition of community justice by the Bolivian state exemplified the profound changes that the country experienced following the election of Evo Morales in 2005 (he was reelected in 2009). For centuries indigenous peoples of Bolivia had been denied any sort of voice within national politics. Now they found in Evo an advocate in the Palacio Quemado (the Bolivian White House), a self-identifying *indigena* who actively promoted the agenda of expanding indigenous rights and representation in the country, while valorizing indigenous cultures and traditions and giving them formal legal recognition. With Morales in power, struggles that formerly took place in the nation's streets moved to its courts and legislature, as the law itself was transformed to reflect the ruling party's ideology and objectives. The community justice provisions in the new constitution represented an official acknowledgment of Bolivia as legally plural: the constitution put indigenous *usos y costumbres* (usages and customs) on an equal footing with national law and required the latter to recognize the legitimacy of the former, creating spaces within the national territory where state law might be discretionary and contested, rather than hegemonic. Even as the constitution co-opted indigenous tradition through recognition, this was still a remarkable move, running contrary to five hundred years of history in which indigenous Latin Americans had been subordinated within a national racial hierarchy, and their beliefs and customs denigrated within national society.

Despite its rather heroic implications, the promotion of community justice and, more generally, the valorization of original indigenous peasant peoples and customs within national law and national ideology was a project fraught with contradictions. As this book explores, even as rural traditions of community justice have been elevated to national prominence, vast numbers of indigenous peoples living on the margins of Bolivia's cities remain without any legal protections whatsoever. In these so-called *barrios marginales* (marginal neighborhoods), no system of law —neither state nor indigenous—operates to provide support or recourse to the residents, and few authorities—neither official nor traditional— exist to administer justice. In these marginal urban spaces (particularly in Cochabamba, Bolivia's fourth largest city), vigilante or "self-help" practices of apprehending and punishing suspected criminals have emerged as a frequent response to crime, as some barrio residents take the law into their own hands to administer a locally understood form of collective "justice." The indigenous residents of the barrios are, in various ways, outlawed—they live outside the protections of state law, yet they are multiply subjected to its constraints; they must do without the law's benefits, but they are criminalized as illegal occupants of urban space and perpetrators of mob justice. The experience and consequences of this precarious position—of being outlawed—is a principal theme of this ethnography.

The MAS-led effort to refound Bolivia as a nation that includes (one might even say that it prioritizes) indigenous peoples and their traditional languages and customs was a radical political project, representing a sharp break with the past (perhaps most especially with the recent neoliberal past) and defining a new era in Latin American politics and social life. And at the time of its drafting, the new Bolivian constitution, with its formal recognition of indigenous rights and practices, may have been the most radical document of its kind in the world (Goodale 2009). In terms of its vision and governing philosophy, the MAS project was undoubtedly a step forward for Bolivians of indigenous heritage, the realization of a long-held ambition of moving from the margins to the center of Bolivian national politics. The rise to power of Evo Morales marked the culmination of decades of political work by those representing the indigenous movements in Bolivia, and the rewriting of the constitution signaled the remarkable overhaul of the Bolivian state and the laws governing the Bolivian nation (Pearce 2011; Sivak 2010; Webber 2011).

However, despite the many transformations in Bolivian law, state, and society, the important processes that have the most impact on the daily lives of indigenous Bolivians unfold at the most local of levels, and these processes are in many ways disconnected from the ideological and legislative work performed at the level of the state. In some senses, despite the MAS government's rhetorical and political efforts to include indigenous people in the fabric of the Bolivian nation, many of those people have continued to enjoy more or less the same basic relationship to the MAS state as they did with its earlier incarnations. Marginal urban areas in particular—where the majority of Bolivia's indigenous people now live (Instituto Nacional de Estadísticas de Bolivia 2001, 2003)—are marked by a continuous experience of poverty and neglect, characteristic of Bolivia's urban indigenous communities since at least the middle of the twentieth century. As subsequent chapters of this ethnography explore, urban indigenous people fit poorly in the legislative agenda of the MAS government and its conceptions of what constitutes indigeneity, leaving a considerable sector of the indigenous population to experience an ongoing exclusion from the protections and benefits of the state.

For urban indigenous people themselves, their condition of quotidian poverty, vulnerability to violence and criminal predation, and lack of access to the most basic forms of public services and infrastructure is encapsulated in a single concept: insecurity. To be insecure is to occupy a habitus of fear and uncertainty that is at once social, psychological, and material. Living in one of the poorest cities on the planet (M. Davis 2006),[6] the residents of Cochabamba's marginal barrios feel insecure: insecurity colors their entire worldview, the way they relate to their neighbors, residents of nearby communities, and strangers in their midst; it shapes their relationships with entities as distant as state and municipal authorities, and as close as their spouses and children. To be insecure is to lack the power to make effective change in your own life, to protect those small investments you have made in your home and livelihood, and to defend your family from crime. Insecurity physically shapes your home; it structures your movements through space and conditions your relationship to personal property. Insecurity means there is no reliable police force in your neighborhood to whom you can turn in times of crisis—it means instead that you call 911 over and over again, and if anyone answers they offer promises but no actual help. Insecurity is having to leave your children alone and untended while you go to work, never knowing if a robber or a rapist might visit while you are away. It is about vulnerability, especially to the work of petty thieves, embodied in the spectral figure of the *ratero*—a quasimythical being who haunts the margins of the city, preying on the unwary and posing an unending challenge to local peace and stability. Insecurity is fundamentally about disorder: It is a sense that the world is unpredictable, out of control, and inherently dangerous, and that within this chaos the individual must struggle desperately just to survive. It is about uncertainty, the unknowable, what Ellen Moodie (2010, 170) has called "not-knowing," an inability to know how to manage risk, which emanates from spectral sources that seem to transcend the local, the recognizable, the real (see also Taylor 1997). It is in some ways part of what Michael Taussig identifies as a culture of terror, "based on and nourished by silence and myth in which the fanatical stress on the mysterious side of the mysterious flourishes by means of rumor and fantasy woven in a dense web of magical realism" (1984, 469). This is the lived experience of insecurity for the marginalized urban poor in Cochabamba—as it is in many other cities throughout Bolivia and elsewhere in Latin America—and it is a condition that remains unchanged despite the many political reforms that Bolivia has experienced in the administrations of Evo Morales.

In a place of insecurity, a variety of personal dispositions and social phenomena can arise. The insecure place is dangerous, both for those who live there and those who visit. The insecure place is highly unstable, characterized more by fragmentation and unpredictability than by order and routine. People living insecure lives cannot rely on what generations of social scientists have called traditions or norms or cultural patterns, much less on state laws or government institutions, to regulate their lives and behavior. In the space of insecurity, people have to continually reinvent themselves and their behaviors, calling on what they know or think they know about the world in order to act purposively and meaningfully in it. In this way, they hope to establish the very sense of order and pattern that their worlds otherwise lack, a sense of control over their environments, their livelihoods, and their lives. For this reason, the marginal barrios—like other marginal zones (Das and Poole 2004)—are spaces of tremendous creativity, where people must assemble modes of living and making do outside the guarantees of the democratic state and its rule of law.

Despite this disorder, however, the insecure space of the marginal barrio is not devoid of law; it is not truly outside the reach of the state, though it may feel that way to those who live there. Indeed, as the chapters of this ethnography explore, the law operates with power in the marginal barrio, as the state attempts to make legible and minimally control the outlawed settlements on its urban fringes.[7] This observation runs counter to the claims of many barrio residents, who describe the state as absent and their relation to it as one of abandonment, and to the critiques of many social scientists, who similarly regard the neoliberal state as having been negligent and abandoned its responsibility to its citizens. But although there is law in the marginal barrio, the law does not protect against insecurity: it does not give residents a sense that they are protected from the work of criminals, or that they have somewhere to turn if they are the victims of a crime. The law operates instead to erect obstacles, sometimes to the very security that people so desperately crave; it strains to impose its own conception of order, which may not conform well to the kinds of social order that barrio residents desire. The law excludes people by failing to attend to their needs while including them in select regulatory regimes of its own devising—a double outlawing that leaves people both outside the law and problematically within it, but in neither sense secure. Contrary to expectations in the global north, the distinctions between legal and illegal, just and unjust, can be blurry in the marginal barrio, and matters of class, race, gender, and social position influence its operation. "The law is like a snake," poor people sometimes remark. "Its bite is worse for those who must go barefoot."

Take, for example, the question of land legalization. As I discuss in chapter 3, establishing legal title to land is a lengthy bureaucratic process requiring barrio residents to jump through an inordinate number of hoops in order to receive state recognition of their land claims. For poor people on the urban margins—who have little time, fewer resources, and scant knowledge of the arcane workings of the legal system—the process is onerous, confusing, and often fruitless because the irregular manner in which they originally purchased their land renders these transactions un-legalizable from the outset. Barrio residents in such circumstances are thus unlawful squatters in the eyes of the state. From their perspective, though, the state and its laws failed to protect them from the unscrupulous tactics of the land speculators who originally sold them their lots, and the laws of land titling impose further damage by making this circumstance painful and unresolvable, consigning them to a perpetual limbo in which legalization and the rights of citizenship that it conveys remain forever out of reach. The law, then, becomes not a force for ordering things and making them knowable and predictable (as the foundational theories of legal realism seem to suggest; see, for example, Llewellyn and Hoebel 1941), but something that in local perspective is barely distinguishable from illegality. A similar point can be made about criminal law and the prosecution of criminal cases. In the absence of a reliable police or judicial presence in their communities (see chapters 3 and 4), barrio residents are again left outside the law, which gives them no avenue to the resolution of conflicts. Indeed, the law perversely seems to require evidence to sustain a conviction, evidence that the absent and corrupt police are obviously incapable of producing—which leaves criminals free to continue their practices and crime victims unable to claim restitution. In the way it apparently favors criminals over crime victims, the law (along with transnational notions of human rights; see chapter 6) again presents itself as a force of illegality and chaos, rather than of peaceful and equitable ordering.

In such a context, in which fear and a sense of vulnerability characterize daily life and the law is seen as either absent or as an obstacle to one's well-being, people seek other remedies to cope with the generalized insecurity they regularly experience (Salcedo Fidalgo 1998). These include a range of behaviors that I describe in chapter 4. But the most dramatic response to insecurity, the one that has most captured national and international attention and sparked public ire, is the vigilante lynching of rateros and other criminal suspects.[8] In some cases, when a ratero has been apprehended, local people have turned to violence in response, characterizing this violence as an effort to create *seguridad* (security or safety) for themselves and their families. Ironically, even as they violate the due process rights of their victims and demand harsher laws (including the death penalty) to punish the accused, some lynching participants assert their own right to security as the paramount right that trumps all others, and that justifies the use of violence to attain it. So even as transnational conceptions of rights provided the fuel that brought Evo Morales and the indigenous social movements to power in Bolivia, many people in the marginal neighborhoods regard human rights as a foreign imposition, an alien concept that privileges the perpetrators of crime against its victims and so contributes to the greater insecurity of the community (see chapter 6). What's more, local people often rhetorically appeal to community justice, using the new constitution's legitimizing imprimatur to justify their own violence as a traditional mechanism for creating citizen security, while subordinating transnational concepts of individual rights to a local rendering of the concepts of the indigenous collective (see chapter 5).

In this discussion, however, it is critical to note the tremendous diversity that exists within the phenomenon known as *linchamiento* (lynching). In my earlier writing about violence in the barrios of Cochabamba (Goldstein 2003, 2004, 2005a; Goldstein and Castro 2006), I explored the lynching as an instrument of public communication, a spectacular means by which the marginalized and silenced could claim a voice and express their discontent with state neglect. In this book, I go beyond the public and performative dimensions of this process to examine lynching ethnographically, exploring the motives, behaviors, and responses of individual barrio women and men to the use of violence as a means of crime control in their communities. This discussion reveals lynching to be a far less unitary practice than the notion of mob justice would suggest, characterized instead by a profound ambiguity and heterogeneity of action and opinion. Lynching, like so much else in the context of insecurity, reflects the uncertainty with which local people go about their daily business, prompting a reconsideration of the mob and the ways in which collective violence are practiced and experienced. From this discussion, lynching emerges as one strategy among many that barrio residents and their leaders adopt as they try to manage the insecurity that they confront every day. The consideration of lynching in this book also differs from my earlier work because the broader political context in which it occurs is different. With the passage of the new constitution and the recognition of the validity of indigenous justice in Bolivia, lynchings now occur in a context in which the discourse of community justice has become a powerful frame for understanding local violence and extralegal forms of justice making. As I demonstrate in chapter 5, the national attention given to community justice in Bolivia has shifted the political terrain on which lynchings are enacted, providing an entirely new dimension to how these acts of violence are interpreted both by external observers and local actors. The question of how these acts violate the human rights of their victims is another emerging context for the consideration of lynching (see chapter 6), a point that further distinguishes this consideration of lynching violence from earlier treatments.

This book, then, examines the lived experience of insecurity for Cochabamba's urban indigenous poor, set within the context of broader national and global concerns with security and human rights. It asks: Can we speak meaningfully of a right to security, as a property that adheres to all individuals regardless of gender, race, or economic position and that the state is obligated to protect and defend? Or, as so often seems to be the case in a post-9/11 world, are security and rights inherently antagonistic, with an expansion of the one necessarily entailing a limitation of the other? This debate is being waged in the barrios of Cochabamba, as this ethnography describes. In the chapters that follow, I explore the conjunction of two powerful transnational discourses—security and human rights—examining their deployments and transformations in daily social practice to reveal the ways in which security ultimately can work to defeat rights as local actors operate within and against national and transnational formations of politics and law. Despite the protracted Global War on Terror and the primacy of security concerns in contemporary life worldwide, few ethnographies have treated the subject as a lived dimension of daily experience for the indigenous poor. This book calls attention to the ways in which security plays out on the ground, deployed not only by states but by citizens and community groups as well. It demonstrates the complex interconnections that exist between security and other global or local phenomena that are frequently the objects of anthropological concern—especially the idea of rights—and points to the cultural and legal contradictions emerging within what some have optimistically called the post-neoliberal societies of Latin America.[9] By focusing on the quotidian nature of insecurity in the barrios of Cochabamba, *Outlawed* shifts the focus of what security and security making are often understood to entail—principally, the fight against terrorism by the United States and other governments worldwide—to consider the daily preoccupations and practices that constitute the lived reality of insecurity for the marginal urban poor.

Finally, *Outlawed* embraces the highly uncertain dimensions of life in outlawed communities. As the discussion above foreshadows, and as many of the subsequent ethnographic chapters demonstrate, life on the margins of the law—where the disorder of daily life competes with the often painful ordering imposed by what I identify in chapter 3 as the "phantom state"—can feel destabilizing. People live with doubt, fearful for their safety and mistrustful of official institutions and promises of support, while lacking their own established mechanisms for resolving the problems they confront. In their search for solutions, they encounter further confusion and ambivalence, wrestling with ethical conflicts and other, more pragmatic considerations about the effectiveness of their responses to insecurity. This uncertainty colors ordinary experience and defies easy analysis. Understanding it requires an approach that is open to multiple and contingent possibilities, including the simultaneous expression of contradictory understandings and practices. Approaching uncertainty in this way can itself lead to murky interpretations that lack the definitive clarity that social science often seems to demand. It suggests instead the emergence of what might be called an uncertain anthropology, which by definition aspires to capture the empirical uncertainty of life amid insecurity. The theme of uncertainty appears throughout the chapters of this ethnography, and I explore the possibilities of an uncertain anthropology in more detail in the book's concluding chapter.

Anthropology, Security, and the State

What do we mean when we talk about "security"? Scholars of international relations typically locate security and the ability to create it within the state, and certainly any understanding of security must consider both the role of the state as a security-making entity and the importance of security for legitimizing and maintaining the state. For some scholars (whom Buzan, Wæver, and Wilde [1998] call the "traditionalists"), security pertains solely to matters of military affairs, with defense of the state being the single most important factor in defining a particular crisis or threat as security-related (see, for example, Chipman 1992). The slippage away from such a seemingly straightforward definition begins almost immediately, however, as we consider what might in fact constitute such a threat. Does a challenge to national identity—for example, posed by the increased presence of minority or immigrant populations—constitute a threat to national security? Does the destabilization of a national economy represent a security crisis? Opposing the traditionalists are the so-called wideners, those scholars who view threats emerging in a variety of arenas as worthy of the "security" designation, rejecting the traditionalists' insistence on a military facet or threat of international nuclear war as the sole criterion for such labeling (for example, Wæver, Buzan, Kelstrup, and Lemaitre 1993). This latter perspective understands security as a response to anything that can be persuasively identified as posing a threat to the very existence of the state or society.[10]

For classical political philosophers like Hobbes (1985 [1651]), Montesquieu (see Robin 2004), Weber (1946), and Marx (1967),[11] fear was a powerful motivation for the formation of states, be they autocratic or liberal democratic, and the purported ability to protect citizens against threats to their peace and well-being was central to any state's raison d'être (Goldstein 2010b).[12] In the twentieth century, individual state security was often envisioned as being best achieved through strategies of collective security, the joining together of nations into coalitions of mutual support and defense like the League of Nations and the United Nations. Collective security rested on the belief that by banding together, nations could provide better security for all against an aggressor because "regulated, institutionalized balancing predicated on the notion of all against one provides more stability than unregulated, self-help balancing predicated on the notion of each for his own" (Kupchan and Kupchan 1995, 52). Such coalitions were thought to be particularly beneficial to smaller nations, which would have more difficulty defending themselves individually against a hostile foe. By the same token, however, smaller nations might be drawn into conflicts in which they had little stake by virtue of their membership in collective security pacts, as in the aftermath of 9/11 and the invasion of Iraq by the "coalition of the willing" (Anderson, Bennis, and Cavanagh 2003). This logic was frequently invoked during the Cold War, when the collective defense organizations of NATO and the Warsaw Pact faced off, occasionally coming to the brink of global war in the effort to secure the perceived interests of the superpowers. In the West, the fear of communism and nuclear annihilation produced a new geopolitical vision and political strategy that not only "colonized everyday life with the minute-to-minute possibility of nuclear war" but also provided the US government "with a new means of engaging and disciplining citizens in everyday life" (Masco 2008, 361). In terms of economics, the creation of global financial institutions like the World

Bank and the International Monetary Fund was motivated in part by a logic of collective economic security, a doctrine of liberal capitalism that assumed the integration of small national economies into global markets would provide greater economic stability and development for everyone, while guaranteeing the public loans and private capital of foreign and transnational investors (Cable 1995; Nye 1974).

But collective security could not be achieved without national security, which after World War II became a paramount concern of many nation-states, again framed within the logic of a clash between communism and freedom. Treating security as identical to national security became an equation with great appeal to a variety of state regimes. In Latin America, authoritarian governments of the 1960s through 1980s based their authority on what was known as the national security doctrine, which identified the military as the institution charged with defending democracy and, indeed, Western civilization against the incursions of world communism (Leal Buitrago 2003). An extension of the broader Cold War emanating from the Western and Soviet blocs, the national security doctrine in the Latin American context provided a powerful exception to the protection of human and civil rights, as the war against internal enemies—communist subversives—had to be fought at any and all costs (Mares 2008). Under this doctrine, the military assumed a domestic policing function, and special units responsible for maintaining public order were created to identify and deal with perceived threats to society and state, however they saw fit. Vital US political and economic support for these regimes was often justified by their demonstrated ability to hold off the communist threat throughout the Americas. The equation of security with social order was quite clearly established in the national security doctrine, a theme that persisted in later versions of state security in Latin America.

As the Cold War came to an end, dictatorships turned into democracies—enjoying support from the United States both before and after the transition (Grandin 2006)—and the state-led, import-substitution developmental model of the 1960s and 1970s was replaced by the free-trade, market-driven model of the 1980s and 1990s. The political, economic, and social consequences of this neoliberal model for the societies of Latin America and elsewhere have been amply documented, including greater income inequality and expanding poverty, reduced state and social services, rising unemployment, and mounting crime and social violence (see Gledhill 2004; Schwegler 2008). Even so, under neoliberalism the official sense of what security might entail remained limited to the political, particularly as the communist enemy of the Cold War morphed into the terrorist enemy of the twenty-first-century Global War on Terror. As economies weakened and the daily lives of people in a range of societies became more precarious, broader conceptions of security that would include such things as employment, health care, and education—what the United Nations has defined as "human security" (United Nations Development Programme 1994)—were slow to emerge, so that security continued to be framed largely as safety from external attack or internal destabilization, and freedom from fear of terrorism or violence. The traditionalist understanding of security seemed to prevail in neoliberal society, overcoming any attempt to widen security's domain.

The emergence of what we might call the security state is the logical counterpoint to neoliberalism's privatization of civil society, its attempt to devolve onto civil institutions, local communities, and individuals the tasks of governance that had once been considered the responsibility of the welfare state. In its neoliberal mode, the state relies on individualizing techniques of governmentality to free itself from the various responsibilities of maintaining its subjects, conferring on those subjects themselves the daily obligations of self-maintenance and self-regulation (Foucault 1991; Inda 2005; Merry 2001). Meanwhile, the state claims for itself the exclusive right and responsibility to define and impose security (maintaining, of course, the prerogative to subcontract that responsibility—for example, to private security firms and proxy armies; see Nordstrom 2004). The state is authorized to assess risk, maintain secrecy, and control dissent, all as part of its reframing of the "care and moral duty" of the state to its citizens, the provision of security as social welfare (Hay and Andrejevic 2006, 339; see also Bratich 2006; on the risk society, see Beck 1992; Giddens 1990, 1999). In Antonio Gramsci's terms, the liberal state supposedly becomes a "night-watchman," "a coercive organization which will safeguard the development of the continually proliferating elements of the regulated society, and which will therefore progressively reduce its own authoritarian and forcible interventions" (1971, 263). Thus even as it warns of imminent security threats, the state seeks to reduce its own role in security provision through expanding individual "responsibilization" (Goldstein 2005a, 391). As James Hay and Mark Andrejevic note about the George W. Bush administration's National Strategy for Homeland

Security, the state assumes for itself a "supportive" role in administering security, while "making each of us 'accountable' for and accountants of our own security, calculating the many forms of risk and exposure" to which we find ourselves regularly subjected (2006, 337). A corollary to this is the apparent need to limit basic rights, which, according to the Bush administration's strategy, make a democratic society "inherently vulnerable" to attack by "the invisible enemies, lurking in the shadows" (Hay and Andrejevic 2006, 337). The proper disposition of the neoliberal subject in this security society, inculcated by the state's immanent securitization techniques, is one of perpetual alertness and individual preparedness, being continually on one's guard against the emergence of any and all possible threats (Elmer and Opel 2006). Suspicion is a key component of this neoliberal disposition, with each individual encouraged to be prudent and responsible and to assume a habitually anxious, cautious engagement with anyone or anything deemed unfamiliar and potentially threatening (O'Malley 1996).

From the perspective of the scholars known as the Copenhagen School of security studies (see, e.g., Buzan, Wæver, and Wilde 1998), security is best understood not as a matter of assessing real dangers to determine their threat level—no objective measure exists whereby such a determination might be made (color-coded threat-warning indicators notwithstanding). Rather, the Copenhagen scholars emphasize securitization, a process of constructing a collective understanding of something as a particular kind of danger, a threat to the very existence of the state, the society, or "our way of life." From this perspective, security is fundamentally social and in a sense performative: in terms of speech act theory (Austin 1962), the ability to make a security declaration—to utter the word "security" in reference to a particular threat or crisis—is an indication of the political power of the speaker, demonstrated by his or her ability to declare something a security threat and to have that declaration publicly recognized as legitimate. Security is thus inherently intersubjective and socially constructed: successful securitization depends on an audience's willingness to accept the legitimacy of the security speech act, based on the perceived existential threat that the object of securitization poses (see, for example, anthropological studies of migration and the securitization of national spaces in an age of globalization, including Bigo 2002; Coutin 2000, 2007; De Genova 2002; De Genova and Peutz 2010; Menjívar 2006; Walters 2002, 2004). It is also highly self-referential: security is that which authorized actors are able to securitize, not what might actually exist as a real social threat.

As scholars of "moral panics" (Cohen 2002; S. Hall et al. 1978) earlier perceived, the labeling of such threats can incite public demand for a force—the state—capable of controlling or policing the crisis that securitization itself has called into being. In a democratic context, a security matter is inextricably linked to the state's ability to declare a state of exception, a condition under which ordinary rules do not apply and individual rights can be suspended in the best interests of the state (Agamben 2005). The power of the security speech act is that it authorizes the speaker to take extraordinary action in response to a threat that is deemed so potentially damaging as to preempt all other threats and concerns. Security in itself, then, supersedes politics: by naming something a security matter, the speaker claims the authority to employ extraordinary measures, to set aside the customary rules of the game because a security threat by its very nature cannot be dealt with through customary means. A security threat is that which "legitimizes the breaking of rules" (Buzan, Wæver, and Wilde 1998, 25), which in general means normative law and the guarantee of rights that law is meant to entail. Security, in other words, is about survival, and matters of law or rights cannot be allowed to interfere in ensuring the survival of a society or the state that leads it.

All of the preceding analyses of security share an emphasis on the state as the singular locus of and agent for producing security.[13] But as anthropologists should be quick to recognize, an entirely state-focused, top-down approach to security—even one that recognizes its important constructivist dimensions, played out in official pronouncements and political discourses—marginalizes subordinated groups and alternative voices, including indigenous people, women, and the poor (Hansen 2000). It is here that what I have elsewhere (Goldstein 2010b) called a critical anthropology of security can make important contributions, both to a broader understanding of what security entails and to its theorization. A critical anthropology of security can explore the multiple ways in which security is configured and deployed, not only by states and authorized speakers but by communities, groups, and individuals in their engagements with other local actors and with arms of the state itself.[14] As in other areas of political anthropology (for example, Arias and Goldstein 2010), a perspective on security as made and understood by actors and groups outside of the state and its official institutions helps to broaden our perspective on what security means, how it is produced, what it includes, and what it excludes in the ordinary and exceptional struggles of daily life. Such a perspective brings to light the manifold ways in which global discourses are adopted, manipulated, transformed, and deployed in quotidian interactions and events, revealing the full range of security as lived social experience in a variety of contexts.

Security and Neoliberalism in Latin America

By the time of the terrorist attacks in the United States on September 11, 2001, the foreseeable impacts of the neoliberal model were already becoming realized, especially in the developing world, where this model did not emerge organically but was imported by national governments or imposed by forces from without.[15] In these societies, the individualizing and responsibilizing strategies of neoliberal governmentality brought immense difficulties for citizens and states alike. Having dismantled the welfare state (or, as in Bolivia, the patronage state) while relaxing many of the barriers to the movement and operations of transnational capital, many national governments had to contend with rising public doubts about their defense of national sovereignty and the rights and security of national citizens in a context of political and economic globalization. In Latin America, for example, where the prescriptions of the so-called Washington Consensus—including deregulation of transnational industries, the removal of tariffs and other barriers to trade, and the reduction of government involvement in the national economy and social service provision—failed to deliver on their promises of trickle-down economic improvement, organized social movements launched powerful challenges to the state and its claims to be working to provide security to all. Even as more and more nation-states in Latin America explicitly renounce the neoliberal paradigm, the impacts of this approach's ascendancy over several decades continue to be felt within Latin American society, with consequences for national prosperity and citizens' civil and human rights.

Who or what is the proper object of security in a neoliberal context is a matter of some debate, as recent conflicts in Latin America have revealed. Under the neoliberal regimes of the last few decades in Latin America, as elsewhere around the world, nation-states have increasingly been required (by the burden of debt and the repayment schedules imposed by multinational lenders like the IMF) to adopt the role of security providers for global capital, which often forces these states to act in ways that undermine the security (economic, physical, and otherwise) of their own citizens (Ferguson 2006). Nations that cannot guarantee security to transnational corporations risk an investment downturn, as foreign companies and financiers may refuse to do business there, depriving those states' governments of the capital they require to keep themselves in power and service their national debt. By "security" here I mean both a guarantee of a stable economic environment for foreign investors, with minimal state intervention in business or finance (for example, taxes or laws that attempt to regulate industrial activity and so impose unacceptable costs on investors), and a guarantee of political stability, with popular challenges to transnational corporations being limited and suppressed by the state. States find themselves caught between the dictates of various foreign bosses and the demands of national citizens, who expect that in a democratic context the duly elected authorities will work to serve the interests of the electorate. Democratically elected governments that are unable to reconcile the security demands of transnational corporations and lenders with citizens' demands for rights face a crisis of legitimacy, as citizens question the loyalties and priorities of national law and policymakers. Such contradictions are particularly fraught when played out across the "neoliberal securityscapes" (Zilberg 2011, 6) that characterize the modern world, unequal distributions of military force and technology that are simultaneously keyed to other forms of power and inequality within and among nation-states from north to south (see Gusterson 2004).

Bolivia experienced such a crisis in 2000, when what came to be known as the Water War erupted in Cochabamba. In 1999, Bolivian officials had granted the lease to Cochabamba's water supply to a subsidiary of the multinational Bechtel corporation, responding to an offer from the World Bank of a $14,000,000 loan to expand service if the city's water system were privatized (Schultz 2000). As a result, monthly water bills for poor urban residents increased by as much as 400 percent, sparking local anger that quickly mobilized in repudiation of the Bechtel deal and a demand for the return of public water management (Morales 2010). The Water War marked the emergence of a discourse of natural resources as collective rights, recognized as part of Bolivia's national patrimony; it also marked a broader claim to indigenous heritage by urban popular sectors, as a means of establishing citizenship claims and the right to participation in democratic politics (Albro 2005). This series of events was repeated in 2003, as internal disagreement over how to manage the sale and export of natural gas resources to foreign markets led to increasingly violent clashes between indigenous protestors and national security forces. Fearing that gas revenues would be misappropriated by a government that did not appear to have their best interests at heart, many Bolivians refused to accept President Gonzalo ("Goni") Sanchez de Lozada's hydrocarbon policy, paralyzing trade in the nation's most viable export commodity and imperiling Goni's neoliberal economic agenda for debt reduction and national economic security. These events culminated in the Gas War of October 2003, as Goni attempted to forcibly impose his export plan, angering the popular opposition and leading to public violence in which national police and military forces killed sixty-seven protestors and injured hundreds more in the highland city of El Alto. Goni was forced to resign and flee the country, bringing to an end a series of regimes in what had till then been one of South America's staunchest bastions of neoliberalism. The Water War and the Gas War, understood as conflicts between rights for indigenous people and the stability and security of the state, called into question who was actually being represented under what people locally identified as neoliberal democracy (Albro 2005, 2006a), and led ultimately to the election of Evo Morales as Bolivia's first indigenous president.[16]

These events challenge the meaning of security in neoliberal democracies, which proclaim a commitment to security for all when in fact they prioritize the security of transnational capital, which ultimately underwrites the state itself. In Ecuador, for example, Suzana Sawyer (2004) has detailed the responses of indigenous Amazonians to the environmental destruction engendered by transnational oil corporations' exploratory and extractive industries. These industrial activities threaten the health and livelihoods of tropical communities, whose members are exposed to pollution and disease and whose local economies are crippled as oil extraction poisons the soil, water, fish, and game on which they rely for subsistence. As these groups mobilize to demand government intervention in this crisis, they reveal the extent to which the national state has fully aligned itself with the interests of transnational capital against those of its citizens, calling into question its legitimizing security function (part of what Sawyer [2004, 15] calls the "crisis of representation" in neoliberal democracy). As Sawyer's work illustrates, a key irony of neoliberalism lies in the contradiction between its rhetoric, which depicts the state as a minor player in the open field of free capitalist activity, and its reality, in which the state operates as manager, actuary, and cop—maintaining an open field for transnational business by creating laws, enforcing policy reforms, and controlling dissent among citizens whose own economic interests run counter to those of industry, and whose social rights impose unwanted and expensive restrictions on transnational commerce (see also Ong 2006). The personal security of indigenous Amazonians is secondary to the financial security of the global corporations at work in the region, a fact clearly revealed by the Ecuadorian state's legal maneuvering as it nullified laws that protected citizens' rights and drafted new codes for industry that protected foreign interests. In this and in the Bolivian case, the state resists popular groups' efforts to broaden the meaning of security beyond threats to the state itself and their mobilization of the transnational discourse of human rights to challenge the neoliberal democratic state's abandonment of its obligations to its citizens. Indeed, one of the first efforts in Bolivia to codify "security" came in the form of the Law of Citizen Security, passed by the neoliberal Sanchez de Lozada administration in August 2003. Articles 213 and 214 of this law banned the use of roadblocks and other forms of popular protest that would obstruct the flow of traffic on the nation's roads, declaring such forms of political action to be detrimental to the "security" of the national population. As in the era of the dictatorships, "security" here meant security of the state, maintaining the political status quo through whatever means might be necessary.

Meanwhile, security means something quite different to most citizens of Latin American nations, especially to the urban poor. Measures of criminality have shown a steady increase in that behavior throughout Latin America since the 1980s, intensifying in the 2000s (Ungar 2011). Despite the inadequacy of data from most countries (police often fail to record accurate crime statistics, and underreporting due to mistrust of the police is rampant), by all existing measures, crimes against property and persons are high across the region (Ungar 2003), with the incidence of violent crime worsening since the 1990s (Carranza 2004). Latin America has a homicide rate that is virtually off the charts: the global average for homicides is 5 per 100,000 people, with a rate of over 10 considered to be dangerously high, but the average for middle- to low-income countries in Latin America is 27.5, the highest regional average in the world (Moser,

Winton, and Moser 2005; World Health Organization 2002). Within Latin America, most violent crimes are committed in large cities, and the Andean region reports the highest incidence of violent crimes in both rural and urban areas (Arriagada 2001). Furthermore, although in the last few years crime rates have fallen somewhat in the region's wealthier countries, they have risen in the poorer countries, a function of income disparity that many observers attribute to the inequities that have intensified under globalization (Carranza 2004). It is these inequities, more than absolute poverty, that social scientists have correlated most closely with violence, suggesting that violence is most likely to be found in contexts of extreme inequality and social exclusion. Fear of crime, meanwhile, has mounted exponentially and without necessarily being correlated with crime statistics, spurred on by daily conversations, rumors, and gossip (Caldeira 2000) and by the contributions of the media, which sensationalize the most horrific incidents of violent crime for their own commercial purposes (Briceño-Leon and Zubilaga 2002; Goldstein and Castro 2006). Personal fear and what has become identified as *inseguridad* (insecurity) are further exacerbated by the loud and furious debate in all Latin American countries (as in the United States and Europe) over public security, amid efforts to prepare and protect the public from criminal and terrorist violence. The result is a pervasive climate of dread and fear that makes the habitus of daily life, particularly in urban areas, one of overwhelming anxiety, uncertainty, and despair (Garland 2001; Giddens 1990; Merry 2001).[17]

Contributing to this pervasive sense of insecurity is the absence of a reliable authority, operating according to a rule of law, to which people can turn to report crimes, resolve conflicts, or seek redress of grievances. As I discuss further in chapter 3, corruption is widespread in the Bolivian police force (as it is in other Latin American police institutions), and people reporting crimes to the authorities are likely to be victimized anew by extortionist police practices, with demands for money to initiate routine police procedures being commonly reported. "This sense of the law as worse than crime, the ultimate injustice" (Taussig 2003, 30), is widely held and contributes to the sense of powerlessness that crime victims typically experience. Additionally, the court system is beyond the reach or comprehension of most poor urban residents, who have an incomplete knowledge of the workings of the system and lack the financial or cultural capital to access it (Domingo and Seider 2001). The

FIG. 1 A private security guard in Cochabamba, 2008. Photo by Lisa Berg.

spaces of policing and justice making vacated by the state are increasingly occupied by private security firms, often staffed by both former police officers and former convicts, who know the workings of the official system and now profit from this knowledge by selling security services to those who can afford them (see fig. 1). These private security firms are increasingly coming to operate like paramilitaries or mafias, dividing the city into turfs under their control and pressuring all local residents to pay for protection or else become the next victims of crime in the neighborhood.[18]

Despite the many problems with the formal justice system, many poor urban residents nevertheless advocate for a stronger and more aggressive police presence in their neighborhoods, contending that crime would be reduced and security enhanced were the authorities to take a heavy-handed approach (*la mano dura*) to crime in the streets. Throughout Latin America, political candidates have been elected on "get tough on crime" platforms that promise to circumvent the due process rights of the accused. (For example, the election of the former dictator Hugo Banzer in Bolivia in 2001 was in part due to his strong anticrime pledge [Prillaman 2003].) Some states are adopting a zero-tolerance approach to crime, a now-transnational philosophy derived from Mayor Rudy Giuliani's administration in New York City. Exported throughout the hemisphere by luminaries like William Bratton, former chief of the New York Police

Department and proponent of the "broken windows" philosophy of crime prevention, zero tolerance justifies a strong police response to relatively minor crimes in order to deter the commission of more serious ones (Escobar et al. 2004).[19] Though studies have shown that zero tolerance is not a realistic approach to crime control—indeed, no city in the world has actually instituted all of its principles (Petrella and Vanderschueren 2003) —zero tolerance has become a powerful discourse for states attempting to project an image of efficacy in the fight against crime (Prillaman 2000). It also appeals to many citizens within these societies, who are willing to surrender some basic rights and freedoms, and to accept harsh penalties and violent police practice, in exchange for enhanced security.

For those who feel themselves abandoned by the state, the idea of taking matters into their own hands can become an attractive option. Indeed, during the last two decades, Bolivia has exhibited one of the highest incidences of vigilante violence in the world, with a majority of this violence concentrated in the southern zone of Cochabamba (Goldstein 2003).[20] Attracted by the city's large informal economy, centered around its huge outdoor market, the Cancha, and its easy access to the lowland coca-growing region, the Chapare, many peasants have migrated to Cochabamba from the countryside over the last thirty years. The result has been an expansion of illegal urban settlements on the periphery of the city. This pattern, common throughout Latin America and other parts of the developing world, is made worse in Bolivia by that country's deep and prevailing poverty and the inability of the state to provide adequate infrastructure and services to the residents of these so-called marginal communities. This poverty also drives a high crime rate, and these barrios are frequently the targets of thieves who prey on the homes of poor people, left unattended during the day while their owners are working. For people who have little, any loss is devastating, and the rage and fear that such victimization generates can be channeled into violence, as some seek retribution against those presumed to be guilty of these crimes. Most people in these marginal barrios are extremely reluctant to call in the authorities, fearing that they might have to pay fees or bribes or get involved in a complicated legal system that they neither understand nor know how to use. Instead, some residents turn to violence as the most expedient and, they believe, most reliable means of deterring future crime in their neighborhoods. Such violence, however, is ineffective as a crime-control measure; instead, it feeds an ongoing cycle of fear, revenge, and erosion of trust in local communities and state institutions. The use of lynching is also highly contested: although most reports describe it as a uniform practice in which all barrio residents unreflectively participate, it is in fact a highly diverse set of behaviors around which no local consensus has actually emerged (see chapter 4).

The consequences of this violence and the climate of fear it engenders are legion, and the security frame compounds the problem by providing a justification for violence, intolerance, and the rejection of human rights. As chapter 3 demonstrates, the vigilance encouraged by neoliberal securitization is robustly present in the marginal barrios, where people regard with suspicion any outsider who enters their neighborhood, fearing that the person is a potential housebreaker, child molester, or rapist. Women's freedom of movement especially is strictly curtailed, as they fear leaving the home, going out at night, or talking to strangers. Community life itself is highly constrained, with people reluctant to attend public events out of mistrust and a generally degraded sense of collective identity. Furthermore, the Bolivian government does little to meet the security needs of its poorest and most vulnerable citizens. Today, if a barrio resident has a conflict or legal problem or experiences abuse or violence, he or she has to figure out where in the downtown area to go for attention, often having to take time off work to spend hours in line at some government office. If the resident lacks funds to pay a bribe, can't afford the cab fare downtown, can't speak Spanish, or doesn't want to leave his or her children or home unattended, he or she is unlikely to get service, and the problem will remain unresolved. For some problems—domestic violence, for example —the government provides few services, and far too few people take advantage of these, for lack of knowledge of how to access them, or for fear of state authorities or spousal retribution. In general, people are more likely to just endure their problems, despite the suffering these cause them, rather than to deal with the labyrinthine and nightmarish bureaucracy in search of official help. Thus, although Evo Morales's MAS government has transformed the sociopolitics of the Bolivian nation, many people in the marginal barrios continue to experience a profound and uninterrupted insecurity that shows no signs of resolution.[21]

Citizen Security and Human Rights

A new and apparently more progressive variety of the security discourse has emerged in recent years, one that seems to combine the longing for security with the quest for rights in the transnational discourse of citizen security (*seguridad ciudadana*) (Goldstein 2004). Across Latin America, governmental policymakers, international development organizations, academic analysts, and average citizens have adopted the language of citizen security to characterize the struggle for greater personal and social security guaranteed by a democratic rule of law. By one definition of this new security paradigm, "citizen security" refers to "the protection of the normal functioning of democratic institutions, the defense of the citizenry from criminality in all of its facets and typologies, [and] the defense of citizens against corruption and other asocial acts that impede or problematize the normal development and enjoyment of the fundamental rights of persons" (Delgado Aguado and Guardia Maduell 1994, 20). Implicit in this definition is the right of citizens to a safe and secure life, and to demand that the state respect and guarantee this right (del Olmo 2000). This new wrinkle in the transnational discourse of security is clearly distinct from earlier meanings of "security" in Latin America, distancing it from the idea of state security and embracing one that more explicitly targets the needs of the populace. Rather than pitting rights against security, citizen security acknowledges security to be a right, guaranteed by the state to its citizens.[22]

In an expanded sense, citizen security has become a platform for the realization of other rights, or for the attainment of security that facilitates equal opportunity and the expansion of economic, political, and social rights for the poor and marginalized (Bobea 2003). Therefore, improving citizen security in the region has become a major goal of transnational development activity in the last few years. Since 9/11, security has become extraordinarily attractive to funders, and many international development organizations (including the United Nations Development Programme, the World Bank, and the US Agency for International Development [USAID]) have recently made grants to Latin American states with the aim of heightening citizen security.[23] The United States now regards security in Latin American nations as critical to its own national security: In the words of a USAID report (in which the agency quotes its own congressional budget justification for 2005), "Establishing the rule of law also helps to fight crime more effectively, and in the process improve security in those countries and throughout the region. In the new environment of security concerns and the War on Terror, the stability of the hemisphere is a high priority for the United States, especially as it recognizes that, in the post–Cold War environment, 'the greatest threats to U.S. interests at home and abroad stem not from conquering states, but from failing ones'" (United States Agency for International Development 2005). Similarly, at a 2003 conference on Security in Latin America and the Caribbean sponsored by the Inter-American Development Bank, a representative of that organization noted that "the effects of the terrorist attacks of September 11 have radically modified the security agenda, and new threats have deepened the consciousness of the Western Hemisphere on the interdependence in facing this problem" and stressed that security should be "the political axis of international cooperation" in the Americas.[24] Not surprisingly, on the heels of this transnational funding impetus, concepts of citizen security have recently been written into some Latin American constitutions, and the language of seguridad ciudadana has been incorporated into a number of hemispheric pacts and programs of transnational cooperation (Gabaldón 2004).

Citizen security as a transnational discourse of rights encounters problems, however, in the daily practice of security in Latin America. Given the high incidence of crime and violence, the profound mistrust and ineffectiveness of police and judicial systems, and the generalized climate of fear and suspicion that clouds everyday life, talk of security experiences a slippage away from this progressive language and back into the inherited meanings of the authoritarian past (Dammert and Malone 2003; Neild 2002). Old equations of security with public order reassert themselves, and violence targeting the enemy within reemerges (if indeed it ever went away) as a publicly acceptable method of dealing with social disorder. Citizen security becomes a discourse of this condition, demonizing a criminal element that pervades society and is responsible for myriad social ills. Delinquents (*delincuentes* or *malhechores*), as they are frequently called in Bolivia, embody the general unease that people (of all races and social classes, but particularly the indigenous poor) feel as they confront the perils of daily life in a context of pervasive poverty, inequality, and personal disempowerment. Like communists during the Cold War, delinquents today are characterized in the language of citizen security as an ongoing threat to democratic stability and security and are made the targets of repressive campaigns at the national and local levels and demonized in official proclamations, media pronouncements, and daily conversations. Youth are especially vulnerable: young people may be criminalized as potential delinquents simply by virtue of their age (see chapter 3).

From the vantage point of what might be called the security paradigm (Agamben 2002), security can be attained only if the forces of insecurity and delinquency are opposed by the superior force of state repression, and rights become obstacles that have to be circumvented so that law and order in the streets may prevail. For the state, this equation creates a space of exception (Agamben 2005) whose logic postpones the realization of citizens' or human rights until such time as delinquency can be controlled and the threats to the social order that it poses permanently quelled. Such an approach allows for the remilitarization of policing, reversing human-rights groups' hard-won gains in excluding the armed forces from the daily work of internal security (Machillanda 2005); the expansion of police latitude in the use of violence in criminal investigations; the adoption of harsher criminal penalties, including the death penalty—now resurgent in Latin America (Dammert and Malone 2003); and the prosecution and punishment of minors as adults. For citizens concerned with their own security but lacking confidence that the state will provide it, the idea of the right to security emerges as a justification for extralegal violence, permitting the adoption of local forms of violent revenge as instruments of crime control and security promotion. The right to security takes its place as the paramount right, the right that trumps all others, and violence—either state, collective, or private—is justified as the means to its attainment.

However, while violent measures to enhance security enjoy broad support across classes in Bolivia, suspicion of the state remains extremely high, support for la mano dura is not universal, and popular responses to state violence not apparently connected to crime control can be swift and severe.[25] In terms of daily life, the contradictions generated by the security-versus-rights debate—a debate transacted not only in Cochabamba but in the United States, across the hemisphere, and around the globe—result in an existential murkiness that only increases the lived sense of insecurity for those on the urban margins. At once aware that rights can be valuable protections and liberating tools as well as apparent threats to their safety and security, residents of marginal barrios often feel torn between embracing and rejecting the discourse and practice of human and civil rights, and ambivalent about the uses of violence in the effort to increase security. In the following chapters, I explore these ambiguous, uncertain states in which barrio residents live, reflecting on the complex and often competing frames through which people interpret their experience of insecurity and determine how to act from an insecure disposition. The resulting ethnography is at times indeterminate, suggesting not some clear-cut set of perspectives unfolding within an organized social order, but a social field in which people must continually grope for solutions to problems that seem unsolvable, and for frames to make sense out of what often seems entirely senseless. It is a picture of uncertainty, lying at the root of the insecurity with which people live.

Outlawed

In a strictly geographical sense, security in Cochabamba is very much keyed to space and the rural/urban divide common throughout Latin America, and it reflects broader ideologies and practices of social exclusion. Since Spanish colonial times, indigenous people in Latin America were assumed to belong in the countryside, with the city being the domain of white and upper-class elites (Radcliffe and Westwood 1996; Weismantel 2001). Although the demographic distribution of colonial and (later) national populations never did conform to this idealized model, the urban landscape was transformed after the 1960s, particularly during the neoliberal era that began roughly in the mid-1980s. At that time, a large-scale rural-to-urban migration produced a massive influx of indigenous people, seeking a better life in the cities than the existence that failing agrarian economies could offer them. In Cochabamba, they settled on available lands on the urban periphery and created new communities that municipal authorities deemed illegal because of their failure to conform to existing norms of land legalization established by the municipality (discussed further in chapter 3; see also Goldstein 2004). As these poor, so-called marginal neighborhoods or barrios continued to grow, the city became unable or unwilling to extend municipal and state services to their residents, denying the people access to what many of them regarded as their basic rights as citizens—rights that included access to the law and to state institutions responsible for maintaining social order and creating official justice. The distance of one's residence from the city center became correlated with one's ability to access citizenship rights and the services of the state justice system, while race continued to dictate one's ability to legitimately claim urban residence and citizenship itself. Insecurity, then, coincides with spatial location: the marginal neighborhoods of Cochabamba fall on the wrong side of a spatial and racialized legal frontier, recalling the same historically constituted inequities of race- and class-based exclusion that have endured throughout Latin American history.

Anthropologists who study the margins have long been aware of the fundamental misnomer contained in the term "marginal," recognizing that supposedly marginal people are in fact deeply connected to the mainstream of social life (Peattie 1974). Marginality is not an innate character flaw that locates some people beyond the pale, but the outcome of a complex political and social process: Peripheries are often peripheral because they have been actively marginalized by the state, with their inhabitants barred from the benefits of citizenship and belonging (Goldstein 2004). At the same time, however, these places are also problematically included in the domain of the state through various official techniques of making order, rendering the excluded legible to power's gaze (Scott 1998; Trouillot 2001). As Veena Das and Deborah Poole (2004) have observed, the margins are in fact critical sites of the nation-state's ongoing self-reproduction: precisely because of their location at the supposed limits of state authority, marginal spaces are those in which the state's attempts to reconstitute itself through its forms of legal ordering may be most robust (see Risør 2010). Because they are both inside and outside the formation of the state, at once included and excluded, these marginal locations might be thought of as spaces of "organized abandonment" (Harvey 1989, 303, quoted in Gilmore 2008, 31): Particularly difficult to reconcile with state projects of historicity and nation formation, these localities are deliberately excluded from national consciousness and identity, yet they must still be regulated if the state's authority is to remain legitimate and opportunities to contest it foreclosed. Such marginal spaces are characterized by poverty, underdevelopment, and neglect, as a host of studies of urban slums and squatter settlements has shown. But they can also be spaces of invention and creativity, as marginalized people explore new ways of resolving local problems, relatively unfettered by broader political or cultural considerations (Appadurai 2002; P. Hall 2004).

An awareness of the ideological and juridical complexity that fills the seemingly marginal spaces of the urban periphery is critical for understanding their relationship to the state and the ways in which their residents try to establish order on its margins. As discussed above, to live on the margins is to be interstitial, both included in and excluded from the domain of the state and its legal apparatuses. As a result, many marginal people find themselves subject in unfavorable ways to the law's dictates. In the barrios of Cochabamba, this can mean lacking legal title to one's land and so effectively being reduced to a squatter, an outlaw illegally occupying urban terrain; it can mean being a participant in or even merely an observer of a lynching, and so situated outside of or made antagonistic to the domains of both state law and transnational human rights regimes. Alternatively, barrio residents may find that their poverty, race, or geographic location on the margins disqualifies them from the protections of state law, including honest policing and access to legal institutions, and so effectively they are "out-lawed" again—written out of the state's legal purview. These dual modes of outlawing—negative inclusion and perilous exclusion—represent different ways that the state produces or perpetuates insecurity in the marginal barrios, even as it establishes a certain kind of order on its periphery.

However, understanding the relationship between the state and its margins, particularly in terms of security and justice making, again requires us to move beyond a limited vision of the law's spatial distribution and connection with nonstate forms of ordering. From one perspective, security making in the barrios is a case of intersection between multiple systems of meaning and ordering. In a given social space—in this case, situated on the margins of the state, in a kind of two-dimensional center-periphery model—state law either maintains order or fails to do so; it extends to the fringes or it doesn't. And where state law fails, vigilante practices or other alternative modes of legal ordering supposedly emerge to fill the gap. These forms are seen to coexist and conflict, vying for legitimacy on a contested legal terrain. This perspective shares an approach with much legal anthropology, in which the notion of legal pluralism—the existence within a single social space of multiple forms of legal ordering—has been dominant, especially as a way of understanding colonial and postcolonial legal contexts. The legal pluralist approach has been extremely useful as a way of conceptualizing forms of local ordering that do not depend on state law, reminding us that law and order do not necessarily emerge from the center and spread to the periphery (Merry 1988). Legal pluralism can be counterhegemonic and potentially radical, suggesting that one national space can contain multiple, equally valid legal systems. Bonaventura Santos's well-known examination of "the law of the oppressed" in a Brazilian squatter settlement provides a good example of what he calls the "plurality of legal orders" that characterize modern society, particularly in cities where the state's legal order may not extend to many poor and marginal communities (Santos 1995, 114). Bolivia, too, can be understood in such terms: as I mentioned at the beginning of this chapter, the academic notion of legal pluralism has influenced the Bolivian state itself by providing the intellectual rationale for the constitutional recognition of community justice, within a nation that officially envisions itself as culturally, linguistically, and legally plural.

But we must be careful here to avoid attributing stability to situations that are better characterized by flux and contradiction—a fallacy toward which pluralist conceptions can lead. In the ethnography that follows, I hope to indicate the ways in which the reality of these marginal spaces are characterized not by stable forms of social ordering and by plural systems of law and legality, but by fractured, ever-shifting planes of law and lawlessness, order and chaos, on which barrio residents unsteadily reside and try to make their way. To insist on a plurality of systems is to risk imposing our own analytical categories on others' realities. Simon Roberts has critiqued legal pluralism as an analytic approach: "We must remember whose understandings we are working with when we conceptualise social space in terms of plural fields/domains/discourses/systems; actors on the ground may not experience or articulate the repertoire of norms available to them in that way at all" (1998, 105). Rather than stable sets of referents, then, or a competition between or the coexistence of coherent systems of meaningful practices and beliefs, the quest to establish order in the marginal barrio is characterized by individual and collective creativity, imagination, and what I call "legal bricolage," a process by which people assemble "whatever is at hand" into responses to particular situations (Lévi-Strauss 1966, 17).[26] These may become routinized with time and so take on the appearance of systems or orders, but they maintain a quality of spontaneity and possibility. Lynching is a good example: rather than a unitary phenomenon in which all barrio residents participate, lynching is a loose rubric under which a range of practices might be grouped, and it is regarded with ambivalence by the majority of barrio residents with whom I have spoken. Rather than an overlapping in space of discrete, contained systems, people's legal understandings may be better understood temporally as the simultaneous expression of multiple, incoherent legal fragments, bits and pieces that present themselves all at once to people facing critical situations (on simultaneity, see Mascia-Lees and Himpele 2006, 2007). In a highly unstable and unpredictable social environment, barrio residents call on a range of resources in their efforts to create security, as they understand it; these include local renderings of state law, transnational human rights, indigenous tradition, and media representations, all assembled through the residents' creative imaginings and expressed through negotiation and confrontation.[27]

The result is a highly uncertain social reality whose parameters are continually open to negotiation. To live as outlaws—subject to the law through their transgressions, yet forced to make their way without the law's protections—is deeply destabilizing for local people, who are perpetually unsure about the nature of social threats and the proper responses to them. People must draw on all their resources, including the forces of imagination, spontaneity, and a kind of juridical creativity, as they struggle to control the uncertainty in which they live. The chapters of this book detail that struggle, as barrio residents make their way across this uncertain terrain.

Organization of the Book

The ethnography presented in the following chapters was conducted in the zone of Uspha Uspha, part of District 8 on Cochabamba's southernmost periphery. Within Uspha Uspha, most of my time was spent in the barrio of Loma Pampa, a community of about 120 families that creeps up a hillside at the farthest end of the district. During the principal fieldwork period, between June 2005 and September 2007, I became very close friends with the president of Loma Pampa, don Miguel; his wife, doña Senobia; and their extended family.[28] From 2007 to the present, I have maintained frequent contact with my friends and collaborators in Uspha Uspha and Cochabamba, and I have pursued a variety of initiatives to try to improve conditions there, all of which fall under the rubric of what has come to be known in the discipline as engaged or activist anthropology. I document this engagement—along with its challenges and pitfalls, as well as its successes—in chapter 2. After examining the different understandings of engagement in anthropology, I describe my own attempts to become engaged during and after the conclusion of my fieldwork, exploring the ways in which the reciprocity asked of me by my Bolivian friends and collaborators both facilitated the research that led to this book and imposed obligations on me that I am still struggling to discharge. The chapter suggests that the goals of engaged anthropology, although in many ways vital to the future of the discipline, present challenges to the fieldworker and academic scholar to which we must pay close attention.

To deepen the ethnographic and historical context of Loma Pampa and Uspha Uspha, chapter 3 provides an ethnography of insecurity, including a description and analysis of the relationship between local communities and state law on the margins of Cochabamba. In contrast to the Western assumption that the law operates to provide protection and support to national citizens, this discussion demonstrates the ways in which law actually can be antagonistic to the rights and welfare of the indigenous urban poor. This chapter consists of an ethnographic description of the law and legal institutions, including the Bolivian police, and of how they work to perpetuate problems of insecurity in Bolivia. In particular, it makes the argument that rather than a complete absence of law—so often asserted by both outside observers, including anthropologists, and barrio residents themselves—the law is in fact a powerful force in the marginal barrios, attempting to regulate and order urban life although it does not provide the protections that might make residents feel more secure. This is what I identify as the absent presence of the state, a form of ordering that imposes some kinds of legal regulation while neglecting others, making the state simultaneously there and not there, a ghostly presence that haunts the margins of the city. How people deal with what I call "the phantom state" and the problems it creates for them is an important theme of this chapter.

In what they perceive to be the absence of the state, people in the marginal barrios must find ways to contend with the problems of insecurity that they regularly confront, especially the predations of rateros and other perpetrators of delinquency and violence. The analysis of chapter 4 focuses on three principal techniques or processes by which barrio residents attempt to manage insecurity: watchfulness, reliance on local forms of leadership, and vigilante violence. In each case, I consider the ways in which a sense of community, or lack thereof, figures prominently in local efforts to deal with insecurity, which tends to promote individualization and isolation. Dealing with rateros seems to require eternal vigilance on the part of barrio residents, and in some cases seems to demand a violent response to contain their ever-present threat. This chapter, therefore, discusses the vigilante lynching as a way in which people deal with the rateros whom they apprehend in their midst. However, unlike most popular and academic accounts of lynching, which characterize it as a collective phenomenon marked by the undifferentiated rage of the actors, this ethnography of lynching demonstrates the deeply contradictory and fragmented nature of this violent behavior. Indeed, what this analysis shows is the profound uncertainty within which barrio residents must manage the insecurity of their lives: in the absence of formal legal institutions or cultural systems for resolving conflicts, the residents of marginal barrios and their leaders grasp for solutions wherever they can find them, struggling to respond to the problems of insecurity that arise in their communities.

As a means of addressing the lack of judicial efficacy in marginal zones throughout Bolivia, the administration of President Evo Morales has promoted a reinvention of community justice, a supposedly indigenous system for the establishment of order and crime control that does not rely on the state or its institutions, but that nonetheless is recognized as legitimate in Bolivia's new constitution. Such a program is part of the state's ideological reinvention of indigeneity itself, an attempt to positively reimagine the negative stereotypes historically associated with indigenous people in Bolivia. This move, however, ends up remarginalizing urban indigenous people, whose basic reality does not conform with the spatial and temporal ideologies of race that are implicitly contained within the constitution and the community justice movement. Chapter 5 explores the controversy surrounding the idea of community justice in Bolivia, while examining the larger question of indigeneity that underlies it. It examines local beliefs about the nature of community justice, and the ways in which people sometimes appropriate this national discourse to justify or explain more local, violent practices of justice making. The chapter argues that, rather than depending on custom or tradition to make justice in their barrios, residents instead rely on their own creativity, assembling responses to insecurity that are appropriate to the circumstances without being formal examples of either official or traditional legal custom. Rather than legal pluralism, the discussion of this chapter points to legal bricolage as the principal means of making justice in the marginal barrios.

In chapter 6, I look more closely at the relationship between ideas about security and beliefs about human rights, as they come into conflict in the marginal neighborhoods that I have studied. In Bolivia, amid a stagnant economy and the failure or absence of state social services, citizens of all social strata perceive grave threats to their physical safety and are increasingly willing to submit to extreme measures to obtain this elusive goal. In this context, human rights (including such legal rights as the right to a trial, habeas corpus, and freedom from arbitrary arrest and punishment) are increasingly coming to be viewed as extravagant, a luxury afforded to violent criminals at the expense of law-abiding citizens. This chapter suggests that the quest for security in Bolivia today poses challenges to the very idea of human rights itself, as those who feel threatened by criminal predation blame the transnational concept and its defenders for their current predicament. In a context of pervasive and quotidian social violence, it is, ironically, the idea of human rights that is coming to be seen as productive of violence and exculpatory of its effects, while other forms of violence emerge as acceptable alternatives to state policing and as legitimate mechanisms for defending the rights of citizens. Part of the problem here lies in the way in which the transnational discourse of human rights is translated in the context of the insecure barrio. I rely on the concept of human rights vernacularization (Merry 2005) to explore the ways in which nonlocal human rights ideals and language are locally reinterpreted and deployed. This analysis reveals that the process of vernacularization itself can involve different sets of human rights translators, trading in multiple and often conflicting notions of human rights. While some of these represent effective adaptations of transnational ideals to local realities, others appear to be in direct opposition to the normative values encoded in the transnational discourse of human rights.

Finally, in the book's concluding chapter, I turn to a fuller consideration of the idea of uncertainty and its relationship to insecurity in the context of the marginal barrio, and beyond. In contrast to anthropological efforts to understand and render coherent diverse cultural meanings, the chapter suggests that uncertainty, rather than clarity, may more closely reflect the quality of life amid insecurity. An uncertain anthropology can capture local and global realities in all their murky inconclusiveness, an insight toward which the ethnographic chapters of this book seem to point.

Getting Engaged

REFLECTIONS ON AN ACTIVIST ANTHROPOLOGY

Like many other fieldworkers, I began to explore the possibilities of an engaged or activist anthropology long before these concepts became familiar ones in the discipline's vocabulary. Defined concisely by Charles Hale as "research in collaboration with an organized group in struggle for social justice" (2010), activist anthropology is often framed as a subset of engaged anthropology, a more broadly understood anthropology that goes beyond the narrow limits of academic social science to explore the possibilities for contributing to the societies that anthropologists study, for critiquing social inequality and injustice, and for initiating or advancing positive social change. Depending on how one conceptualizes "engagement," this kind of engaged praxis is either something radically new or a longtime foundation of the discipline. In any event, the question of whether and how to engage—the extent to which an engaged or activist anthropology is appropriate or even possible in the contemporary world—is a matter of great concern to professional anthropologists and students of the discipline. In my case, the research on which this book is based was conducted using a collaborative methodology and what I identify as an activist approach, one that I believe was indispensable to the success of the research. Rather than presenting science and engagement as dichotomous poles between which the anthropologist must choose, in this chapter I argue that engagement in fact makes for better social science, and that the commitment to advocacy and activism is today a critical precondition for much ethnographic work—claims I support with examples from my own field experience. Activist anthropology is not only an ethical responsibility for many ethnographers of contemporary society. Instead, it may be the only kind of anthropology possible in the twenty-first century, involving a commitment by its practitioners that is essential if the discipline is to have a future as a viable producer of knowledge about the human experience.

My desire, then, to combine anthropology with social justice work—what I identify here as a kind of activism, a distinction I will make in more detail below—did not emerge from any sort of inherent nobility on my part. I did not come to this commitment from a long-standing desire to change the world, thinking that I somehow had the answers to how to reduce social violence and eliminate poverty for Bolivia's urban indigenous people. Nor did I come from any kind of activist tradition—frankly, I have never felt comfortable as an activist at home, and lack any extensive experience with social protest, in contrast to other anthropologists (see, for example, Graeber 2009). But for many years I have lived among and studied the lives of Bolivian people who are deeply engaged in struggles for social justice, or whose worlds are colored by a profound, lived sense of injustice, and at some point—like many others who may or may not identify themselves as activist anthropologists—I decided I had to get involved. I felt that in a context of intense violence and suffering, especially because that violence and suffering was the very focus of my research, it was simply unethical to practice an exclusively academic anthropology, one that spoke only to other anthropologists without contributing to the struggles I was witnessing (Bolton 1995).

But I cannot take all or even most of the credit for arriving at this decision to become engaged. In many ways, it was an obligation thrust on me by my friends and collaborators in Cochabamba as well as a strategic move that the research process itself demanded. As I will go on to demonstrate in what follows, cultural anthropology today is practiced in a milieu in which our research subjects or informants are well aware of the global market for knowledge on whose fringes they reside, and they recognize that their contributions to that knowledge have a value, even if they themselves might have trouble calculating it. In the mercantile economy of Cochabamba, to give away such value freely would be the height of idiocy. In such a context, people require some kind of return for their time and their willingness to share the details of their experience. This is not necessarily a new phenomenon—to some extent, the expectation of give and take has always been part of the reciprocal nature of ethnographic fieldwork (see, for example, Rabinow 1977)—but it seems particularly important in the wake of neoliberalism and its destructuring effects on local communities. Additionally, when the topic of investigation is one that is of great and immediate concern to the people being studied, they have a vested interest in seeing some sort of return to themselves and their community from that research. In other words, giving back to the community was not an option for me, but rather a precondition for doing research in the barrios of Uspha Uspha.

The practice of activist anthropology is not easy, however, with costs that sometimes seem to eclipse the benefits. In my case, the journey has been arduous and the results have not always been pretty—my experience has been equal parts failure and success, as perhaps all such experiences must be. Indeed, in writing this chapter I have struggled with what to include and what to leave out, frequently questioning whether what I did can really count as engaged or activist work. But, as Stuart Kirsch (2010) has suggested, engaged anthropology cannot take hold more firmly in the discipline unless its practitioners are willing to be honest about both their successes and their failures, and reporting on these can afford us new opportunities to define the possibilities and limits of engagement itself. So, before turning to the ethnography and analysis of the subsequent chapters, it is important to first explore the process—engaged, activist, academic—that I followed in the course of this research experience. I begin by interrogating the notions of engagement and activism, examining some of the principles and dilemmas of the engaged anthropology movement. I then consider my own research process in Bolivia as a kind of activist anthropology, tracing its highs and lows and final outcomes, so as to sketch the paths that have led to the book you now hold in your hands.

Engaged Anthropology

How can anthropologists in particular (and academics in general) fail to engage with the fear, suffering, and hope that infuse our conversations with repressed people? How could one justify a research methodology or project . . . in which these turbulent lives are peripheral to the research questions at hand?
—MONIQUE SKIDMORE, "SCHOLARSHIP, ADVOCACY, AND THE POLITICS OF ENGAGEMENT IN BURMA (MYANMAR)"

Anthropology—the most humanistic discipline of the social sciences and the most scientific of the humanities, as Eric Wolf (1964) famously described it—has always been concerned with lived human experience, its insights gained through direct interactions with other people. Equally characteristic of anthropology's history is the struggle of its practitioners to locate themselves politically and ethically in relation to those people, the subjects of our research. In our fieldwork we become intimately acquainted with the lives of our collaborators, forming deep and abiding friendships, even ties of kinship, with them, and we often come to feel a great empathy with them as they face the many challenges in their lives. Are anthropologists—who so often work and study alongside the poor, marginalized, and oppressed—morally obligated to intervene in situations of clear injustice? That is, what is the nature of our commitment to the people whom we study in our research? Do we have a commitment to help resolve their suffering and aid them in their struggles against oppression? Or is our commitment instead to the production of scientific knowledge, which might be hindered by other kinds of more direct interventions in the communities that are supposedly our living laboratories? The question of researchers' ethical obligations to the subjects of their studies has long been an important issue in anthropologists' reflections on their own fieldwork experiences and on the work of participant observation more generally (Adams and Jones 1971; Albert 1997; Berreman 1968; Gjessing 1968; Jackson 1999; Kirsch 2002; Maybury-Lewis 1985). Engaged and activist anthropologies represent the most recent efforts to think through these matters, developing insights to guide our ethnographic practice, research methods, and critical theorization.

ENGAGEMENT VERSUS ACTIVISM

For many practicing and would-be anthropologists, including many undergraduate students, the answer to the above questions is clear: anthropology can and should be fully engaged, using all of its resources to advance the struggles of the people with whom we conduct research. The ways in which this might be done vary widely, but Setha Low and Sally Engle Merry (2010), in an important review of what has come to be called "engaged anthropology," have defined it to include the following categories: (1) social and cultural critique—excavating that which is hidden and shining a light on inequality and social injustice (Clarke 2010); (2) sharing, support, and empathy—expressing solidarity or connection with people in ways both small and large; (3) collaboration—sharing knowledge with, and including in the research process itself, those with whom we work; (4) teaching and public education—dissemination of knowledge through pedagogy and public communication; (5) advocacy—using the language of policy to translate grievances to a wider public; and (6) activism—working closely with groups in the struggle to advance their causes. Another kind of engagement is witnessing (Sanford and Angel-Ajani 2008). The anthropologist here serves as a kind of "keeper of the records" (Scheper-Hughes 2004, 175), writing the history and experience of marginalized and oppressed people as a way to preserve that which might otherwise be lost. In this way, engaged anthropologists can "advocate for the histories of terror and misery to be retained in the contemporary world . . . to puncture the hegemonic reading of past and present" offered up by military regimes or other repressive authorities (Skidmore 2008, 47). Applied anthropology is another frame within which anthropologists concerned with public engagement have been located. Though often less obviously political than other forms of engaged anthropology and so in some ways shielded from the critiques that dog them, applied anthropology has a long history as that branch of the discipline concerned with the practical deployment of anthropological knowledge for the public good (Lassiter 2005; Peattie 1958; Singer 1990). These categories of engagement are not discrete—in practice they overlap extensively, and any one individual may practice some or all of them during any particular project.

Typologies inevitably lead to debate over what to include and what to leave out, and typologies of engaged anthropology are no different. Where to draw the line around engaged anthropology can be a challenge, sometimes leading it to be defined in the broadest possible terms (as the Low and Merry typology seems to do). There is something to be said for the broadly inclusive, big-tent approach, which eliminates the need for internecine squabbling over what constitutes real or legitimate engagement. But if nearly everything anthropologists do counts as engagement —baby-sitting at community gatherings, teaching our classes, writing about environmental degradation, and so on—then what is the point of naming a subset of the field "engaged anthropology"?[1] The big tent threatens to stretch engagement to the point where it loses its utility as an identifier of particular kinds of knowledge production or research practice. Overly broad definitions can also lead to ethical complications. For example, throughout the discipline's history, one of the most public forms of anthropological engagement has been collaboration with the US military (Price 1998). During World War II, the Cold War era, the Vietnam War, and more recently in Iraq, Afghanistan, and the deterritorialized Global War on Terror, some anthropologists have presented themselves as professionals capable of providing expert knowledge on alien and combatant culture, helping the military to better understand and hence defeat its enemies (Goldstein 2010a). Although many anthropologists object to this use of anthropological knowledge, those anthropologists who choose to work with the military or other government intelligence institutions—for example, those who identify themselves as "security anthropologists" (Selmeski 2007)—view themselves as practicing a kind of engaged anthropology, using their knowledge and experience to advance a cause about which they care deeply (American Anthropological Association 2007; McFate 2007).[2] The fact that this kind of engagement, even activism, conflicts with the more transformative projects of resistance that other anthropologists (for example, Aggarwal 2010; Sluka 2010) envision points to the potential hazards and ethical complexities inherent in a loosely defined engaged anthropology. It also suggests problems of accountability, and with whom within a particular community or society an anthropologist's primary loyalties lie (Hodgson 1999).

Among the different categories of engagement, perhaps the greatest tension exists between cultural critique and activist research. Although cultural critique as a form of engagement is vitally important as a way to reveal the workings of power and the hegemonic forms of inequality and injustice in contemporary society, its primary audience is typically other academics and students, or at most an educated, usually English-speaking public. It can therefore remain at a significant remove from those people who are most directly affected by, and most formidably engaged in, struggles against those forms of oppression and injustice that the anthropologist critiques (Hale 2008b, 16).[3] Activist anthropology, in contrast, seeks to directly engage the subjects of anthropological research at the level of daily life, to join them in their struggles and use the tools and insights of anthropology to aid them in those struggles. Activist anthropology relies on cultural critique to provide insights into extant forms of social inequality and injustice and to identify their sources, but it goes beyond critique to try and effect change in the current situation. In doing so, activist anthropologists try to deconstruct their own implicit power, accrued not only from their institutional positions and comfortable salaries but also from their ability to set the agenda for research, determine the critical questions to be asked, and produce the final analysis for public consumption (Martínez 2008). Much activist anthropology, therefore, attempts to democratize the research process by including local collaborators directly in it, allowing them to influence the priorities and help to define the terms of the research itself (Fals-Borda 1991).[4] Such a destabilizing of anthropological authority is a challenge to traditional modes of doing research, requiring constant dialogue between ethnographer and subjects and a willingness on the part of the former to allow the latter a hand in shaping the research project and its goals and outcomes.[5]

In contrast to overly broad definitions of engaged anthropology, activist anthropology can be overly exclusive, its parameters at times too narrowly defined. For example, to define "activist anthropology" as supporting organized groups in struggle (as in Hale's definition, quoted above) is to leave out the many anthropologists whose field projects do not consist of work with formally organized groups. Jemima Pierre makes this point convincingly in her discussion of her work in Ghana, arguing that "activist research" too often seems to imply that the group in question is "organized and self-consciously working against a particular system or hierarchy of oppressions" (Pierre 2008, 117; cf. Marcus 2005). Such a requirement excludes the majority of anthropological field sites and seems to restrict the possibility of activism to those who work with social movements engaged in a struggle against a specific issue or problem. Additionally, the exhortation that the marginalized group that is under study actively contribute to directing the course of the research project can be daunting to many anthropologists. That approach simply is not possible in many field situations, where people lack the time, preparation, or basic interest to collaborate to such an extent. US-based funders of anthropological research have yet to recognize the value of activist work and are loath to provide resources to adequately compensate local collaborators for their time, making it even more difficult to encourage participation from local people exhausted from working all day and struggling with poverty. Where these conditions do not apply, as in Pierre's work and my own, the anthropologist may feel insufficiently activist, not living up to the rather stringent standards that "real" activism seems to set (Pierre 2008).

Nevertheless, activism, more broadly conceived, can be an important umbrella under which many anthropologists working today can comfortably fit. Activism can be understood in "broad and pluralistic" terms, in recognition of the many contradictions and debates within the movement and the need to work on resolving them (Hale 2008b, 20). Shannon Speed's definition of activist research as "the overt commitment to an engagement with our research subjects that is directed toward some form of shared political goals" is useful in this regard (Speed 2008, 215). In such a pluralistic approach, I believe, activist anthropology can include work that attempts to use ethnographic knowledge not only to inform other academics, but also to create positive transformation in the lives of the people with whom we do ethnography. Such work can and should be collaborative whenever possible, with constant dialogue between researcher and subjects, and the participation of local collaborators in the research process should be encouraged and facilitated. Cultural critique from this perspective can be a kind of activism, if it is made available to local communities through translation, dialogue, and direct communication and structured to create positive social change. This kind of engagement can require a great deal of work, but that is another feature of activist anthropology: activism often requires the extension of one's academic role rather than being a convenient fit with it, thus involving an additional investment of time, energy, and resources. Accordingly, activist commitments by anthropologists should receive institutional recognition and reward befitting the investments that these efforts demand (Pulido 2008).

ACTIVISM OPENS DOORS

The extent to which anthropology can be said to be engaged, in any or all of the forms discussed above, is also subject to some debate (Low 2011). Based on the typology listed above, engagement has always been a hallmark of the discipline.[6] Low and Merry date the politically engaged stance to the post–Civil War era of Reconstruction, when anthropologists protested the genocide of native peoples in the American West (Low and Merry 2010). A concern with issues beyond the academy was an important element of the anthropology of Franz Boas and his students, who were strong public critics of racism and fascism prior to World War II (Susser 2010). Margaret Mead famously used her knowledge of non-Western societies to offer public criticism of US society (Lutkehaus 2008). Engagement—understood as a "politically conscious critical perspective" (Low and Merry 2010, s203)—characterized much work in postcolonial anthropology during the 1960s and 1970s (Hymes 1969; Silverman 2007) and influenced subsequent calls for a larger role for anthropologists in discussions of and participation in the drafting of US public policy (Forman 1993). A concern with collaborative research and the uses of anthropological data in addressing social problems has long been a dimension of anthropology, particularly in its applied variety (Rylko-Bauer, Singer, and van Willigen 2006) and in African American activist anthropology (Gwaltney 1993), a position advanced further by the flowering of activist anthropology in the 2000s (Hale 2006; Kirsch 2002; Speed 2006). And while North American anthropology has debated the appropriateness of collaboration and engagement, these have become established principles in other regional anthropologies—particularly in Latin America (Bonilla 1982; Nolasco Armas 1984; Ramos 1999)—as well as in other national disciplinary traditions, a point that Joanne Rappaport (2008) makes clearly for Colombia (see also Jimeno 2008; Riaño-Alcalá 2006).

From another perspective, however, one could argue that while historically North American *anthropologists* may have been engaged, North American *anthropology* has not been (Starn 1991).[7] Modern anthropology in some ways has been characterized by a durable incitement to objectivism, limiting the extent to which the discipline can truly claim to be engaged. Despite our poststructuralist critiques, which clearly recognize the political contexts within which all knowledge is produced, the positivist strain within anthropology remains strong, the sense being that political engagement in the struggles of our field research partners will somehow delegitimize our research results. Even after the "writing culture" moment of the 1980s, which called attention to the ways in which the authorial techniques of ethnographic writing could obscure the intimate nature of the anthropologist-informant relationship and the movement from fieldwork to final product (Clifford and Marcus 1986; Marcus and Fischer 1986), mainstream anthropology still seems to require a certain distance between ethnographer and the ethnographized, for fear that objectivity will be compromised and science sacrificed to politics. How can we conduct rigorous field research, some anthropologists ask, if we are politically and emotionally engaged with the subjects of that research? Low and Merry acknowledge this point as one of the major barriers to a fuller emergence of engaged anthropology, noting the expectation that anthropological work be "scientific, objective, and neutral rather than humanistic and personal" (Low and Merry 2010, S213). The resulting work is often laden with jargon and inaccessible to a wider readership, particularly to those in the field who might wish to use the results of anthropological research to advance their own causes. This incitement to objectivism has significant career impacts as well: "graduate students and junior faculty members are regularly warned against putting scholarship in the service of struggles for social justice, on the grounds that, however worthy, such a combination deprives the work of complexity, compromises its methodological rigor and, for these reasons, puts career advancement at risk" (Hale 2008b, 2).

I encountered precisely this kind of resistance when I first started down the road of engaged anthropology. At a department faculty meeting, the discussion had briefly turned to some of the not strictly scientific work I had begun doing in Bolivia. Following the meeting, one of my senior colleagues, a well-known scientific anthropologist, came into my office looking concerned. He closed the door behind him and proceeded to explain to me all the reasons why I should not get involved in this sort of work, principally because such involvement would damage my research and, ultimately, my professional prospects. Though well intentioned, his words were chilling; had I not already been tenured, I certainly would have reconsidered my plans. His argument was based on the distinction between social scientific research and what he called "do-gooding," a task best left, in his opinion, to social workers (see Johnston 2010, S235). In the end, my colleague's warning to me can best be summarized by his concluding observation that, as anthropologists, "we're just not good at this kind of thing."

Though frequently invoked in conversations like this—and more implicitly through institutional practices of hiring, promotion, publication, and reward—the supposed dichotomy between objectivity or methodological rigor and engagement or activism is a false one (Hale 2008b). The question of objectivity in anthropology has been much debated, with some anthropologists still clinging to the notion that ethnography must be conducted from a stance of detachment, distance, and neutrality, so that the data collected are not compromised by the inherent biases of the investigator.[8] Activist anthropology turns this concept on its head, arguing that anthropological work can proceed from a place of positioned objectivity, which recognizes that any social scientific practice is culturally and historically situated, its practitioners ethically and politically positioned subjects whose basic affinities and predispositions inevitably shape their actions, including the methods and topics they choose to investigate (Hale 2008b). Explicit attention to this positioning leads not to unreflective bias but to a more careful research practice, characterized by methodological rigor and an ongoing questioning of one's goals and behaviors. Such observations emerge from a by-now well-established stream within anthropology, stemming largely from feminist and postcolonial work that understands all knowledge as situated—never removed from the context of its production and interpretation (Haraway 1988).[9] These traditions and the activist-research movement view the objectivist stance as both professionally untenable and personally unsatisfying. Jennifer Bickham Mendez observes: "Proponents of activist research explicitly reject the role of the disinterested researcher and actively seek ways to be politically relevant in the 'real world'" (2008, 140).

Critiques of activist anthropology as lacking ethnographic detachment also rely on an antiquated understanding of anthropological research itself. Ethnographic fieldwork does not, in fact, occur in a laboratory, in which the investigator can be hermetically sealed off from the subjects of his or her research. Whatever the intentions of the researcher, fieldwork is a profoundly messy process, requiring above all flexibility and a willingness to respond creatively to the challenges that arise when working with people who may be much more interested in the practical realities of daily life than in the concerns of one's research. In such a context, the idea of detachment is laughable. The only way to secure the cooperation of local people in a research endeavor and to overcome the inherent mistrust and suspicion of the anthropologist's motives and purposes, particularly in those marginal places where so many of us work, is not through detachment but its diametric opposite: engagement. Putting anthropology to work in the service of local concerns can galvanize local support, opening doors that might otherwise have stayed closed and greatly facilitating the research process. This is not to suggest cynically that all engagement need be instrumentally motivated, but in my experience it has been the case that people are much more willing to participate in ethnographic research if they see some benefit in it for themselves, particularly if it might help them to address some fundamental problems that seem intractable or beyond their ability to resolve. In my research the issue was personal security, including barrio residents' lack of access to formal institutions of justice and law. The possibility that my research might provide some relief from the constant insecurity that local people experience enabled me to collect data that no investigator, Bolivian or foreign, could have otherwise acquired. In exchange for this access, I made a deeply held commitment to follow through on the implicit promise that my research might benefit the communities in which I worked, and I tried to use my knowledge and insights to help transform the local security situation, a process that I will describe more fully below.

The point here is that contrary to objectivist expectations, engagement can be a critical component of the research process, one that makes rigorous research possible rather than obstructing it. Through collaboration and the promise of social transformation, activist scholarship can make anthropology relevant to local people and elicit their enthusiastic participation. Collaboration and close consultation can yield important theoretical insights that might not present themselves to the lone anthropologist in the field (Rappaport 2008); through collaboration, new questions may be posed and new answers found. Engagement therefore "has the potential to yield privileged insight, analysis, and theoretical innovation that otherwise would be impossible to achieve" (Hale 2008b, 20). Activist research of this type is a deliberate balance between the production of ethnographic knowledge and the deployment of that knowledge in both academic writing and the promotion of social justice. Though it involves significant costs, it produces significant rewards, both professional and personal, for the individual who practices it. I describe both of these in the next section of this chapter.

Activist Anthropology in Uspha Uspha

My Bolivian work included a number of different forms of engagement, according to the typology laid out above, though I recognized this only in retrospect. When designing the project and then putting it into action, I did not believe myself to be guided by any particular movement or philosophy or feel any special a priori commitment to engagement. Perhaps for that reason, the engaged research process was one of continuous discovery and invention, and I had frequent occasion to recall my colleague's warning that I just might not be good at this kind of thing. I often felt as though I were groping in the dark, trying to concoct solutions to problems that were well beyond my financial means or practical experience, guided only by my own intuition and imagination and that of my local friends and collaborators. Again, the decision to do activist research emerged out of necessity—the pragmatic need for access, the ethical imperative to act, and the expectations held of me by my friends and collaborators in the study communities. I followed no clear "activist" program. At times I had to blur familiar boundaries, moving between academic and applied anthropology, research and pedagogy, lone anthropologist and team leader, professor and director of a nongovernmental organization (NGO), calling on a range of resources in an effort to generate positive local impacts. The results, as I stated above, were not always positive but instead contradictory, suggesting that engagement for the anthropologist can be a truly challenging endeavor and the outcome of our efforts never entirely foreseeable. Nevertheless, as I have said, the effort to engage was so critical to both my sense of personal satisfaction and the research process that neither would have been possible without that effort.

STRICTLY ACADEMIC: THE CHANGING FORTUNES OF A RESEARCH PROJECT

Although I did not begin this research from an explicitly engaged stance, I did intend from the outset that the research should be collaborative, involving the participation of a Bolivian research team that would be directly involved in the collection of data. Before I even submitted grant proposals to fund the project, I recruited three former associates, trained researchers and friends from my earlier work in Cochabamba, to serve as research assistants for the project. This was made possible by the support of the National Science Foundation, which allowed me to include funds for hiring research assistants in my project budget. As the project advanced, this original research team grew to include three additional people, two of whom lived in barrios in Cochabamba's southern zone and were familiar with the realities of life in those communities. Team membership fluctuated over the two-year life of the research project, but by the second year a core group had emerged, consisting of two men and two women, with another woman working part time as messenger and assistant. Under my supervision, these people participated actively in data collection, doing participant observation, taking field notes, and conducting interviews in the study communities.[10]

Working with a research team had both advantages and drawbacks. The team helped to bridge a number of immediate gaps, particularly in the areas of language and gender. Though I speak Spanish fluently and have some knowledge of Quechua, my understanding of the latter is not adequate to the tasks of the ethnographic researcher. Several of the re-searchers on my team were native Quechua speakers, and although nearly all residents of the study communities were fluent in Spanish—often speaking Quechua and sometimes Aymara as well—my assistants could conduct interviews with those few individuals, usually women, who were monolingual in Quechua. Having female researchers on the team was also helpful in doing interviews with women, who often felt more comfortable talking with another woman than with a man, especially a gringo. Additionally, working with a team meant that I was able to do much more extensive research than I could have accomplished on my own. Together, we conducted hundreds of individual and group inter-views, wrote thousands of pages of fieldnotes, and gathered reams of secondary source materials. The fieldnotes were especially collaborative: in their own notes, team members would often comment on, correct, or contribute additional information to the notes of another team member, including mine. The team members were also able to work indepen-dently, allowing me to spend several months of the year in the United States while the work in Bolivia continued, under my supervision via e-mail and Skype. However, I soon realized that being the leader of an international research team was not something for which I had any training. Conflicts among the team members were frequent—questions about hierarchies and roles within the group were common, as were problems arising from different understandings of the project's goals, interpersonal disagreements, romances between colleagues turned sour, and the like—and I was often at a loss as to how to handle them. I often felt forced to take a side in these conflicts, and I was unsure about whom to support at any given moment. At times I felt more like a manager than an anthropologist and would question my decision to do team research. But then things would settle down, the team would return to a rhythm of harmonious productivity, and I would feel better about things once more. This fluctuation—both in group harmony and my feelings about working in a group—was a constant throughout the project's life.

Perhaps owing to the group nature of the project, the residents and leaders of the barrios with whom we worked often seemed to mistake our team for an NGO, as these are the most familiar kinds of outside entity present in the marginal communities. The topic of insecurity was also very compelling to local people, especially as no NGO, let alone any gov-ernment agency, was locally active in addressing this issue. This may explain the eagerness that many local leaders expressed when we approached them for permission to work in their barrios. When we first set out to identify a research site in Uspha Uspha, a zone consisting of thirteen different barrios, we directed our attention to Loma Pampa, whose president, don Miguel, was known to someone in our group from a prior encounter.[11] Miguel welcomed the team warmly to his home, served refreshments, and quickly announced his decision that we would be doing our research in Loma Pampa. The visit had been planned as only an introductory meeting to evaluate the appropriateness of Loma Pampa as a research site, but Miguel had already made up his mind. "These people," he told the other members of the barrio's executive committee present at the meeting, "have come to do research to improve the security in Loma Pampa. We are very happy that they have chosen to do this important project in our barrio." And with that he rose and shook everyone's hand, and it was a done deal. We had been caught up in the force of don Miguel's personal will and magnetism, and there was no saying no. This private meeting was followed by a larger public gathering in the barrio, where we were introduced and presented an outline of the project to barrio residents for their approval. In Loma Pampa, people made welcoming speeches, plied us with food and drink, and readily gave us leave to work in their community. This was similarly the case with leaders and residents elsewhere, whom we approached later as we expanded our research beyond Loma Pampa to other barrios, including Uspha Uspha Central, Mineros San Juan, Concordia, and Juan Pablo II. In each of these communities, early skepticism was replaced by eager delight, as we explained that we would be studying the sources of and responses to insecurity in the barrio. At these initial meetings, people would often tell long stories of their own personal security problems, obviously hoping that we might be able to do something about them. Though we always took pains to explain, both in these group contexts and in individual conversations and interviews, that our work was strictly academic in nature, we were not in any position to discourage people's enthusiasm, as we needed access to the communities in order to conduct our research.

The research began in July 2005, and by autumn of that year we were well settled into Loma Pampa. We rented a small house to serve as a local office, hanging out our shingle to declare the headquarters of what by then had come to be known in the barrio as Proyecto Rutgers. (Because Rutgers, the name of my home university, is extremely difficult for Spanish speakers to pronounce, it often came out sounding like "Proyecto Root-Hairs.") Don Miguel became our best collaborator and my close personal friend, and he was always available to help with practical and intellectual matters. He and several other individuals in Loma Pampa, some of them his friends and members of his executive committee, helped to direct my inquiries and devise better research questions. Miguel would point me toward people to interview in his community, and when the time came he introduced me to the leaders of other barrios where we hoped to conduct research. A well-known local figure, Miguel allowed me to accompany him on barrio business, and through him I met a range of politicians and bureaucrats in the municipal government, whom I returned to interview and who provided me with valuable secondary source material. Miguel and I would converse at length about the project, often seated in the shade sharing a two-liter bottle of Coca-Cola ("matando la tarde," he laughingly called it [killing the afternoon]); and he provided me with an ongoing analysis of the research and its findings. Miguel, his family, and his friends became my close confidants and collaborators, whose friendship and contributions to the research I soon became eager to repay.

The tradition of reciprocity, as many ethnographers have noted (for example, Alberti and Mayer 1974), is an important component of Andean social life, especially in the rural communities from which many of the residents of Loma Pampa and other barrios of Cochabamba have migrated. The sense of generalized exchange—I receive something from you today, and though no strict record is kept, I know I can count on you to repay me something at some unspecified future date—is a core component of Andean sociality. Reciprocity is also a fundamental element of the ethnographic research process. Though anthropologists may be reluctant to admit it because of the obligation to reciprocate that it imposes, the knowledge that we collect in the form of data and that in turn constitutes the basis of our scholarly publications is gleaned from the life experiences of other people who are willing to share that information with us. It may be given freely or with the implicit expectation of some future return; but in whatever form it is given, our willingness to receive it binds us to those who have shared it with us (Pulido 2008). Of course, we can refuse to reciprocate, return to our home countries and universities and publish our books, and forget all about that implicit commitment, denying that it even existed because, well, "I *told* them my research was strictly academic, I didn't promise anybody anything." But in our hearts, we know better.

In Uspha Uspha, despite our assertions of being an academic research team, it was clear from the outset that my barrio interlocutors, including don Miguel, expected that some kind of return would be given in exchange for the cooperation of local informants and collaborators. In our initial encounters, barrio leaders would often ask if our project could provide large-scale infrastructural improvements—running water, perhaps, or a sewer system. Once persuaded that our project was not equipped to deliver any major public works, barrio leaders were disappointed but not deterred. They then asked us for *asesoramiento*, professional advice on how to deal with problems facing their communities. This was something we felt more comfortable offering them. Because two of our team members were lawyers, we were able to provide advice on certain matters that had been troubling local residents, particularly on questions of the legalization of land ownership and the many obstacles to that process. We were also able to help by drafting letters for barrio people trying to resolve other legal disputes or conflicts with the municipal government, of which there were many (see chapter 3). Finally, though unable ourselves to provide many direct services, we agreed to use our connections with other Bolivian and international NGOs to try and attract them to the barrios in which we worked.

It is from such small seeds that larger commitments are born. As time went on, I began to feel increasingly obligated to reciprocate the privilege of being allowed to conduct research in Loma Pampa and people's collaboration in that work, and our project gradually began to offer more direct services to the community. Throughout the fieldwork period (which lasted from June 2005 through August 2007), Proyecto Rutgers functioned as a small research NGO, collecting data while performing many services within the barrio of Loma Pampa and elsewhere in Uspha Uspha. These services were always intended to benefit the community as a whole and were tied to the goals of research and reciprocity. For example, it became evident early on that women were extremely reluctant to participate in the project. For reasons discussed in more detail in chapter 3, women were much less likely to respond to our overtures than men, often refusing to be interviewed despite Miguel's exhortations that they should open their doors to us. Miguel put us in contact with some of the more personally dynamic women in the community, who told us that women have a hard time setting aside the obligations of work and family even for an hour, unless they can somehow justify it to themselves and their husbands. These women suggested that a class that taught women practical skills would offer such a justification and also provide a valuable service to the women of the community.

So in the fall of 2005 in our small, hillside office, Proyecto Rutgers held its first knitting class for the women of Loma Pampa. About eight women showed up that first day, shyly peeking around the doorframe to see who was inside, then shuffling in to take their seats on the benches that lined the walls of the sparsely furnished room. They gathered their long skirts about them, sitting quietly in their seats while their children played on the floor or on the dirt patio outside. We had hired a teacher, a professional knitting instructor, who came to the barrio to give lessons, and the project supplied the materials. (For purposes of the National Science Foundation, I think this all got budgeted under "other" in the "other direct costs" category.) Despite my assumption that all Andean women learn how to knit as children, this was not in fact the case, and the women were extremely grateful to be given the opportunity to learn. Over the months the group grew to about twenty women, who formed a kind of *club de madres* (mothers club), a familiar institution in urban barrios but one that had never existed before in Loma Pampa. The women elected a leadership board and planned other events, including a soccer tournament in which they would compete against women from neighboring barrios, and a series of expositions to display publicly the results of their handiwork. They learned to make socks, scarves, and sweaters for their families and themselves, and they entertained hopes of making money selling their products in the market—a hope later realized, when Proyecto Rutgers helped them to organize sales at local crafts fairs. While they knitted, they talked and shared stories, with each other and with us: the knitting class provided them with a space for socializing with other women, a rarity in their busy lives. It also provided the researchers with an opportunity to get to know the women, to talk with them individually and as a group, and to schedule appointments for individual interviews that we later conducted.

And these classes established Proyecto Rutgers as both a counterpart and a contributor to barrio life. There were plenty of NGOs in Uspha Uspha, supported by private foundations, transnational entities, and the governments of several different nations, including the United States,

Germany, Holland, Denmark, and Japan. But these organizations always arrived with their own agendas, providing what they had already determined that the barrios needed, and demanding all kinds of compliance from barrio residents to receive those benefits. One NGO, for example, funded by a transnational religious organization, offered health services to residents of the barrio Mineros San Juan, in exchange for which the residents had to sit through lectures on personal hygiene and family health, a quid pro quo that many found patronizing. Proyecto Rutgers, in contrast, was not an NGO and had no local service mission, so it set no preconditions for participation in its activities. Though we obviously hoped that our service would benefit the research—which indeed it did —we did not make participation in the research a requirement for involvement in our other activities, and this helped to establish more horizontal relations between researchers and community members.

Proyecto Rutgers offered other classes and workshops throughout the two years of the project. Most notably, these included martial arts classes for children, taught by one of my research assistants, himself a master of judo, tai chi, and kung fu. Though at first an apparent contradiction— Why is a project concerned with violence offering classes in violence to children?—the martial arts classes were in fact perfectly attuned to the themes of the project. The instructor taught martial arts not as a way to injure others but as a path toward personal growth and responsibility, teaching the children to respect the bodily integrity and basic human rights of themselves and their opponents (Olivero n.d.). Through martial arts, he taught the children of Loma Pampa that they could respect themselves and control their bodies, protecting themselves from the many harms to which they are routinely exposed without succumbing to anger or personally destructive behavior. Parents in Loma Pampa were thrilled with this instruction, which the project offered without charge to all barrio children, and some thirty or forty kids would show up every Sunday morning for classes on don Miguel's patio.

Proyecto Rutgers became a familiar part of daily life in Loma Pampa. We were a regular presence at all barrio events, including monthly community meetings, special occasions and celebrations, and even a lynching (see chapter 4), and through our interviews we came to know about the work and family lives of many barrio residents. We made contributions to the community at Christmas and for the anniversary of the barrio's founding, and I personally came to be regarded as a close friend, publicly referred to, jokingly, as the *padrino* (fictive parent, or godfather) of Loma Pampa. But as time went on, a certain awkwardness began to creep into our relations with barrio people, including don Miguel. What, people began asking me, were we intending to do about security problems in the barrio? Knitting classes were nice, but they didn't make people feel any safer walking in the streets. Though we had arrived in Loma Pampa talking about insecurity, we had so far done nothing to address the problems we were studying. Wasn't that the goal, after all, of our research?

It did not surprise me that local people had this expectation of the project. For them, living every day with problems of insecurity, the topic was far from an academic concern: it was a matter of daily survival. And though I had been careful to present myself as doing strictly academic work, there was always the implicit assumption that this work—interviewing, arguing, and analyzing in meetings, focus groups, public events, and individual encounters—would lead to something more, some final product. At times I even encouraged this assumption, suggesting that although our project was only diagnostic, it might form the basis of some later project that was more practical in nature, something that would benefit the participants in the research. This, of course, was what motivated people to participate—the possibility of this second, subsequent project, not the present academic one. Again, this relates to the question of reciprocity, though here it was more a matter of direct exchange than some generalized obligation. Although an officially socialist state, most Bolivians work daily in the capitalist economy, struggling to support their families and improve their personal situations. Cochabamba is a deeply mercantile society, with the vast majority of the indigenous poor finding work in the informal markets that dominate the local economy. On the margins of Cochabamba, people recognize that knowledge has value and require something in return for the knowledge they provide to an outsider. In both public and private settings, discussion of the research and Proyecto Rutgers increasingly came to be framed in terms of how these were going to benefit the people of Loma Pampa and Uspha Uspha. The willingness of people to collaborate in the project was predicated on their expectation that once the diagnostic part was completed, additional kinds of results would be delivered. And though I and my colleagues never made any promises, as the months went by we began to feel increasingly enmeshed, tied to the suggestion of a possible future project that we had allowed to hang in the air, overshadowing all of our strictly academic interactions.

At this point in the project, I had to make a decision. How far did I want to take this engaged anthropology business? Proyecto Rutgers was in some ways an NGO, but it was an unfunded one, supported entirely by a research grant whose purposes were wholly focused on research. I could justify using some of the funds from that grant to support local projects to the extent that those projects produced direct benefits for the research. But to do more than that would require additional financing and a more concerted effort to create a different kind of project. Ultimately, through long conversations with my research team and my friends in the barrio, particularly don Miguel, I decided to pursue a new project with very different objectives.

ACTIVISM INSTITUTIONALIZED

The question of institutionalization has been widely debated by activist scholars. Does activism require an institutional home, with the resources and political power that institutionalization entails, in order to be effective? Or does institutionalization, paradoxically, subvert the goals of activism, situating it within a system that is inherently conservative and hierarchical? Some have argued that locating activist practice and goals within an institutional structure inevitably leads to co-optation and the emergence of ideologies and governing structures that are inconsistent with the spirit of activist scholarship (Ribeiro 2006). But in the absence of a robust and well-funded local organization with which the activism of an individual scholar may be joined, it can be exceedingly difficult to effect any kind of profound social transformation. In Uspha Uspha, though I worked closely with the leaders and residents of several barrios, none of these groups could be described as "organizations" in the sense of providing an institutional platform for the coordination of ongoing social struggle by a coherent population. The people of barrios like Loma Pampa are loosely joined as residents of a particular geographical and sociopolitical space, but they are riven by internal conflicts and lack a strong collective social life, a point I explore in more detail in chapter 4. Although individuals like don Miguel provide leadership around issues of concern to barrio residents, the urban barrio—officially known as an Organización Territorial de Base (Territorial Base Organization, or OTB) —is a political entity in the structure of Bolivian municipal governance, and as such it is part of a hierarchy, has insufficient resources, and is subject to the demands and restrictions imposed by Bolivian law. My collaboration with the leaders and residents of Loma Pampa and other barrios was useful in conducting research and running the small programs that emerged through Proyecto Rutgers, but it was not adequate for larger projects that might address the critical problems of insecurity that these communities faced.

My decision to help found a real NGO, then, came about in response to these structural inadequacies that limited my ability to create positive social change in the barrios, whose residents had been so welcoming and generous to my research. The organization evolved out of the work that I and my collaborators had accomplished through Proyecto Rutgers, and at the time it seemed like the necessary next step in our efforts in the barrios, where no other institution, either state or nongovernmental, existed to address questions of justice, security, and the realization of basic rights. Our organization would provide a platform by which we could be recognized by the political establishment of Cochabamba and Bolivia and by international foundations that might be willing to support our projects. Although speaking of academic institutions, Hale's prescription ably captures our intentions with our NGO: "We need to create and defend safe spaces from which to carry out activist scholarship within often inhospitable environments; this requires us to wage a struggle from within, to negotiate and even to wield the modest quotas of institutional power to achieve our goals, while remaining especially vigilant toward the destructive allure of the elitism and hierarchy that surrounds us" (Hale 2008b, 17–18).

So in the spring of 2007, as the research project known as Proyecto Rutgers began to wind down, my colleagues and I entered into discussions with the OTB Loma Pampa about forming a real NGO. We called the organization that emerged out of these discussions El Centro para Justicia y Derechos (the Center for Justice and Rights, a pseudonym),[12] or "the Center" for short, and it received legal recognition by the Bolivian government in the summer of that year. Some members of the research team decided to leave at that point, doubting that the Center had a very promising future and choosing to pursue other opportunities; other people joined, hoping to break new ground with this new organization. During the remainder of 2007 and much of 2008, the Center took over the work of Proyecto Rutgers, operating on a shoestring budget to continue offering the knitting and martial arts classes in Loma Pampa and to begin some new activities in another barrio called Alto Cochabamba. I returned to the United States and began the search for funding to support the Center and its initiatives. On its website, we described the Center as "a nonprofit organization whose main goals are the promotion and enforcement of human rights, access to justice, and the improvement of quality of life. The Center's work is interdisciplinary in approach, specializing in research, action, and dissemination of findings, and offering alternative solutions to problems facing our constituents, with the aim of reducing human vulnerability and insecurity. The Center's main objective is to foster the growth and expansion of citizenship rights and human security, and the respect for diverse cultures, in a context of legal pluralism." By August 2007, I had written a proposal to a major international grant-making foundation to create access-to-justice centers in the barrios of Uspha Uspha. The idea for these centers and the details of what they would involve had emerged through my research, including many hours of discussion with barrio leaders like don Miguel and interviews, private conversations, and focus group discussions with ordinary barrio residents. In all of these interactions, I and my research team had explored with the residents their perceptions of the security problems they faced, the causes of these problems, and their suggestions of how to fix them. The varieties and effects of violence came up frequently in these discussions, as did questions of citizenship and human rights— questions that later chapters of this ethnography explore in detail. The plan to create local justice centers, which we called Casas de Acceso a la Justicia (CAJs; Access to Justice Houses), came out of these many conversations, as a way to address local problems by empowering local people to resolve them without the use of violence and without relying on state institutions for help. We hoped to create a model that could be replicated in other impoverished marginal communities, in Bolivia and elsewhere in Latin America, where lack of access to justice is a familiar problem.

The CAJ project, put into effect in the fall of 2009, adhered very closely to the original plan for the project, as described in my proposal to the foundation:

> After years of research among and discussion with the indigenous leaders and residents of one district (Uspha Uspha) in Cochabamba's

southern zone, the Center for Justice and Rights now seeks funding to implement a program to alleviate the problems of intense interpersonal violence that exist in these communities. Through a network of Casas de Acceso a la Justicia (CAJs), the Center proposes to facilitate access to legal advice, family counseling, conflict resolution, education, training, and violence-reduction services for the poor and indigenous residents of Uspha Uspha. . . . Through the CAJs, the Center hopes to create local understanding of and respect for the law and human rights, and to create local mechanisms for the resolution of conflicts without resort to violence. The CAJs will help to develop local capacity for conflict management and non-violent approaches to crime control by providing training in human and civil rights and their protection, particularly among youth and young adults; they will create a corps of local justice advocates and rights defenders who can advise their neighbors on laws and legal procedures, offering them non-violent courses of action and helping to broker relationships between residents and police, judges, and other judicial authorities. The CAJs also bring together a variety of needed services, providing not only access to legal services but to the kinds of counseling, education, and training that local people require to make their own worlds more peaceful and sustainable. Having established close personal contacts both within the target communities and with municipal and state officials responsible for these areas, the Center can ensure that the program has significant local support—both moral and financial—that will enable it to be sustainable beyond the funded period.

The CAJ project was designed to be different from other, existing programs of this sort. Although other access-to-justice projects had been implemented in communities underserved by state legal institutions (including one that also used the acronym CAJ, sponsored by the US Agency for International Development in El Alto, Bolivia), these projects used a legalistic conception of justice, operating only to extend existing state services—such as police, courts, and municipal bureaucracies—into these marginal communities. Many of the projects were less concerned with creating justice than with bringing illegal settlements into accordance with state and municipal norms and legal codes, or with bringing order to the chaotic and rebellious urban frontier. Other projects, while concerned about the degree of criminality and insecurity experienced in marginal communities, limited their activities to improving policing and increasing use of the courts, areas that fell under the rubric of official justice administration. For such projects, "justice" is limited to state law, implemented through state institutions, and "access to justice" means being able to take advantage of the legal services provided by those institutions. Such projects encounter difficulties in contexts in which fear and suspicion of state institutions is widespread, ignorance about the workings of official justice is virtually complete, and language barriers are high—in other words, in contexts like that of the marginal barrios of Cochabamba. My original proposal noted:

> In contrast to the above [projects], the Center understands justice not only to include state law and legal services, but also equality, rights, and security; justice involves creating the conditions by which people can live in harmony, peacefully and without fear or desire for retribution, in order to earn their livelihoods and live their lives under the protection of basic rights guarantees. Making justice involves educating and training people to use existing services, eliminating those obstacles that prevent access to formal institutions. But justice here goes beyond the formal public sector to the family and domestic life, where a range of injustices—from domestic abuse to child exploitation to fraudulent land transactions—are experienced on a daily basis, and tries to intervene in these problems. For the Center, justice is much more than formal state institutions; justice should be part of the fabric of everyday life in poor communities.

No project of its kind had ever before been seen in the barrios of Uspha Uspha, but the CAJs had no problem attracting constituents. Perhaps because the project had been designed in consultation with barrio residents, many were quick to enroll in its various programs. People came to the CAJs to consult the staff lawyer or psychologist, seeking advice on legal issues, marital and family problems, and local conflicts. Especially popular were the workshops that the CAJs offered that taught practical skills to barrio residents: electronics and electrical repair drew many men to the Center, while the ongoing programs in knitting and baking attracted women and children. The martial arts classes in particular were packed every weekend, and a group of children from Loma Pampa became so adept in judo that they competed in and won a city-wide tournament, defeating kids from much more well-to-do communities on Cochabamba's north side. Many people of both genders attended the workshops on practical legal issues that were run at the CAJs. Center staff solicited local input on the kinds of issues that people were interested in learning about, and the results included a series of workshops on marriage, divorce, and concubinage, which were very well attended by local women. Twice a year, the Center organized educational fairs, at which the staff displayed a variety of informative posters on a range of legal issues, and representatives of government institutions like the Brigade for the Protection of the Family—rarely if ever seen in the barrios on other occasions—explained the services provided by their offices and encouraged residents to visit.

Unfortunately, people seemed less interested in the CAJs' workshops on human rights (for reasons explored in chapter 6)—a core element of the program's plan—and it soon became apparent that the project would have to give them incentives to attend the workshops. Like the NGO-run health project in Mineros San Juan mentioned above, the CAJs began to require attendance at human rights workshops as a prerequisite for participating in the more attractive knitting and electronics classes. Although smacking of paternalism, this was a necessary move for the CAJs. The project funder had very stringent monitoring requirements, and the staff had to continually report on the numbers of constituents being served by these workshops, and whether these numbers were reaching the levels that our original proposal had guaranteed. This became a source of great stress for my Bolivian colleagues who dealt with these issues on a daily basis, and tensions arose in the group when the numbers dropped below quotas. Additional problems were created by my poor budgeting: I had written the original proposal with very little understanding of the ways in which such programs were administered in Bolivia, so the budget contained little money for such necessities as annual Christmas bonuses; in addition, I had budgeted too little for more routine matters such as car repair and electrical bills. The funder was also very concerned about limiting the percentage of the budget devoted to salaries, and as a result the staff members were chronically underpaid. Management of funds also caused them tremendous anxiety, due to the lack of funds in certain categories and the poor reporting of expenditures by some team members, which led to further anxiety and suspicion of misappropriation of funds. The foundation's twice-yearly audits of the projects were occasions of terrible stress for staff members, some of whom became physically ill in anticipation.

Problems like these arose continually, as people who were effective as researchers proved less so as administrators. The CAJs were a major project for the Center, which had little institutional experience in managing a budget and administering a project of such magnitude. It became extremely difficult for me to participate in the work of the project, as by that time I was required to be in the United States and had to rely on my Bolivian colleagues to communicate with me to keep me in the loop on the daily operations of the CAJs. Of particular concern was the question of institutional organization. Several of us on the team were strongly in favor of a horizontal approach, in which all members of the team would have an equal say in decision making. This grew out of our work on Proyecto Rutgers, in which I was the leader of the project but worked collaboratively and democratically with a team, all of whom were relatively equal in their roles and responsibilities. Given the success of this earlier project and our own commitments to equity, a horizontal arrangement seemed the best approach for organizing the Center and the CAJs.

But several factors worked against this desire for equality, pushing us inevitably toward hierarchy. Some of the problems were structural: Bolivian law, the sponsoring foundation, and the bank in which the Center had its account all insisted on identifying the project's officers and their relative degrees of authority and responsibility. These requirements forced us to depart from our organizational goals by elevating certain individuals over others and establishing a de facto hierarchy instead of the horizontal structure we wanted. But interpersonal conflicts were responsible as well. Those with academic degrees and research experience sometimes had trouble regarding those without such credentials as equals on the project, a status difference that was further compounded by differences in race and class. The team included white, educated lawyers and Quechua-speaking, darker-skinned "technical" personnel, and when the sponsor demanded verticality, it was members of the former group who quickly stepped up to assume those roles. Although the justification for these moves was expressed in terms of the level of university training that these individuals possessed, education here became a proxy for other forms of invidious distinctions—not surprisingly, given the ways in which racism and education are deeply intertwined in Bolivia

(Canessa 2004). For at least one of my Quechua-speaking colleagues, being subordinated in this hierarchy was an intolerable injustice (and blatantly ironic, given the Center's stated mission of justice promotion, as he was fond of pointing out), and he would frequently decry the Center's loss of focus and betrayal of its original vision. I was problematically positioned within this emerging race- and class-inflected hierarchy. As the educated white professional, I was "clearly" the leader of the project, but I was also rather easily marginalized when I had to leave the country for reasons related to work and family. Although I was ostensibly the head of the project—I was listed on the original proposal as *asesor técnico principal* (the principal technical advisor)—I was not able to be present full time in Bolivia as the CAJ project began operation, and I therefore had very little say in—or even, at times, understanding of— what was occurring on a daily basis. By the end of the first year of the project, I was already feeling extremely alienated from both the Center and the CAJs, stressed out by my lack of connection, concerned about the emerging inequities and the conflicts these generated, and depressed by my inability to influence the direction of things.

The CAJ project ran its two-year course and by fall of 2011 had concluded its operations in the barrios. By that time, though, I had already left the project. By December 2010, I had become exasperated with the constant infighting among my colleagues and frustrated by their lack of communication with me, which made me feel that I was being deliberately cut out of the loop. Though I maintained my friendships with some individuals on the team, I withdrew from the CAJs and resigned my membership in the Center, leaving behind the project I had helped create and the organization I had helped to found. I was relieved to be out, but I remained deeply saddened by my decision to resign. It felt like a personal failure, although the CAJs did much good work with the people of Uspha Uspha. I have maintained my contact with don Miguel and other friends in Loma Pampa, to whose struggles for peace and justice I remain committed.

To speak of success and failure is too simple a dichotomy to characterize the experience of the CAJs. Don Miguel was always enthusiastic about the project, though he frequently grumbled about the top-down decision making of some of the team members, who never could embrace the idea of collaboration and whose tendencies toward hierarchical leadership infuriated him. Many people were served by the various workshops and training programs (ultimately the project actually surpassed its quota of constituents reached), and during the life of the project no lynchings occurred in Loma Pampa—the reduction of public violence having been one of its principal goals. Many women and children in particular benefited from the classes and activities that the project organized, and residents of both genders learned a great deal about the law and rights from the workshops they attended. In terms of achieving the goals as set out in the original proposal, the CAJs were a success.

As a form of activist scholarship, however, I am less enthusiastic about them. Though they were based on local input and designed on the basis of knowledge derived from a two-year research project, the institutionalization of this knowledge in the form of the Center and the CAJ project drifted far from my original vision. The tendency toward elitism and hierachicalization of which activist scholars have warned was fully in evidence in the CAJs and, along with poor communication and a sense of having my role usurped, led to my own decision to withdraw from the project. Institutionalization in this case threatened to sap my activist spirit. Fortunately, through another type of engaged project, I was able to sustain it.

INTERNATIONAL SERVICE LEARNING AS ENGAGEMENT

While I waited for the foundation to make a decision regarding the Center's application to fund the CAJ project, I tried to imagine other ways in which I could support initiatives in the marginal communities, particularly in Loma Pampa. Again, the problem was financial: having worked for two years in the barrio and formed close relationships with many of its leaders and residents, I had a fairly clear idea of the range of local needs and desires, but I had no idea of how to get the money to achieve the residents' goals. It is important to recognize that in the context of a community-based research project, the struggles that people are engaged in and that the anthropologist can support are not always as dramatic as a court battle, a fight for land, or a blatant violation of human rights. In Loma Pampa, the struggles were quotidian and prosaic: water was constantly in short supply, roads were unpaved, schools and health services were poor and distant, the police were absent, and government attention to local needs at every level was lacking. Local struggles, then, were daily, ongoing affairs, as people worked to acquire some of the basic necessities of life, especially urban infrastructure. It was this struggle that my barrio friends frequently asked me to engage in, and to which I hoped, in some way, to contribute.

It was at this time, in the winter of 2007–8, that I first learned of international service learning (ISL). More than just study abroad or volunteerism, ISL represents a form of (if you will) engaged undergraduate education that, if done right, skillfully blends academic work with community service to go beyond either of those things done separately. According to one definition, service learning is "an educational methodology combining the academic or classroom study of a particular problem or issue (e.g., social, educational, health, environmental), together with the practical experience of collaborating with a community seeking to resolve such problems or issues. It means, quite simply, that you take a course thematically connected with a targeted service agenda, and immerse yourself in problem-solving interaction with a coordinated community or group with whom service is welcome and negotiated, in its home location."[13] Meant to push students beyond the limits of classroom learning, ISL makes the academic study meaningful by joining it directly to participatory work in service to a particular organization or community. Linda Chisholm describes the potential of ISL in these terms:

The very heart of higher education, especially the liberal arts, lies in opening ourselves to see beyond our individual experience. Our knowledge and understanding are extended by entering, however vicariously, the thoughts and experiences of others. . . . Combining formal study and immediate encounters with those who experience life differently brings a power to both. The service makes the academic study immediate and relevant as the study informs the service. Whether at home or abroad, the joining of study and service enlivens, enriches, and reinforces both, and helps the student use them in making life choices. (2000, xvi–xvii)

Though ISL is intended primarily as a way to enrich undergraduate education, it was immediately apparent to me that it could also be used to bring concrete benefits to a community like Loma Pampa (see fig. 2). Through an ISL program, I could join the labor of students and community members to perform work locally identified as useful and productive, funded by the tuition dollars that students would pay to participate in the program. All could potentially benefit from this relationship, with students earning credits as they improved their language skills and learned about another society, while the people of Loma Pampa received material support for projects of interest to them. Additionally, I realized that while ISL could be joined with any academic discipline, it was par-

FIG. 2 Students in the ISL program work alongside residents of Loma Pampa to construct a patio behind the barrio's community center, summer 2009. Photo by the author.

ticularly well suited to engaged anthropology. The anthropologist's deep local knowledge and personal connections could ensure that the service work was not merely a token contribution but something of real and lasting significance to the community. By including training in anthropological field methods alongside theoretical and ethnographic readings related to topics of concern in my own research, I could expose students to the work of ethnography while introducing them to the principles of engaged anthropology, as their fieldwork would be intimately connected to their community service. The prospect was exciting, though I realized it would require a great deal of work on my part and a willingness to devote the next few summers to teaching and supervising students, rather than writing up the results of my already completed research.

In February 2008, I wrote a proposal to the Rutgers Study Abroad office to establish an ISL program in Cochabamba. The program would join academic study—including training in ethnographic field methods and language study—and community service, all based in Loma Pampa and focused on issues of law, justice, and rights. In the words of my proposal, I would create:

> a summer study abroad program/field school with a strong community-service component, based in Cochabamba, Bolivia. The academic focus of the program will be on law, justice, and rights in Bolivia, with a wider reference to Latin America more generally. Working through an in-country NGO called the Center for Justice and Rights, students will have the opportunity to learn first-hand about the workings of the Bolivian legal system, access to the law, and the expression and realization of rights, with a special focus on poor, indigenous people living in a Bolivian city. Students will meet and study with justice professionals in Bolivia, to learn about how a foreign judicial system operates, and will meet with human rights advocates to develop a sense of how human rights promotion and defense works "on the ground" in Latin America. Students will also learn techniques of anthropological field research, and apply these in the preparation of their own independent research papers. Additionally, through the Center, students will work directly with residents and leaders of one indigenous neighborhood helping to improve local community services. The six-week program will thus provide students with a unique opportunity to both learn about law, justice, and human rights issues in an international context, while contributing their own energies to helping improve the quality of life for people on the social margins.

Enthusiasm for a faculty-led ISL program was high at Rutgers, and my proposal was quickly approved, with the first group of students set to go that very summer. In April 2008, I returned to Cochabamba with a representative of Rutgers Study Abroad to sort out the details of the program. We met with my colleagues at the Center to discuss program administration, and with my friend Lee Cridland at Volunteer Bolivia (a Cocabamba-based business that coordinates travel and service experiences for foreign visitors),[14] who would organize home stays and language classes (in either Spanish or Quechua) for the students. Most important, we talked at length with don Miguel and other leaders of Loma Pampa, to identify their specific needs and desires for the service component of the project. Miguel was very excited by the prospect: something like this was completely unprecedented in any of our experiences, but we all could imagine the possibilities. Through these discussions, Miguel and I decided that the program's principal contribution to the barrio would be construction of a community center, a building where public meetings and events could be held. Loma Pampa had no administrative offices, no place to hold a wake for a deceased neighbor, nowhere for visiting doctors to set up and run a vaccination clinic or provide free dental care, no space for civic life to unfold. Monthly community meetings were held under the barrio's lone tree, with residents standing or squatting in the dirt to conduct local business. A community center, Miguel and his colleagues decided, would benefit the entire community.

And so the Rutgers ISL in Bolivia program was born. We initially had twelve or thirteen students each year, growing to eighteen by 2011, with students from seven different universities participating. Each year we had a diverse group of students from various ethnic and class backgrounds, reflecting Rutgers's diverse student body and our determination to keep cost from being an obstacle to a student's participation. Each year, students were involved in various service activities, working in small groups on a variety of projects: to assist the women's knitting group or the martial arts classes in Loma Pampa; to start a baking cooperative in the barrio of Alto Cochabamba; to set up a lab of donated computers and offer classes to children and adults in the barrio Concordia; and to create a film documenting the struggles of a group of street vendors, another group with whom I had conducted research in Cochabamba. In 2011, our work expanded to include collaborations with local water committees, barrio-based associations of neighbors struggling to improve the delivery of potable water to marginal communities in the aftermath of Cochabamba's Water War. In addition to these small-group projects, the entire group of students worked every Sunday, side by side with community members, to construct the community center in Loma Pampa. In 2008, the first group of students helped lay the foundation for the building; in 2009, the second group continued work on the walls and roof and helped clear the ground for a covered concrete patio behind the center; in 2010, the third group painted the center inside and out, including a giant mural on the rear exterior wall of the building, executed in collaboration with barrio children; and in 2011, the fourth group worked

FIG. 3 Students and children of the barrio play together on the patio behind the community center in Loma Pampa, summer 2011. A mural painted by students and community members in 2010 is visible on the center's back wall. Photo by the author.

on landscaping and exterior design and construction (see fig. 3). In addition to their labor, the students and the program provided the financial resources to carry out the construction projects. Indeed, the vast majority of the work on the community center was done by barrio residents, working in groups after the students had left the country, using the funds the program had brought in to complete the building and its surroundings. Throughout the life of the project, new ideas for engaged activities continued to emerge, as students interacted with community members and generated ways to contribute that I had not anticipated.

I commented on these various activities in the blog I kept for each of the first four years of the program, which captures the excitement and sense of possibility that surrounded all of these encounters. One entry was about our first day of doing construction work.

| | | "BUILDING THE COMMUNITY CENTER IN LOMA PAMPA," JUNE 9, 2008

At first the people on the construction crew—men and women both—seemed skeptical about a bunch of gringos showing up offering to help in their work. But after watching our students labor for a few hours, everyone was very impressed. As was I—our students took to it with great enthusiasm, hacking away at the rocky earth with picks and shovels, sweating in the midday sun. Jacob, who worked like an old pro, was given the honor of laying the first stone of the foundation in the newly dug trench. During breaks, some of the students got up the courage to make conversation with the people there, and learned a little bit about life in the community. Some people asked if we could offer an English language class to kids in the barrio, an idea that our students readily embraced. We will initiate this activity next Sunday.

By the second year of the program, the community center that we had helped to build was already in use, though we continued to work to refine and expand it.

| | | "A GOOD DAY IN LOMA PAMPA," JULY 13, 2009

We began with construction work on the community center (the *sede*), which our group began last year and which has progressed to a remarkable extent. Half the students worked alongside community residents, moving rocks and shoveling dirt to level the ground for a large concrete floor and aluminum awning that will be erected outside of the sede, for public meetings and events. The other half painted inside, sanding the wooden doors and frames before applying the reddish-brown paint that I had helped don Miguel to select the day before. After a while the groups switched, so that everyone had the opportunity to get blisters on their hands and paint on their clothes. After three hours of hard work, the students were treated to ice cream by members of the neighborhood executive committee.

After lunch in the shade, some students went up to watch the women's *fútbol* league tournament, before returning to the sede to teach classes to the barrio children. Fewer showed up than the previous week, probably due to the fútbol tournament, but there were still plenty on hand. We divided into three groups—one for English classes, one for drawing classes, and one for photography lessons. Though the sede is still incomplete, it was wonderful to see it already in use, buzzing with activity as the children and students worked on their various lessons.

On their way down to the sede, four students were stopped by a woman who came running out of her house, yelling excitedly and waving her arms. At first the students were unsure of what she wanted—was there some sort of emergency? But no, she just wanted them to come inside her house, which they obligingly did. Inside, the woman and her husband invited them to eat birthday cake and drink soda with them. The man explained how grateful he was that we were here working in the community, that in all his years he has never seen outsiders come into a community for the purposes of doing work for and with the people who live there. He was very moved, as were the students by this encounter.

Each week in Bolivia, the group of students gathered for reflections.

| | | "REFLECTIONS," JULY 10, 2010

Last night was our first "reflections," when we gather to share our thoughts and emotions as recorded in our daily journals. Reflections is an important component of the service-learning process, requiring participants to think carefully about what they are feeling and experiencing even as they are living through it. Their insights as a result are deeper than they might be otherwise, and through sharing they come to realize the commonalties and divergences in their collective experience.

An interesting theme to emerge last night was the question of whether the Bolivia program could "change your life." Some thought it would, or had, while others were skeptical. I am not a big believer in the idea of "life changing," as it implies that our lives are stable and constant and can change suddenly from one particular state or condition to another, rather than being more of a continuum that is always in flux. But I think that living here in Bolivia for six weeks, doing the kind of work we do with women and children in poor communities, can change one's *perspective*. Students reflect on their own privilege and the lack thereof of their barrio friends. They recognize how difficult it is to create lasting and meaningful change in the lives of others, despite our best intentions, but also how even the smallest efforts are significant and appreciated. And through this kind of awareness, they begin to understand their own positions relative to others in entirely new ways. They begin to relativize their own problems through juxtaposition with those of others, and they start to think differently about what role they might be able to play in building a new kind of society. So while their "lives" may not necessarily change by being in Bolivia, students do, I think, come to see the world, and their place in it, through a different set of lenses.

On our last day in Bolivia in 2010, I reflected on the successes of this program (see fig. 4).

FIG. 4 The community center in Loma Pampa, 2010. The building was constructed with funds and support from the ISL program, with students and barrio residents working together in the construction process. Photo by the author.

| | | "GOODBYE AGAIN," AUGUST 9, 2010

Yesterday we celebrated the twelfth anniversary of the barrio with our friends in Loma Pampa. The day included various speeches and words of thanks, followed by games and performances. Some of our students sang and played guitar, others danced, and some competed in the races, highlighted by Carolyn's big win in the spoon-and-egg relay. It was a proud day for New Jersey.

The events of the day were all set against the backdrop of the community center, now beautifully painted inside and out, and the incredible mural that our students created over the course of the last ten days. This mural represents hours of work by students, program faculty and staff, and members of the Loma Pampa community, all of whom devoted their time, energy, and creativity to this project. The result is a unique work of art, unlike anything to be found anywhere in Cochabamba's impoverished southern zone.

Watching the events of the anniversary celebration unfold, with hundreds of people gathered in the space of the community center, all talking, laughing, eating, and playing, I was powerfully struck by the fact that all of this was made possible by the generosity and hard work of so many people, both in the United States and Bolivia. In the space of three short years, we turned a barren patch of ground into a thriving social space, where people can gather and a host of social services can be provided. This project stands as proof that international collaboration need not happen only at the level of governments. Individuals and communities (and universities!) have the ability to make powerful contributions, improving people's quality of life, producing new kinds of friendships, and promoting cross-cultural understanding. Maybe no one of us can change the world, but we can make positive change. This project is proof of that.

Although in some ways the Bolivia ISL project could be seen as a type of applied anthropology, I prefer to view it as an example of what in this chapter I have identified as an expanded notion of activist anthropology. Although I am an anthropologist, I did not particularly apply anthropological knowledge in the interest of local development, and I never used that discourse to characterize the program's philosophy or objectives.[15] Instead, the project was about collaboration and mutual transformation. It invested foreign resources (money especially, but also willing student workers and my own logistical talents) in locally selected projects. The work was fundamentally collaborative and entirely locally driven in terms of both planning and execution, with barrio leaders and residents determining its goals and coordinating the work needed to achieve them. I created the program in a spirit of reciprocity, born from the research process and the recognition that real engagement that benefits local people also benefits anthropology and its broader social and scientific goals. By putting people from very different backgrounds into direct proximity with one another, asking them to work together for mutual benefit, the project also contained an implicit political dimension, challenging the barriers of race, class, and culture that separate the global north and south. The project represents a replicable model that other anthropologists can follow in using their institutional positions and resources to benefit their local collaborators.

Conclusion: The Future(s) of Engaged Anthropology

O limed soul, that struggling to be free, art more engaged!
—SHAKESPEARE, *HAMLET*

The term "engagement" has a range of definitions, several of which capture critical dimensions of what "engaged anthropology" is meant to imply. In a generic sense, to engage is to become involved with someone or something; to join or participate in a project, program, or activity. In this sense, most ethnographic work, founded as it is on the method of participant observation, is inherently engaged—to participate actively in the life of another society or community has long been the basis of ethnographic research. From this perspective, a broadly inclusive definition of "engaged anthropology" makes perfect sense. "Engagement" also expresses the sense of interconnection that one has with other people, and the potential that this interconnectivity has for creating momentum and change, just as the gears of a car engage one another and cause the vehicle to move. On a more profound level, engagement represents a pledge or a commitment—people who are engaged to be married enter into an agreement to intimately join their lives, further deepened by their subsequent vows of matrimony. Other, less positively inflected definitions of engagement that further this sense of interconnection suggest entanglement: to be bound by a formal promise, thereby exposing oneself to risk. As in Claudius's lament in *Hamlet*, to be engaged can be a curse, a trap of one's own making, from which one feels there is no escape. All of these definitions suggest a strong moral if not legal connection binding the engaged parties one to another. As with a marriage or a murder, such relationships are not to be entered into lightly.

I offer this brief etymological review as a kind of warning, lest we come to think that engagement with field collaborators can be lightly undertaken. It cannot. To practice any variety of engaged anthropology is to enter into a committed and ongoing relationship with other people that at times threatens to overwhelm one's research agenda, overtax one's resources, and lead one down paths that are ethically murky and politically—perhaps even physically—dangerous. Engagement cannot be easily added to the ethnographic bag of tricks, like digital photography or snowball sampling. It requires a fundamental reordering of the research relationship and has lasting professional and personal implications for those who truly wish to practice it.

As I stated at the outset, my own experience with what I choose to identify as activist anthropology was marked by both successes and failures, which I have described above. In providing this account, I have tried to present my experience with all of its attendant ambivalence. Engagement, I think, must be practiced and reported on with humility, rather than using the triumphant tone that too often seems to accompany our self-descriptions. In my case, my attempt to create social change through an NGO and its access-to-justice project was a mixed bag, successful in many ways but also extremely challenging and in the end personally frustrating. On a much smaller scale, but ultimately more rewarding, was the international service learning program, which proved to be an adventure in pedagogy and participatory education, bringing benefits to the students involved and, critically, to the barrio of Loma Pampa and its residents. The program satisfied a desire expressed by many undergraduates, particularly anthropology students, to put their studies to work in the service of others. In this, engaged anthropology again demonstrates its rich potential, and the way it serves the larger discipline as a whole. Too many students become discouraged by what they perceive to be anthropology's negativity, its relentless focus on racist oppression, capitalist exploitation, environmental degradation, and the like. And when they ask, "How can I work to change these situations?," their professors too often are at a loss to respond. Here, the limits of engagement as cultural critique are very clear: unless it is joined with action—personal or political, collective or individual—cultural critique can feel more like impotence than engagement. Activist anthropology provides students with the tools they need to be more effective in the world, using the insights of critique to contribute in some small way to the struggle they see going on around them.

In contrasting my two engagements in Uspha Uspha, the CAJ project and the ISL program, it is clear to me that change can come in ways both large and small—but, for an anthropologist, small is beautiful (Schumacher 1973). Having run both a big, externally financed project and a small, internally funded one, I have come to conclude that change can sometimes most effectively emerge from small, inexpensive, targeted interventions that proceed directly from the needs and desires of the people being served. A small project like the Bolivia ISL program allowed me to make direct material contributions to local communities that the residents of those communities themselves felt were priorities, and to do so without a lot of institutionalization, with its attendant hierarchies and hidden costs. Whereas trying to coordinate a big NGO project took me far from my interests and abilities, the ISL program proved an easy extension of my roles as researcher and professor and allowed the possibility of engagement inherent in those roles to emerge. When I think back on my experience with the Center and the CAJs, I am discouraged and doubt the possibility of effective anthropological engagement. But as I watch children laughing and learning as they study English or art or dance with my students, within the walls of a community center that our project helped construct, the positive impacts of this engagement are readily apparent.

As my experience with the CAJ project demonstrates, the line between academics and engagement is also played out in the funding sector, where academic projects have trouble supporting engaged initiatives due to the restrictions of our research grants. In my case, I felt compelled to venture into the realm of social service provision, a path that took me away from my scholarship and into the world of NGO administration, an area that I found mystifying and personally challenging. A broader acceptance of the legitimacy of activist anthropology would make such digressions unnecessary—were funders to allow academic research projects to provide some direct benefits to the subjects being studied, the need to invent other, parallel projects to accomplish those goals might not be so urgent. Funders of ethnographic research must recognize the extent to which activism is not an unscientific diversion from the real work of anthropology, but rather, as Kirsch has noted, "a responsible extension of the anthropological commitment to maintain reciprocal relations with the people with whom we work" (1996, 15). Thus, as I have tried to suggest in this chapter, activism and engagement are fundamental components of the research process itself. Engagement demonstrates a commitment on the part of the anthropologist to use his or her knowledge, resources, and connections to advance the struggles and improve the situations of the people with whom he or she works. This commitment opens doors to the researcher that otherwise would have remained closed, allowing for a deeper, richer understanding of the social worlds that anthropology has dedicated itself to recording.

3 | The Phantom State

It is often said that the state is absent from the barrios of Cochabamba's periphery, but the death of seven-year-old Wilmer Vargas demonstrates both the truth and the lie of that statement.
Wilmer's death and the events that followed reveal the dual
nature—what I call the absent presence—of the state and its law
in marginal barrios like those of Uspha Uspha. The events are
best summarized in my blog.

| | | "A PASSING," JULY 13, 2010

Yesterday afternoon, Wilmer Vargas, a seven-year-old resident of
Loma Pampa, was trying to cross a busy highway with his older
brother when he was struck by a speeding taxi. He died instantly.

Wilmer was a constant presence in the community center in
Loma Pampa. All our students knew him, in 2008, 2009, and 2010.
He was a regular participant in all of our activities in the barrio,
joining our classes and trying to help out in the construction projects in his own small way. On our first Sunday in the barrio this year,
he participated in group games with other children and a few of our
students. One student remembered fondly how Wilmer just couldn't
grasp the subtleties of duck, duck, goose—he would just keep running around the circle, unaware that he was supposed to sit down
once he returned to his spot. Eventually someone had to grab him
and force him to sit so that the game could proceed.

Wilmer came from one of the poorest families in Loma Pampa. He lived in a single adobe room, bare of furniture, sleeping on the dirt floor with his four brothers and sisters. His mother speaks only Quechua, his father is prone to drink, and they struggled to provide him with the kind of care that a young kid needs. But things seemed to be improving. The first year we came to Loma Pampa, Wilmer was covered in warts—on his face and especially his hands, which were thick with them. I had never seen anything like it and would hesitate when he would beg to handle my camera. By this year, though, he seemed to be improving. The warts were mostly gone, and he seemed happy and cleaner than in the past.

But Wilmer was from a poor family, and like so many other poor kids was encouraged, even at a young age, to go out and try to make some money to support his family. When he was killed, Wilmer was down on the main road with his brother selling frozen popsicles from a small Styrofoam container that hung from a strap across his chest. It is not uncommon to see young boys doing this and other kinds of work, to be able to bring a few pesos home to their families.

It is the poorest, here and elsewhere, who are the most vulnerable. Poor children like Wilmer stand very little chance of making it out of poverty. More likely they wind up like him, with nothing but a blog posting for an obituary. It is a tragedy beyond measure.

Wilmer's death lays bare the contradictory ways in which the state and its laws and legal institutions operate on the margins of Cochabamba. In many ways, as this case illustrates, the law does not operate at all—it neither accords with reality as experienced by people living on the margins, nor is it enforced to any extent that would demonstrate its utility or inspire confidence in those subject to it. From the time he was old enough to walk, Wilmer was out on the street working, selling small items to bring in money for his family, despite the existence of child labor laws in Bolivia and transnational agreements concerning the rights of the child, to which Bolivia is a signatory.[1] He had to work—that's what poor kids do—and no law was going to stop him. By law, Wilmer should have been in school, though his parents were often lax in sending him, and no one followed up to find out where he was when he didn't show up—with fifty children in the classroom, the teacher was unlikely to miss the presence of one warty little boy. And when the accident occurred, the law appeared to be entirely absent as well. Wilmer was hit by a *taxi-trufi* while trying to cross the old two-lane highway that leads from Cochabamba to the lowlands of Santa

Cruz. A taxi-trufi is a taxi that follows a fixed route (hence the name: *taxi de ruta fija*, or *trufi*); trufis are often minibuses, but some are cars and so are called taxi-trufis to distinguish them from the larger trufis. All trufi lines are controlled by *sindicatos* (workers' guilds), which drivers pay to join and from which they get certain guarantees and protections, including the right to drive the route and support in case of trouble. When the driver killed Wilmer, he immediately radioed for help—not from the police or the fire brigade but from his fellow sindicato members, who came to clean up the mess and handle the aftermath of the accident. These men were supposed to return the body to the family, arrange the funeral, and make reparations to the family—all of which, as it turned out, they did, at least, according to their own standards. From start to finish, these events transpired with no apparent intervention of the state. During the three days from Wilmer's accident to his burial, no police officer, investigator, or other state official appeared in Loma Pampa to speak to the family, make inquiries, impose or suggest courses of action, or make sure that things were handled according to a formal set of procedures.

However, several additional factors need to be considered, which point to what was in fact the state's critical involvement in this series of events. For one thing, it turned out that the taxi that struck Wilmer was *chuto*—slang for illegal, but specifically illegal as a result of having dodged the rules. Vehicles brought into the country without paying customs duty or licensing fees are frequently referred to as chuto, and Cochabamba's busy roadways are packed with *autos chutos*, unrecognized and unregulated by the state. In this case, the vehicle was triply chuto—in addition to being an illegal import, the driver of the taxi didn't have a driver's license, and the car was uninsured—it lacked the state insurance coverage known as Seguro Obligatorio de Accidentes de Tránsito (SOAT) that all automobiles are legally obligated to carry. Vehicles with this coverage are designated by a triangular sticker on the lower left-hand corner of the front windshield, so that the traffic police can easily verify their status as drivers circulate through the city. (Unlike many divisions of policing, the traffic police force is well staffed and constantly on the prowl, a point to which I will return below.) As with many autos chutos, the driver of this taxi had simply purchased one of the stickers illegally—off-duty traffic cops will sell them for about 20 Bs (twenty bolivianos, or US$3)—and did not actually have the insurance, which would have provided a monetary indemnification to Wilmer's family of about US$1,000. This put the driver and his sindicato in a vulnerable position should the victim's family choose to file a complaint, as all sindicato drivers are required by law to have licenses and carry insurance—without them, both the driver and the sindicato are potentially subject to a heavy fine and lots of hassles from the traffic police.

So almost immediately following Wilmer's death, the sindicato leaders came to Loma Pampa to put pressure on Wilmer's father. They offered him money—no one would say how much—to keep the matter from the traffic police and to let the whole thing drop. Given that there had been no police investigation at the scene, it was unclear to me how a case could be prosecuted, but the agitation of the sindicato leaders was clear enough. They pressured the father to accept money from them, threatening that if he didn't accept their offer he would get nothing, and in fact he would end up having to pay for the burial himself. Ultimately the father accepted this offer and the matter died there, just like Wilmer, his head crushed like a melon against the road surface. Though the lawyers on our team threatened to follow up, there was little that anyone could really do without further imperiling the family's precarious situation. Whether the amount paid was enough to help the family to put another room on their tiny house, or whether it would just buy *chicha*—a locally fermented alcoholic beverage made from corn—for them to drown their sorrows, remained undetermined.

The disposition of Wilmer's body became another point of contention. In Bolivia, a person who dies must have a death certificate to be buried in a public cemetery. To receive a death certificate, the body of the deceased must be presented for inspection to the state medical examiner and the required fee must be paid (about 200 Bs). Of course, it might be possible to bribe the attendants at the cemetery to bury one's loved one without a death certificate, but such a request would be highly risky because it might provoke further investigation. In the absence of a death certificate —if, perhaps, one cannot transport the body to the medical examiner's, doesn't have the money to pay the fee, or doesn't particularly feel like explaining how the person died—one might pay to have one's kinsman buried in an illegal cemetery, of which there are several in the southern zone of Cochabamba: bodies, too, can be chuto. This became another point of leverage for the sindicato, which threatened to withdraw its offer of support in burying Wilmer if the parents wouldn't accept their indemnification money. Once the parents agreed to do so, the sindicato was able to have the body inspected and certified as an accidental death and received the certification for burial. They also arranged for a hearse to transport the body to the cemetery—such vehicles are rarely seen on the margins of Cochabamba, but the sindicato had connections—and paid for the interment. So although the law was not enforced in this case, and official representatives of the state were nowhere to be seen, the existence of the law and the threat that it might be enforced still exerted an influence over the entire proceedings, shaping—if only indirectly—the unfolding of events in the aftermath of this tragedy.

The death of Wilmer Vargas suggests the complex ways in which the state is simultaneously there and not there in barrio life, a ghostly, shadow presence that haunts daily and—as in this case—extraordinary encounters, menacing but prosaic, erecting obstacles that seem to perpetuate injustice rather than preventing it. Jacques Derrida (1994) referred to the contradictory condition of being and nonbeing as spectrality, a key element of his "hauntological" approach to history, in which, as Avery Gordon puts it, "that which appears absent can indeed be a seething presence" (1997, 17). Meant as a pun on "ontology" (the words in French sound very similar), hauntology is about the nature of being, of reality, based on a contemplation of nonbeing. It calls into question the "stability of presence" (Sconce 2000, 7) in the world around us, which we perceive to be spatially continuous and temporally linear. The specter, for Derrida, is a challenge to our established understandings of the world, cloaked as they are in binaries and absolute beliefs about the real and the unreal: "Derrida's specter is a deconstructive figure hovering between life and death, presence and absence, and making established certainties vacillate" (C. Davis 2005, 376). Though primarily used by literary theorists concerned with understanding assemblages of texts (for example, see Christiansen 2011), I apply the notion of spectrality here to bring into focus the contradictory condition of law, at once both present and absent in the marginal context. As the ethnography of this chapter shows, many people in the barrios feel that there is no state or state law at work in their neighborhoods, that in any crisis or official encounter, they are left to fend for themselves and inevitably get screwed in the process. Certainly Wilmer's family would attest to that. The state requires every car to have SOAT coverage and every driver to have a license, but even in the case of a fatal accident, there is no police presence and no official report made on the case. Everything is left to private negotiation, and the victim and his family suffer doubly. Though a death certificate is required, in the end this is a formality and does not provoke an investigation or any further attempts at restitution. So the sindicato paid for the burial and showed up with lots of cars to convey people to the cemetery, and its representatives made fancy graveside speeches about how Wilmer didn't deserve this, but now he is with his Maker in heaven and we have to be brave and soldier on, and they probably bought the boy's alcoholic father a barrel of chicha to boot. So a family loses a child and receives no real kind of compensation or justice. "Nothing, but nothing," said a neighbor, "the authorities don't know if we exist or we don't exist. I wonder if they ever even think about Loma Pampa."[2]

But to assert simply that the state is absent is to miss the critical ways in which the state—an analytical shorthand conflating the federal, departmental, and municipal governments, all of which play a role in passing ordinances, imposing limits, and making laws that influence local realities in various ways—in fact operates on the margins of its own domain. "Absence" suggests nonpresence, which is clearly not the case in the marginal barrio: the death certificate, for example, was a significant obstacle to Wilmer's family in attempting to bury their son, forcing them to accept a bad deal from the sindicato; and the driver's failure to acquire mandatory insurance coverage prompted the sindicato to issue a series of threats and evasive maneuvers to avoid state intervention. Nor is it accurate to talk of state failure in this context (for example, see Fukuyama 2004; Krasner and Pascual 2005). Failure implies a set of intentions gone awry, that the state somehow intends to have a particular effect but for whatever reason—incompetence, corruption, lack of resources, neoliberalism —cannot live up to these intentions. The state clearly does fail to live up to the expectations that barrio residents have of it, but that does not therefore mean that the state—its functionaries, leaders, and institutions— ever shared those expectations and assumptions about the role of the state, its obligations to its citizens, and the possibilities for its positive intervention in people's lives and communities. Far from being absent, the state is subtly present in the daily lives of barrio residents. From birth to death, as the case of Wilmer shows, the state inserts itself into people's lives at various points, demanding their attention or encouraging their dissimulation. The state is present through the law, which imposes certain requirements and restrictions on citizens, encouraging certain types of behaviors and punishing others; and through the deadening rituals of its bureaucracy, which consume time and money but are often arbitrary and seemingly punitive. At the same time the state is nonpresent, in that it does not consistently enforce the law, protect citizens' rights, defend them against threat and harm, or offer a way for them to secure justice when their rights are violated or they are injured through willful negligence. For the residents of the marginal barrios of Cochabamba, the state is a spectral entity, both there and not there; people can feel at once burdened and abandoned by the state, simultaneously oppressed and ignored. This basic relationship to the state has remained constant from at least the neoliberal period of the 1980s and 1990s through the present, and it shows no signs of abating despite the changing political configurations at the national level.

What I want to call attention to here is the way in which the state—incorporeal, sometimes terrifying, always flickering at the edges of perception—and its laws and institutions haunt the urban margins, making people less, not more, secure. Philip Abrams famously described the state as a mask, an illusion concealing the basic reality that there is no "there" there, no state subject hiding behind the curtain of state forms (1988 [1977]). It is that fundamental emptiness, shrouded in the trappings of rule, that I am calling the phantom state. It is a set of formalities, encoded in law and administration but only intermittently realized in the practice of daily life, restricting certain kinds of behavior while turning a blind eye to others. People in the barrios of Uspha Uspha rarely encounter the state unless they are compelled to do so, and their experience in these encounters is usually stressful, costly, and unsatisfying. Rather than working for the economic and physical security of the population, in its absent presence the phantom state produces insecurity, using law to intervene occasionally in the chaotic reality of the margins and to force that reality into a kind of legibility, striving to create a legal order within urban space without providing it with a stable social order. Legibility is an act of statecraft, a technique of modern governance or governmentality (Foucault 1991; C. Gordon 1991; Inda 2005). To make a population legible is to simplify its complexity, to cast it into a more easily accessed, "readable" form, so as to know it and subject it to various forms of government (such as the regulation of civic identities and the habitation of urban space, discussed below), and to more effectively discourage popular protest (Scott 1998; see also Trouillot 2001). Such are the tasks of the phantom state, and the principal points of its intersection with the lives of its marginal populations. Though not the only source of insecurity on the margins of Cochabamba, the phantom state is one of the most loathsome, for to it is attributed all the responsibility for the others and the insecurity they produce.

In offering this critique of the phantom state, I want to caution against the notion that people in Bolivia would be better off if there were no state at all. As I write, the Tea Party is ascendant in US politics, largely because of a platform that condemns the venality of the state and advocates for its radical diminution, a severe limiting of its ability to tax and otherwise interfere with individual livelihoods. My critique of the state should not be read in those terms, nor should the Bolivians I cite in these pages necessarily be viewed as politically conservative. In their own understandings of the state and its relationship to their personal security, barrio residents hold complex, sometimes contradictory views, at once condemning the government for its inability to provide protection from crime in the barrios and firmly supporting the policies of Bolivia's avowedly socialist president Evo Morales—whose mandates on social security and pensions, for example, have had direct material benefits for the marginal poor (Müller 2008). Unlike Tea Partiers, many people in the barrios want more state, not less. They rose up in protest against neoliberal attempts to reduce state programs and services during the 1990s and 2000s, and under Evo they endorse state efforts that promote such progressive initiatives as land reform, the redistribution of wealth, the nationalization of private property, and the greater representation of minority voices in national governance. At the same time, they remain critical of the enduring neoliberal tendencies of the Bolivian state in the 2010s, including its approaches to policing and judicial administration, and its rhetoric of citizen security, all of which are discussed below. Thus, even as they decry state negligence and abuse, many residents of the barrios subscribe to a notion of the state as something that should secure their rights and protect their interests, providing them with a kind of security that includes protection from crime but extending beyond that to offer them a broader sense of stability and safety in their lives. In contrast to state projects that limit governance to making things legible, barrio residents imagine other forms of state-subject relations, dreaming of a state that legitimately represents them and serves their interests, what Winifred Tate (forthcoming) has called the "aspirational state." My critique of the phantom state, then, should be read not as an argument for abandoning the state, but as an assessment of the impacts of its retrenchment, celebrated during the neoliberal period and maintained, by necessity or default, in the supposedly post-neoliberal era. It is a description of how the (post)neoliberal state works in practice, with a particular emphasis on the role of law in the processes of ordering the unruly margins, and it points to alternative visions of what the state might be.

The following discussion outlines the nature of people's engagements with the phantom state and the ways these are linked to insecurity in the barrios of Uspha Uspha, on the southern fringes of Cochabamba. Together with chapter 4, it constitutes an ethnography of insecurity in those communities, detailing local people's perceptions of insecurity in the barrios and their responses to it. The discussion in this chapter focuses principally on the role of the state—and its laws, actors, and institutions—in constituting insecurity, including an exploration of barrio residents' understandings of and relations with the police and the law. The chapter also offers a discussion of the nature of security problems from the perspective of the police and legal professionals, looking at the meanings of "citizen security" in Bolivia and how these have affected, but not really changed, the organization and practice of policing and judicial administration in the country. The discourse of citizen security reduces security to problems of crime and delinquency, circumscribing state responsibility in resolving other kinds of security problems, even when these problems have resulted from state laws and practices. This is the doubly problematic position of those people I am calling the outlawed, who are at once excluded from the law's protections but subjected to its power to make legal—or illegal. What emerges from this discussion are the ways in which the phantom state's absent presence invalidates it as a resource for resolving barrio problems, setting the stage for the consideration in chapters 4 and 5 of the strategies—violent or not—that people adopt to handle the insecurity that they must confront every day.

Insecurity and the Absent Presence of the State

Uspha Uspha (the name means "ashes" in Quechua, which is how the first settlers to arrive there characterized the consistency of the soil) is a dusty, rocky area of about forty-five square kilometers where some thirteen barrios, home to about fifteen thousand families, perch uneasily on the sides of dry washes and low, scrubby hills. Uspha Uspha was first settled in the mid-1990s, as Cochabamba's southern perimeter pushed ever further southward. Older, closer-in settlements—established by migrants from the rural *altiplano* (highlands) and Cochabamba valley during the waves of migration that began in the 1960s and intensified from the 1980s through the 2000s—had become too densely populated, pushing land values higher in the rare places where a vacant lot for construction could be found. Villa Sebastián Pagador, for example, the site of my earlier ethnographic research (Goldstein 2004), grew from about thirty thousand to more than one hundred thousand people during the course of the 2000s, and this demand contributed to the steady rise in property values there.[3] So many newer migrants looked south to Uspha Uspha, where abundant land could still be purchased for a reasonable price, albeit a full nine kilometers from the city center. As the city has expanded to the south, the same problems that earlier, more northern settlements experienced have reproduced themselves: Even as some older barrios like Villa Pagador have seen some improvements in their conditions (the main avenues of Villa Pagador are now paved with asphalt, for example), newer southern communities lack the most basic of necessities. Roads in Uspha Uspha are unpaved, there is no running water or sewer system, telephone service is limited, and of course there is no Internet. The district has one school for the thousands of children who live there, one private hospital that most people can't afford, and no police station or patrols. The urban frontier has rolled south, a lava flow creeping slowly across the valley floor, bringing with it all the same problems that the frontier has always had in Cochabamba (see map 1).

Uspha Uspha doesn't really look like most people's definition of "urban." Most of the streets are made of dirt, although several of the main thoroughfares have recently been paved with stones. The streets are not laid out in a grid fashion but wind in different directions, skirting ravines and wrapping around hills or marching up their sides at perilous slopes. The houses are made of adobe, mud brick of local manufacture that does well in the arid climate of the lower valley. Roofs are made of tin. Most houses have only one story, with several rooms clustered around an open patio; some have two stories and others are in the process of construction, the second story awaiting completion until the owner gets enough money together to continue the work. A two-story house is a good index of foreign migration: families with one or more members working abroad (usually in Spain or Argentina, less often in the United States or

MAP 1 Map of Bolivia.

elsewhere) will invest the remittances sent back by their relatives in home improvement. Some homes have an exterior wall that surrounds the property completely. This wall is also made of mud and is topped with shards of broken glass, intended to keep intruders out. Entrance is through a locked metal door, behind which is a savagely barking dog.

The landscape in Uspha Uspha is almost entirely brown. There is very little vegetation, most of the usable wood having been torn up for construction or cooking fuel long ago, so dry, dusty winds whip through the area unimpeded. On the way to Loma Pampa, one of the most distant and inaccessible barrios in Uspha Uspha, one passes a long empty field of low, desiccated bushes whose branches clutch plastic bags that the wind has tossed up, giving the impression of a farm cultivating a strange polymer crop. Many people keep animals to supplement their diets or incomes, and chickens, pigs, goats, and sheep roam freely through the barrio streets, as do skinny, scabby dogs who probably have owners but look as though they don't. Loma Pampa has one tree, an *algarrobo* (a variety of mesquite) about ten meters tall, whose dusty, low-hanging branches afford a modicum of shade to those who sit under it. The tree grows at the side of Loma Pampa's basketball court—which is more often used for *fulbito*[4]—halfway up the hill, and until the construction of the community center (see chapter 2), it was the site of monthly barrio meetings. The barrio is built up the side of a long rise, at the very end of the road leading from the main highway (the old road to Santa Cruz, where Wilmer was struck and killed) through the barrios of Uspha Uspha. The road climbs several hundred meters up the hill, through Loma Pampa, terminating at a flat expanse atop the hill—hence the barrio's name (*loma* meaning "hill," *pampa* meaning "flat"). The sun is intense in Uspha Uspha—there is very little cloud cover most days, and though the average high temperature in Cochabamba (altitude about 2,500 meters) is a comfortable 27 degrees Celsius (about 80 degrees Fahrenheit), it feels much hotter under the scorching rays of the sun. The best times of day are early evening, when the sun is just beginning to descend, and an early moon may be seen rising above the hills overlooking the barrio; or early on a fall morning, when the sky is blue, the smog has yet to rise, and the view across the valley to the city and the mountains in the distance is unobstructed. At such moments Uspha Uspha is actually quite beautiful, and one can understand why people chose to leave their rural pueblos or the cramped quarters of the city center to make a life here on the margins.

They may not look it, but Loma Pampa and its neighbors are urban communities. They belong administratively to the province of Cercado, the urban district of Cochabamba Department, a belonging that was determined after an extended political struggle between Cercado and the neighboring province of Arbieto, which tried to claim the furthest southern barrios for itself. But this effort failed, as most barrio residents felt it important to belong to the larger urban agglomeration of Cochabamba City. Residents of Uspha Uspha look to the Cochabamba municipal gov-

ernment (the Alcaldía) as their source of official support and representation, recognizing that it is from the municipality that improvements to
their living conditions might eventually arrive—although no one is holding his or her breath. People are also economically linked to Cochabamba
City. Nearly everyone in Uspha Uspha earns their living in the city, or
through connections to other urban areas in Bolivia. Many men work in
construction, some in skilled trades like plumbing but most as unskilled
laborers; others work as *transportistas*, driving buses, taxis, or trucks
within the city or between cities. Many men and women work as street
vendors, selling small items illegally on the downtown sidewalks or in the
city's enormous open-air market, la Cancha.[5] Others earn money by pushing wheelbarrows to transport the purchases of market shoppers. A few
women work as domestic employees in the homes of wealthier families,
but more find work through the Plan Nacional de Empleo de Emergencia,
a government program that hires women to do short-term maintenance
projects in the city, like sweeping streets or picking up trash in the parks.
Children attend the one city-run school in the district. In general, barrio
residents feel themselves to be urbanites—they have left the countryside
and its stigma of backwardness behind them and have established residency in the city. The city is where they have bought land and built homes.
The city is where they see their futures, and their children's futures.

In its own small way, Loma Pampa reproduces internally the same set
of problems that the southern zone demonstrates at a greater scale. Just
as barrios further north are better off than barrios further south, so are
residents at the bottom of the Loma Pampa hill better off than those at
the top. Although almost everyone in Loma Pampa is poor and of indigenous (Quechua and Aymara) descent, the people at the top of the hill
tend to be more recent arrivals to Cochabamba, and they are the most
poor, living in the most marginal conditions. Many of their homes are of
one or maybe two rooms, lacking even the basic exterior wall to provide
them with privacy and a sense of security from intruders. Until the
arrival of a new trufi line in the barrio (the same one that killed Wilmer,
incidentally), the x-10 bus line was the only transportation connecting
Loma Pampa to the city center, and it stopped at the bottom of the hill,
unwilling to risk its buses' transmissions hauling up that tremendous
incline. So people who lived at the top of the hill would have to trudge a
great distance, often carrying children and heavy bundles, to reach their
homes, which could be especially challenging at night. Curiously, many

FIG. 5 A view of Loma Pampa, 2005. Photo by the author.

of the people at the top of the hill—they are sometimes called *arribeños* (highlanders, or those from above)—are migrants from the real highlands, often from the rural parts of La Paz and Oruro Departments, and Aymara speakers; the people at the bottom of the hill—*abajeños* (lowlanders, those from below)—are more often Quechua speakers from the Cochabamba Valley. Though themselves poor and marginal, Quechua-speaking *cochabambinos* in Loma Pampa nevertheless belong to the dominant ethnolinguistic group of the region, and to the numerical majority not only in the barrio but in the city and the department as well. So the spatial distribution of marginality, which across the southern zone is arrayed along a horizontal access from north to south, is arrayed vertically within Loma Pampa (see fig. 5).

THE URBAN STAIN

The history of the city of Cochabamba, like that of many Latin American cities, has been marked by spectacular urban growth and expansion. Founded in 1571 by a mandate of Francisco de Toledo, the Spanish viceroy of Lima, Cochabamba (a name derived from the Quechua words for flood plain) originated as a small colonial market town that supplied the mines and cities of the highlands with the produce of the relatively verdant Cochabamba Valley (Larson 1988). Cochabamba began to grow during the 1930s: the end of the Chaco War left many indigenous former combatants unwilling or unable to return to their rural pueblos, and they settled instead in the city (Solares Serrano 1990). During the second half of the twentieth century, Cochabamba's growth soared. With a population of about fifty thousand at the time of the national revolution of 1952, Cochabamba had almost eight hundred thousand inhabitants by 2000 (Instituto Nacional de Estadísticas de Bolivia 2001). Most of this growth occurred as a result of rural-to-urban migration, with people leaving the villages and towns of the Bolivian altiplano and the high valleys of Cochabamba Department to seek economic opportunity in the city (a process described in detail in Goldstein 2004). Growth accelerated particularly during the period of structural adjustment of the 1980s, as government efforts to adopt neoliberal reforms resulted in the closure of the state-owned mining industry and the relocation of twenty-five thousand former miners to Cochabamba (Hinojosa 2007). The settlement pattern of these migrants usually began with a rental in the city center, where prices were high and space was limited. But after a short while, the migrants typically turned their eyes to the city's southern zone, where they might purchase their own plot of land and build their own home, to live as *propietarios* (land owners) and not as mere *inquilinos* (renters)— an unpleasant condition for independent people accustomed to being lords and ladies of their own, albeit humble, domains. Often people found land in barrios where they had friends and relations, contacts from their hometowns who had preceded them to the city and purchased lots in a particular neighborhood, and who could now assist the newcomers in finding land of their own to buy. (Loma Pampa was first settled by a group that included migrants from the town of Pocona, located in the high valley of Cochabamba; subsequent settlers included a large number of people from Pocona who followed the trail blazed by these pioneers.) Through this process, what government officials and journalists call the *mancha urbana* (the urban sprawl—more literally, the urban stain) of Cochabamba crept ever further to the south.

At various moments in its history, Cochabamba's municipal authorities attempted to govern and regulate the city's expansion. The municipal government put into effect master regulatory plans in the late 1940s and again in the early 1980s, both times in response to the perceived invasion of the city by indigenous peasants and the transformation of urban space into disordered, unregulated chaos (Urquidi Zambrana

1995).[6] The mayor and city council passed laws governing urban growth, in an effort to define those areas of acceptable urban settlement and to preserve the open spaces of parks and agricultural land that had been the basis for Cochabamba's long-standing identity as the "garden city" of Bolivia (Urquidi Zambrana 1967; 1986). These laws did little to discourage settlement outside of the designated areas of urbanization, however, as the demand for housing outstripped the approved zones of habitation and the city, bowing to the inevitable, did little to enforce its own regulations. In these unregulated zones on the urban periphery, people who knew little or nothing of municipal ordinances purchased lots from *loteadores* (land speculators), who sold them property without the legal papers the owners would subsequently need to formalize their land claims; the loteadores provided only a *minuta* (a bill of sale), which seemed legal enough to the purchasers but was insufficient in the eyes of the municipality. Throughout the southern zone, new barrios sprang up in violation of municipal law; city authorities labeled them *barrios ilegales* or *zonas rojas* (red zones). People who had purchased property in such zones were not recognized as the legal owners of their land, and their barrios had no legal claim to urban services and no political voice in the municipal government.

This process of legally codified exclusion was subsequently reversed, as successive municipal administrations grappled with the problems of the margins and tried to impose some measure of state control. During the 1990s and 2000s, periods of amnesty were declared during which land owners could legalize their holdings if they agreed to follow a series of time-consuming and expensive bureaucratic *trámites* (procedures), including paying back taxes, enclosing their lot with a mud wall, and producing a topographic diagram illustrating the limits of their claim (Goldstein 2004). Similarly, illegal barrios could be officially recognized if they also undertook a lengthy trámite that included presenting survey plans and maps to demonstrate that the barrio had dedicated adequate space to roads, sidewalks, and public *áreas verdes* (green areas), ownership of which they then had to formally cede to the municipality.[7] Such legal requirements, however, were often difficult if not impossible to satisfy—they demanded a significant investment of resources and time and often exceeded the comprehension of barrio residents, who lacked legal representation and knowledge of the process. In many cases, the loteadores involved in the original sale had disappeared, and the frustrated buyer had no witness to the transaction, left with only the minuta to prove that money had changed hands. Often illiterate and unfamiliar with the workings of lawyers and legal bureaucracies, many residents felt completely lost in dealing with the situation and so remained in limbo, unable to become legal owners of their own land. Nevertheless, land legalization is something that many barrio residents continue to crave.[8] Without it, they cannot enjoy the benefits of being urban propietarios. Illegal landowners cannot use their land as collateral to take out a loan or make an investment; they cannot pass the land on as inheritance or sell it to another buyer. Perhaps worst of all, they live in fear that at any moment someone else might claim their property or the state might evict them from their homes.

Being illegal in this sense is a fundamental form of insecurity for barrio residents, motivating them to go to great lengths to try and legalize their claims. Don Segundo, a resident of Loma Pampa, made this connection quite clearly: "The papers for the land, that they haven't given us yet, I think that if they give them to us soon we will feel happier and more secure, no? For the investment we have made. If for some reason there should be some kind of problem, who knows, we could lose the land, no? We run that risk now."[9] Lacking a solid understanding of how the system works, people remain confused about exactly where the obstacles to legalization lie, leading to greater uncertainty: "It is a problem with the doctor who sold us the land, many people say that the problem is with her, but I don't know what the problem might be, why they don't legalize our trámites and all that. Maybe it has to do with the authorities who are in charge of all these cases. And it's a problem because you need papers for your house, for example, if you want to get a small loan or something. We always lack the papers for the lot and the house."[10]

Another source of insecurity around land ownership stems from the fact that if one cannot legally demonstrate one's *derecho propietario* (ownership rights), one's land might easily be claimed by another party. This has happened frequently in the barrios, where unscrupulous loteadores often sold the same parcel of land to multiple buyers (the infamous *doble venta* [double sale]), before skipping town and leaving the competing owners to sort things out. Elsewhere, the marginal status of barrio land—not quite rural, not fully urban—has led to complications and conflicts. One barrio in Uspha Uspha that has had particular problems in this respect is Mineros San Juan. Initially established in 1995 by a group of former miners and their families from the highland departments of Oruro and Potosí, Mineros San Juan was settled by families who bought chunks of a seventy-six-hectare parcel close to the border between the provinces of Cercado and Arbieto. However, in 1996 the federal government passed a law known as the Ley INRA, creating the Instituto Nacional de Reforma Agraria, intended to continue the work of land distribution and to facilitate peasant smallholders' claims to land allocated under the 1953 agrarian reform. As part of this process, twenty-seven individuals from the nearby agrarian community of Llave Mayu were granted ownership of land already purchased by people in Mineros San Juan. This sparked a prolonged controversy, pitting different sets of claimants against one another in the dispute over the legal ownership of the land. For several years the former miners and their families lived in tents on the lots they had purchased in Mineros San Juan, afraid to construct proper homes. Then, tired of waiting, they began to settle the area. They built houses and, with their own money, cleared streets, laid out a public square, and started a transport line. In the meantime, yet another set of claimants had appeared, insisting that they were the descendants of the original owners of the land, who had been dispossessed as part of the postrevolutionary agrarian reform of 1953. Don Reynaldo, then president of Mineros San Juan, wryly described this ghostly presence: "Even the dead were showing up to claim ownership of this land."[11]

The matter was finally resolved in favor of the former miners, when the government of President Eduardo Rodríguez decided in 2006 that, as the area under discussion had already been declared part of the city of Cochabamba, the 1996 Ley INRA—which applies to rural areas—was not relevant, thereby nullifying the competing claims. But the problems did not end with that decree. Conflicts continued between Mineros San Juan and Llave Mayu, and acts of terrorism were perpetrated against the settlers by those whose claims to the land had been denied. Violent attacks have been committed against residents of Mineros, often at night. In addition, *casabobos* (booby traps) were laid near the homes of barrio leaders and residents, and a young boy was killed in 2009 when he accidentally detonated a land mine buried outside his house. Don Reynaldo attributed the problem ultimately to economics, and to the derecho propietario that his people continue to lack: even after the conflict had been decided in favor of Mineros San Juan, individual residents still had to complete the legalization trámite, and with only the minuta to demonstrate their ownership, the process remained an arduous one. For barrio residents, such problems are clear threats to local security. Don Reynaldo observed: "It's not only the leaders who deal with this insecurity, with this worry, but the residents themselves, who have great fear about what can happen, not only to themselves but to their families. That's why we want the authorities to take this very seriously. They talk so much in the media, on television, that they will bring security to Cochabamba. But we see that it is not such an easy task."[12]

PHANTASMIC ENCOUNTERS

Residents of barrios like Loma Pampa, Mineros San Juan, and Uspha Uspha Central encounter government authorities and institutions in the mundane interactions that usually take place across a counter or a desk, when they must approach low-level functionaries to execute their trámites, as in the land-legalization process. One reason why barrio residents describe the state as absent is because state functionaries and institutional representatives do not come to the barrios. Rather, residents must present themselves and their papers at the downtown offices of the Alcaldía or the Prefectura. It is in such corporeal encounters that the phantom state momentarily assumes flesh, manifesting itself in the body of a bureaucrat working in an administrative office. There, the indigenous person is likely to encounter the calculated indifference that Michael Herzfeld (1993) has identified as characteristic of modern bureaucracies, as matters of race, gender, language, and so on delegitimize the client as worthy of official attention (see also Bernstein and Mertz 2011). Although this situation improved following the election of Evo Morales, with more indigenous people employed in administrative positions and indigenous languages like Quechua and Aymara officially recognized as legitimate languages of the public sphere, for many barrio residents, the experience of encountering government bureaucracy remains a frightening and discouraging one. Indigenous women in particular dread these encounters. To access state institutions, they must leave their children at home unattended for extended periods, or give up work sometimes for days at a time, while they wait in long lines to receive instructions that they don't understand or lack the resources to comply with. The land-legalization trámite, for example, requires them to deal with a range of professionals, often white male Spanish speakers, whom indigenous women may find to be intimidating and incomprehensible. In addition to officials like bureaucrats and topographers, these may include private-sector individuals like lawyers, architects, and *tramitistas* (professional trámite processors), all of whom will take a fee and make a variety of promises that they seldom keep. The insecurity of lacking legal land title is compounded by the legalization process itself, which requires one to invest scarce resources in a process that one imperfectly understands and feels powerless to influence.

Other kinds of encounters further reinforce the absent presence of the state, at once remote yet deeply implicated in the daily lives of the urban poor. One of these is in the area of personal credentialing. As with a land title, acquiring a *carnet* (identity card) from the state is both a symbolic as well as a practical instrument of national citizenship, signifying belonging while entitling one to a range of rights guaranteed under the constitution. For barrio residents, the carnet also signifies a specifically urban belonging, containing an implicit promise to reverse marginality. One reason that residents of Uspha Uspha resisted the effort by the neighboring province of Arbieto to incorporate their barrios was their desire to belong to the urban province of Cercado, and their carnets signal that achievement. In the words of one woman, a resident of the barrio Uspha Uspha Central: "Our children are marginalized because we are from a rural area, so . . . we have to belong to [the urban province of] Cercado. Our children will have children and they will continue to be part of Cercado—we won't be marginalized, see? Because now we live in the city, on our carnets it says 'Cercado.'"[13] This observation suggests the importance of the carnet, like the land title, to marginal urban people. Recognition by the state implies the promise of belonging, citizenship, and hence rights—to a job, to live in peace, to educate one's children, to have a voice, to be secure.

Yet the carnet can be an elusive quest for many urban residents. Many indigenous people lack a birth certificate—those born in the countryside often do not know their own birthdays or ages, as such information was never recorded by the local midwives who delivered them in their mothers' villages, and their births were not recorded by the federal government. Getting a birth certificate can be a nearly impossible task, often requiring adults to return to their communities of origin to conduct research in municipal or parish church archives in the hopes of encountering some kind of proof of their existence. Men are required to have completed twelve months of obligatory military service and must present papers attesting to that service along with their birth certificates to receive a carnet. In addition, until 2011 the Bolivian National Police was in charge of the administration of identity cards, forcing people into direct contact with the hated police and their bureaucratic machinery. Outside police headquarters on Calle Baptista near Cochabamba's Plaza Principal, where the identity-card trámites were processed, the line of hopeful residents stretched around the block as people waited for days, missing work as they tried to bring their identities into line with government requirements. Even when successfully acquired, the carnet is often rife with errors, requiring more time in lines, more money, more paperwork. Don Miguel confessed to me that he had only recently learned that for his entire life he had been spelling his last name incorrectly. After meeting a distant cousin, he discovered that the spelling on his birth certificate was incorrect (because he had been born in a mining town, he was fortunate enough to have a birth certificate), and this error had been perpetuated on his carnet throughout his life. Miguel's daughter's carnet lists her as a boy. To correct these errors, Miguel will have to navigate the system and persuade it of its mistakes, a daunting task that he has been putting off. In a previous encounter with a state bureaucrat, Miguel had asked why the carnets and other official documents contain so many errors. Making errors is a form of job security, the man explained, straight-faced: "We make work for future bureaucrats who have to correct our mistakes."[14]

Such a remark, though amusing, contains an element of truth. The trámite requires people to maintain an ongoing engagement with the state as they try to make themselves and their property legible, in hopes of attaining citizenship and the rights it conveys. The typical trámite requires months—sometimes years—to complete, as people fill out forms, have them notarized, pay fees, receive stamps and seals at different offices, fill out more forms, have those forms notarized, pay more fees, lobby to correct mistakes that slip into their documents . . . the process feels endless. For those who wish to complete it, the trámite brings them into constant contact with state functionaries and institutions—phantoms whose malevolence is revealed by their insatiable demands and dehumanizing manner of interaction—and places the intimate details of their personal situations under the scrutiny of these entities. For private people who already harbor a profound mistrust of the state, such exposure can feel devastating. And like Russian nesting dolls, one trámite is likely to contain a multitude of other trámites hidden inside of it, so that once one enters the process, it can be exceedingly difficult to get out. For that reason, whenever possible people will dispense with the legal process altogether and simply cobble together a solution to the problems facing them. This might mean living chuto—doing without identity papers and the kinds of things that those allow one to get, like a bank account, a driver's license, or a loan. In this way people avoid the state entirely, living with the insecurity that comes with being chuto, but avoiding its crushing, dehumanizing demands. Rather than successfully ordering social life, in this case the requirements of state law encourage people to *esquivar*—to dodge the law and live without its recognition. Entire industries grow up around this willingness to dodge the state, as people find ways to adopt the appearances of legality while lacking the law's true approbation.

Take, for example, my own experience with car ownership in Bolivia. Though I had worked in Bolivia since 1993, I had never actually owned anything in the country, and it was through the experience of property that I initially encountered the Bolivian legal system as a user, rather than as an anthropologist. My first encounter, or perhaps nonencounter, with the state was when I purchased the car, a 1996 Subaru Legacy wagon, which had entered the country without paying import duties and was thus itself illegal, an auto chuto. Through the services of an attorney, I was able to obtain legal ownership, though this was a complex process involving numerous trámites and a rather large outlay of cash—so large that most Bolivians would probably have avoided it by just getting a minuta (in this case, a letter from the previous owner acknowledging the sale) and ignored the paperwork and the state. Of course I needed license plates, and Milton, the car dealer, was able to provide these, though where he got them from I was afraid to ask. As in the United States, I also needed an inspection sticker, but because this was January, the time for inspections had already passed. Fortunately Milton knew a guy, a traffic cop, who was happy to sell me a sticker for 50 Bs (about US$7), which I glued on my window next to my SOAT sticker, indicating that I had paid my federal accident insurance premium. This I did buy officially for US$12, though I could have bought a fake sticker for less if I had known anyone who sold them.

The driver's license was another trámite altogether. Though expatriate friends insisted they'd driven for years on their US licenses, on the advice of my Bolivian attorney (rather prudent and risk averse, as attorneys tend to be), I decided to go the legal route and get my official Bolivian driver's license. This required me to have Interpol verify that I was not an international criminal; however, to process that trámite, I needed a Bolivian resident's card, and to get that I would need a resident visa, which was another huge and expensive trámite that I didn't feel like undertaking. The nice official at the federal offices of Migración assured me, with a smile, that something could be worked out for me—which, my attorney explained, meant that something would have to be worked out for the nice official. On the other hand, meanwhile, my friend Josias, a taxi driver and don Miguel's son, knew a guy who for 100 Bs could make me a Bolivian driver's license, no questions asked. In the end I elected not to get a license at all but to just drive chuto and hope I wasn't pulled over by a traffic cop—in which case I would have paid him 20 Bs and he would have let me go on my way. Cheaper and easier in the long run for all concerned.

I could choose to avoid the state because I had the security of my passport and my bank account with grant money in US dollars. For most Bolivians that I know, living chuto is no laughing matter, and they are much less flippant about the entire undertaking. That doesn't mean, however, that they are humorless about it. People laugh all the time about the state and its functionaries, and they relish pointing out the ironies of a state that doesn't pay attention to its own laws. Someone recently told me that Cochabamba's giant statue of Jesus Christ, supposedly the tallest in the world (a few inches taller than the one in Rio de Janeiro, people say), which stands proudly on a hill overlooking the city, was built on land that the government itself never bothered to legalize. When I told this to Miguel, he laughed and laughed. "Only in Bolivia," he said. "Even Jesus is illegal!" From then on, he referred to the Christ statue as the *Cristo chuto*. An entire genre of jokes and stories catalogs the experience of dealing with the Bolivian justice system ("What are the three things one should avoid when traveling in South America?" "Peruvian men, Chilean women, and Bolivian justice"), and people frequently recount anecdotes of their encounters with the police and the law. Miguel's story about bureaucrats making work for other bureaucrats is one example. Taxi drivers like Miguel are great tellers of jokes revolving around their work driving about the city. For example: When driving in Bolivia, remember that red means go and green means stop. Why? Because you always run a red light unless there's a policeman (in his green uniform) standing there. Article 20 of the Bolivian constitution? It's the 20 Bs you pay the traffic cop to let you go without a ticket. *Taxistas* call the cops "*loros*"—parrots, again for the color of the uniform. Josias told me of a time that a traffic cop stopped him on the road and demanded a bribe to let him go, and so Josias gave him one boliviano (about fifteen cents). Outraged, the cop replied: "Come on, man, that's not even enough for a Coca-Cola! You're making a mockery of the law!"[15]

MEN IN GREEN

The jokes and stories try to minimize the real fear that many barrio residents have of the police, the very embodiment of the state's absent presence. As the joke about the traffic light suggests, cops are occasionally present, particularly on streets in the business district downtown, and their visible presence does discourage transgressions. But these are the traffic police (La División de Policía de Tránsito), who circulate through the downtown hoping to catch people who have violated traffic laws or otherwise stepped out of line and thus made themselves a target of police attention (for example, stopping for a red light but blocking a crosswalk). The "rent-seeking" behavior (Kohl 2004) of many of these policemen consistently reinforces peoples' belief that the *pacos* (cops) are corrupt and self-serving, and that the police force as a whole is out for its own enrichment, rather than to provide security for the population. Indeed, in the minds of many barrio residents, police and other legal professionals are producers of insecurity, rather than agents working to counteract it.

If the traffic cops are overly visible, other kinds of police officers are much less in evidence, leading people again to conclude that the state is absent from their communities. People widely insist that the cops are not present in the barrios, and indeed in all of Uspha Uspha there is not a single police station or barracks, nor any roving police patrols or police officers walking the beat. The nearest police station is eight kilometers to the north, near the Laguna Alalay, where the Policía Técnica Judicial (PTJ), the investigative arm of the national police force, maintains one of its headquarters. It is to this distant outpost that crime victims must report, to file papers in the vain hope that items stolen from their homes might be returned, or that some kind of investigation into the violence committed against them might be initiated. Emergency phone calls to the police typically go unanswered. Although there is a 911 emergency hot line, people who call it often get no response to their pleas, or if they do it is long after the emergency has passed. Doña Dora commented: "El policía hasta que llegue . . . taaaaaarda" (the police come slooooowly).[16] Some barrio residents attribute the lack of police protection to the fact of their marginality and the discrimination they experience for living on the margins. A woman in Mineros San Juan said: "I have seen how there in the northern zone of the city, you can see cops on motorcycles any hour of the day, they are always up there making their rounds, but down here they never come, not even on a Sunday to make one little round."[17] This perspective is disputed by friends of mine in the northern zone, who make statements about the police similar to those of barrio residents to the south. One friend, an automobile importer who lives in a fancy gated high-rise condominium, said that the police are inattentive to him and his neighbors: the police are of no use, "not for the poor, not for the rich, not for the middle class, not for the white, yellow, brown, nobody."[18]

Many barrio residents understand the pacos to be corrupt, refusing to investigate a crime unless they are paid by the victim. One woman said: "The first thing they ask for in the PTJ is money. My niece was murdered, and when we went to the police so that they would investigate, the first thing they asked us for was one hundred dollars to begin the investigation. Imagine how much they would want to complete the investigation! Because we didn't have money, we had to leave it at that. She was killed, she was buried, but nothing."[19] Another woman described her experience reporting a crime to the police: "I go into the PTJ—which at that time was operating out of the main plaza—I go in and, 'Yes, I recognize him, there he is.' They have photos of those malhechores all over the place in there, and I go, 'That's him,' I say . . . 'Ahh! Of course that's him, *señora*, tomorrow we'll go and recover [the money]. But only half.' 'Okay,' I said, 'half.' I accepted, no? Such blackmail! But I accepted, half. And to this day I haven't gotten my half."[20] While some people want there to be local police stations in their barrios, others resist this suggestion for fear that a greater police presence would end up costing them more money. Police officers frequently insist that the impoverishment of their institution requires them to ask barrio residents for money to carry out their basic functions. Several policemen have their residences in the barrio Concordia in Uspha Uspha, and they have suggested trying to establish a police substation in the barrio. "But," said another Concordia resident, "we would have to pay their salaries, their meals, who knows what else they might need. So it's not really possible for us to maintain them. They even want gasoline for their vehicles!"[21]

Because the police appear to be in business for their own enrichment, many people harbor a basic mistrust of them, viewing them as agents of insecurity, rather than citizen security, in their communities (Rocabado Rodríguez and Caballero Romano 2005). Again, it is the absent presence of the police that is at the root of the problem: people have contact with the police, but these contacts are typically negative, resulting in extortion, a sense that their concerns are not taken seriously, and a deepening sense of victimization rather than of restitution. The police come to be seen as identical to the malhechores and delincuentes they are supposed to be controlling. Doña Irma speaks for many when she claims that the police have *un convenio* (an agreement) with the thieves to release them in exchange for a payment.[22] People assert (often erroneously) that the cops show up quickly in the event of a lynching, underscoring this point in the minds of many—the cops don't appear in response to the calls of barrio residents, but they come in a hurry when their accomplices are in jeopardy. A resident of Mineros San Juan told me: "I want to be clear about police corruption. When we catch a delinquent, the police arrive immediately, because there is so much contact between the delinquent and the police. But when we have a terrible problem among the *vecinos* [barrio residents] . . . then the police never appear. So the police coordinate with the delinquents."[23] A resident of Concordia said: "The police come when we tell them we have caught someone, they come to defend the thief, but when we tell them that we have been robbed, no. Twice my house has been broken into and nobody came."[24] Said another vecino: "The police are always on the side of the *maleantes* [bad guys]—everybody says that, not just me. The cop is a thief, too, the same as a thief."[25] And another commented: "Any case you have, they ask you for something, always, 'you give me this amount and I'll help you,' that's what they say to us, right to our faces. Sometimes it's for gasoline. . . . If we call them, they tell us, 'Yes, we're coming, but I have to put twenty pesos of gasoline in my car, you have to give me that no matter what.' There is no confidence in that institution, many vecinos, many of us have no trust in it [*desconfiamos*]."[26]

The lack of confidence that many have in the police extends to the justice system more broadly, including prosecutors, judges, and the law itself. Again, it is not a question of the law's absence but of the problematic engagements that people have with the individuals and institutions that represent the law, and the partial, selective nature in which law affects their lives. This is perhaps best symbolized by Bolivia's election laws, which require every citizen over the age of twenty-one (over eighteen if married) to vote in local and national elections.[27] The consequences of not voting include a stiff fine and, perhaps more important, a future inability to process one's trámites, many of which require that one present proof of having voted. Thus a law intended to guarantee universal suffrage becomes for citizens a burden and a means of subjecting them to state oversight. And although free and fair elections remain perhaps the most significant indicator of democratic governance for the academics and transnational entities that monitor such things (see Arias and Goldstein 2010), the experience of the electoral process can feel coercive and in some ways authoritarian for those who participate in it.

For many people living on the margins, the law seems a distant and perverse creature, something beyond their ability to comprehend. In an abstract sense, some people recognize the importance of the law and appreciate its possibilities. For instance, don Angel of Loma Pampa, when asked if there are laws in Bolivia and if they protect or harm the average person, stated: "There are laws, they always work, you have to obey the law. . . . They protect me, they don't harm me. . . . They serve us, because under the law we can do certain things, if there is no law, one can't function well."[28] Others disagree and regard the law as an obstacle that harms them more than it helps to protect them and their interests. In part, they say, this is because of the great gulf that separates the realities of barrio life from those who make and enforce the law. Judges, prosecutors, and lawyers are all viewed in a similar light as the police: corrupt, self-serving individuals with no sense of responsibility toward the public and no knowledge of what life is like for the poor and marginalized. Josias said: "Really, I believe that the law obstructs things. If there were district governments I think that would be much better . . . there would be much more communication with those who govern, they would know our problems, how we live, no? In reality, though, they are in their houses, in their beds, they have money probably for their whole lives, including for their children, no? So they don't know how we live."[29]

This sense of distance between the law and barrio reality is in part due to the spatial separation that locates law and its institutions in the city center, with barrios and their populations on the urban periphery. Here it is a question of horizontal distance that divides the law and lawmakers from citizens. But, as Josias's comment above indicates, there is also a matter of the vertical distance between these entities, a hierarchy in which the law is above social reality, and those who make and benefit from the law are far superior to those who live at the bottom. The distance here is not so much a matter of space as it is of race and class, social differences that separate people from the law and the government institutions that make and enforce it. A resident of Juan Pablo II attributed this gulf to the innate deficiencies of the urbanized *campesino* (peasant), who speaks only Quechua and lacks the refinement to present him or herself before the law: "If I go to the Alcaldía, they're not going to let me in. . . . First of all, I have to know how to express myself in front of them, because we from the countryside, we are basically stupid, uncouth (*brutos*). I'm just telling you my reality. I'm not a lawyer, I'm nothing, I'm there speaking in my own language, so they are not going to let me come in."[30] Some believe that the laws are not intended to protect people like them. One man described his problems following a car accident, in which not only was he unable to gain restitution from the driver who struck his car, but he somehow ended up having to pay 380 Bs for the damages, as well as a 50 Bs bribe to the traffic officer and 300 Bs to a lawyer. He concluded: "These laws are for people who have money."[31] Don Baltazar of Loma Pampa captured the multiple distances separating barrio residents from the law: "There is no justice. There are laws, but in serious cases the prosecutors say, 'Article such-and-such, we are going to proceed,' but they never do. . . . The laws are very far away from the poor."[32]

The poor also lack the personal connections with lawyers, police, and judges that could help them to get the system working on their behalf. People are cynical about lawyers, whom they regard as entirely self-interested, invested in promoting conflicts so that they can then be paid to resolve them. Of lawyers, doña Elena of Loma Pampa said: "They fix things, but they only do it for money. They take a lot of money out of you, 40, 50 bolivianos. But they fix things fast."[33] For those with money to hire a lawyer, or for those few with a relative or compadre (fictive kinsman) in the legal profession, having legal representation can help to give confidence in the law. The laws function "sometimes," said doña Dora. "But I have a very good lawyer. With him I have done the papers for my mother's house, we only go to him, to Dr. Ramiro. He also helped me get my son away from the police [when he was arrested]."[34] Without these kinds of contacts and the *muñeca* (influence) that they provide, people find the law much more remote and antagonistic. Don Armando of Loma Pampa said: "I believe that, for those who have money there is [justice], because here in Bolivia everything depends on money. When you have money, you can make contact with any authority you like, but if you don't have money then there is no justice. In Bolivia it's like that, if you don't have money, they don't attend to you, they kick you out instead."[35] From the perspective of many barrio residents, the law is for others, not for them, and in a sense this excuses them from having to pay the law any attention. In a group interview in Uspha Uspha Central, some women exchanged comments on this point:

> FIRST WOMAN: [The laws] protect those who are, for example the MASistas [supporters of the ruling MAS party], obviously, now they protect the MASistas. If you are from MAS you have support; if not, you don't have anything.
>
> SECOND WOMAN: I'm from MAS but nobody supports me [laughter].
>
> FIRST WOMAN: Nobody supports you, have you needed some help [more laughter]?
>
> *Are the laws important? What kinds of laws should there be?*
>
> SECOND WOMAN: Obviously the laws are important, you have to obey them. But who obeys them nowadays?[36]

Another important element affecting people's relationship to the law is their often basic ignorance of it and how it operates. Having had no legal education and often little experience with legal professionals or institutions, barrio residents express confusion about the law's basic operations and purposes. This is particularly problematic when one is a victim of a crime and doesn't know how to access the authorities. A woman in Juan Pablo II observed: "We don't even know the phone number of the police."[37] Many barrio residents feel completely lost when dealing with the law and legal institutions, and powerless as a result. A man in Concordia put it like this: "In the southern zone of Cochabamba, the majority of us have few resources and don't understand much, and in the case of these laws, nothing. So the only thing to do is to get a lawyer, which takes money and time. For those of us who survive from day to day, it is impossible to think in terms of a trial."[38] Some attribute their inability to legalize their land claims to this lack of knowledge. Another resident of Juan Pablo II characterized the illegal land sales this way: "We suffered a serious rip-off, so we need an orientation in how to defend ourselves, to know the laws. He who knows the laws has a lot of knowledge, but we are not all on the same level. For example, in my case, I sincerely think that you all should come and teach us how to defend ourselves, because I don't know what the 110 [the mobile police patrol] is, I don't know what 911 is, I don't know where to go, and I'm sure that the majority of people here don't know either."[39] It was requests like these that prompted me and my research team to consider ways of intervening more directly in the problems we were studying, leading to the creation of the CAJs project described in chapter 2.

Because of the extensive corruption they witness and must sometimes participate in, their poor understanding of the law, and the lack of its enforcement, many barrio residents view the law in general, and its various personnel and institutions more specifically, as actively antagonistic to their own well-being. For example, under the New Penal Procedural Code (El Nuevo Código de Procedimiento Penal, introduced in 1999), Bolivian law provides for habeas corpus and prohibits preventive detention of the criminally accused (see chapter 6). As a result, many criminal suspects are released after only eight hours of detention due to lack of evidence or the failure of the crime victim to make a formal accusation, an expression of people's unwillingness to engage the state legal system. Even if they feel inclined to use the justice system, people may be afraid to do so. In part this stems from the fear of having to pay a bribe or of being treated poorly by officials. But it also is based on the fear that the system will not work properly, and that they will suffer repercussions for having denounced a criminal to the authorities. People are terrified of revenge and so hesitate to engage the justice system even when they suffer directly from crime. Describing an incident in his community, a male resident of Juan Pablo II related how "in this case no one denounced the criminal, even though he was 100 percent guilty. The victim didn't make a denunciation because there are threats—the very same thieves will threaten you, 'if something happens to me, you will pay.' So many won't make a denunciation; they are afraid of revenge."[40] Without a formal denunciation, the accused cannot be prosecuted, and the case ends there. Many people view this apparent failure of the law as a kind of leniency that favors the criminal over the crime victim, and as an illustration of how the law protects the rights of criminals over the rights of victims (see chapter 6 for a more detailed discussion of this point). Another resident of Juan Pablo II interpreted it this way: "Right now we have laws, but these laws—one has to have money, time. So these laws don't do anything for us. A thief shows up, we catch him, and seven, eight, twenty-four hours later, they let him go. So these laws don't do anything for us."[41] If the laws don't serve them, many vecinos say, there is no motivation for them to pay attention to the law. My friend Josias said: "The truth is, in many barrios they don't comply with the law, including here. We don't pay any taxes, we don't pay any kind of tribute to the government. There are people who don't pay attention to the laws because we aren't served by them. They don't benefit us in any way. Rather, in other ways, they harm us."[42]

Josias told me the story of a buddy of his, an electrician falsely accused of car theft, that captures this perception of how the law and the legal system operate:

> One of my friends was just walking along when there happened to be a robbery of a car further up the street. He is an electrician, and he was carrying his little tool kit, so when [the police] grabbed him they checked his bag and found screwdrivers and pliers. So they said to him: "You are a car thief." He replied: "I am an electrician." But because of what he was carrying they thought he was a thief trying to take apart cars, they mistook him for a thief, and they put him in jail. . . . They put him in San Sebastián [prison]. He was there for six months, trying to proclaim his innocence. There was a trial, but it was a big mess. I went to visit him and he told me: "You know, Josias, I have to plead guilty, I have to say that I was the thief if I want to get out of here. They are going to give me a long sentence otherwise." I said to him: "How can you plead guilty when you haven't done anything?" But his lawyer had told him it's easier for a thief to get out of jail than for an innocent person. So he had to say in another trial that he had done it, that yes, he was the thief. . . . He had to pay the judge something like

three hundred dollars. So, there might not be too many more electricians around after this [laughs]. . . . You have to declare yourself guilty to get out. So we realize that the law in Bolivia is in favor of the thieves. If a thief can get out faster than an innocent person, then we have no reason to trust in the laws.[43]

Speaking with Phantoms

Lack of understanding, disappointment, alienation, revictimization—all contribute to barrio residents' feeling that they have no reason to trust in the laws, or in the institutions that make and enforce them. It is important to note here that many people who work in the enforcement of law and the administration of justice in Bolivia have similar sentiments. Much as poor city dwellers feel that the law works against their interests and that the state is an obstacle to their well-being, so do many police officers, bureaucrats, lawyers, and judges regard themselves as victims, powerless and exploited by a system that has more to do with individual enrichment than with administering justice or ensuring citizens' rights. Though the politics of citizen security have gained momentum in Bolivia in recent years, the practice of justice administration has changed little, and many working in the system experience levels of dissatisfaction similar to those whom the system is supposed to serve.

With the rising crime rates in the country following the introduction of neoliberal reforms[44]—statistics show an increase in crime of 360 percent from 1990 to 2001[45]—the Bolivian state adopted the language of citizen security to frame its efforts to protect the population from delinquency, shifting attention away from security as protection of the state or promotion of *orden público* (public order) and toward security as protection of the population (Comisión Andina de Juristas 1999; Curbet 2006). Beginning in the mid-1990s, the Bolivian state issued numerous proclamations and decrees, creating a host of programs and initiatives intended to improve citizen security—understood exclusively as protection from crime, in contrast to broader conceptions of what security might entail (see chapter 1)—in the country. Most of these programs focused on institutional reorganization, aiming to increase cooperation and communication between different policing entities while maintaining a centralized, hierarchical operation. Despite changes in government (Bolivia had six different presidents in the 2000s),[46] the state's approach to citizen security remained consistent throughout the decade, with successive governments introducing new laws to create additional levels of institutions and bureaucracy without putting significantly more resources into policing or the justice system, or developing new programs to encourage citizen participation in law enforcement.[47] Citing a "climate of citizen insecurity," in 2000 President Hugo Banzer created (through Supreme Decree 25676) the Dirección General de Seguridad Ciudadana (the General Department of Citizen Security), a bureau in the Ministry of the Interior to coordinate the crime-control efforts of the national police and the departments, municipalities, and members of civil society.[48] In 2003, the government of Gonzalo Sanchez de Lozada approved Law 2494, the Law of Citizen Security, which created the Consejo Nacional de Seguridad Ciudadana y Orden Público (National Council of Citizen Security and Public Order), charged with developing master plans to reduce what the government identified as the crime wave in different departments in the country. And in 2006, President Evo Morales issued Supreme Decree 28631, expressing even greater concern for security by establishing the Vice Ministry of Citizen Security. Through his own Plan Ciudad Segura (Secure City Plan), introduced in 2010, Evo's government also mobilized the Defense Ministry, enlisting the services of the military in everyday police work to fight crime.[49] Of potential significance was Supreme Decree 28421, which directed that the tax revenues from sales of natural gas be channeled into efforts at the municipal level to improve education, health, economic development, job creation, and citizen security. Given the wide array of unmet needs, however, and the stipulation that these monies could not be used for salaries or benefits for police or judicial personnel, the practical impact of these reforms was minimal.

These national-level changes were reflected at the departmental and municipal levels. In 2005 the Prefecture of Cochabamba created the Dirección Departamental de Seguridad Ciudadana (State Department of Citizen Security), whose principal project was another plan called Ciudad Segura (Secure City), intended to decentralize police functions, raise public awareness of security issues, and create district-level police departments. And in the same year, the Alcaldía of Cochabamba City created the Unidad de Seguridad Ciudadana (Citizen Security Unit) to coordinate efforts at the municipal, departmental, and national levels. For its part, the Departmental Police created an office called the Jefatura de Seguridad Ciudadana (Citizen Security Headquarters), with the aim of promoting community policing and establishing police units in twenty-two barrios throughout the city.[50] However, resources were lacking to fund this project—the Jefatura had only one officer, one secretary, and one motor scooter permanently assigned to it—and the costs of supporting the barrio police units fell to the local barrios themselves. In 2006 the Jefatura ceased operations, and the barrio units were withdrawn. Today, policing in the city is coordinated through the Organismo Operativo de Orden y Seguridad (Operative Organization for Order and Security), a centralized entity on Avenida Heroínas downtown. The Organismo includes the first responders such as Radio Patrol 110, firefighters, and the Brigade for the Protection of the Family; it is also the entity directly charged with protecting the departmental and municipal authorities in times of social disruption and protest.[51] For this purpose they have created the Delta Group, a specially trained unit to intervene in times of public disturbance. The group consists of male and female officers with distinctly gendered assignments: in confronting angry mobs, for instance, they form two lines, with a line of women in front to try to negotiate with the protestors, backed by a line of heavily armed male officers who can intervene forcefully should the negotiations fail. Given the strong backing that the Morales administration receives from the *movimientos sociales* (social movements) in Bolivia, these units can find themselves in an awkward situation, as happened when they were called on to disrupt protests of angry coca growers—government supporters—marching on the Plaza Principal of Cochabamba, where the main government buildings are located.[52] Nevertheless, it is interesting to note that through the development of this series of organizations meant to deal with security matters, the notion of citizen security—which originated as a way to move the idea of security away from protection of the state to meeting the needs of citizens—has now once again come to mean public order and state security.

Despite these organizational changes and the attendant promises to increase the police presence on the streets of Bolivia's cities, to provide more resources for policing, and to encourage popular participation in the work of increasing security through such approaches as community policing,[53] few changes were seen in the daily reality of police and judicial practice. The shortage of resources that these institutions experience are felt by officers from the top to the bottom of the hierarchy. The commandant of Cochabamba's Organismo Operativo de Orden y Seguridad, for example, complained that the government does not provide his office with the resources its staff members need to improve their physical conditions or adequately carry out their functions.[54] The same complaints were heard from his subordinates.[55] Froilan Mamani, a sergeant in the Cochabamba force and a leader of the Asociación Nacional de Suboficiales, Clases y Policías de Cochabamba, an organization much like a union that represents the interests of police officers at the departmental and national levels, said that the institution lacks even the most basic necessities to allow officers to perform their duties. For example, no accommodations have been made for the increasing numbers of women entering the police force in recent years; as a result, there are no separate dormitories for men and women in the police barracks, an uncomfortable situation for officers of both genders. The dormitories where these officers sleep for a few hours during their extended shifts are equipped with shabby, broken furniture, and if cops want sheets or blankets on their beds, they have to bring them from home. Nor are the salaries and benefits provided to individual officers adequate. A police officer just graduating from the academy can expect to earn 750 Bs—about US$107—a month, while being expected to work twenty hours a day in forty-eight hour shifts. Police officers have to buy their own uniforms and equipment out of their salaries, including their own handguns. If an officer can't afford to buy a gun, he or she will have to enforce the law using only a nightstick. Sergeant Mamani also said that each officer gets a certain ration of gasoline for his or her vehicle each morning, but if the day's duties call for more gas, the officer must pay for it out of his or her own pocket. For this reason, he said, cops will sometimes ask crime victims to help them buy gasoline for their vehicles, a request that citizens view as an example of police corruption.[56]

Statements of this sort are typical of the Bolivian police force, which has a long history of denying responsibility for its transgressions (Quintana et al. 2003). The police force is governed by a set of unofficial codes that regulate internal behavior and the face that the institution and its officers present to the public. Corruption, for example, is indeed widespread in the Bolivian police force—most cops will privately admit to using their uniform to extract payments from citizens, including those who have done nothing wrong (Mansilla 2003)—but many officers deflect the accusation, insisting that corruption is no worse than in any other Bolivian institution or branch of government. "Where is there no corruption?" asked another officer, Sergeant Alejandro Bravo, rhetorically. "There is corruption everywhere."[57] At the same time, the constant accusations of corruption damage the morale of the force. Sergeant Mario Huanca, another leader of the Asociación Nacional de Suboficiales, Clases y Policías de Cochabamba, said: "To be a policeman now is an embarrassment. The cop is the worst element of society—that's how we are made to feel. And they demand so much from us and they give us nothing."[58] Rather than corruption, he insisted, much of the force's infrastructure has been provided through private donations from corporations and private individuals. For example, a local company that makes pasta and crackers has assumed the role of padrino of the police, helping to maintain Radio Patrol 110's station house and donating baskets of food and other gifts at Christmas. Such private financing of course implies that the financier will receive better attention from the police and thus verges into the realm of privatization of public functions. In addition, to make up for the lack of institutional resources, the police will sometimes call on a forced labor draft—for example, requiring street kids and other "delinquents" to perform physical labor in the construction of a station house. Nevertheless, most low-grade officers point to the higher levels of the police hierarchy when the issue of corruption is raised. Both Sergeant Mamani and Sergeant Huanca complained that in cases of corruption, it is typically only the lower-ranking officers who are accused and investigated, while the captains and colonels enjoy impunity. The sergeants claim that what looks like police corruption is only the street officers trying to do their duty, requesting money to buy gasoline and the like, while the real corruption is taking place at the higher levels of the hierarchy.

Indeed, the police force is a vertical institution, with those at the top enjoying a much greater range of privileges than those at the bottom (Mansilla 2003). In addition to having better pay, benefits, and working conditions, chiefs treat the lower-level officers like their personal valets. Sometimes the abusive treatment includes physical abuse, with officials kicking or beating their subalterns in the ordinary course of duty. Although such behavior is officially prohibited, lower-level officers rarely complain, knowing that the institution will take the side of the chief against the paco.[59] The police hierarchy is not exceptional; it is similar to other hierarchies of race and class in Bolivian society. Poor and indigenous candidates to the police force, lacking the required preliminary education or the resources to pay tuition at the Officers' Academy, generally attend the Escuela Básica Policial (Basic Police School), from which it is impossible to enter the higher ranks of the institution. Low-level cops live in fear of higher-ranking officers, who often pressure them to do anything that they require. "Whatever the problem, we are the ones who pay," said Sergeant Huanca, "because we are the front line. If there is a popular demonstration, we are the ones that have to confront the demonstrators, while the chiefs—no. The chiefs just give orders."[60] This fear and what we might call insecurity of the ordinary officers contributes to an overall sense of discouragement and a lack of loyalty to the police force.

Oddly enough, many police officers see themselves as a constant and active presence in the communities they are assigned to protect, a view that runs contrary to the one expressed by most barrio residents. Whereas barrio residents describe the police as absent from their communities, the police see themselves as deeply enmeshed in barrio life. In fact, some officers said, it is precisely because they are so close to the community that they are the ones who are singled out for blame for the problems of insecurity. Corporal Manuel Palacios, another low-ranking officer, said that he feels very close to the population, because every day he sees problems, attends to emergencies, helps people who have been in accidents, receives calls and visits from complainants, breaks up fights among drunks, and so on. Every aspect of his job, he said, involves relations with the public, so he doesn't understand how they can say that the police are far removed from the citizenry: "The politicians are far away, the judges are far away, the mayor is far away, but the police officer is in permanent contact, responding to the needs of the population."[61] Of course, such an assessment flies in the face of most barrio residents' assessments of the police and their work, as described above. But the discrepancy points again to the absent presence of the police, who feel themselves to be fully engaged in public life while for most barrio residents they appear only as shadows.

In terms of relationships between institutions, there is a great deal of hostility, suspicion, and finger pointing between the police, who are supposed to apprehend criminals, and the judicial authorities, who are supposed to try and incarcerate them. Each institution blames the other for the ongoing problems of citizen insecurity in Cochabamba, with accusations of ineptitude, corruption, and negligence of duty flying from one side to the other. Police officers, for example, insist that while there may be some problems with corruption in the police force, the real abuses occur within the legislative and the judicial organs of government, particularly with the prosecutors and judges who let criminals off the hook, and that they are the ones the public should blame for problems of insecurity. From the commandant to the low-ranking officers like sergeants, the police are defensive about accusations of corruption and deflect blame onto others. Corporal Palacios, for example, complained that people should direct their accusations against the higher levels, especially the judges: "But for the people it is easier to attack the police, the class that is barely able to maintain their families. They don't want to get involved with these big corrupt guys."[62] Police also blame the judicial system for their inability to control crime in the city, claiming that judges are bound by the leniency of the law. The police state that even when they apprehend criminals, they are quickly put back out on the street by judges who inappropriately insist on material evidence to incarcerate them. Police spokesmen frequently appear in the news media, displaying pictures of violent criminals and blaming judges and the lack of suitable laws for the fact that these delinquents remain at large. The New Penal Procedural Code has come under particular fire from the police, who claim that the mandate of habeas corpus and the elimination of preventive detention make it impossible for them to do their jobs, releasing detainees back onto the streets in the absence of evidence that the police claim they lack the resources to provide. Although such laws might work well in more advanced societies, they say, such laws are not appropriate to the Bolivian situation. This line of reasoning has been taken up by some barrio residents as well. For example, a male resident of Uspha Uspha Central observed: "I personally think that the penal law that we have does not accord with our reality. It is copied from other latitudes and doesn't work for us."[63] Criticism of the judicial system even comes from very high-ranking officials in the MAS government. Then-Minister of Government Sacha Llorenti, commenting on the need for better crime control programs like those embodied in the national Plan Ciudad Segura, asked: "How many cases do we have in which the police act with diligence and opportunity, apprehending the delinquents with proof of guilt, but a few days later some bad district attorneys or judges let them go free, as has happened in Cochabamba and Santa Cruz?"[64]

Judges and lawmakers believe that the police are hostile to laws like the New Penal Procedural Code because such laws limit the ability of the police to use with impunity harsh techniques in criminal investigations. Blaming the law, the judges and lawmakers say, is a good way for the police to exculpate themselves for their own lack of efficacy in doing their job of collecting evidence to support a criminal conviction. Instead, in cooperation with the media, the police have campaigned against legal reforms and have been generally effective in persuading the public that the law is against the citizen and in favor of the delinquent. In this regard, one prominent judge stated: "This perception of the citizenry is the product of bad information, a kind of disinformation, that has been given out by the mass media and by certain authorities, above all the police, in respect to security and the fight against crime. I think it has been a kind of escape valve, to justify police inefficiency in conducting investigations. Because let's not forget, from the judicial perspective, everything is based on the investigation. The judge bases his decision on the evidence presented to him, the proof. And how do they get this proof? Through an effective investigation. If this investigative work is poorly done, obviously the results they get, the incriminating evidence, will be poor as well, and the final result will be impunity, the result of bad police work."[65]

Judges reject the police claim that they lack the resources to investigate crimes properly, arguing, for example, that the lack of well-equipped police laboratories is just "a pretext. Obviously they need laboratories, but with a little initiative, good will, and imagination they could still do an effective investigation with the means in their possession."[66] Judges and prosecutors manage an overwhelming caseload, with the typical prosecutor handling up to three hundred cases at any one time.[67] Like the police, judges and prosecutors complain of having insufficient resources and insist that they can't do their jobs properly without additional funding. Without support from the state, these judges argue, the law cannot be enforced and security cannot be guaranteed. Especially in large departments like Cochabamba, which have experienced so much growth in recent years, there is simply not enough judicial capacity to process all the conflicts that occur. Without an expansion in this regard, said one judge, "justice is going to collapse."[68]

Meanwhile, of course, as these various institutions and their members squabble and point fingers at each other, the people of the barrios remain without police attention or the services of the state justice system. Despite what may or may not be a truly felt commitment on the part of police officers, bureaucrats, and judges to the cause of citizen security, a

FIG. 6 A roadside memorial to Wilmer Vargas, erected by his family on the spot where he was killed, 2011. Photo by the author.

sense of stability and well-being remains elusive in the barrios. From a barrio perspective, the police, courts, and law are not real working institutions but phantoms, entities occasionally sensed at the edges of awareness but lacking substantive reality. More real are the bureaucrats that barrio residents sometimes must encounter, who send them on an endless paper chase that in its own way points to the state's reality but underscores its refusal to serve the needs of its subjects. The absent presence of this phantom state contributes to the insecurity of barrio life (see fig. 6), driving people to look for other remedies to resolve it.

Conclusion

| | | "THE FUNERAL," JULY 14, 2010

I got the call notifying me of Wilmer's death early yesterday morning, from some students who had just arrived in Loma Pampa for their service work. I immediately notified the rest of the students, and as a group we headed to the barrio. We viewed the body, strangely doll-like in its wooden box, surrounded by candles and sobbing relatives, laid out in the same one-room adobe house where Wilmer had spent his days. Eventually a hearse arrived—no small feat, there on the far fringes of the city—and a group of men carried the small white casket from the house to the street. People piled into vehicles for the long, slow procession to the cemetery. There we gathered around the grave, where prayers were said, coca leaves were chewed, and alcohol was sprinkled on the ground. The casket was lowered in. People threw flowers into the grave as men shoveled dirt into the hole. It thudded heavily on the lid of the box. Important people made speeches. We watched as the day gradually faded away, and then we retired to our vehicles to return home.

It is difficult to write in standard blog-speak about Wilmer's passing. The linearity of the narrative, reflecting the linear nature of the day, does not capture the experience. My mind was all over the place. I thought of Wilmer, two years ago and just five years old, making a nuisance of himself during the construction work in Loma Pampa. I thought of the future he would not have, and what it means for people to live in this kind of a situation. Most of all, I thought of the structural conditions that precipitated this tragedy. How alcoholism destroys families. How Wilmer's father would toss him out of the house at 5:00 AM to go sell popsicles. How Wilmer, cold and lonely in the darkness of the morning, would sleep on the street corner until the day brightened and he could head out to work. How a family of seven could share one room with no furniture. No furniture! And how Wilmer would always show up at the community center whenever our Rutgers students came around, finding there the friendship and affection he couldn't get elsewhere.

Should we cry over such things? I don't know whether to be sad or angry—probably both.

Over the course of several years, the Bolivian state elaborated a politics of security predicated on the notion of citizen security, a concept meant to orient state security making toward the protection of citizens from crime. But in practice, citizen security in Bolivia remains a mirage, a discourse used for talking about local problems without actually engaging the population at the level of lived reality. Although the Bolivian state issued numerous proclamations and decrees, creating a host of government bureaus and initiatives intended to improve citizen security, these have done little to produce any discernible changes in the daily lives of most Bolivians. For many residents of Cochabamba's marginal barrios, the inability of the discourse of citizen security to actually contribute to a lived sense of security is interpreted as an absence, another indicator of the state's abandonment and neglect of the residents of its marginal barrios. But the state, its laws, and its instruments are virtually present in the barrios, affecting local life even as they remain difficult for the living to perceive. In this sense they are phantoms or ghosts, neither fully present nor absent but somehow in between, their absent presence felt in a host of daily encounters and requirements. And even as they are haunted by the ghosts of the state, the residents of the barrios struggle with their own kind of nonbeing. They are trapped in various forms of illegality, forced to navigate the legal bureaucracies of the state to try to achieve official recognition of their urban identities and citizenship rights. Unable to formalize their land claims through the land-legalization process or to establish their legal identities through the carnet, barrio residents are chuto, outlaws residing beyond the limits of the law and its protections, spectral denizens of the marginal spaces that seem to register only peripherally in the consciousness of the state. We can again recall the words of Wilmer's neighbor, commenting on the state's lack of response to his killing: "The authorities don't know if we exist or we don't exist. I wonder if they ever even think about Loma Pampa."

What is clear from this discussion is that whatever its intentions—and these may have shifted during the transition from the neoliberal era to the period of Evo Morales and MAS—the Bolivian state does not operate to provide peace and security to the people of the marginal barrios. Instead, it functions to maintain a set of laws and procedures with which residents must comply if they hope to enjoy a legal identity and, ultimately, to access the rights of citizens. Rights in this context extend not from the basic guarantees of democratic society, but through compliance with state regulations and participation in the rituals of rule (Corrigan and Sayer 1985) that are meant to establish public order and shape identities, part of the quotidian routines that provide the basis for an ongoing process of state formation (Joseph and Nugent 1994). The phantom state's absent presence is felt in the contradictory ways in which it and its laws are at once entirely unhelpful in creating conditions of security in the marginal barrios yet remain active in the ordering and regulation—the legalization, if you will—of the illegible marginal population.

This chapter has explored some of the problems for local security to which the absent presence of the state contributes in the marginal barrios. In the next chapter, I look at other sources of insecurity and fear, including crime and the lack of infrastructure in the barrios. Mainly, though, chapter 4 considers the ways in which barrio residents manage the insecurity that they daily confront, looking at the disposition of alert watchfulness, the role of local leadership in resolving problems and conflicts, and the role of violence as a means of handling insecurity. What emerges from that discussion are the ways in which, in a context of profound and unmitigated insecurity, barrio residents often opt to leave the state out of things entirely, turning to much more local sets of resources to resolve their problems and to establish for themselves their own definitions of security—the work, once again, of the outlawed. The results of these strategies and techniques, however, are profoundly uncertain, often leading to a deepening, rather than a lessening, of insecurity in its many forms.

4 | Exorcising Ghosts

MANAGING INSECURITY IN USPHA USPHA

The state's absent presence in the marginal barrios, chronicled in chapter 3, is experienced by residents of those barrios as abandonment. Although state law touches their lives in various ways—sometimes subtly, sometimes not so subtly—the people of Uspha Uspha by and large do not recognize the state's presence, feeling instead that they have been left entirely to their own devices to deal with insecurity. This is of particular concern in facing crime and delinquency in their communities—what most people think of when they think of citizen security. Don Silvio Lopez, the representative of District 8 to the Subalcaldía, referred to the neoliberal retrenchment of the state (discussed in chapter 1) this way: "There used to be police here, three, four, now there are none, they've locked up the station and withdrawn. . . . The southern zone is completely abandoned in terms of security, we don't have any citizen security. The prefecture has a citizen security plan to build barracks, police stations, but it is not happening, it's just a project, a proposal from the prefecture. . . . In respect to citizen security we are really—we are abandoned."[1]

But the residents of these barrios are not passive in the face of their perceived abandonment. Unconvinced by state discourses and policies of citizen security, and highly dubious of the phantom state and its laws, many barrio residents—as individuals and in groups—have assumed responsibility for dealing with the problems posed by delinquents and other forces of insecurity in their communities, adopting both violent and nonviolent techniques to police their neighborhoods and ward off the forces of insecurity. Although some practices target external audiences, most barrio efforts to increase security are focused closer to home, employing local resources to create security at the most local of levels, the marginal barrio or Organización Territorial de Base (OTB). The result is a complex sociolegal terrain on which people adopt particular dispositions and deploy a variety of practices in an attempt to do what they believe the state has failed to do: bring security to their neighborhoods. Their success in these efforts is dependent in many cases on the quality of the local leadership and on the willingness of the local residents to collaborate, both violently and peacefully, in making the barrio space secure. However, one of the most powerful effects of insecurity is the individualization of local populations, making truly collective action in the marginal barrio a difficult prospect and an infrequent occurrence.

The sources of insecurity against which barrio residents feel they must defend themselves are legion. As chapter 3 showed, the police, the justice system, and the law itself all seem to be sources of insecurity in the eyes of the majority of barrio residents with whom I spoke and interacted during my field research. But the phantom state is not the only source of insecurity on the urban margins. Other kinds of phantoms populate the marginal spaces of Cochabamba, specters of violence embodied in the various characters who also haunt urban life. They include the delincuente, who appears suddenly outside your home, looking to harm your children or steal your meager possessions; the loteador, who took advantage of your ignorance and sold you a parcel of land but not the legal title to it; the ratero, often scarred and hideous, completely unscrupulous, always watching you and tracking your movements; and the *pandillero*, the gang member on the corner whom you have to pass on your way home from the bus. All of these ghostly characters are sources of insecurity in the marginal barrios, and it is only through their own direct interventions that people feel they can defend themselves against these threats.

One of these interventions is watchfulness, an alert disposition through which barrio residents hope to protect themselves from harm by spotting it before it strikes. Driven by fear—both a product of and a response to insecurity—barrio residents form loose collectives of vigilant neighbors, who are constantly on guard to recognize and intercept malevolent forces as these move into barrio space (Mollericona, Tinini, and Paredes 2007). The fear generated by insecurity and a sense of abandonment—of being left outside the law's protections, or out-lawed—contributes to a certain kind of solidarity among barrio residents, who join together to police their neighborhoods through informal chains of alertness. But fear more strongly produces a sense of isolation, leading people to withdraw into their homes and cut themselves off from one another, making them unwilling or unable to call on one another for support in times of crisis. The barrios of Uspha Uspha are thus also characterized by individualization, as people feel themselves only loosely to be members of a community joined in a common struggle. Though they refer to themselves as vecinos —which literally means "neighbors" but in other Andean contexts is a reference to a place-based citizenship and sense of solidarity (Lazar 2008; Risør 2010)—for most barrio residents in Uspha Uspha, the term is more a description of proximity than a statement of sociopolitical belonging.

Another important local resource that barrio residents draw on in responding to insecurity is the system of leadership that exists at the level of the OTB. Although they feel abandoned by state authorities, people rely heavily on their local barrio *dirigentes* (leaders) to help them with a host of bureaucratic, legal, and personal problems. As the OTB's chief political figure, the barrio president is particularly critical in this regard, and a barrio that has an honest, capable leader truly committed to the welfare of his community can make strides toward legalizing land claims, deterring criminal activity, and generally increasing the sense of security in the barrio. Such is the case in Loma Pampa, and I use the example of don Miguel to illustrate the importance of the barrio dirigente in resolving conflicts and managing problems of insecurity at the local level. In some ways the reliance on local dirigentes represents a form of patron-client relations, replicated in the dirigente's own relations at a higher level with other political figures and political parties (Forman and Riegelhaupt 1979; Wolf 1966). As I discuss below, however, these clientage relationships can be exploited for the patron's own benefit or, as in the case of don Miguel, can help to produce a greater sense of collective solidarity within the barrio. As with watchfulness, the efforts of leaders like don Miguel are limited by a lack of solidarity within the outlawed community, which is constrained by the poverty, fear, and insecurity of daily life.

Finally, as a third kind of local intervention in problems of insecurity, barrio residents sometimes employ violence as an instrument for increasing security in their neighborhoods. Through the lynching (or attempted lynching) of criminal suspects, barrio residents understand themselves to be taking direct action in response to insecurity, delinquency, and state abandonment, donning the mantle of security makers that the state, through its inaction, has ceded to them (Castillo Claudett 2000; Fuentes Díaz and Binford 2001; Godoy 2006; Guerrero 2001; Vilas 2001). However, in contrast to how this violence is typically portrayed in media and academic accounts, lynching[2] is far from a unitary, communal practice in which all barrio residents participate. While many vecinos feel that lynching is an appropriate response to insecurity, many of them also feel a deep ambivalence about the use of violence to control delinquency. Women in particular are fearful: afraid for their children, whom they realize could easily fall victim to a lynch mob in another barrio; afraid of vengeance by a lynching victim's family; afraid of being accused of complicity with the victim if they express any kind of support for him. Moreover, instead of reducing the overall sense of fear permeating barrio life, the fact of lynching violence contributes to it, and lynching transforms those excluded from law's protections (out-laws, as I have called them) into active violators of the law (outlaws in the more familiar sense). Rather than a species of collective violence, then, the ethnography of this chapter demonstrates lynching to be an overly reductive category of social description within which a variety of behaviors and attitudes are conflated and subsumed. Again, as with other local responses to insecurity, lynching emerges not as an expression of community or group solidarity but more as a result of the absence of such solidarity; far from being collective, lynching is actually fraught with contradiction and debate (Colloredo-Mansfeld 2009).[3] Although lynching is highly visible and dramatic—elsewhere I have called it spectacular (Goldstein 2004)—it is in fact one intervention among many that are locally deployed by individuals and groups in an attempt to manage the insecurity that they experience on a daily basis. The results of these processes are fragmentary, inconsistent, and at times contradictory, and rather than reducing insecurity they may actually serve to increase it.

The Scars of Insecurity: An Urban Hauntology

Don Omar opened a little store in his barrio, where he and his family sold bread and various other small domestic items that people typically need to keep their households running. Omar decided to open the store because there were no others in his neighborhood: "I saw that and I said, 'I'm going to put a nice store right here, I want to open a store.'"[4] Omar invested the little money he had managed to save up, and people in the barrio were very happy with the results. "'Congratulations,' they said to me, 'How nice that you opened this store.' 'You should sell *garrafas* [propane tanks for cooking], you would make more money.' Whatever they asked for, I tried to accommodate them and brought in more things to sell. I was doing very well, very well, I was making money. But overnight everything changed."

One Sunday morning while Omar and his family were at church, some men pulled a taxi up to his store and took everything that he had. Some of his vecinos had seen the thieves at work, but they had assumed them to be some new renters and did nothing to stop them. The thieves also robbed Omar's house, which was adjacent to the store. He says: "They stole my television, my stereo, money. I had a store that I had made with so much effort. The garrafas, they took eight garrafas." After the fact, Omar didn't want to call the police because he doesn't "have much confidence in the police." Besides, Omar said, he would just have had to pay them to investigate, and after the robbery he had nothing left to spend. Omar tried to conduct his own investigation, going to the Barrio Chino, a section of the Cancha marketplace where vendors notoriously resell stolen items, often to the original owners trying to buy back their stuff. But he was unsuccessful. Then he started freaking out: "I went crazy for a bit. I was going up, down, I saw the entire world with mistrust. I saw someone looking at me and I thought, 'That could be [the thief], why is he staring at me?' *Desconfianza* [total mistrust]." Finally, Omar said, he came to his senses, deciding to leave the matter in God's hands. He opted not to reopen the store and moved out of the barrio, though he remained mistrustful: "My wife and my daughter, there were times when I had to work in the city and leave them alone in the house. And someone could enter the house when they were there alone. I didn't want to put anything more into the store, so I sold what I could and I decided to leave."

Thieves—often called rateros or delincuentes—weigh like a nightmare on the brains of barrio residents.⁵ Like the phantom state, they constitute another ghostly absent presence, always possibly there, lurking and waiting to prey on the unsuspecting.⁶ Rateros are merciless, otherworldly, inhuman. Women in particular seem to regard them as monstrous, fundamentally different from normal people, lacking basic human relationships and therefore basic human feelings. Said a woman resident of Mineros San Juan: "The ratero is shameless, for him it is only about robbing and selling. The ratero doesn't say, 'This is a poor person, I won't steal from him,' the ratero doesn't say that. He just grabs stuff, he robs you, he has no compassion for you. Others of us have compassion, it hurts us, because we have children. . . . But they don't feel pain. The ratero grabs your earrings or your money, he takes you away and kills you. He has no compassion."⁷ Rateros are cornerstones of barrio insecurity, semimythical creatures who manifest themselves at times to commit real harm to vulnerable residents. They are the urban counterpart to the *pishtacos* or *kharisis* of the countryside, ghostly spirits who waylay unwary passersby, drawing out their vital fluids for the spirits' own nefarious, and profitable, purposes, leaving the body weak and the soul depleted (Canessa 2000; Weismantel 2001). Much as the trails and villages of the altiplano are haunted by these figures, life in the barrios of Cochabamba is colored by the risks to which people feel themselves to be exposed, having to live with the perpetual threat of ratero violence and violation.

The ratero is also said to be physically distinct from normal people; in body as well as in spirit, he is "a different kind of person."⁸ Doña Casilda concurs: "It's easy to tell who is and who isn't a ratero, it's obvious, you know, the thieves are another class entirely."⁹ Although rateros can look like anybody else and often do, there are always discrepancies, people say, that the careful eye can discern. The ratero may be dressed much more nicely or much more sloppily than normal people. His eyes are always alert, watching those around him. He has scars on his face, hands, and torso from where he has been cut in fights or as part of a gang initiation, which often requires prospective gang members to carve things into their own flesh. Supposedly one can read the relative status or danger level of a ratero by the nature and style of his cuts. If he has just a few, then he is probably a petty thief who steals people's wallets and the like. A more expert criminal will have deeper cuts and scars on his abdomen and arms and legs. Cuts on the face are most likely the result of knife fights with other thieves, in bars or in the street. Those elsewhere on the body are probably self-inflicted and indicate the degree of toughness of the individual bearing them. However, such signs can be deceptive, and uncertainty creeps into people's evaluations. It is said, for example, that as these cuts have become more recognized as signs of a ratero, thieves have begun to take more care, especially of their hands and face, so as not to be immediately recognized. In addition, there are other ways of getting cut, and someone who has been in an accident, for example, may be indiscernible from—and possibly stigmatized as having the face of—a ratero. It also makes it extremely difficult for rateros to leave the criminal life, as they are permanently and publicly disfigured. The main thing is that one can never be entirely sure who is or is not a ratero, and this uncertainty enhances the overall sense of threat. Rateros are either physically distinct or they look just like everybody else, and this contradiction also adds to the sense of insecurity. Josias, don Miguel's son, told me a story about his encounter with a possible ratero, trying to scope out his house for a future break-in:

> [Rateros] look normal like any other person, that's what the thieves look like now. One time a man came to our house, with his helmet, his overalls. "I'm from the gas company," he said, "I'm coming to check the gas tanks, I'm from Yacimientos [the gas company], I work here." My mother called me over just as this man was trying to enter the house. I looked at him and his face had been like all cut up, and I said to him: "Show me your credentials." And he was wearing gloves, so he took them off and his hands were all cut up. He showed me his credentials, I took his card, and I said to him, "Now show me your [personal] carnet." He took his credentials out of my hand and said to me: "I don't have to give you any explanations, I am from the gas company." "But give me your carnet, if it is as you say I will let you come in," I told him. "But if not we are going to sound the horn and all the people [of the barrio] are going to come here, we will take care of things and right here we will kill you. . . . The man left quickly, and a bus came just then, and he got on and left.[10]

Rateros are always on the prowl, hoping to take advantage of people's vulnerabilities. "They study us," said a woman in Concordia, "or perhaps they send someone to spy when we are going out, and they take advantage of that."[11] The threat they pose is compounded by the lack of barrio infrastructure and services, which in itself constitutes another source of insecurity. Though people recognize that most robberies occur during the day when people are at work and their homes are unattended, night is especially frightening, when the dark streets and lack of public illumination increase the feeling of vulnerability: "At night I am very afraid, because they say that recently a ratero broke into someone's house in [a nearby barrio]. This just happened, so I am very afraid at night."[12] A resident of Grupo Domingo, a sector of Mineros San Juan, said: "There is fear, because we are always in the dark. So when the bus leaves us off at the corner, and some of us live further on, you know very well, Doctor, that in a short distance a lot can happen. So getting home, in one or two blocks, that is the fear."[13] Another resident of Grupo Domingo said: "So when we speak of security, what security am I going to have if all is dark around me? I am insecure in every respect." Lack of telephone service is another obstacle to security, enhancing people's sense of being isolated and alone: "It's very dangerous, since there's no telephone here. When something happens we can't call anybody." The sense of isolation and marginality plays on people's imaginations, throwing out new and terrifying possibilities: "Because we are so isolated here, we are a little afraid because wild animals could pass through, no? At night. Maybe not, but we always run that risk."[14] Not everyone is afraid, but having a home on a main street with good sight lines up and down, near public transportation, helps to enhance a sense of security: "I am not afraid, but others say that they are afraid. . . . They say there are rateros, but nobody has ever attacked me. My house is very well situated, [very visible] too."[15] Occupants of the most isolated houses, high on a hill or on a small side street, are often the most fearful: "[I fear that] at night thieves will come and enter my house, because they are always walking around in these parts. They can kill me and my children and take everything we have. I have to live with fear here, no? What else can I do? And my house being so hidden from the others, worse still, no?"[16]

Land legalization issues are also a threat to security in the physical sense, in that the requirements of the trámite can leave people feeling more vulnerable to crime. In the barrios of Uspha Uspha, the most basic form of protection one can have is a mud wall, topped with broken glass, surrounding one's house and limiting access from the outside (see fig. 7): "When I first came here my house didn't have a wall; even now the back

FIG. 7 A house in Loma Pampa, 2007. The lack of an exterior wall surrounding the property makes this an insecure dwelling in the eyes of barrio residents. Photo by the author.

part is missing. So this made me afraid. I didn't sleep at night, thinking that someone could come and attack the house, because it didn't have a wall, not even a dog to bark, nothing."[17] In addition to providing a protective enclosure, such a wall also demarcates the boundaries of one's property and is one requirement for land legalization. But an inability to define the exact parameters of one's lot can leave one unable to construct such a wall:

> Right now we are having trouble with our lots, we are not able to enclose them yet because we have problems with the measurements. The previous mayor sent around a new architect to measure. He was in charge of measuring these lots, he came to measure, and our lot was oversized here [points to one side], and with this new measurement it stuck out. That is, I have too much land here and here [points to the other side]. And now for that reason I can't enclose my lot yet. Many people have this problem, and even though some have already enclosed their lots, now they have to make room for a sidewalk. So we have enclosed our lots and we have problems. . . . There was a guy hanging out on the street corner all day until the night. As soon as I got home he left, [but] all afternoon he was waiting around. And a few days ago someone broke into a house.[18]

While people in the marginal barrios attempt to barricade private spaces, they also tend to avoid public ones, as these are seen as inherently dangerous, gathering places for rateros and other *antisociales* (antisocial elements). Electronic game rooms, parks, fields, bars, stores—all can be places of danger. *Pandillas* (youth gangs) in particular may hang out in these places, frightening older residents and attracting kids to their ranks. Said a woman in Mineros San Juan: "It used to be [that] you didn't see these young men, but now they're there, there are gangs. They [gang members] are young, ten, eight years old. They hang out at the ball court, they watch who is coming and going, what they are doing, what you do or don't do, this they watch."[19] *Chicherías*—bars where people gather day and night to drink chicha—are another source of insecurity in the barrios. Don Miguel calls them *focos de infección* (sources of infection) because they attract an undesirable element to the community, and from them emanate all kinds of bad effects. Of course, many patrons of chicherías are often themselves local community residents, but many people nevertheless consider the chicherías to be a problem because they draw outsiders to the barrio, who then proceed to get drunk, noisy, and occasionally violent. People will sometimes petition the municipality to shut down a particularly problematic chichería, and occasionally this will have an effect: the chichería will shut its doors for a few days, until its owner pays some "fines" (more likely payoffs to municipal officials) and is allowed to reopen. What's more, those who complained may subsequently feel threatened by the owner of the chichería for having tried to shut down his business. So again people are left feeling powerless to affect a situation that they feel threatens their security, and they regard appeals to authorities as likely to make things worse.

DANGER ZONES

The barrio is a frightening place, but many residents are also afraid to leave it. Although the downtowns of most Bolivian cities appear to be much more tranquil than those in other countries, barrio residents who venture there often do so with great trepidation.[20] Doña Casilda is afraid of walking downtown or going to the Cancha, where she must go everyday to sell her small wares. She once had her wallet stolen, losing all her proceeds for the day, and now she clutches her bag to her side as she makes her way through the crowded streets. Doña Eva worries about her twelve-year-old son, who the year before had begun working as a shoeshine boy in the main plaza downtown. Every day he goes alone to the city center to work, and she fears for his safety: "Don't trust anyone," she advises him.[21] Because rateros are stereotypically young males, it can be extremely dangerous for adolescents and young men to visit other barrios, to hang out with friends, visit a girlfriend, or go to a club. Young men are often the victims of lynchings, when they are mistaken for a thief prowling about an unfamiliar neighborhood. Taxi drivers run similar risks, as their work often takes them into far-flung barrios where they are not recognized by local residents. In addition, many people insist that thieves always travel in white taxi cabs, and the *taxi blanco* has become another semimythical entity whose presence augurs ill. Josias, who works as a taxi driver, admits: "It's a problem. Sometime people look at you, sometimes you drop off a passenger [in a barrio] and you are heading back alone and they watch you. Twice this happened to me, they threw stones at me in the night."[22]

The danger of going to another barrio is very real because of the widely held belief that the ratero is always somebody from outside the local community. Conceived of as a quasihuman, antisocial presence, the ratero is by definition an outsider, someone not of the locality and inherently antagonistic to it. Not everyone subscribes to this belief; a resident of Concordia observed: "If we analyze the situation, where they are from, who they are, from where they have appeared, these criminals or these *delincuentes*, they are from here, from those same places that we are from."[23] And a resident of Mineros San Juan stated: "Thieves from outside, we don't have. The thieves are internal to the barrio, they are young men from right here that rob us."[24] Sergeant Mamani, leader of the policeman's union, put it this way: "The delinquents don't come from Mars or Venus, they come from ourselves, they are our own children."[25] But many more people believe the rateros to be from outside their barrio. "The bad guys are from outside," said a woman from Concordia,[26] and doña Casilda from Loma Pampa agreed: "People from other barrios, you can't trust them, we are not all the same."[27] Some of this mistrust is conditioned by competition over land in the zone of Uspha Uspha, where people of different barrios have sometimes clashed over who has access to land in a particular area. Residents of Mineros San Juan still hate residents of Llave Mayu because of the earlier dispute over land claims in the zone. And residents of Concordia hate residents of Mineros San Juan, because the latter have tried to invade and settle their áreas verdes, which were deliberately left unoccupied according to the statutes of land legalization, while residents of Loma Pampa hate residents of Concordia and other neighboring barrios for similar reasons. On one of my first days in Loma Pampa, I joined with residents of the barrio in laying out clear lines of demarcation in the barrio's área verde atop the main hill, to ward off possible settlement attempts by hostile neighbors.[28]

If local neighbors are dangerous, foreigners are particularly threatening. Peruvians especially are widely regarded in Bolivia as inherently criminal and are blamed for various crimes in the country (recall the joke in chapter 3 about avoiding Peruvian men). The news media drive home this perception with frequent reports about Peruvian miscreants engaged in elaborate schemes to rob, rape, and murder innocent Bolivians.[29] More local forms of gossip—what Caldeira has called "talk of crime" (2000)—feed perceptions that the unfamiliar person, no matter how seemingly innocuous, is inherently dangerous: "[When a stranger comes to the barrio, people feel very] suspicious. For example, there was an ice cream man who came around—I don't know how much of this is true. My husband went to the meetings, and he said that the ice cream man—I don't know much about it, but surely he was checking out the houses. He came around with his ice cream and surely he knew where no one was home, and in the night or a few days later he broke in to rob them. This is what people said, but I don't know how much of it is true."[30]

Knowing one's neighbors and being alert to the movements of strangers is one way people try to establish a sense of security, enabling them to distinguish familiar and hence reliable faces from unfamiliar ones. On this basis, some barrio residents have made suggestions for increasing security by regulating access to their neighborhoods. Most of these have to do with the privatizing of public space. In group discussions in both Concordia and Juan Pablo II, several men suggested barricading the streets of their barrios to limit access only to those known to be safe: "we have to close the barrio" was the general sentiment. Doña Irma suggested putting up signs or plaques on people's homes, so that everyone would know the identities of who resided there. Because unfamiliar or transient people can be dangerous, renters may be regarded with suspicion by those who own homes in the barrio. Doña Dora said that in her barrio, efforts were particularly targeted against renters; some people there suggested that a prospective renter should have to provide his or her previous address and a certificate of good conduct in order to be allowed to rent a house in the barrio. Others spoke of hiring private security to patrol the barrio, as wealthier neighborhoods do, but the expense of this measure was generally considered to be too high for residents to consider.

Paradoxically, watchfulness is at the heart of both security and insecurity in the barrios of Uspha Uspha: it is a disposition of both delinquents and upstanding citizens concerned to protect themselves from delinquency. Rateros, people say, are always watching: They stand outside your house, scoping it out for a future robbery. They hang around, noting the times of day when houses are left unattended, planning crimes, waiting for their opportunity. And there are plenty of opportunities, for people must leave their homes to go to work each day: "There have been so many [robberies] here, because we all leave to go to work, husband and wife, the kids go to school, so in that moment outsiders take advantage. They are from the city, I don't know. From other places, they come, they watch, and straight away they enter the houses and take what they want."[31] Many barrio residents perceive the delinquents to have an almost supernatural ability to observe their activities and their whereabouts. Even during a lynching, the thief is superhumanly alert: "The ratero is always watching you, he doesn't even feel it when you are hitting him. But he's watching you from above."[32]

But if the rateros are always watching, barrio residents adopt this same watchful disposition in response to the insecurity produced by delinquency. Only through perpetual alertness, many of them feel, can they hope to save themselves from victimization. Because women are expected to be the principal caretakers of the home, this responsibility falls most heavily on them: "When I am here, I am always watching, when strangers walk by."[33] The zone is "dangerous, the rateros are always out there, at night they walk around, so sometimes we don't sleep, we are always watching, we wake up nights and watch."[34] Women are always on the lookout for strangers in their neighborhood, and while some watch from their windows, others are not shy about confronting passersby. When doña Licia spots a stranger in Loma Pampa, she will approach him to find out if he has a legitimate purpose in the barrio, asking: " 'Who are you looking for? Who are you waiting for?' I know almost everybody around here, their names, so according to how he answers me I will know [if he is a ratero]."[35] Doña Casilda, who lives near the top of the hill in Loma Pampa, uses a similar technique, which relies on familiarity with one's neighbors: "Up here, we all know each other. Down below, I don't know how it is. Here for example when someone is walking up the hill, we watch him. Where is he going, how far up the hill? Covertly we watch."[36] Women rely on one another to watch each others' houses on those occasions when they have to leave home, such as when they have to go to work during the day. They depend on a neighbor's willingness to keep an eye out for any strange activity when they must leave their homes unattended. The practice of being alert and watchful is in fact official policy in Loma Pampa, where residents decided in a public meeting to be vigilant and watch for the presence of strangers in the barrio. Josias said: "For our security, any stranger who ends up in the barrio is suspicious." He told me:

> One time I found a man in front of my house. I watched him as I went in, and I kept watching him and he stayed there. Ten minutes passed and he was still there, fifteen minutes, still watching my house. So I went out and I said to him: "Are you waiting for someone?" So he in turn said to me: "What does it matter to you? I'll do as I please, I'm in the street," he said. And I said to him: "You know, I'm on the executive committee of the OTB, so you have to prove to me what you are doing here, who you are looking for. Maybe I can help you find them," I said. And he said to me: "No, I am waiting for a friend who lives here." "Well, let's go find him," I said. He changed his mind and left.[37]

The perception that the barrio is under constant surveillance by thieves provokes new behaviors in its residents, who alter their lives in response. Women especially adjust their movements, so that they can defend their homes against crime. One woman from Concordia said: "We are very attentive, because there have been so many robberies, we are attentive. If we have to leave the house for a minute, one person leaves, one stays home, one leaves, one stays home, that's how it is in the houses. We don't leave it [the house] alone; if we leave it alone they can empty us out. If they empty us out, who can we turn to?"[38] Some people refer to this as *inseguridad domiciliaria*, a fear of leaving one's domicile unattended. While their husbands go to work, women give up employment opportunities because the house must always be occupied: "If I leave my house they will empty it out. I can't leave it. . . . I was going to work in PLANE [a government employment program], but if I go the house will be left unattended."[39] Another woman said: "I can't go out, I don't go out, not even for a moment. We used to go to the market, we could leave the house with confidence because there was security. Now we are afraid to leave our houses. Especially on Saturday when we go to the market, we come flying home."[40]

Although people cooperate in watching each other's homes, they are much less likely to collaborate on other kinds of communal or collective activities, a situation that especially affects women and their families. Women who rely on their neighbors to watch their houses when they have to go to work or the market are reluctant to call on those neighbors in times of trouble—if someone is sick, for example, or if there is not enough food in the house for the week. Some women will assist their friends—doña Casilda and her neighbor doña Samuelia help each other out by exchanging food and other small items. And when someone dies, the dirigente will sometimes ask for contributions from barrio residents to help the family with the burial costs. But in general, women say, they do not go to their neighbors' aid, nor do they receive aid from the community. Some compare it unfavorably to life in the countryside, where systems of mutual assistance (including those known as *ayni* and *mink'a*)[41] helped to sustain individual families and provide the labor for collective work projects that benefited the entire community (see, for example, Painter 1991). In the urban barrio such systems do not exist, and women frequently express the sentiment that they must face their problems on their own. While some women like doña Casilda claim to know everyone in the barrio, and hence to be able to recognize strangers and delinquents, others say that they know only their neighbors and so cannot rely on the larger community for assistance: "When someone gets sick no one contributes. One time I saw that when someone died, they took up a collection, but when someone gets sick I don't think they give. When someone dies I think they do, for the burial, but not for everyone either. For example, my father-in-law died, and nobody helped me, nobody visited me. Perhaps many people don't know me? I hardly know anybody in the barrio, only my vecinos."[42] Many women express a terrible sense of loneliness and isolation, feeling cut off from everyone, even their own husbands. Doña Delina described the birth of her first child: "When I was pregnant with my son, I was alone, I didn't tell anyone, I was alone. When I could no longer bear the pain I went to the hospital, I took a taxi. I went alone to the hospital. When I arrived the doctor told me, 'Don't push!' He screamed at me. Many doctors appeared, they said my water had broken when I was coming in. In the emergency room they attended to me. I was all alone in the hospital, nobody came to visit."[43]

Poverty and racism are both factors that internally divide the marginal barrio, leading to disharmony instead of unity and cooperation. Although in some instances poverty can contribute to group solidarity, it can also divide people, producing conflicts over resources and jealousy between families. Doña Delina, for example, said of the women in Loma Pampa: "We are not united because there is jealousy, some people are envious of others, some envy those who have two, three rooms [in their houses] while they only have one or two, so they are jealous: 'Her husband makes more than my husband.'" She went on to explain that competition over scarce public resources also produces conflicts. Some women, for example, have claimed exclusive rights to a natural spring near Loma Pampa and don't want to let other women have access to the water. Asked how they might resolve this conflict, Delina admitted: "We don't resolve it, that's what we say, what I tell myself. What are we going to do? If there is jealousy, we just leave it like that."[44] Some people explain the disunity that exists in barrios like Loma Pampa by biologizing the difference between the different groups of people that inhabit the zone. I have already mentioned the tensions that exist between abajeños (those who live at the bottom of the Loma Pampa hill) and arribeños (those who live at the top), and how these locations correspond with Quechua and Aymara language and culture, respectively. Many Bolivians see the differences between these groups as being fundamentally biological—that is, racial—properties, which make the two groups basically incompatible. The tendency toward violence, as manifested in lynchings, "runs through the veins" of Aymara people, according to doña Altamira of Loma Pampa, reflecting a common stereotype in Bolivia of the Aymara as a tough, hard people; Quechua people, meanwhile, are seen as inherently docile and *humilde* (humble). Don Miguel himself describes the Aymara culture as *cerrada* (closed) and points to this as a reason for the problems that exist between arribeños and abajeños in his barrio.[45] Some women agree that this Quechua-Aymara divide is at the heart of the disunity in Loma Pampa: "[The barrio] is not very united, because some of us are not from this place. There are *cochalas* [women from Cochabamba], as we call ourselves, and there are *paceñas* [women from La Paz], as they call themselves, and we can't understand each other. That is why there is disunion."[46]

People in Loma Pampa and other barrios recognize this lack of collective sentiment and bemoan it as another source of their insecurity. For example, referring to a neighboring barrio well known for its high levels of delinquency, a resident of Uspha Uspha Central described it as a place "where there is very little sense of community, the people feel themselves to be very much up in the air [*al aire*; at loose ends]."[47] Because they are not unified, people say, they cannot protect themselves effectively against crime. Though people in different barrios have suggested trying to organize communal rounds whereby barrio residents could police their own communities, such proposals have rarely gotten off the ground owing to the general unwillingness to collaborate in such an endeavor. Watchfulness, therefore, remains an individual disposition and practice and does not develop into a collective form of patrolling, as is the case in some rural Andean contexts (Starn 1999). Nor are people willing to contribute the money it would require to hire private security guards for their barrios—the residents of Loma Pampa experimented for a time with hiring one of their own neighbors to patrol the barrio during the day, but the money for this ran out after a few months, and residents were unwilling to revive the system. Instead, people seem to prefer to barricade themselves in their homes, adopting a watchful disposition and hoping that harm passes them by. Again, the sense of isolation, of being overwhelmed by poverty and insecurity, pervades people's commentaries. Don Omar, whose store was burglarized, said: "People are extremely busy, everyone in their homes, trying to get by each as they can. There are times when we don't know who is coming, who is going, because we are thinking about, 'How am I going to make money, how am I going to make money, what do I have and what do I need?' You have to pay the light bill, you have to pay the water bill. So people are just desperate."[48]

Local Leadership and the Problems of Insecurity

Despite the lack of community sentiment in marginal barrios, every neighborhood is organized politically as though it were a coherent, unified entity. In each barrio of Uspha Uspha, an elected *directorio* (leadership council, or executive committee) makes decisions on behalf of the barrio residents, providing representation for the neighborhood at higher levels of municipal organization. The members of the directorio, and in particular the president (often referred to simply as the dirigente, the leader, and almost always a man), also provide important counsel to barrio residents on matters of concern to them, including personal and legal issues on which they seek advice. How the dirigente conducts himself in his office can mean the difference between whether or not barrio residents feel completely helpless to resolve conflicts and to confront problems of local insecurity. Though Loma Pampa is a marginal barrio whose residents face terrible problems of insecurity, it has a strong dirigente in don Miguel. Through his own intelligence and imagination, he has been able to guide the barrio through various problems and crises, improving the conditions in Loma Pampa relative to some of its neighbors.

Although many of its individual residents remain without legal title, as a barrio Loma Pampa has received legal recognition from the municipal government of Cochabamba. Founded in 1998 and legalized in 2007, Loma Pampa is an OTB, the fundamental structural unit of urban Bolivia. Barrios in Bolivia are recognized by the state either as OTBs or *juntas vecinales* (neighborhood organizations). (Barrios without state recognition are simply referred to as *urbanizaciones* and have no legal standing in the eyes of the municipality.) Until the mid-1990s, all urban barrios with official state recognition were juntas vecinales, represented politically at the municipal level by the powerful Federación de Juntas Vecinales. With the passage of the Ley de Participación Popular (Law of Popular Participation) in 1994, which aimed to decentralize the state and put resources directly under local control, juntas vecinales could receive legal recognition from the state and an annual operating budget (the Presupuesto Operativo Anual) if they reorganized themselves as OTBs.[49] This reorganization required a lengthy set of trámites, including the establishment of a Comité de Vigilancia (Vigilance Committee), a leadership body charged with managing the budget, mediating between the state and the residents of the OTB, and working to ensure that individual landholders continue to legalize their claims. Once established as an OTB, the barrio would have the right to request basic services and infrastructure from the state (though the success of such petitions would continue to depend largely on the patronage connections that the local dirigente had established with municipal and regional authorities). Recognition as an OTB, then, was a key step toward gaining recognition and rights for barrio residents.

The zone of Uspha Uspha consists of thirteen OTBs and juntas vecinales. Each of these units is represented at a larger Consejo Zonal (Zonal Council), which has regular meetings that each barrio president is supposed to attend. These councils have no governing power in the zone, but they serve as nodes of organization above the level of the individual barrio and are able to coordinate local action on matters of shared concern and to present a unified front to the higher levels of organizations of which they form a part. Other important bodies within the zone are the Comité Impulsor, which makes decisions regarding the allocation of the zone's own operating budget; and the Junta Escolar, the governing body of the local school, which has authority to convoke meetings of parents and to initiate political actions outside the educational realm in the name of children's welfare. The Zonal Councils of the different zones within each urban district are represented in a Consejo Distrital (District Council); Uspha Uspha is part of District 8, which contains over forty OTBs and juntas vecinales. The districts are represented on the Consejo Municipal (Municipal Council), whose members are elected every four years, and who together comprise the critical governing body of the city, capable of passing ordinances that affect every dimension of urban life. Also important is the Alcaldía, the office of the mayor, which has its own suboffices (Subalcaldías) at the district level, to which residents and barrio leaders can appeal for assistance with infrastructural improvement projects, and to which they must present their papers in the land legalization process. The Subalcaldías are small, however, and have few resources of their own to support projects or initiatives; those sorts of decisions are made in the Alcaldía, which is located in the city's central plaza and is much further removed from the realities of daily barrio life. In addition, the Prefectura represents governance at the departmental level, and the prefect of Cochabamba controls the operations of the national police force based in Cochabamba City.

Although nested within this elaborate system of governance, the average barrio resident has few if any encounters with political leaders beyond her own barrio president, the dirigente. As in the case of Wilmer Vargas, described in chapter 3, even times of extreme crisis rarely seem to bring barrio residents into contact with state officials, political office holders, or government entities. Though she is forced to deal with minor bureaucrats as she tries to get her papers through the legalization system, it is her dirigente to whom the barrio resident turns for advice and guidance as she deals with problems of a legal, procedural, or even personal nature. Conversing on don Miguel's patio on Sunday afternoons, we would continually be interrupted by people knocking at his door, as one or another of Miguel's vecinos would come to him for a consultation, often clutching manila folders crammed full of legal papers, topographic maps, house plans, tax receipts, and so on, seeking help with the next stage of the trámite. Others would come with more delicate issues, including complaints about their children's behavior, conflicts with a neighbor or a relative, or excuses for not having attended a recent meeting or event. Miguel would attend patiently to each of them, providing concrete instructions on the proper course of action to take, often speaking in Quechua to the vecinos on whom he waited. Though Miguel was not equipped with any formal training or official resources, the *cargo* (office) of barrio dirigente required him to be a one-stop service center for all of his vecinos on a variety of official and unofficial business.

In many ways don Miguel is an exceptional barrio president, with personal qualities that allow him to serve as a strong and popular dirigente who exemplifies the possibilities of that role. Now in his late fifties, Miguel was born in Oruro, where his parents, natives of Cochabamba, were working on a temporary mining job. Shortly after his birth, Miguel's parents returned to their village in the countryside of the province of Arani, in the high Cochabamba Valley. The oldest of three boys, Miguel was raised by his maternal grandmother while his parents (peasants who had abandoned agriculture in the unpredictable valley climate) worked as market vendors in Cochabamba City. He spoke only Quechua until the age of eight, when his grandmother died and he came to Cochabamba to join his parents. As the oldest child, Miguel had the obligation of caring for his siblings when his parents were out working, which instilled in him a sense of responsibility for those in his charge. This carried over into his working life, and as a young man he quickly assumed a leadership position in a local sindicato. In the early 1960s, Miguel and his father opened a stall selling books on a patch of ground south of Punata Avenue, just below the heart of downtown Cochabamba, an area that would soon grow to be called La Pampa and that was later absorbed into Cochabamba's enormous outdoor market. Miguel helped to organize the various market vendors in his sector, founding one of the market federations that still control commerce in the Cancha. In becoming a union dirigente, he took advantage of his natural speaking ability and his heartfelt commitment to the underdog: "I have always tried to support the people with few resources, the poor, the people who can't defend themselves. There are many people in our society who suffer the consequences of abuse of authority, and I don't like that. I can speak better than many of my *compañeros*, better than my vecinos, and I use that to defend them in all sorts of ways. That is why I have assumed the [leadership] responsibilities that I now have."[50]

Miguel credits his earlier experiences of organizing workers with helping to develop his skills as a dirigente. He determined not to join any political party, preferring instead to operate as what he called a *dirigente cívico* (an unaffiliated civic leader), so as not to get caught up in the corruption and favoritism that he sees as characteristic of party politics in Bolivia. Though having a party affiliation can help a leader to bring resources and projects into his community, it also obligates him to the party, with which he must then perpetually cooperate. Most barrio leaders are affiliated with a party, and they must deliver their constituents on election day to vote in support of party candidates and otherwise perform services for the party organization. They also constantly face the temptation of enriching themselves at the expense of their vecinos, using their offices and contacts to advance their personal careers. For many barrio residents, their experience of the state is often mediated by these dirigentes and other sorts of political brokers, to whom they must make various sorts of pledges and to whom they in turn owe various kinds of favors, in exchange for their help accessing or manipulating the political and bureaucratic systems to produce favorable outcomes (Albro 2010b). Not wanting to participate in the game of patronage and clientage, Miguel prefers to remain outside the party system—though he sympathizes with the parties of the Left and generally supports the goals and ideals of Evo Morales's MAS.

Miguel and his family were among the first people to settle in Loma Pampa, purchasing a lot at the bottom of the steep hill back when there were only about eight other houses in the zone. Earlier he had purchased land in the barrio Primer de Mayo, which came with papers showing the land title to be clear and legal. Along with a number of other buyers, Miguel had taken out a loan from the Banco Sol (a Cochabamba microlender) to buy the lot, only to find out subsequently that the documents had been forged and that someone else had also purchased the land and had received the legal title. So Miguel lost his money and his land and was left homeless. Shortly thereafter, he learned that a distant cousin was selling land far to the south, on the edges of Uspha Uspha, with papers that were not yet legalized but that had the potential to be. The land at that time was reasonably priced, going for about four to five bolivianos (less than a dollar) per square meter.[51] So in 2000 Miguel and his wife, doña Senobia, settled in Loma Pampa, constructing a house and beginning the process of making a life on Cochabamba's furthest periphery.

Loma Pampa at this time lacked every kind of urban infrastructure imaginable. It had no electricity or running water, no roads or public transportation, no streetlights, no telephones. However, in the initial division of the parcel into lots, plans had been made to allow for the future development of infrastructure in the barrio—space for streets, sidewalks, and public areas were designated, for example—needing only local initiative to begin the process of bringing improvements to the area. But the directorios in charge of the barrio during its early years were inept and corrupt, and initiatives that began strongly soon petered out. Particularly troubling was the effort to bring electricity into Loma Pampa. The electric company, the Empresa de Luz y Fuerza Eléctrica Cochabamba (ELFEC), at that time a privately held company,[52] had no great incentive to run power lines and deliver service to newly emerging barrios on the margins of town, so the vecinos themselves were required to raise the funds to pay the installation costs.[53] In 2005, the dirigentes of Loma Pampa collected about US$6,000 from a hundred barrio families— an enormous sum for people in that zone—to pay ELFEC's costs, but instead of going directly to ELFEC, the dirigentes subcontracted with a third-party engineer who never delivered on his promises and—many residents believed—pocketed the people's money instead. In addition, the dirigentes conveniently lost the *libro de actas*, the official record of barrio finances, minutes of meetings, and so on; they also consistently failed to provide accounting reports to the vecinos on how they were spending the money they had collected. Accusations against these dirigentes were many, and included the charge that the barrio's treasurer had financed his own emigration to Spain with misappropriated funds. Disgusted, the vecinos threw the dirigentes out of office; several were forced to flee the barrio in fear for their lives.

It was at this moment that don Miguel emerged as a local leader. Building on the momentum generated by people's anger at their financial loss, Miguel led a contingent of barrio residents downtown to the gates of ELFEC, where they declared themselves to be on strike, demanding that the public utility provide basic electrical service to their community. Under this public pressure ELFEC relented and installed the high-tension wires to bring power from the main line out to Loma Pampa. In the aftermath of the 2000 Water War in Cochabamba and the 2003 Gas War in El Alto, Bolivia, it is likely that the utility company was not willing to risk a major public uprising over electricity. Individual residents still were required to pay to connect their homes to the line, but as a result of these efforts about 80 percent of the homes in Loma Pampa today have electricity. Miguel also tried, unsuccessfully, to negotiate with the third-party engineer for the return of the residents' money. He still holds out hope of a resolution but resists any suggestion of taking the case to the official justice system: "With our justice, more in favor of the rich person than the poor, we have to try to work something out in a friendly way. . . . The poor person is always a good loser."[54]

Don Miguel has continued to serve as president of Loma Pampa, elected by acclamation to three consecutive two-year terms. Most barrio residents view him as an honest alternative to the corrupt and self-serving leaders of the recent past. Some attribute this to Miguel's religion: they say that because he is an evangelical Christian, his beliefs won't allow him to deceive the people. (Curiously, Miguel's refusal to join any political party is mirrored in his religious practice. Though a Christian, he belongs to no recognized church, leading his own prayer service every Sunday morning on his patio with a few fellow believers.) Whatever the explanation, Miguel has proven himself to be a strong advocate for his community, not needing party support to bring local improvements to Loma Pampa. He is also a natural democrat, running the monthly meetings of the OTB with openness and transparency. He will cede the floor to anyone who wishes to speak, inviting the contributions of everybody, including women— who usually sit quietly, content to observe the public debate. Unlike his predecessors, Miguel makes a great show of his public rendering of accounts, carefully delineating at each monthly meeting his directorio's expenditures of public funds collected from barrio residents.[55] In the eyes of many of his constituents, this is exactly how a dirigente is supposed to function: honestly, openly, and sincerely, like the father of a family (see Goldstein 2005b). One resident said: "The dirigente has to be here in the barrio, like a father. He has to watch over (*vigilar*) everyone, everything that is going on in the barrio, what needs we have or don't have. He has to watch over everything, he has to be attentive, like a father."[56] Doña Delina agreed: "A dirigente has to walk around [the barrio], he has to hold public meetings, he has to go to the Alcaldía to get them to help us. . . . In the barrio he has to look after the people."[57] Nevertheless, the role of dirigente takes its toll on don Miguel, requiring enormous investments of his personal resources, not to mention his time and energy, to do the job right. His wife, doña Senobia, frequently urges him to step down and let someone else lead the barrio, but Miguel feels committed to the projects he has begun and enjoys the prestige and authority that comes with being barrio president.

The dirigente also has to play a role in the settlement of local disputes, which sometimes include matters of criminal activity. Though he has no formal legal authority over such matters, the dirigente and his colleagues in the directorio sometimes must intervene in conflicts within the barrio, either because they feel that no other authority is likely to respond, or because (as with don Miguel and the third-party engineer in the electricity dispute) they are reluctant to involve outside authorities in barrio conflicts. Again, this pertains to the sense of abandonment that people express vis-à-vis the phantom state: although they are well aware that a formal justice system exists in Bolivia, it is beyond their experience and ability to access. Thus Miguel understands his own role as local leader to include serving as a kind of legal agent, set outside of an official state justice system that provides him with no training or resources to play that role and that affords no security to his neighborhood. Miguel says, "This is a community without law. . . . I am the law in this barrio."[58]

In such a context, local dirigentes may be the only ones able to bring about a peaceful settlement of a conflict, though they often lack the authority to do so. In the barrio Juan Pablo II, for example, vecinos view the state as absent; the police as corrupt, ineffective, and invisible; and local intervention as the only possible solution to local problems. Said one dirigente: "There have been fights among the vecinos here, between family members, too, in which the directorio has intervened in the problem, has made recommendations, has totally calmed down the situation. They put an end to it, and people paid attention. . . . The directorio has every right to go and hear the case and make a verbal solution."[59] However, this idea of "making a verbal solution" (*poner solución así verbalmente*) suggests the limited authority of local leaders in these kinds of conflicts, which legally are the purview of the state. Dirigentes are often hesitant to impose solutions on vecinos, for fear of overstepping their bounds and having their authority questioned. As president of the Comité Impulsor for Uspha Uspha, don Fulgencio has had occasion to intervene in situations where local children were running with gangs, calling the behavior to the parents' attention and trying to broker a solution, but "one has to have a great deal of tact, a great deal of authority, and a great deal of proof, if one hopes to make people comply. Otherwise, they will just laugh at you."[60] The problems that urban dirigentes have to deal with are also extremely challenging, with some questions exceeding the experience and competence of many local leaders. More quotidian problems —gossip among neighbors, for example, or someone's goats getting into a neighbor's garden—can be relatively straightforward. Other matters— like domestic violence, disputes over land, and closure of an establishment known to serve alcohol to minors—require legal knowledge and resources to resolve adequately.

Without any formal legal authority, dirigentes like don Miguel tread very carefully when dealing with local conflicts, and the solutions they adopt may not always produce a satisfactory resolution. Sometimes the dirigente might bring local offenders (in a case of domestic violence, for example) before the community at a monthly meeting of the OTB, where their behavior can be criticized publicly in the hope of shaming them into reforming, but lacking any formal ability to sanction the behavior, the dirigente has no real means of enforcement. In some barrios, the dirigente will impose a fine on offenders in certain types of cases, but in Loma Pampa people have resisted this measure, fearing that they themselves might some day be called on to pay. This leaves the dirigente with very few options to resolve a dispute in his barrio. Some dirigentes fear retribution by angry parties if they impose harsh decisions; they also run the risk of sparking further conflicts, as jealous rivals perceive the dirigente as favoring one side or another in a dispute. In addition, as discussed below, dirigentes can be especially vulnerable when vecinos turn to violence. In cases of lynching or attempted lynching, the police will often seek out the local dirigente and blame him for the incident, in an effort to identify a culprit responsible for the violence. Though sometimes barrio residents will protect their dirigentes or other individuals by adopting what the newspapers like to call a "pact of silence,"[61] the police (incompetent to investigate other kinds of crimes but under enormous public pressure to identify the perpetrators of lynchings) will single out the barrio leader as synecdoche for the amorphous mob. Dirigentes thus have great incentive to resolve conflicts peaceably before vecinos, frustrated with lack of action, decide to employ violence to settle them. This was the case in Loma Pampa following the electrification scandal, as angry vecinos threw bricks at the home of the barrio treasurer, demanding the return of their money and threatening to lynch his wife if it was not forthcoming. Miguel had to mediate this situation, arranging an exit from the barrio for the wife of the accused man and finding other means —the protest march—to allow people to vent their anger while successfully bringing electricity to the OTB.

Although the dirigente has persuasive power and a certain degree of authority to influence decisions in the barrio, his work is made more challenging by the lack of internal coherence—what people describe as "unity" —among the residents of his OTB. In many ways, under Miguel's leadership, Loma Pampa became much more organized than it had previously been, and more so than other barrios that lacked similar leadership. During Miguel's three terms of office, he organized numerous public events— soccer tournaments, public works projects, political protests, barrio anniversary celebrations—all of which engaged the residents and encouraged or required them to turn out and participate. In this way, some people feel, Miguel increased the general sense of security in the barrio. Josias said: "During [Miguel's] term of office, he united the barrio, with the various events that he did. The people have come to know each other more, they talk to one another, they take care of each others' houses. When I go out my neighbor says to me, 'I will watch it for you, don't worry about it,' he says to me. When he goes out I too tell him not to worry, that I will watch [his house]. We sometimes invite each other to share a meal. . . . Because of [Miguel's leadership] it is more like that."[62] But others continue to feel the sense of isolation and disunion described above. Participation in public works projects, for example—which each year include a crew assigned to repair the crumbling road leading into Loma Pampa—is done under duress, with vecinos facing a fine if they fail to participate. Doña Tadea commented about these communal work activities: "If there wasn't a fine, they wouldn't show up."[63] Attendance at the monthly meeting of the OTB is similarly mandatory, with fines imposed on those who do not come or send a representative on their behalf. Every meeting or event is marked by a stampede at the conclusion, as all the vecinos descend on the poor barrio secretary, whose job it is to register their attendance on his clipboard.

Others note that the lack of unity—the individualization of barrio residents—makes it impossible to intervene effectively in conflicts in the barrio. Cases of domestic abuse or violence can be particularly challenging, as they are often widely known to occur within the barrio, yet no one feels authorized to take action. In addition, people fear the gossip that can come to dog them if they mix themselves in the problems of other families. This goes both for leaders like Miguel and ordinary barrio residents, who prefer not to make themselves the targets of gossip or revenge by getting involved in other people's business. Don Casto, for example, recounted a case in which abuse was widely known to be taking place, but nobody wanted to get involved:

> Rarely do [the dirigentes] intervene, no? Like I told you, so as not to make enemies they just watch from afar, they let problems pass. When there is a big problem here everyone knows about it, with the gossip and all. For example, they say there was a case of mistreatment of the parents [by an adult son]. Everybody knew about it; the whole barrio knew that such and such person had abused his parents. So we said to ourselves, what can we do? The majority of the people didn't say "What are we going to do?" They just let the problem slide. . . . Everyone was aware of the problem, but no one intervened. They stayed quiet, and finally the problem just went away."[64]

Don Miguel and others in Loma Pampa understand that while people in the barrio may at certain moments appear to be unified, underneath there remains a sense of fragmentation and individualization that limits the possibilities for security in the barrio. As doña Irda put it: "If we were united, we could be more advanced, we wouldn't have anything to worry about. If we were united, we could do anything and advance, helping ourselves as poor people. That is how it is to be united."[65]

Violence as a Path to Security

Most if not all anthropologists who write about lynching violence have been spared the agony of having to actually experience a lynching in person. We rely on secondhand sources to support our analyses, including video recordings, news reports, anecdotes, and, of course, interviews with people who witnessed or participated in the violence. It is extremely difficult to study lynching using other basic techniques of ethnography, especially participant observation, which in the case of lynching sounds like a grotesque contradiction in terms. Perhaps for that reason, lynching is a fertile field for interpretation. Despite the difficulty of gaining direct experience of the practice about which we write, anthropology can contribute to an understanding of lynching, not to justify it or to sanitize its ugliness through relativist explanation, but to situate it within the larger set of experiences that characterize life on the insecure margins of the state. In doing so, we must confront the host of popular, official, academic, and media-generated interpretations of these acts, not to arrive at "the truth" about lynching but, as I try to do, to offer the actors' perspectives on what they are doing and why. In this way, I demonstrate that what we think of as "lynching"—typically characterized as a single phenomenon in which all members of a community participate—is in fact a highly diverse and internally contradictory set of processes.

A key question in many analysts' considerations of lynching is the communal, collective nature of the practice. In some ways, as the event in Loma Pampa described below suggests, lynching appears to be a collective act, expressing the rage and frustration of a community where state law does not operate and people take the law into their own hands to punish criminals in their midst. This is the point at which many scholarly interpretations of lynching conclude. But on closer inspection, the Loma Pampa event—like other lynchings and attempted lynchings in this and other barrios—is characterized less by unified action on the part of a community than by a deep ambivalence among the actors, many of whom remain profoundly conflicted about violence and its potential for creating security and justice. In addition, rather than proceeding according to some established pattern or plan, the attempted lynching in Loma Pampa appears to have been a rather ad hoc affair, which might have ended in the killing of the suspect but did not, due precisely to the ambivalence of the crowd and the timely intervention of an able dirigente. A closer consideration of lynching violence demonstrates the ways in which an apparently collective action can in fact mask a deep diversity of opinion, revealing barrio residents' complex and contradictory views of violence. Though many people understand lynching violence to be an appropriate response to insecurity, they are also deeply conflicted about its use and uncertain about the ways and circumstances in which it should be deployed. The resulting picture is an unstable one, characterized by disagreement, doubt, and uncertainty, rendering any attempt to identify a singular meaning, objective, or explanation of lynching highly suspect.

A LYNCHING IN LOMA PAMPA

Although I have not physically been present at a lynching, members of my research team in Bolivia have, and their fieldnotes of this event provide a fascinating anthropological record of participant observation in a lynching.[66] On February 19, 2006, while I was in the United States, three members of the team were in Loma Pampa teaching martial arts classes and chatting with vecinos at don Miguel's house on a sunny Sunday afternoon. Hearing noises in the street, they went out to investigate. There, tied to a lamppost on the corner was a man, in his early to mid-forties, seated on the ground beneath the post staring blankly into space. A few vecinos stood around observing, including the person who was the supposed victim of the man's aggression, a young woman from up the hill. She claimed that the man had entered her house and threatened her and her children, at which point she called her neighbors, who appre-hended the man, tied his hands, and carried him down the hill to the main corner by the bus stop. Shortly thereafter someone lit off some rockets and a larger crowd gathered, though one of my colleagues re-marked that people arrived "gradually, walking calmly" to see what was going on. A crowd of about fifty or sixty people gathered, standing around and observing with curiosity; another colleague recorded in her notes that people kept a distance of about three meters between them-selves and the man tied to the post, "as it seemed that nobody knew what to do."

Indeed, from these observations an atmosphere of uncertainty appar-ently prevailed, and debate rather than consensus characterized the atti-tude of the people in the crowd. People talked in small groups, with louder opinions sometimes being voiced to the larger assembly. Some people discussed the events surrounding the crime and the apprehen-sion of the criminal, with some confirming the woman's version of events (the man entered the house, threatened the occupants, and violently resisted the attempts of the neighbors to subdue him). Others suggested that the man had been wandering about Loma Pampa for several days, intent on finding young girls to rape. This second version seemed to take hold of people's imaginations ("Good thing this is Sunday, because we were home and they could catch him. If this had been a Monday or a Tuesday, we would have been working, and he could have easily entered our houses and raped our daughters." "He came to rape, and they rape boys, too, you know, not just girls"). Other people debated the nature of the criminal. Some said he was drunk, while others said they couldn't smell alcohol on him. Someone said he was mentally ill, and his manner did suggest a certain lack of engagement with reality, as he continued to stare blankly into space, not reacting to the events going on around him. Some in the crowd interpreted this as a sign that he was actually staring at them, memorizing faces so he could later return and exact vengeance, which scared some people and amused others ("[Nervously] Did you see how he looked at us?" "He was watching all of us!" "[Laughing to a friend] He was looking at you! He's going to come back! You're screwed, you're not going to be able to go out drinking anymore!"). People also debated what action to take. Some were in favor of calling the police, but others were opposed. An old woman said: "They [criminals] have to be killed." Someone suggested that if the man was indeed mentally ill, all the more reason not to call the cops; given the lack of public mental health facilities in the city, the cops were more likely to release the man than to prosecute him.

In the midst of all this, some people decided that the man had to be interrogated, to find out who he was and what he wanted in the barrio. But perhaps due to a mental disability, the man did not reply to any questions put to him and remained mutely staring out at the crowd. This was particularly unnerving, and some began to insist that it was all an act, with the man pretending to be mentally disabled in order to confuse the crowd. This made some people view him as an expert criminal, someone who could handle a situation like this in cold blood ("He's a live one, he doesn't speak, he doesn't plead, he doesn't apologize. Anyone else in his place would be scared to death").

Throughout this period there were no screams, no insults thrown at the man bound to the lamppost, or attempts to strike him. After about an hour, though, new people began to join the crowd, some of them coming from a nearby chichería where they had been drinking all afternoon. These people began to speak of the need to deliver a warning so that the man wouldn't come back and take revenge on the barrio. Three of these people—men, quite obviously drunk, and not residents of Loma Pampa —got right up in the man's face to interrogate him further, adopting a much more aggressive attitude than previously seen. They kicked the bound man and struck him on the head, opening a wound that gushed blood into the dirt on which he sprawled. Seeing violence, others in the crowd surged forward, trying to get a better view of the action. After delivering the beating, the drunks began to vociferously egg on the crowd, inciting them to kill the bound man.

Until this point, don Miguel had been standing by the post, quietly trying to calm the more agitated members of the crowd. Twice he had called the police, but nearly two hours into the event none had yet arrived. My colleagues had also tried calling the police, but to no avail. Then Miguel responded, stepping forward to engage the drunk men, supported by a number of his vecinos who stood behind him as he confronted the men. One of my colleagues, a lawyer and human rights activist, also stood with Miguel. These two groups argued, with Miguel insisting that they wait for the police, that they respect the law, while the other men yelled for the bound man to be burned, frequently calling to the crowd, "Bring gasoline!" There were also some women in the crowd, Loma Pampa residents and also apparently intoxicated, who urged that the man be burned right away, lest he come back and rape their daughters. These women accused my colleague of somehow supporting the delinquent by objecting to his being burned, screaming: "If our daughters are raped, it will be your fault!" According to her fieldnotes, "although the people did not take direct action against the man there was much tension, people confused by each other's arguments, arguing, shouting, etc." Meanwhile, the children who had been participating in the martial arts class sat nearby, observing the entire event.

Finally the three drunk instigators moved away from the crowd, and though they continued to yell exhortations ("He has to be burned!" "Justice by our own hands!"), these seemed to lack force and were repeated simply by rote, as the energy for violence gradually diminished. The crowd of vecinos continued to debate, with many sober people still worried and wanting to send a warning by administering physical punishment to the man. However, nobody moved to hit or burn the man, nor did they insult him or address him directly. With time, more people seemed to hear the arguments of don Miguel against using violence, and some in the crowd began saying that they should listen to Miguel because he was the authority in the barrio ("Even though I wanted to burn or kill [the man], I have to pay attention to what don Miguel says"). A half hour later, the drunk women continued to exhort the crowd, but they received little in the way of response. New people arrived and in soft tones tried to interrogate the man, but he remained mute. One man, winking at the crowd, shouted in jest, "Bring gasoline, he doesn't want to talk!" and people laughed, including, bizarrely, the bound man.

At last, some four hours after the beginning of the event, the police arrived. They came in force, a whole team clad in riot gear, driving four trucks and two motorcycles, commanded by a colonel who spoke with Miguel and several vecinos, trying to verify what had happened. While some of his officers freed the bound man and loaded him into one of the vehicles, the colonel spoke with those remaining in the crowd, listening to their complaints about lack of police service in the zone. He suggested that they write a letter to the prefect of Cochabamba, asking him to install a police station in the barrio. The police then departed, taking the accused man with them. The crowd lingered for a while longer, conversing in the dusk before dispersing.[67]

VIOLENCE AND CONFUSION

In some ways the practice of lynching is a collective act in which many barrio residents, perhaps the majority, participate to some extent (Achá 2003). In the event of an emergency, such as a possible delinquent being spotted or apprehended, barrio residents can be quickly summoned and a previously quiet street transformed into a meeting ground, filled with a crowd of people talking, arguing, trying to understand the specific circumstances in which they find themselves. On many such occasions, people will blow whistles or set off bottle rockets as a way of alerting their neighbors to the presence of a delinquent in their midst, and men and women alike will come running to investigate. In the excitement of the moment, finding themselves suddenly face to face with the spectral delinquent, now rendered harmless and subdued before the angry crowd, people do feel a sense of unity and solidarity, even security, through their actions. A resident of Juan Pablo II described the situation in terms of organization (albeit with some redundancy). "Here in our organization we are organically organized," he said. "We watch each others' houses, we take care of ourselves, too. We see someone strange walking around, that is when we sound the alarm. Then a rocket. When the rocket sounds we have to gather, come what may, all who live close by here. Sometimes we trap him. That is more or less how we organize ourselves and how we protect ourselves."[68] The rocket is the signal, the call to arms to which all are expected to respond. Another resident of Juan Pablo II said: "In this we are united."[69] One member of my research team wrote in his fieldnotes that in the event in Loma Pampa, he had sensed a "fusión comunitaria" (collective fusion) as people "conversed intensely" in a way that they seldom do in the marginal barrio. This was emphasized by the

FIG. 8 An effigy wearing a sign that says "Residents on alert" hangs from a lamppost on the approach to Alto Cochabamba on the city's south side, a warning to criminals to stay away, 2010. Photo by the author.

explicit utterances of some in the crowd, who commented on the need to be "united" in these kinds of situations.

At the same time, however, some residents recognize that unity, rather than being "organically organized," is in fact a kind of performance put on for the benefit of the captured criminals. For example, another resident of Juan Pablo II said that in times of emergency, "we have to come out to support each other, to see what is going on. The people gather here, and the thief thinks that we are all united, that we all support one another. And that is what we want. When something is happening, then the people appear. This shows unity, and it makes the thieves afraid."[70] A resident of Mineros San Juan echoed this sentiment, saying that lynching "makes [the rateros] a little scared, seeing us all united. . . . Maybe they will give a little more respect to our community."[71] Many people describe lynching as a warning, a way to scare thieves away so they won't come back, a way "to make them respect the barrio." The use of effigies in some barrios is another way to communicate this message (see fig. 8), while also an attempt to render recognizable the mysterious countenance of the delinquent (Risør 2010).[72] The spectral nature of the ratero, always possibly present, requires a constant system of warning, conjoined with the behaviors of alertness to enhance a feeling of security. The lynching itself, like the effigy, is a warning given flesh. Josias said: "The truth is, with the state we're in now, poorer all the time, more thieves will appear, so hitting or killing a person intimidates other thieves who might want to come rob the barrio."[73] This performance of unity and of dangerousness through lynching is also an attempt to conceal the fundamental disunity that characterizes the marginal barrio. And it masks the chaos that is the act of lynching itself, as in Loma Pampa. A resident of Juan Pablo II admitted: "For now we don't have our own security system, the only way we communicate [an emergency] is by shouting, sounding an alarm. With that we are there. But we are not organized in that situation."[74]

Indeed, though observers and analysts describe lynching as though it were a singular phenomenon, it is in fact a highly diverse set of practices about which people have a range of opinions and perspectives. Commentators in the media and the academy, in Bolivia, the United States, and other countries, describe lynching as a "sociological phenomenon" (Tórrez 2005, 33) and labor to interpret the meaning of this behavior. The agent of lynching violence, according to most reports, is "the mob" or "the crowd," a coherent mass that acts with a single mind to torture, maim, and kill. For example, "last Sunday a mob falsely accused two students of being thieves, tortured them, killed one and left the other in a coma."[75] The police, unable to control lynchings and themselves occasionally their victims, cannot identify individual perpetrators and so consider the entire mass guilty of the crime; journalists and scholars pick up on this conception, describing the crowd as "drunk," "irrational," "barbaric," "sadistic," "hysterical," or "brutal,"[76] with no attempt to distinguish between, say, actors and observers, the drunk and the sober, the titillated and the horrified. And while various researchers struggle to compile exhaustive lists of lynching events,[77] such lists end up demonstrating the real diversity—in terms of the types of victims, the methods used, the people who participated, the sequence of events, the sites in which the events occurred, and so on—that exists within this group of phenomena that are lumped together under the lynching rubric. Although exhibiting certain commonalties (for example, the perpetrators usually interrogate the captured individuals), lynchings do not unfold according to some established pattern or routine that is known to all participants. Most important, the lynchings that I have studied actually occur in a context of tremendous uncertainty. People are unsure of what to do, and rather than extreme and unanimous rage, the so-called mob exhibits a profound ambivalence that leads to a diversity of outcomes: the victim may be killed but usually is not.[78] Indeed, as in Loma Pampa, the emotions of people in the crowd shift constantly during the event, with rage, boredom, amusement, irony, grief, shame, and pity surging to the forefront at different times.

People in the barrios agree that something needs to be done about crime and delinquency, and many residents, especially those who have been victims of crime, feel that violence is a possible solution. Having been abandoned by the police and judicial authorities, some say that taking the law into their own hands is the only realistic response to insecurity. Because of their inattention, doña Irma says, "the police themselves oblige us to make justice with our own hands [*por las manos propias*]."[79] As discussed in chapter 3, the lack of confidence in the justice system is extensive among barrio residents, and many people feel that because of the extreme levels of corruption among the police, violence on the part of residents is a reasonable response to crime. The delinquents, they say, are in cahoots with the police, and if the police arrest a thief they will simply let him go in exchange for a small bribe. In addition, the laws are weak and favor the criminal over the victim of crime, again rendering the justice system ineffective. Doña Tadea, on the lynching of criminals, said: "You have to burn them, or they will be set free!"[80] This mistrust of the authorities is one factor motivating lynching violence. Said don Angel: "Any suspect that we see, we have to launch a rocket and the people gather, we ask him where he is from, who he is, why is he here, from what barrio, all of that we have to ask. If he doesn't say anything, he has to be burned straight away, without notifying the authorities. Otherwise the police are going to come, today he is here, tomorrow morning he is out, he gives them a few pesos and that's it. And later the police say he escaped, but really they themselves let him go."[81]

Many barrio residents with whom I have spoken are quite certain that lynching is a correct and proper response to insecurity. For these individuals, men and women alike, the ratero is unredeemable, a threat to their security—and there is no alternative but to eliminate him. Though Miguel is strictly opposed to lynching, his son Josias feels differently: "I would do it personally, I would burn him with my own hands. . . . I think that these people have to be killed, because they are beyond hope."[82]

People like Josias seem to embody the stereotype of the enraged mob participant, the person so full of anger from having suffered the abuses of criminals and the ineffective justice system that he is willing to torture and kill to try to put an end to the situation. Friendly, quiet people who on other occasions might happily invite you to share a meal or have a glass of Inca Kola can talk about the details of lynching in truly horrific ways. One woman from Mineros San Juan suggested that one way to punish a thief is to cut off his fingers, because "without fingers what can he do? He can't rob with his feet."[83] Doña Birgith described a lynching she had witnessed in especially graphic terms: "His flesh melted away like lard, the police took him away half dead. . . . He was screaming in pain, 'Waaaay!' And they were burning him, and he suffered so much."[84] A male resident of Mineros San Juan expressed a willingness to kill his own children if they turned out to be delinquents: "If I have a child that makes someone cry, better that he no longer can make someone cry. There is a refrain: an eye for an eye, a tooth for a tooth, he who lives by the sword dies by the sword. It is beautiful, and it goes for our children, too."[85] And a man from Juan Pablo II coldly stated: "It is necessary to burn them, even if it be my child, even if it be your child, it has to be done. . . . They have to be burned."[86] Some families use burning to punish children for misbehavior—a child who breaks a dish or fails to do a chore, for example, might have his fingers held over the fire as a correction. Some women use this to justify the violence of lynching: in Loma Pampa, one of the drunk women arguing that the accused man should be burned said that when her children don't listen to her or steal from her, "I burn their hands so that they will learn." The same lesson, by extension, can be taught to delinquents.

Such certainty, however, is balanced by a kind of ambivalence, observable in the ways in which many barrio residents talk about lynching not with conviction but with grave doubt and hesitation. Most people, for example, would not be willing to execute their own child, despite the rhetoric of the men quoted above. Indeed, even lynching one's own vecino is problematic. Asked if such a thing could happen, another male resident of Juan Pablo II stated: "I don't think so, I don't think we would let him go, but to lynch him, I don't think we would go to that extreme. We are all human beings. I don't think we would go to that extreme, we would have to take other measures."[87] Of course, this doesn't preclude the possibility that a vecino might be lynched elsewhere. Another man responded: "In this barrio, for example, in all of Uspha Uspha, we are almost all migrants from the countryside, and you know that peasants are more honorable than city dwellers. . . . So I don't think it would be necessary to rob in [one's own] barrio. If he wanted to work as a robber, he would have to go rob in another place, and in that other place they would have to lynch him."[88] Such remarks reveal the doubt that slips into people's perspectives on lynching: it is appropriately applied only to outsiders, rateros who are spectral but not fully present like an actual vecino. Some people describe themselves as similarly torn between their anger over being victimized and their unwillingness to actually kill someone in anger. For some this is a religious conviction: doña Irma emphasized that while stealing is against God's wishes, "to make justice [that is, to lynch] is also a sin."[89] Don Omar, whose store was robbed of all its contents, described his ambivalence following the event and his fear of being tempted to sin: "I too had a desire to kill, not to kill myself but to kill those who assaulted me, took my things. . . . Justice is divine, it has to be the work of the Lord. . . . Better to leave it to God, and He will make justice. I can't do anything. I just hope that I never find myself in a situation where someone is being lynched, I wouldn't want to fall into that." He went on to speculate that even those who participate in a lynching may later regret it: "I think that those people don't feel so good after they lynch someone, after they have burned a person. I don't think that they have a clear conscience, to say, 'Ah, I have made justice.' In the moment, yes, when they are enraged, but I think that afterwards they are not so well."[90]

Women especially express their deep internal conflict about using violence to control delinquency. Expected—because of their gender—to care for the home and protect it, its contents, and their children from harm, women feel especially vulnerable to crime and especially torn about how to respond to it. This is clear from the Loma Pampa incident, in which women were some of the most vociferous in calling for the burning of the captured "rapist," but also some of the most reluctant to actually take action. Part of women's ambivalence stems from their frequent exposure to violence in the home. As mentioned earlier, domestic violence is a constant problem within poor families, and women are often the victims of abuse by their husbands. At the same time, many women will themselves use violence as a technique for disciplining their children, as with the women quoted above who burn their children's fingers to teach them proper comportment. As both victims and perpetrators of domestic violence, women may regard the public violence of lynching from this dual perspective, simultaneously empathizing with the victim while demanding that he be physically punished for his crime. Women's ambivalence is also linked to the competing stereotypes of indigenous women that abound in Bolivia, and to individual women's uneasy attempts to straddle these while caring for a family and a household in the context of poverty and insecurity. On the one hand, indigenous women are supposed to be weak and subordinate to the men in their lives. Some women express a sense of helplessness in confronting insecurity as a result of this weakness and feel that lynching is the only possible protection they have. In addition, women hold themselves responsible for the behavior of their children, as does society—which views the mother as equally guilty of the crimes of the child. Doña Pacífica, for example, stated that the child's decision to dedicate himself to crime "depends on the mother who raised him."[91] A woman in Mineros San Juan echoed this, and justified the lynching on the basis of maternal failure: "Kill him. What can we do? We are just women, we can't teach our sons. When a woman has children and is poor, she can't maintain them."[92]

On the other hand, in contrast to the stereotype of the weak but responsible mother is the image of the urban indigenous woman—the *cholita*—as tough, indomitable, and resourceful (Albro 2000; de la Cadena 1995; Rivera Cusicanqui 1996). From this perspective, indigenous women don't let anybody push them around, as is evidenced by their willingness to use violence to discipline their children or to punish a thief. Some of the accused thieves in different barrios are in fact women —*rateras*, for whom the punishment of a lynching may include cutting off their braids, erasing both their femininity and indigeneity in one fell swoop. In an interview, doña Casilda captured both dimensions of these stereotypes—women as weak, women as strong—in her comments about dealing with thieves:

> DOÑA CASILDA: What can we do? Hit them? For example, say a ratero came by here, we women are going to grab him? Men have to grab him!
>
> *But they say the women more than anyone . . .*
>
> DOÑA CASILDA: . . . are those who *chasquean* [hit, in Quechua], no?
>
> *The most chasqueadoras [hitters] [laughter].*

DOÑA CASILDA: These *kjateras* [market vendors][93] from the countryside are terrible, no? When they are selling, if you stop for a minute in front of their stall they tell you, "Move it! Move it!"[94]

Amid dueling stereotypes, women remain uncertain about the appropriateness of violence as a response to insecurity. Some women express strong convictions on the matter and condemn the practice of lynching: "Those who burn [another person] don't have a heart" (doña Birgith).[95] "Some say you have to beat them [rateros] up, there has to be justice by our own hands. But the ratero is a human being, too. The only thing we can do is to advise the police. That is the only thing we can do" (doña Casilda).[96] "It is craziness, I tell you. How that poor man screamed!" (doña Irma).[97] "There are people like us with feelings, and there are people who just react. In my case, to see someone burn, no, I can't watch, better get me away from there. I go, I escape" (resident of Uspha Uspha Central).[98]

Other women are less sure. Many fear for their own children's safety, recognizing that many lynchings involve cases of mistaken identity. Asked whether all are in agreement about the appropriateness of lynching, a woman from Mineros San Juan said in a group interview: "If I had sons . . . I would not agree with the lynching. If I had sons, because I only have daughters—but I have male cousins, and one day by some bad luck, they could find themselves in the same situation. It can befall an innocent person, so if I think of my cousins, then no."[99] Another woman said of lynching: "It hurts us, and it makes us want to cry. We have our children, too."[100] Others fear that if the captured person is not executed, he will return to the barrio to seek revenge. The fear of vengeance can be a powerful motivator of lynching violence, but it is not enough to erase women's ambivalence. Doña Isabel put it this way:

DOÑA ISABEL: He has to be killed, *pues*, but they can come back and take revenge, we say.

Many have that fear, no?

DOÑA ISABEL: Yes. Even now they are still trying to find out who was the person who killed the man up there [in another barrio], the man that they burned. They are still looking; the police are investigating as well. They say that his relatives can come back to the barrio, and this is worse, we say—this makes us very afraid. I say tie him up and take him to the police, or just beat him up. Others say burn him. This causes me pain, too.

Yes, it is painful. Why do you feel pain?

DOÑA ISABEL: I feel as if it is my own son that they are burning.[101]

Doña Casilda expressed similar views about lynching, simultaneously holding two competing opinions on the matter:

DOÑA CASILDA: Sometimes it scares me. It hurts me, too, when they burn a thief. How can they burn someone, one asks oneself sometimes. On the other hand, it's good that they burn him like that.

You think both things?

DOÑA CASILDA: Yes, both things.[102]

The ambivalence and uncertainty that many people experience in reflecting on lynching in the abstract is also manifest in the event itself, destabilizing the certainty that most analysts ascribe to it. Rather than the actions of a unanimous, undifferentiated mob, the lynching unfolds amid doubt, fear, and debate about the proper course of action. As mentioned above, for example, lynchings often involve interrogating the accused by members of the group that has captured him, but the reasons for doing so relate more to the fundamental uncertainty of the moment than to the unfolding of an inexorable pattern. For some, questioning the victim is an attempt to extract a confession, mirroring their own notions of what justice should look like, perhaps garnered from some television program or movie in which the forces of justice break the will of the criminal and secure a conviction. But for others, the interrogation is a diagnostic tool: in a context in which so many cases of mistaken identity occur, barrio residents often try to verify that the person they have apprehended is, in fact, a criminal. This is surprising, in light of the broad claim in media and academic accounts that "popular rage does not discriminate between delinquent and innocent," a symptom of the "irrationality" that lynching embodies (Tórrez 2005, 34). But given the ambiguity surrounding the identities of these spectral beings, people employ the criterion of local knowledge to determine the true nature of the person before them:

In these cases they investigate, they ask him: "Where are you from?" If the thief is innocent, he sings: "I am such and such person, call this telephone [number] and tell them to come and get their relative." But if the thief doesn't say anything, is mute, says, "I am from [the nearby towns of] Quillacollo, I am from Sacaba," says anything, one suspects that he is a thief. If he is saying, "I am from there, my phone number is such and such, call my family to come get me," nobody is crazy enough to kill him. His family will come in no time. Then he is innocent. But if he doesn't say anything, if he is confused, he names various places, gives numbers that are not from here, unknown cellphone numbers, one realizes automatically [that he is guilty].[103]

The desire to know the truth about the person's identity is partly driven by a desire to unmask his inherent spectrality, to distinguish between a real person who has a legitimate reason for being there and a phantom who is only looking for an opportunity to make mischief: "You have to ask. If a person knows the barrio, has family there, then he has to speak, he has to sing: 'I am looking for such and such family, I am his family, his relative, his son.' Someone who doesn't know anybody, it means he is a ratero."[104] "Sometimes we don't know if someone is a ratero or not. Maybe they are drunk or crazy. That has to be known, from my perspective, no? Some have no fear and are immediately hitting him. Maybe he is, maybe he isn't, we don't know yet."[105] "It could be a problem if they burn him and he wasn't a thief, no? If we are not sure, better that we do nothing, no? His relatives could come, they would ask about him. That's why they question him. And if he doesn't answer, then obviously he is a thief."[106]

Uncertain about the nature of the person they have apprehended, the so-called mob is also unsure about how to handle him. As discussed above, many women are ambivalent or actively opposed to lynching, and though they may stay and watch, they do not want to see violence done. In such moments, it is often the loudest, fiercest opinions that are heard and taken by some observers to represent the views of the majority. While some women might be very vocal and opinionated, others are less so. Women tend to remain silent at public gatherings (like the monthly meetings of the OTB), and they may hesitate to express their feelings when these run contrary to those of the loudest people in the crowd. Said doña Fausta, describing the women at the lynching in Loma Pampa: "We were quiet, we said to ourselves, 'We have sons, too, you don't have to burn him.' Others said that they should burn him."[107] In addition, many people are afraid to speak out against the violence for fear of being accused of sympathizing with the criminal, or of being his active accomplices, as my colleague discovered when she objected to the use of violence in Loma Pampa.

Indeed, it takes only one person to throw the gasoline and light the match that sets the accused aflame. Lynchings most often take place on weekends, when people are in the barrio in large numbers (the barrios can feel deserted during the weekdays) and often drunk. Drunk men and women, who (as in the case of Loma Pampa) may not even be residents of the barrio but merely patrons of the local chichería, are often the principal instigators of the violence. Though many in the crowd may be in favor of lynching, the action itself requires someone to initiate it, and the drunk person, less inhibited than he or she otherwise might be, can take that role. A woman from Mineros San Juan described the situation, capturing both the diversity within the crowd and the intense fear that surrounds the event; she referred specifically to *sulfúricos* (enraged individuals) as the prime movers of the lynching: "There were drunk people, young people—so many people. Not all the people kill, only the sulfúricos. You know, all people are not the same. There are people who react strongly, they kick him around, but there are people who are just watching out of curiosity. There may be a crowd, but not all kill—only some people, the most drunk or the most sulfúrico. One hits him, the other brings gasoline, they throw it, and bang! Others are just watching. What are you going to say? If you oppose them, they will hit you, too. If you say 'Don't do it, poor thing, why are you attacking him?' they will call you his accomplice."[108]

The fear of being accused of being an accomplice, the strong doubts about the morality of what they are doing, the concern for their children, the worry about possible revenge or retaliation by the relatives of the accused, the fear of God's wrath—all are present in the minds of people before, during, and after a lynching. Though enacted in the name of security, the violence of lynching perpetuates insecurity, reinforcing existing problems and creating new ones. The trauma of seeing someone tortured or killed before their very eyes raises the general level of fear, both for adults and for the many children who gather silently to watch the event as though it were a form of horrific entertainment. The sound of the alarm calling people into action emerges as a new signifier of insecurity in the barrio. One woman from Mineros San Juan said: "When

I hear the rocket, it makes me nervous."[109] In addition to sending the warning that so many desire, the lynching also provokes thoughts of vengeance, and barrio residents after the event remain fearful that the friends and relatives of the victim will come in search of revenge. Nor does violence deter crime, as people in the barrios have learned. They lynch thieves, said one man, "so that they won't come back, so they won't do it any more. But it seems that the more they [lynch], the more they return."[110] Perhaps, then, another source of people's ambivalence about violence is their recognition—explicit or not—that it does not make them feel more secure but does precisely the opposite.

Conclusion

I have identified three ways in which the out-lawed residents of the marginal barrios of Uspha Uspha attempt to manage the insecurity that they confront daily in the localities where they make their homes.[111] These include watchfulness, an alert disposition through which people try to identify and intercept delinquents before they can do harm; reliance on local leaders, especially the barrio president, who provides guidance and tries to broker solutions to conflicts in his OTB; and violence, which people deploy as a mechanism to scare or punish delinquents, though not without a great deal of ambivalence and contradiction. In each case, I have examined the ways in which these efforts affect, or are affected by, the question of collective unity, a sense of community and solidarity that is largely absent from the marginal barrio, but that many residents believe would help them to feel more secure.

In making this analysis, one might be tempted to call on the older concept of social anomie to account for the seeming lack of norms in the marginal barrio, and the emergence of violence as an apparent response to the absence of firm social control. From this perspective—stemming from Durkheim's (1951 [1897]) classic sociological work on suicide and Merton's (1938) subsequent extension of the concept to analyze social deviance in the United States—anomie is a condition of social instability and individual alienation resulting from society's failure to impose limits on human feeling, "a breakdown of the regulatory order" (Braithwaite, Braithwaite, Cookson, and Dunn 2011, 1) that defines people's aspirations and the appropriate ways of attaining them. Derived from the Greek *anomia*, meaning lawlessness, anomie can lead to deviance as people seek to satisfy their desires in ways typically not sanctioned by society, thus challenging institutional and cultural norms (Orcutt 1983). Violence here is one possible outcome, perhaps the clearest indication (from this point of view) of societal breakdown and the failure of social order. Particularly in urban situations characterized by migration, racism, and social exclusion, anomie is seen to characterize the so-called marginal man—someone who has been separated from his former cultural norms but not fully assimilated into new ones, and who thus finds himself internally divided, lacking the normative signposts to guide his actions and perceptions and so, essentially, lost (Park 1928; Stonequist 1935). Such analyses are echoed in the writings of critics like Robert Kaplan (1994), whose projections of "the coming anarchy" decry the chaos and criminality of modern nations in the context of failing central governments and broader societal dissolution (points critiqued by Besteman 2005).

The lack of a robust community sentiment, combined with the propensity for violence, does suggest that there is an element of anomie at work in the lives of barrio residents in Uspha Uspha. As I have observed, the lack of legal institutions or firm cultural patterns for dealing with delinquency leaves people feeling uncertain of how to handle the problems facing them, in a way that at times seems especially anomic. Certainly this conforms with many observers' perceptions of life in what are variously called barrios, *favelas*, slums, squatter settlements, *villas miseria*, and so on, found in every city in Latin America and sometimes considered the "dumping ground for a surplus population" (UN Human Settlements Programme 2003, 46) that has no other place in the new world order of neoliberal capitalism. Given the extreme poverty, spotty infrastructure, and deficiency of official attention in these neighborhoods, it would not be surprising to find total societal chaos, a complete lack of order, institutionality, and social normativity. By all expectations, barrio residents should be entirely anomic, completely disconnected from the norms and values of mainstream society.

But rather than breakdown, loss, and an unbridled tendency toward violence, the residents of the marginal barrios of Uspha Uspha exhibit an awareness of the importance of community, a local system of political leadership that at least occasionally is capable of nonviolent resolution of conflicts, and a profound reluctance on the part of many to resort to violence to resolve social problems. Although in various ways barrio residents' behavior expresses certain elements of neoliberal security cul-

ture (see chapter 7), they are not automatons who unreflectively reproduce these dispositions and behaviors. In spite of living with a sense of
isolation and at times paralyzed by fear, barrio residents are capable of
great creativity, sorting through their options, arguing their points and
listening to the arguments of others, and struggling to arrive at workable
solutions to their problems. These are not always successful and, as I
have shown, sometimes serve to augment the lived experience of insecurity rather than to diminish it. But the search for solutions continues, as
people draw on whatever resources present themselves to help create
security. One of these resources is the idea of community justice, which
has recently come to the fore in Bolivia as a powerful but problematic set
of discourses and practices by which indigenous people attempt to account for lynching violence in their neighborhoods. It is to this issue that
I turn in the next chapter.

At about four o'clock one morning, someone pounded on don Miguel's front door. Miguel was tired, having worked late, and he had no desire to get out of bed into the early morning cold. But the knocker was persistent, so Miguel and his wife, doña Senobia, both got up to see what was going on. The person at the door was a woman who lived in the neighboring barrio of Monte Rancho. She told Miguel that her husband had captured a man trying to break into their house, and they weren't sure what to do. Several residents of Monte Rancho wanted to lynch the man. Don Miguel said that it really wasn't his jurisdiction and she should talk to her own barrio president, but she said her president didn't want to get involved, and who else could she turn to? No one wanted to call the police. So Miguel went out to investigate. He first went to the home of the president of Monte Rancho, but the man refused to come out of his house. Miguel thought he seemed drunk. Miguel told him that if anything happened—that is, if the man were lynched—he as president would be held accountable, but he still refused to come out and begged Miguel to intervene. Miguel then walked to a nearby street corner, where he found a young man tied to a lamppost, with a crowd of people from both Monte Rancho and Loma Pampa standing around. After talking to some of the vecinos to assess the situation, Miguel squatted down next to the bound man and demanded to know his mother's phone number. "You'd better tell me right now, because they are going to kill you," he told the man in a low voice. The man quickly divulged the number, and Miguel used his cellphone to call the captured thief's mother. Very soon the mother showed up in a pickup truck, racing to rescue her son. It turned out that she and the man whose house had been broken into knew each other, and they greeted each other in a friendly manner, which seemed to defuse some of the tension among the observers. "*I* will punish him," the mother said, and taking up a piece of wire lying nearby, she administered five fierce blows across her son's back. Then she took him away in the pickup and everyone went back to bed.

This story was told to me by don Miguel and doña Senobia, a few months after the incident in March 2009. It is an odd little anecdote, expressing the many and sometimes contradictory elements of lynching violence as a response to insecurity in the marginal barrios of Uspha Uspha. The story captures the uncertainty that many people feel as lynching becomes more common and the importance of the local dirigente in helping to resolve conflicts without resort to state institutions or collective violence. Most critically, it illustrates the creative ways in which dirigentes and barrio residents approach problems of insecurity in their neighborhoods. As previous chapters have explored, although "abandonment" is a mischaracterization of the actual workings of what I call the phantom state, as a perspective on local relations with the state it captures the sense of being (as some barrio residents put it) al aire, at loose ends, without any firm notion of what one is confronting or how to proceed in handling it. In the barrios of Uspha Uspha, no established institutions exist for dealing with conflicts, crime, or violence, nor are there any cultural patterns or indigenous traditions on which people can reliably depend. In the absence of any clear paths to security, people have to figure things out as they go, devising responses to insecurity that they find helpful in resolving the problems they confront. They must be creative, drawing on a range of ideas, symbols, discourses, and practices to make what they understand to be justice and security in their neighborhoods.

Critically, however, local security making in the barrios of Uspha Uspha occurs in a context in which the Bolivian state has embraced the notion of community justice as a path to citizen security in the "plurination."[1] As discussed in chapter 1, the new Bolivian constitution recognizes community justice (justicia comunitaria) as the way in which the residents of Bolivia's original indigenous peasant communities (*pueblos indígena originario campesinos*) traditionally handle or have handled judicial affairs and contains provisions for its legitimate exercise alongside state law and legal institutions.[2] The inclusion of community justice in the nation's legal framework reflects the opening of other pathways by which indigenous people in the country can seek a broader kind of inclusion as, after centuries of marginalization and discrimination, the nation under Evo Morales officially recognizes and welcomes their customary cultural usages (usos y costumbres). The judicial practices of indigenous or community justice are understood as properly located in rural areas, where the supposedly traditional indigenous peasant community provides a model for the MAS state's conception of what counts for indigenous in Bolivia. For urban people, however, the process of recognition and inclusion is hampered by the very fact of urban residence, which seems to disqualify them as indigenous in the eyes of the state—despite the fact that, according to the most recent census data, the majority of indigenous Bolivians now reside in urban areas (Instituto Nacional de Estadísticas de Bolivia 2001).[3] Nevertheless, many urban people adopt the language of community justice to characterize their own security-making practices—including lynching—not merely as a cynical attempt to justify violence, but in an effort to overcome their out-lawed status and so transform their insecure conditions. For many barrio residents, their local practices of conflict resolution are examples of community justice, despite official declarations to the contrary. By suggesting that lynching is not a crime but an important element of traditional justice, barrio residents discover a new set of resources for the creative management of insecurity. In this context, the discourse of community justice constitutes a path out of uncertainty, contributing to people's efforts to understand the nature of their predicament and the appropriate means of confronting it.

The community justice debate in Bolivia, characterized by an opposition between supposedly real forms of rural community justice and urban forms of justice making, is highly spatialized, with the rural and the urban understood as fundamentally separate and distinct. Rural and urban spaces may be seen as antithetical, as in the traditionalist vision that regards the country as simple, natural, and harmonious and the city as complex, mechanical, and exploitative (Williams 1977). Or the spaces can be arrayed in a trajectory, in which the migration of people from rural to urban spaces joins the two in a continuum, much as Robert Redfield once envisioned happening in Mexico (Redfield 1941). But purely spatialized conceptions are limited by their failure to consider both the temporal and racial dimensions of their own spatialization, and how these multiple dimensions together help to constitute the ideological and political framework for the nation-state. As Frances Mascia-Lees and Jeff Himpele (2007) have observed, spatially oriented accounts tend to operate in a specifically Newtonian space, one derived from classical Euclidean mathematics.[4] Such accounts paint a picture of society as consisting of highly stable and static spaces, populated by the kind of "stabilized state[s] of affairs" that Bruno Latour laments as characteristic of social science (2005, 1). The incorporation of other factors into this social geometry, however—especially the temporal and racial dimensions of social life—can reveal a much more unstable and uncertain social and political order than one mapped only along the vertical and horizontal axes of Euclidean space (see Coutin and Yngvesson 2008).

Rather than operating within a two-dimensional planar geometry, wherein we imagine discourses, bodies, and objects moving in a sort of linear fashion between dual poles—center and periphery, local and global, rural and urban—we might consider a non-Euclidean approach, characterized by a multiplicity of crosscutting dimensions, in which space and spatial ideologies provide only one set of organizing principles (Alonso 1994; Boyarin 1994; Gribbin 1996; Mascia-Lees and Himpele 2006; Munn 1992). This multidimensionality I call "race-space-time." In race-space-time, the spatial and temporal dimensions of our social mapping are combined with an additional dimension that entwines the discourses and ideologies of time and space with those of race in such a way that any attempt to tease apart their interwoven threads or relative contributions becomes an exercise in futility. In the Andean context, at least, the national project of space-time has been thoroughly washed in "blood," with the framing of the nation, its history, and people intimately connected to ideas of indigeneity and its others.[5] The race-space-time of Bolivia—played out along axes of rural/urban, traditional/modern, and indigenous/not indigenous—has been used to structure the national landscape, imagine national history, and write national law. The Bolivian constitution's frequent invocation of original indigenous peasant peoples and customs as the plurination's new leading edge is the clearest expression of the nation-state's racio ("indigenous") -spatio ("peasant") -temporal ("original") ideology.[6] But although this tripartite framework has a powerful impact at the level of the Bolivian state and the public imaginary, it conforms poorly to the experiential reality of Bolivia's indigenous people, especially those living in the cities. The urban indigenous are a living contradiction to the ideologies that comprise Bolivia's race-space-time; their very presence in the urban landscape places them outside any easy categorization within the official schema, and their means of creating security problematize their relationship with the state and its official forms of ordering.

This framework is particularly useful in analyzing Bolivian community justice. Typically conceptualized—by scholars, media observers, and representatives of the Bolivian state—in fundamentally spatial terms, authentic community justice is understood to be located exclusively in the rural spaces of the countryside, where the plurination's original indigenous peasant peoples supposedly reside. Such an attempt to spatialize community justice—to fix it as properly belonging in one particular geographical and social space, specifically the rural peasant community—runs counter to the efforts of many urban indigenous people, who claim that lynching is also an expression of community justice, transposed to the city via a transspatial, rural-to-urban migration. But any consideration of lynching and community justice must take into account the temporal and racial ideologies that surround them, as well as their spatial dimensions. Critics on the right, for example, conflate lynching and community justice, calling them "savage" acts, practices taken straight out of the "middle ages."[7] The discourse surrounding this position is clearly racialized and temporalized: Lynching or community justice is viewed as a sign of the innate barbarity of Bolivia's indigenous people—as it is in other Latin American countries, including Guatemala and Mexico (Binford and Churchill 2009; Burrell 2008)—as well as an indicator of their retrogression, their being trapped in an archaic past that the Morales regime's recognition of community justice threatens to reinvigorate. The leftist Bolivian state, on the other hand, rejects this conflation, insisting that lynching is not community justice and claiming that community justice can be found only in the ancient (or, perhaps, timeless) spaces of the countryside. Thus the state's recognition of community justice similarly thrusts it and its practitioners into a spatialized, racialized temporality, one that is indigenous and original and hence authentic, predating the modern state and therefore according it some autonomy from the constraints of state law. Both of these positions, left and right alike, disqualify urban indigenous people as authentic practitioners of community justice and so deprive them of their own indigeneity by virtue of their erroneous spatial location in the city—a surprisingly deracinating move on the part of the pro-indigenous MAS state, and one that recalls the colonial definition of urban space as the exclusive property of whites (see chapter 1). For urban indigenous people, then, to assert that their security-making practices are examples of community justice is to stake a specifically temporal and racial claim; it is to declare themselves indigenous practitioners of ancient customs, despite their physical residence in the modern city.

In offering this analysis, I am not arguing for the legitimacy of lynching as a form of community justice. Rather, I am suggesting that the politics of lynching and community justice in Bolivia are embedded within complex racial, spatial, and temporal ideologies and so pertain also to matters of identity and belonging, citizenship and rights, history and nation. They are important both in relation to security—understood as freedom from crime and violence, and from the fear and uncertainty to which these contribute, as documented in previous chapters—and justice, which for barrio residents means fairness, accountability, and, at times, punishment and vengeance for wrongs committed against them. These questions, then, relate back to the local desire for order, stability, and a sense of control in a world that is profoundly disordered, unstable, and unjust, and in which daily life is uncertain and insecure. In what follows, I first consider Evo Morales and the MAS government's conception of indigeneity in Bolivia today, and examine the official vision of community justice and what it is meant to entail. I go on to consider how the language of community justice is being applied in the barrios of Uspha Uspha to local security-making practices. In particular, I consider the ways in which the language of community justice is deployed by barrio residents and leaders to characterize and account for the violence of lynching in their neighborhoods. Rather than the enactment of an alternative order or "unofficial legal system" (Santos 1995, 126), I argue that creativity and incoherence best characterize local legal practice on the margins of the state. In the spaces of uncertainty that insecurity provides, barrio residents confront the possibility of radical invention, assembling for themselves a kind of legal bricolage that transcends the established constraints of race, space, and time to provide solutions for the problems of the day. The discussion reveals that, in contrast to the more encompassing visions of community justice that circulate in government, popular, and academic accounts, local practices are less about indigenous heritage or tradition than they are about making security through creative problem solving, and they are closely tied to the capability, experience, and imagination of local political leaders.

The Politics of Indigeneity in Evo's Bolivia

Evo Morales Ayma, son of altiplano livestock herders and leader of the lowland coca-growers movement, was elected president of Bolivia in 2005, internationally heralded as the first indigenous person to be elected to a Latin American presidency. Morales embraced the transnational language of indigeneity and indigenous rights, both during his electoral campaigns and in his subsequent inaugurations and official pronouncements. In his first inaugural speech, Evo framed his election as a triumph for indigenous peoples everywhere, the culmination of 500 years of resistance to oppression and marginalization. Though indigenous people have suffered, Morales asserted, his election marked the opening of a new era in global politics: "The 500 years of Indian resistance have not been in vain. From 500 years of resistance we pass to another 500 years in power. We have been condemned, humiliated . . . and never recognised as human beings. We are here and we say that we have achieved power to end the injustice, the inequality and oppression that we have lived under."[8] In this discourse, Evo Morales, and indigenous Bolivians in general, are used as a synecdoche for indigenous people around the globe, the various distinctions between populations elided by the assertion of an overarching identity grounded in a common experience of subordination. This political self-presentation has made Morales an internationally celebrated figure, a symbol if not a representative of indigenous peoples and their struggles throughout the hemisphere, holding out the promise of a successful transformation of long-standing structures of inequality.

Within Bolivia, the symbolic content of Evo's politics is similarly broad and encompassing. In contrast to the elaborately grounded and place-based identities and ritual practices of traditional Andean rural communities (*ayllus*)—the ethnographic sites and objects for multiple generations of Andean anthropologists—Morales's indigeneity and the MAS as an indigenous-inspired political project are depicted in broadly inclusive yet distinctly place-based strokes meant to appeal to a wide range of constituencies. Evo routinely characterizes himself as being of highland Aymara heritage, yet formed politically in the crucible of lowland Quechua unionism. He invokes a wide variety of cultural references in his public

speeches and events, a prime example being the 2006 inauguration cere-
monies cited above, held at the pre-Inca archaeological site of Tiwanaku
(de Munter and Salman 2009). Robert Albro (2006b) has described the
heritage-based references of MAS cultural politics as having a generic
character, one that goes beyond even an indigenous audience to speak to a
much broader coalition that includes the urban poor, working, and middle classes of Bolivia. In this sense, the target audience for the MAS includes a broad popular sector of Bolivian society, one that ostensibly
promises to bring an assortment of individuals, ethnicities, classes, and
communities under an indigenous umbrella. Andrew Canessa suggests
that this "new indigenism" is a political stance consonant with the MAS
program and ideology—which itself reflects global indigenist trends
(2006, 256; see Niezen 2003)—so that being indigenous need not necessarily be tied to a rural lifestyle or the command of an indigenous language. From this perspective, "it appears that central political issues, national issues that affect everyone, are represented as indigenous issues. . . .
Indigeneity is becoming the language of protests over resources and the
defense of the *patria* (fatherland) against the forces of globalisation; it is
breaking out of its specific concerns and offering a language of political
engagement for a much broader public" (Canessa 2006, 254). Indigenism
thus remains the central plank of the MAS platform, even as the conception of who the indigenous in Bolivia might be evolves and expands.

This generalizing tendency, in which a generic Indian is imagined and
mobilized for purposes of national state formation, is reminiscent of the
indigenismo movement of the 1920s and 1930s, when Bolivia's indigenous people supplied the rhetorical cannon fodder for an earlier moment
of national self-imagining, even as the indigenous themselves were excluded from the benefits of national belonging.[9] The new indigenism of
the MAS, like its twentieth-century forebears, trades on an essentialized
notion of the racialized Indian—though in the case of the MAS, the
prototype is positively inflected as a full rights-bearing subject, not
merely mined for its cultural heritage and subsumed within a hegemonic
mestizo society. And, perhaps surprisingly, like earlier forms of state
ideology that romanticized a particular imagined authentic indigeneity,
this new indigenism celebrates certain forms of indigenous belief and
practice while excluding others that fail to conform to its broader vision-
ary project. Here the indigenous cultural heritage drawn on by Evo and
the MAS emerges as potentially problematic, containing as it does vague

indigenous referents that, even as they are meant to be inclusive, exclude many contemporary Bolivians—particularly urban Bolivians—who may or may not identify themselves as indigenous. The generic culture that the MAS deploys in public events and moments of symbolic significance derives its content from a specific set of references, located spatially in an idealized version of the rural Aymara highlands (Albro 2010a).[10] It invokes stereotypically rural forms of language, dress, and belief that gesture toward a rural highland referent, one that claims to be original yet does not necessarily correspond to any actually existing highland peasant community.[11]

The imagined rural Andean, Aymara community figures significantly not only in plurinational ideology but also in the governing practices and legislative strategy of the MAS-led Bolivian state.[12] In his calls for national unity around such issues as the passage of the new constitution, for example, Morales draws on the supposed solidarity and internal cohesion of the traditional Aymara peasant community as a model for bringing the country together to address matters of concern to all Bolivians. Morales (and other, oppositional indigenous leaders, including Felipe Quispe of the Movimiento Indígena Pachakuti) invoke a generalized constellation of Aymara ayllu values as an antidote to the problems caused by neoliberal capitalism, both in Bolivia and globally. For example, principles of ayni (systems of generalized reciprocity and mutual support at the community level) are contrasted with the individualist, profit-driven, cash-based structures of capitalism and are invoked by indigenist politicians like Quispe as a fundamental opposition between Aymara and mestizo peoples (Canessa 2006, 259). References to traditional Andean values drive Evo Morales's well-known indigenous socialism and, in addition to basic notions of reciprocity and communal solidarity, include such ideas as renouncing war, imperialism, and colonialism; viewing water, hydrocarbons, and other natural resources as human rights not subject to privatization; and constructing a communitarian society in harmony with the Pachamama (Mother Earth) (Postero 2010). In an interview with Amy Goodman, Morales identified capitalism as the single factor responsible for global climate change and the destruction of Mother Earth; to stop this destruction, Morales advocated for "changing economic policies, ending luxury, consumerism. It's ending the struggle to—or this searching for living better. Living better is to exploit human beings. It's plundering natural resources. It's egoism and individualism. Therefore, in those promises of capitalism, *there is no solidarity or complementarity. There's no reciprocity.* So that's why we're trying to think about other ways of living lives and living well, not living better."[13]

Generic indigenous values also find expression in the new Bolivian constitution, either despite or as a result of the many efforts of the document's framers to be specific and inclusive. The constitution identifies Bolivia as fundamentally plurinational under a unitary state; chapter 1, article 2 guarantees to the "indigenous original peasant nations and communities" (*las naciones y pueblos indígena originario campesinos*) of Bolivia the right to autonomy, self-governance, the preservation of their cultures, and the recognition of their institutions under the law (Congreso Nacional 2008, 3). Chapter 1 also grants official status to thirty-six indigenous languages (plus Spanish), each of them listed in alphabetical order (though for some reason Aymara comes first in the list, preceding Araona). In chapter 2 (which delineates the "principles, values and objectives of the state"), article 8 lists the "ethical-moral principles of the plural society," which include *suma qamaña* (live a good life, from Aymara), *teko kavi* (live well and wisely, from Guaraní) and *qhapaj ñan* (follow the noble path, from Quechua) (Congreso Nacional 2008, 4). These principles, roughly on the order of "life, liberty, and the pursuit of happiness" enshrined in the US Declaration of Independence (Postero 2010), again point to a generic, overarching indigeneity that provides the framing context, if not the operationalized content, of this refounding document.

Given that the constitution locates the source of Bolivia's plurinationalism in the "original indigenous peasant nations and communities" of the countryside, urban indigenous Bolivians may find themselves excluded from the MAS project.[14] In some ways, urban indigenous people are as antithetical to the MAS conception as they were to that of the Spanish colonizers, whose very framing of the modern colonial world was based on a sharp distinction between the indigenous in the countryside and whites in the cities, with urban space being the critical site of the colonial civilizational project (Goldstein 2004; Radcliffe and Westwood 1996; Weismantel 2001). As the following discussion of community justice reveals, the unacknowledged but deep-seated basis of this perspective is a remarkably durable spatiotemporal conception that merges the countryside with the past and the city with the present and future. The rural, in both colonial and contemporary state conceptions, is the locus of tradition, while the city is the site of modernity, but this is given a different valuation in the Bolivian state's vision, turning the colonial conception on its head. Now the rural is the source of all that is original and valuable about Bolivian national culture, and the urban is the source of social decay and problems such as crime. The countryside is both timeless (unchanging and original) and time-bound (stuck, for better or worse, in an unchanging past). Both Spanish colonizers and Evo Morales's ruling MAS party invoke an implicit racial cartography as well, wherein the indigenous are the proper denizens of this timeless rurality, and rural areas are the best and most fitting sites for indigenous bodies. The key term here is "original," an apparently temporal concept that enfolds unexamined spatial and racial elements and that appears over and over again in official Bolivian discourse and law. Rural spaces are also considered the principal—perhaps the only possible—loci of community, another critical spatiotemporal referent in the MAS vocabulary. "Community" here refers to a particular kind of rural sociality, grounded in face-to-face interaction, mutuality, and interdependence (the "solidarity," "complementarity," and "reciprocity" that Morales mentioned above), formed around a set of institutions whose origins can be found only in the ancient past. The presence of the classical anthropological imagination can perhaps be detected in this conception of the rural community, as it is in the ideas of community justice discussed below. Indeed, "the original indigenous peasant community" is not only a key component of national political ideology, it is also the main actor in the MAS state's strategies of governance under the new constitution.

Community Justice and Indigenous Autonomy

Following the passage of the new constitution as a basis for refounding the Bolivian nation, the MAS-led government under President Evo Morales had to determine how to put a host of new constitutional mandates into effect in organizing and governing the country. One of the most important challenges facing the legislature was the implementation of the mandate for indigenous autonomy.[15] Under the new constitution, the state recognized the autonomy of indigenous pueblos and municipalities, giving them the rights of self-government and self-determination and the authority to maintain their own cultures and institutions. Article 289 of the new constitution defined the "original indigenous peasant communities" as being composed of people who share "territory, culture, history, languages, and [that have their own] juridical, political, social, and economic organizations or institutions." In addition, according to article 290, these communities are based in "ancestral territories, presently inhabited by these peoples or nations," who apparently enjoy an unbroken continuity of connection to the lands they occupy (Congreso Nacional 2008, 65). These and other articles also identify the will of the people as being a determining factor in whether or not a community will receive state recognition as an autonomous pueblo or municipality, as all the people must be consulted and through a referendum express their desire to be so recognized. Politically, the autonomy mandate represents a major step forward for indigenous peoples in Bolivia, while also promising to produce dividends for the MAS as it seeks to expand and solidify its base. With the ability to convert preexisting communities and municipalities into pueblos indígena originario campesinos, the new constitution offers an expanded degree of self-government that will probably encourage individuals and communities to identify themselves as indigenous, framing their experience and identity in terms laid out by the state.[16]

It is within these autonomous communities, legally constituted as indigenous jurisdictions, that the constitution envisions community justice being deployed, according to the cultural and legal traditions—the usages and customs (usos y costumbres) or customary law (derecho consuetudinario)—of the indigenous peasant community. Here, the constitution provides official recognition to the various forms of indigenous justice already being practiced in the country's rural communities (see Canessa 2012). Article 190 of the constitution identifies the community's leaders as those charged with the administration of justice: these pueblos "will exercise their jurisdictional and competent functions through their authorities, and will apply their own principles, cultural values, norms and procedures" (Congreso Nacional 2008, 45). Within indigenous jurisdictions, as described in article 304, las autonomías indígena originario campesinas will have the exclusive right within their territory to administer justice "according to their own norms and procedures within the Constitution and the law." This last stipulation suggests that local forms of justice ultimately must be executed in accord with state law ("de acuerdo a la Constitución y la ley") (Congreso Nacional 2008, 73–75). Article 190 also states that indigenous jurisdictions must respect "the right to life, the right to a defense and other rights and guarantees established in the Constitution" (Congreso Nacional 2008, 45). Nevertheless, the constitution clearly grants "exclusive competency" (Congreso Nacional 2008, 73) to the pueblo (the village; the people) in the administration of their own forms of justice. It is this provision that has sparked enormous controversy within Bolivian legal circles, as jurists, politicians, law enforcement officials, and citizens try to figure out what is meant by all of this and how it is likely to affect the administration of justice in Bolivia once it is finally put into effect.

Indeed, there are grounds for confusion. For one thing, while the entire public discussion is framed in terms of justicia comunitaria, nowhere does this term appear in the constitution. "Justicia comunitaria" has emerged as shorthand for the complex of norms and procedures that supposedly exist in rural communities, descended from time immemorial as usos y costumbres, peasant customs of community justice. Although clarifying legislation began to emerge in late 2010 with the passage of the Ley de Deslinde Jurisdiccional,[17] the constitution contains no stipulations of what community justice may include or exclude, apparently leaving it entirely up to the autonomous community to determine its own judicial practices. While it makes indigenous legal systems accountable to transnational human rights norms, the constitution's emphasis on self-rule and autonomy seems to suggest some flexibility in that regard. This failure to absolutely insist on the priority of human rights has alarmed transnational rights agencies (including Amnesty International), which have expressed their concerns both within Bolivia and internationally over the new constitution and its community justice provisions.

For its part, the Bolivian state seems to base its own understanding of community justice on what is known as the Andean code: "Ama suwa, ama llulla, ama qhella" (Quechua for Don't steal, don't lie, don't be lazy). This phrase is occasionally accompanied by the additional "Ama llunku" (Don't be an ass kisser). (My favorite is the version popularly ascribed to Bolivian politicians and other elites: "Ama suwa, ama llulla, ama qhella . . . y si no, a Miami.") This phrase—"ama suwa, ama llulla, ama qhella"— has been elevated to the level of national mantra, appearing frequently in official discourse on the subject of community justice, and it is even encoded in article 8 of the constitution as one of the key "ethical-moral principles of the plural society." This code is popularly and officially imagined to date from the time of the Incas, and it is rhetorically invoked as a preconquest, prestate referent, a way of grounding contemporary practice in a deep history that gives rural practices continuity and legit-imacy. In the same way as autonomous indigenous communities are imagined to be culturally homogeneous and to have maintained un-broken ties to their native territories, the frequent invocation of the Andean code suggests an ancient yet deliberately vague connection to the deeply Andean.[18] For example, Casimira Rodríguez, then Bolivia's justice minister, once described community justice as "ancestral justice, the practices in different communities of Bolivia, especially in our com-munities that are much more original [and] that have maintained justice without needing written norms. It is a tradition that comes from the ancestors."[19] Just as the heritage-based references of MAS cultural poli-tics are highly generic in character, gesturing to a broadly Andean, spa-tially rural, and temporally ancient conception of what constitutes the authentically indigenous, so the idea of community justice most fre-quently portrayed is one that is generally rural and loosely ahistorical, helping to support the constitutional push for the creation of autono-mous indigenous spaces by linking rural communities to a timeless past that nonetheless temporally precedes the modern state (see Colloredo-Mansfeld 2002).

Academic studies of rural forms of justice making in the Andean context have described it as consensual, informal, and collective, with the principal goal being the maintenance of local behavioral standards (Stavenhagen and Iturralde 1990). To this end, justice is more about rehabilitation than punishment, reincorporating the offender into the community so as to repair the damage done and enable collective har-mony to return (compare with Nader 1990).[20] Rural justice making oc-curs in the context of a broader system of local self-governance, in which community institutions and political hierarchies operate to regulate so-cial behavior within established local norms (Ardila Amaya 2010). Of particular importance is the communal system of authorities responsible for maintaining this social regulation, whose judicial competency—among the Aymara, for example (Mier Cueto 2005)—is grounded in both a political and a religious legitimacy, the two being inseparably intertwined and bestowing on these officials an almost spiritual author-ity to address social problems and impose judgments. In all of these ways, rural forms of adjudication differ greatly from the practices of lynching seen in both rural and urban communities and described in detail in chapter 4.

The resolution of conflicts is an important dimension of local justice making, and ethnographic studies of these processes in the rural pueblos of both the Bolivian highlands and lowlands detail the variety and complexity of these practices across a range of diverse sociocultural contexts (Nicolas, Fernández, and Flores 2007). However, violence is not unknown in these systems as a tool for enforcing local norms, and even capital punishment may sometimes be practiced.[21] Marcelo Fernández Osco traces the "pain of death" (2001, 14) as a punishment for serious crimes to the Inca period and finds elements of this and other means of administering justice persisting in the contemporary rural communities of the highlands, in what he calls "the law of the ayllu" (2000). In rural Aymara communities, the pain of death is administered in exceptional cases, based on the consensus of the community and following extended debate (Mier Cueto 2005), and here again one notes the discrepancies with lynching violence (Gutiérrez Pérez 2009; Mayer 1991). Of particular note, however, is the fluidity of these systems of justice making: scholars of these processes observe that rather than the enactment of some ancient system or juridical code, rural forms of justice making are constantly changing and adapting to circumstance (Vilas 2008). In rural Quechua communities, for example, René Orellana Halkyer notes that "the standards of conflict resolution are not a sort of cookbook present in the historical memory of the communities, but practices that are changeable, recreated and reinvented" (2005, 18), and in describing the "dynamic" competency of local Aymara officeholders to resolve conflicts, Enrique Mier Cueto observes that this is "one more indication of the constant changes that occur with respect to the assignment of tasks and functions within the Aymara system of authorities" (2005, 72). These studies indicate that rather than a timeless code, rural justice making is a fluid and flexible set of practices that local communities employ in diverse ways to respond to specific problems that require attention.

Given the diversity and flexibility of local systems, it is interesting to note the role of the anthropological imagination in the invention of community justice. The concepts of "justicia comunitaria" and "indigenous justice" themselves are academic creations, possibly originating in Mexico to describe the various legal systems found in that country's indigenous agrarian communities (Sierra 2005). The concept did not appear in Bolivia until 1999, when the Ministry of Justice and Human Rights, in collaboration with the World Bank, published a series of ethnographic studies by different researchers working in a variety of settings within the country, to document the tremendous diversity of practices, beliefs, and traditions—the usos y costumbres—that underlie the country's many indigenous legal systems, the semi-autonomous forms of legal consciousness and practice found in the nation's indigenous communities (Centro de Estudios de la Realidad Económica y Social, Ministerio de Justicia y Derechos Humanos, and Banco Mundial 1999; Centro de Estudios Jurídicos e Investigación Social, Ministerio de Justicia y Derechos Humanos, and Banco Mundial 1999; Centro de Servicios Integrados para el Desarrollo Urbano, Ministerio de Justicia y Derechos Humanos, and Banco Mundial 1999). It is principally this set of anthropological studies (published under the collective title *Justicia comunitaria: derecho consuetudinario*) that provided the empirical basis for the state's later recognition of community justice. Some scholars have generalized from the diversity of forms that these and subsequent studies documented, to define community justice as "an institution of customary law that permits the sanction of reprobate conduct by individuals without the intervention of the State, its judges and bureaucracy, but directly within the community of individuals in which the natural authorities of the community strike a balance between the two conflicting parties."[22] Many scholars (for example, Fundación de Apoyo al Parlamento y a la Participación Ciudadana 2007; Gutiérrez Pérez 2009) observe that the existence of these various legal forms in Bolivia represents a kind of legal pluralism, in which multiple legal systems occupy a single social field (Merry 1988). In Bolivia, as in many other countries, the existence of a legally plural field is a legacy of the colonial era, and for some analysts it represents a triumph over marginalization and assimilation: "Customary law exists alongside 'official' law, having survived the conquest, the colonialization and the Republic, because the peasant and indigenous communities have mounted a fierce resistance to maintain their usos y costumbres" (Acevedo V. 2004). Critics, on the other hand, have noted that official conceptions of such things as *justicia indígena*, derecho consuetudinario, and usos y costumbres represent state inventions, created and imposed on the people who supposedly practice such forms as part of a broader project of colonialization of justice and the law (Chivi Vargas 2010).

From the tremendous diversity of indigenous legal systems, then, scholars made the "discovery," we might say, of an abstract community justice, a generalizing concept that could contain all of this variety within a single rubric. The discovery in the late 1990s that Bolivia is legally plural provided a theoretical basis for the inclusion of community justice as a generic form in the new constitution—interesting, considering that states typically reject claims of legal pluralism, as these suggest that the state's official justice system is only one among many and thereby (it is feared) diminish its effectiveness and scope through relativization (Ardito 1997; Forsyth 2007; Merry 1988). In Bolivia, in contrast, legal pluralism is foundational to the entire autonomy project (just as plurinationalism is central to the broader refounding of the state itself).[23] Autonomy, meanwhile, is itself foundational to the MAS government's efforts to decentralize the state, empower indigenous jurisdictions, and, in something of a neoliberal twist, devolve responsibility for managing their own conflicts onto municipalities and local communities. The provisions for the constitutional recognition of community justice remain vague and rather ambiguous, intended as they are to be inclusive of a broad range of indigenous practices and norms and thus to facilitate the larger autonomy project.

In the context of present-day reality, the ambiguities—deliberate or otherwise—that envelop community justice have quickly led to problems in the administration of justice in the country, in both rural and urban settings. In the absence of clear legal stipulations of what justicia comunitaria includes and how it is to operate, any number of problems have arisen concerning what constitutes community justice and what is the proper nature of its relationship with state justice, or *justicia ordinaria* (ordinary justice). For example, in the rural Cochabamba community of Laco Laconi, a recent widow named María Chambi ("young and very beautiful," according to the news reports) was accused of having sexual relations with her brother-in-law. *Los Tiempos* of Cochabamba reported that the women of the community denounced María to the local dirigentes, describing her as a danger to community life and demanding her expulsion. The dirigentes "decided to apply community justice," expelling the unfortunate widow, denying her contact with her two children, and imposing a fine of US$7,000.[24] Denying the charges, María took her case to the Defensoría del Pueblo, the state office of the human rights ombudsperson, constitutionally obligated to intervene in cases where people's rights are violated. The Defensoría took up the case, claiming that in this instance "the abuses committed against the widow violated the spirit of community justice,"[25] but was unable to get the dirigentes to change their minds. The Defensoría also observed that the fine applied in this case was exceedingly high and claimed that community justice does not include provisions for the collection of fines, a point that the dirigentes disputed. Although the US$7,000 that María paid was supposed to be used for local improvements, in the aftermath no one in Laco Laconi was quite sure what had happened to the money. In addition, the women of the community refused to allow María to return to see her children unless she agreed to get down on her knees and beg their pardon. María refused and decided to challenge the fine and the expulsion in municipal court.[26]

As discussed above, the Bolivian state's conception of who counts as indigenous is essentially rural in character, a point reflected in the way community justice is conceptualized in the constitution. Indigenous jurisdictions are those in which people have historical ties to their ancestral territories and in which residents share a common language, culture, and history. This insistence on antiquity and homogeneity is essentializing and ahistorical; it is therefore problematic for rural communities because it apparently neglects the hundreds of years since the conquest, during which time these communities have experienced tremendous disruption and change. The problems surrounding the events in Laco Laconi illustrate the lack of consensus in what is supposed to be a homogeneous community, in which harmony and the reintegration of the offender into the fabric of the community are supposed to be the objectives. The imposition of a cash fine is also jarring, coming from a system that is supposedly precapitalist in origin, and the evidence of local political corruption points to the presence of interests that lie far outside the question of local justice.

The official conception of indigeneity also conflicts in some rather obvious ways with the reality of urban indigenous people. Residents of urban neighborhoods like those of Uspha Uspha do not inhabit ancestral land, having established claims to their territories only during the last couple of decades after their migration from the countryside to the city. Nor are these barrios culturally or linguistically homogeneous—Loma Pampa, for example, is a mix of Quechua- and Aymara-speaking peoples, some monolingual in one of these languages, others trilingual with both of them and Spanish, and the residents came from a variety of provinces, departments, and cities around the country. Nevertheless, in many urban neighborhoods of Cochabamba and elsewhere in Bolivia, the discourse of community justice is increasingly being invoked in conjunction with the popular lynching of criminal suspects, like those described in chapter 4. Although Cochabamba has had a high incidence of lynchings since the late 1990s, in recent years, as discussion about community justice has surged in Bolivia, some urban actors have come to frame their violence in terms of ancestral forms of justice making. Such claims transgress the established race-space-time within which national and judicial practices are framed, invoking new framings from which new forms of claim making on the state and its judicial system can be initiated. Local justice, for lack of a better term, manipulates and simultaneously inhabits the various race-space-times of both official and community justice, as individuals and groups piece together their own forms of social ordering through their creative imaginings and practices.

Community Justice in an Urban Key

In response to lynching violence in the context of discussions about community justice, Bolivian academics, jurists, and media commentators from all points on the political spectrum have engaged in an increasingly fierce debate about what in fact constitutes community justice, trying to fill in the space of ambiguity left by official pronouncements on the subject. Many on the right, predictably, take the question of community justice as an opportunity to criticize the entire project of Evo Morales and the MAS, characterizing community justice as a movement away from democracy and toward savagery and mob rule. The tactic from this side is to reduce all community justice to lynching, and to depict lynching as the limit of community justice. For example, the commentator Luis Eduardo Siles Pérez equates *justicia a mano propia* (justice by one's own hand) with justicia comunitaria, identifying "the lynching and the violence of the horde" as the "principal pillars" of community justice. He takes this as evidence that "Bolivia today is living a direct process of regression into medieval times."[27] Such comments are echoed across the Bolivian and transnational blogospheres, as observers denounce the savagery of community justice qua lynching. Similar cries have come from a range of quarters, including the Bolivian Episcopal Conference, which describes community justice as "anti-Christian";[28] and the New York–based Human Rights Foundation, which, though claiming not to equate community justice with lynching, nevertheless blames it for the surge in lynchings during the last several years, calling community justice "barbaric" and accusing the new constitution's recognition of it as "enshrining mob rule" (Human Rights Foundation 2008, 1). It is unclear whether the authors of such comments recognize the obvious racialized content of their denunciations, which invoke historical tropes of primitiveness and the uncontrollable impulses of *los indios* (Indians)—who, now that they are running the country, seem (from this perspective) to be making white society's nightmare a reality by replacing democratic institutions with their own perverted conceptions, leading inevitably to chaos, mob rule, and the end of the world as we know it. These critiques also employ an explicit temporality that situates the practitioners of community justice in the (primitive) past, with references to "medieval times" and "savagery" as counterpoint to the modernity of the ordinary justice system and the neoliberal state.

Supporters of Evo Morales and the MAS respond to these accusations by pointing out the obvious differences that exist between lynching and the idealized version of community justice imagined in the new constitution. Various commentators—myself included (Goldstein 2008)[29]—have taken pains to detail the many ways in which lynching is not community justice in the classic sense. After every lynching event, politicians and left-leaning intellectuals are quoted in the newspapers drawing the distinction. In these cases, the contrast is made between the violence of lynching and the supposedly peaceful and consensual forms of "real" rural community justice. For example, this question surfaced following a particularly horrific event in Ivirgarzama in the tropics of Cochabamba Department, in which three suspected thieves were dragged from their cells in the local police station and burned to death in the plaza by community residents. Waldo Albarracín, a former defensor del pueblo and a human rights activist, observed during an interview in the aftermath of the lynching: "This has nothing to do with community justice. It is an act of the masses, in which an enraged mob surprises a person who may or may not be guilty. They decide to hang him, beat him, and they end up killing him. That has nothing to do with the reality of community justice."[30] Roberto Quiroz, representative of the defensor del pueblo in the Chapare, similarly commented: "The lynching is a crime and is not related to the original justice applied in the communities, now recognized in the Political Constitution of the State."[31] And Denis Racicot, a UN representative in Bolivia, said: "What occurred in Ivirgarzama is not a case of the application of indigenous justice. It is rather the reaction of a population in the heat of the moment. . . . We insist that acts of this kind not be confused with what the country knows as original indigenous justice, established in the new Constitution."[32] Again, the emphasis in these testimonies is on identifying real community justice, which is original and hence authentic, prior to other forms of justice and thus deserving of recognition within the context of the autonomous indigenous community.

The battle over the nature of community justice is waged in the cities as well, where the constitution makes no explicit stipulations for the recognition of community justice. Cochabamba politicians, horrified by the frequency of lynchings in their districts, draw the distinction between lynching and community justice quite clearly. Don Silvio, the representative of Uspha Uspha's District 8 to the Subalcaldía, observed: "There is some confusion here, when they talk about community justice. It doesn't mean to murder, it doesn't mean to kill, it is above all a process. . . . I think they are a little confused about the term 'community justice,' that it means directly to kill. That's not it. It is also to reform the person who commits the crime."[33] In Loma Pampa, where the discourse of community justice is frequently invoked in discussions about policing, crime, and lynching, don Miguel said: "It seems that the people understand community justice to be catching the bad guy and taking his life. I think that that is not community justice. That has to be regulated, it has to be clarified."[34] Like the government spokespeople who contrast lynching with real community justice, some barrio residents point to the judicial practices of the countryside to debunk the notion that lynching is somehow an accepted practice or a cultural norm. Said a resident of Juan Pablo II:

> I would not say it [lynching] is a norm. It's an obscenity. Because the peasants who live in the countryside are more educated than anybody. So it is not a norm. I would say that when there is a robbery, a person gets angry and tries to start an uprising, he makes it happen, and others come, without thinking they do it. So for me it is not a norm. In the countryside the justice is meant to punish, it is not meant to kill. They beat someone up, in the first place, first option. Second, they keep beating him and later they expel him from the community, that is their justice. But in these parts, for example, many lynchings have been about robbery, there have been mix ups, a person comes here

from, say, Quillacollo, he is drunk, he falls down at someone's door and they say he's a thief, and they lynch him. We are talking about something that is against the law.[35]

In contrast to these opinions, many other people in the barrios of Uspha Uspha equate practices associated with lynching—including physical punishments like beating, torture, and execution—with community justice. For them, community justice is about taking matters into one's own hands in order to punish delinquents, establish order, and discourage future criminal acts. Community justice is about collective action, but it also suggests impunity from the sanctions of official justice, which, as we have seen, many regard as absent, irrelevant, or hostile to their interests. According to doña Casilda, for example, community justice "means that when a thief is captured the whole community kills him, and when the police come they don't know whom to arrest."[36] A resident of Grupo Domingo in Mineros San Juan echoed this conception: "How many times here have they stolen garrafas from humble ladies, who barely have enough for their daily bread? They take their garrafa, their stove, this happens. Here in this barrio we have had sixteen houses robbed of their garrafas. But, thank God, on one occasion they caught these delinquents *con las manos en la masa* [literally, with their hands in the dough; in other words, red-handed]. And what did the vecinos do? The only thing we could do, community justice: they grabbed him, they soaked him with gasoline, and they set him on fire."[37]

Official and media critiques of this vision of community justice, like those of the defensor del pueblo and the bloggers cited above, do little to dissuade these people from this position. To the contrary, it is precisely because of official inaction or corruption that people claim community justice is necessary in the barrios today. A resident of Juan Pablo II stated: "Let's say we catch a suspected ratero, the police come and take him away. After a few steps they let him go and the ratero goes off, laughing. For that reason the people have this idea of community justice. It is better to catch the ratero and burn him, liquidate him."[38] Many people whom I interviewed shared this perspective, suggesting that the police and the justice system oblige them to employ community justice. A woman in Uspha Uspha Central expressed her despair over the situation: "Community justice, there is no other way. Because if we call the police, they lock him up for a night and the next day he is free. And the thieves come back with even more desire to do bad things. So I don't know what we can do against these men, I don't know what measures we could take. We have no support from the authorities, none. I leave it in God's hands. Every time I go out. I leave my house in God's hands."[39] A man from Juan Pablo II expressed similar frustration, describing the law as a problem to which community justice is the solution: "For me, [community justice] would be a thousand times better, at least there would be one less of these damned people. . . . In my case, I leave at 5:00 in the morning, I get home 10:00, 11:00 at night, I'm working all day long, and a delinquent comes and takes all my stuff. It is not just. I say we should just make him disappear, there would be one less. But the laws are, if I did that, they are going to put me away."[40]

It is often said in academic and media debates that barrio residents use community justice to justify lynchings, a cynical manipulation of the truth intended to exculpate themselves for their violent behavior (Molina 2010). In some instances this may be so, as people invoke official discourse to account for local forms of security making. This is the case for more sophisticated politicians. For example, don Reynaldo, the dirigente of Mineros San Juan, explained the local rationale for lynching: "The justice system here in Bolivia, if we analyze it, is so flexible, that is why the delinquency is expanding in Bolivia. So facing this situation, the community of Mineros San Juan says: 'A person caught red-handed, what we have to do is what our ancestors did, doing usos y costumbres, we have to make the law of the community, the community justice.'"[41] Here, Reynaldo used the language of both neoliberalism (a key component of which is "flexibility"; Harvey 1991; Inda 2000; Ong 1999) and the national constitution (usos y costumbres) to account for local violence. He also positioned lynching as a truly collective action, the "community" of Mineros San Juan speaking in a singular voice to state its policy on crime control.

But such deliberate expressions are uncommon in barrio discourse, leading one to question the claim that people use official discourse on community justice to justify violent behavior. While this may be the case in some of the more widely publicized lynching incidents in the country,[42] in more quotidian barrio experiences, people hold strongly to the notion that community justice includes a truly violent set of practices, with strong precedents in rural juridical tradition. Some people in the barrios of Uspha Uspha have firsthand experience of rural life, which may or may not include having witnessed or participated in rural justice-making practices; many more have no such experience and rely on stories and rumors for their information. In much the same way as the state derives its understanding of community justice from a set of vague but widely held beliefs about rural life, so the residents of Cochabamba's barrios invoke a rural stereotype to which they link their understandings of community justice. Some talk about this community justice as a prevailing ethos of respect and mutuality, which in itself discourages criminality; others describe a set of practices that rural people can invoke to punish criminals, often violently. This vision of community justice, like the state's, is based on the supposedly collective and communal nature of rural life, but with a violent twist. Don Armando said: "It is worse in the countryside, because if they see a thief, they kill him straightaway, they don't advise the police, they kill him. The whole group kills him. . . . In the *campo* they don't take anybody to the police, nor to the subprefect, nobody—they don't take anybody, they stone him to death."[43] This kind of justice, according to Armando, is not called "community justice": "That justice has no name, we just say it's about justice." A woman from Concordia described rural Cochabamba justice: "In my mother's village, it is a crime to be a ratero. They kill a ratero, no matter what. Having killed him they say, 'Okay, now there are no more thieves,' and the others see that and they don't dare, the young people don't do it."[44] Other practices, like the pact of silence that barrio residents supposedly enter following a lynching, are also sometimes attributed to rural justice, perhaps reflecting the dark side of the unified collective that official visions of "community" prefer to ignore. A woman from Mineros San Juan said: "They do it a lot there in my *pueblo*, in Punata [in rural Cochabamba]. They killed a young man, but all the people were in agreement. If they catch him with his manos en la masa, they lynch him straightaway. They have entered into an agreement, and all the people have to be quiet, nobody can say anything. 'We don't know, I don't know who did what,' that is the only thing they can say. Silence, that is the agreement they have. . . . That is what is called community justice."[45]

In their reflections on rural community justice, barrio residents also echo the state's spatiotemporal positioning, locating the countryside and its judicial practices in the ancient past. They share with the state a vision of community justice that situates it originally in the peasant communities of the countryside—where since time immemorial, people have practiced their own forms of indigenous justice. But unlike the state's vision, community justice here is characterized by a propensity for violence. Because many barrio residents lack direct personal experience of rural life, having either been born in the city or moved there very early in life, discussions of community justice sometimes slip into the realm of legend, as people invoke antiquity, "the time of the ancestors," to situate a violent community justice and establish its legitimacy, like one man in Concordia: "My father used to speak of the old days, when there was community justice, *con sus priopias manos* [with their own hands], in the remote provinces, in the countryside. So I think that that should be maintained. . . . It would be good if we returned to those times, those old days, so to speak, of our grandparents, to make justice with our own hands."[46] Another man in Concordia said: "I believe that, thank God, with this government that has made a statement about community justice, with don Evo Morales, hopefully this will be put into effect and every neighborhood, every community will be permitted by law to exercise community justice. In the past our parents, our ancestors, if they caught someone in adultery they would stone him to death. That was community justice. Now in our times, the authorities are immersed in corruption. We have to return to the past."[47] Don Casto said: "Many years ago, according to what the grandparents say, if they caught someone, say, committing a robbery, then they would apply that justice, no? The people got together, they killed him, and nobody said anything, not even the authorities. They killed a lot of people like that, no?"[48] Even those who are critical of lynching share in this temporalization, which locates the origins of violent community justice in the ancient past. Admitting that he knew little about it, don Segundo said: "Community justice I think is when the pueblo decides, no? At least that is what I think it is, they do what they themselves decide. But to come to this, I think, it's like you were living in the time of [pause] illiteracy."[49]

Creativity and Justice Making

My purpose here is not to support either side in the "yes it is, no it isn't" debate about the relationship between community justice and popular lynching in Bolivia. Rather, it is to understand the ways in which the ideas and discourses of community justice circulate within and, in various and problematic ways, intersect with the security-making practices of local barrios. Given the robust debate over community justice in Bolivia, triggered by the constitutional recognition of supposedly original forms of justice making in the context of indigenous autonomy, it is not surprising that barrio people should appropriate fragments of this discourse to characterize their own local practices. Certainly, this can be understood as an attempt to give local forms of justice making, even the horror of lynching, a degree of legitimacy, justifying their violence to themselves and to an external audience that includes the police and others who might want to punish them for what they have done. But more than that is at work. Amid the insecurity and uncertainty of barrio life, barrio residents deploy the discourse of community justice as part of an interpretive frame through which they try to render meaningful the chaos of the world around them. Describing lynching and other forms of behavior like alert watchfulness as elements of an older way of making security is to situate them within a historical and cultural context; it provides a sense of continuity with the past, imagined as a time when things made sense, and order was created and maintained by local people joined together by the bonds of collective solidarity. To describe lynching as community justice, then, is an act of creative imagining, a surprisingly optimistic move in the present context because it suggests that—through violence—some kind of local order might be established or restored.

It is also a surprising political move. To claim that local techniques of adjudication and punishment are forms of community justice is to insist on an entirely different spatiotemporal framing of the urban indigenous neighborhood, one that breaks with the official identification of indigenous people and their cultural practices. By claiming community justice for themselves, urban people are likewise staking a claim to the mantle of originality and indigeneity, now so politically salient in Bolivia. In so doing, they also stake a claim to the cultural traditions (usos y costumbres) that accompany such a racial identity, and that serve as a gateway to political and civil rights in the new national configuration. This move involves a temporal frame shift as well, transposing the timelessness of the rural indigenous community to the space of the urban barrio. Rather than viewing rural-to-urban migration as a temporal rupture, a form of time travel through which former peasants emerge as modern subjects on arriving in the city, this move reconfigures migration as continuous, decoupling the spatial transition from the temporal one, creating a time-space within which urban migrants can also be original. And finally, it represents a claim to community, positioning the urban barrio as a particular kind of locality within which community justice can exist as a possible social utility. In the Bolivia of Evo Morales, in which the original indigenous peasant community stands as the fundamental archetype of the plurination, barrio appropriations of this discourse represent attempts to frame local reality, both for barrio residents in their ongoing struggles against uncertainty and disorder, and for any external audiences that may be listening.

The story of the attempted lynching in Monte Rancho in which don Miguel was asked to intervene, related at the beginning of this chapter, illustrates the ways in which local people mobilize ideas about community justice to resolve a specific security crisis. In that case, a man was apprehended in the act of robbing a house (*con las manos en la masa*, as people would say), and tied up in what amounts to the public square— here, an illuminated street corner—for judgment. Before violence occurred, Miguel called on the accused's mother, who administered a beating to her son, apparently satisfying the need to punish him for his transgression. A closer look at this and other cases in which local barrio leaders have intervened to resolve conflicts in their OTBs demonstrates the creativity that such men use to successfully avoid violence, as they suggest alternative means of conflict resolution that satisfy local expectations of community justice and security making.

The barrio dirigente is a critical figure in the making of local justice, and his knowledge, wisdom, and sense of duty all contribute to the outcome in a case like that in Monte Rancho. As discussed in chapter 4, the dirigente is in some sense the law in the marginal barrio (as don Miguel stated, "I am the law in this barrio"), and the responsibility falls to him in moments of conflict to produce some sort of resolution. Not all dirigentes are capable of doing this: the dirigente of Monte Rancho, who refused to come out of his house to deal with the problem, was clearly useless in this regard. But one local woman, surveying the available options, called on don Miguel, the dirigente of the neighboring barrio with a reputation for good sense and a reluctance to use violence in response to problems, and Miguel agreed to intervene. As he himself noted, being politic about it: "Some dirigentes are active, others are not."[50] He takes his role and responsibility as dirigente very seriously: "To govern a little ranch, a pueblo, an OTB, or a small village, a nation, whatever it is, I think that you always need a head that is intelligent, and able to distinguish right from wrong, and guide them with prudence, no?

Down the right path."[51] And while he may not like it, Miguel recognizes that the dirigente is the main source of judicial authority in the urban barrio, partly as a result of spatial distance: "Many times, I have been called on my cellphone and had to leave my work and come here, to resolve some issue. It is very important in this zone that the dirigente plays the role of authority, no? Besides being a civic authority, he is always an administrator. In many cases, we even have to be a judicial authority, because the city is nine, ten kilometers away."[52]

Although he regards the police as a necessary evil, Miguel believes that turning a captured thief over to the police is a better alternative than killing him, which will lead to revenge and, as he warned the dirigente from Monte Rancho, blame for the event falling on the dirigente himself. This is not to suggest that all dirigentes are opposed to lynching violence, as the above testimony from don Reynaldo of Mineros San Juan indicates. But don Miguel deplores violence, in part because of his strong religious convictions and in part because of his faith in democratic society and the rule of law.[53] He said: "We have to make every effort [to avoid lynching] because that goes against our law, no? In the case of a lynching, I make every effort. But, if it should happen, it is not with my authorization. But I think that *mi gente* (my people) have confidence in me and they will listen to me, as they have listened to me on some occasions. They have paid attention to me and we have tried to bring suspects to the authorities."[54] As mentioned above, don Miguel does not equate community justice with lynching: having spent the first eight years of his life in a rural pueblo, he has no specific memories of how the campesinos made justice, but he is certain that it did not include killing. Nevertheless, he expresses a willingness to use community justice up to a certain point. Community justice is acceptable, he says, "according to the gravity of the crime. We can give a light punishment, no? As a good father can give a correction with a stick to his son so that his behavior improves, no? But if there is no love and discipline then it doesn't work, no? In the more distant zones [in the countryside] they have done this since antiquity, maybe a little warning, a little *huascaso* [beating, in Quechua] they call it, a little *tunda* [thrashing, in Spanish]. But they don't eliminate him."[55]

In responding to cases like the near-lynching in Loma Pampa described in chapter 4, don Miguel could not rely on an integral community justice system to resolve the conflict but had to intervene spontaneously, using dialogue, persuasion, and the force of his personality and his office to avert violence. Similarly, in the case in Monte Rancho, Miguel was able to call on a set of resources, some of them personal and others appropriated from rural practice, to resolve the conflict nonviolently. Given the sharp lines that so many draw between rural and urban forms of justice making, it might come as a surprise to note that some of these techniques do in fact resemble the judicial practices of the countryside. Calling in the mother of the accused is a clear example. In his discussion of community justice in rural Quechua communities of Bolivia, Orellana Halkyer (2005) explains that being the mother of a known criminal is a mark on a woman's honor, the son's culpability and the suspicion with which the community now regards him extending to all his relatives. In such cases, it is not uncommon for the mother to present herself, along with her son, before the local elders for judgment, and for her to offer guarantees for her son's future behavior. Miguel's decision to call in the mother of the accused thief followed this pattern, echoing a practice that may have been beyond the direct experience of many in the crowd but that nevertheless resonated with certain of their expectations about how justice ought to be achieved and produced the desired effect of reducing tensions and beginning the process of correction. This was continued as the mother beat her own son—not necessarily a traditional practice, but a signal to observers that the family was assuming responsibility for the child's deviant behavior, thereby creating the impression that justice had been served and the future security of the barrio protected.

In similar instances in other barrios, families have been called on to take responsibility for their children's behavior in ways reminiscent of rural judicial forms, which included practices perhaps drawn from rural custom. For example, expulsion from the community is recognized as a significant penalty for offenses committed in the rural peasant village (Fernández Osco 2000). However, in its stead, sanctions may be imposed that are meant both to punish the offender and benefit the local community (Orellana Halkyer 2005, 16). Along those lines, don Fulgencio, president of the zonal development committee and former dirigente of the barrio Uspha Uspha Central, related a case in which the son of a police officer who lived in the barrio had committed offenses against some of his neighbors: "What we did, well, we decided to set a precedent, we did what I call community justice. We met and agreed that this couldn't continue to happen in the zone, we are going to surprise this guy, we are going to throw his whole family out because we can't live with this type of people."[56] After much beseeching by the family members, the barrio residents decided instead to impose a fine of five hundred bolivianos, which was used to buy cement to construct a sidewalk in the barrio. In addition, the boy's parents had to sign a guarantee, pledging to more closely monitor his future behavior—also an element of Quechua rural justice.[57]

The family is important in other ways that link barrio justice to community justice, symbolically and practically. Real people have families while ghostly rateros do not, and establishing the family relations of the accused serves to humanize—we might say despectralize—the accused, making him familiar by associating him with a familial context. This connects with the tendency to interrogate the accused prior to taking any further action, including lynching. As discussed in chapter 4, people state that the reason for the interrogation is to establish the identity of the accused, in order to avoid mistaking a ratero for an innocent person. A woman in Uspha Uspha Central explained: "You have to make him talk. You can put him in a room with his hands and feet bound, and the next day we can go look for his family. Then we can know if he is a thief or if he is innocent."[58] From statements like this, it would seem that merely establishing the existence of a family is enough to exonerate the accused.

Similarly, in deciding how to handle a crime, barrio leaders and residents often require the testimony of witnesses to establish the veracity of the accusation, though the provenance of this technique is less clear. In Loma Pampa, the woman who was supposedly threatened (chapter 4) made her charges against the man who was subsequently tied to a post and almost lynched, her testimony being a key to people's willingness to consider violence in dealing with his crime. Orellana Halkyer describes the presentation of witnesses as a juridical form "more or less general in indigenous and peasant (not only Quechua) communities," without which "the truth remains uncertain" (2005, 13). Don Miguel described something similar in his own adjudicatory practice: "There has to be proof, no? For example, if there are witnesses that saw him enter [the house], no? As dirigente I am very serious and energetic in questioning the witness that saw him commit this crime."[59] However, it is unclear whether barrio residents understand such practices to be dimensions of traditional rural community justice or a more modern technique of official justice—perhaps both, as the good cop/bad cop style of interrogation is well known as a technique of detection, seen in television serials and in news reports on a daily basis. Don Miguel is himself an ardent collector and viewer of North American action movies and police procedurals, buying pirated copies from street vendors downtown and watching them on the old Panasonic television in his bedroom, and some of his ideas about how to administer justice are probably drawn from this interest. The questioning of witnesses, then, is something shared by both community and ordinary justice, and its appearance in the barrios can simultaneously refer to both of these systems without demonstrating the existence of either. In either case, it hardly matters whether or not it is "real" community justice, as the indeterminacy in a way benefits the outcome: as the judicial authority, Miguel can draw on whatever resources he can find to produce a just resolution to a crisis, allowing observers to make different interpretations according to their own expectations and beliefs.

For skilled orators and popular leaders like don Miguel and don Fulgencio, their best hope of resolving a conflict may be through the use of public speaking, where their lack of formal legal authority can be compensated for by the moral authority implicit in their office. Here, people often gesture to memories or imagined ideals of the rural community, where (they say) local leaders had full authority to resolve criminal cases and local disputes. Though the office of barrio president lacks this kind of power, the urban dirigente—as the voice of the community—can channel the authority of his rural counterparts, invoking transcendent values to persuade people to accept his proposed resolutions. For example, don Fulgencio recounted an incident that took place when he was president of his barrio, in which he was called on to resolve a conflict between his vecinos and a young man, a gang member who had physically threatened and tried to extort money from a number of vecinos. Fulgencio called a public meeting at which the accused had to confront his accusers: "One time I faced a very difficult situation in which I felt like I was [caught between] the city and the countryside. Here one can't do the same things that one can do in the countryside, but somehow I had to find a mechanism [to resolve the conflict] that my *base* [my political base, my people] would respect. . . . So I was very cautious and I said, 'Look, compañeros, here is the accused, here is the victim, here is the mother of the accused who is of legal age. Okay, so you all make a decision [about what to do] and I won't decide it, because we live in a democratic country. But if you want,

I will assume the responsibility for the decision, there's no problem with that either.'"[60] Confronted with this responsibility, the vecinos debated what kind of sanction to impose; some wanted to lynch the young man, some wanted to force him to do community service, others wanted to impose a fine of one thousand bolivianos. After they weighed their options, the accused was given a chance to speak. Don Fulgencio, invoking a masculinist discourse to frame his account, described what followed:

> He [the accused] said "Look, Señor Presidente, I would like to clarify a few things. . . . I would ask that you forgive me, please if it is possible. I am going to kneel before all of you. It is true that I don't have a job, and my mother, I thank my mother for showing her face here, [I apologize] for this bad attitude I have taken." And he almost started to cry, and some of the people, too. At least I did. . . . And then I asked all my compañeros to reflect, I said to them, "We all have sons, we are all men, and our sons are going to have sons, too. . . . Let's reflect, let's think, at any moment, how this same kind of thing that happened to this young man [could happen to our sons]. . . . It is important to first hear the apology that the young man just made, but above all, let's not do anything too strong or too weak, let's do something intermediate." And that's what happened.[61]

In the end it was decided that the young man would go off and join the army, a solution that seemed to satisfy everyone—including the young man, who promised not to seek any kind of appeal or retribution against Fulgencio or anyone else in the barrio. For Fulgencio, the decision not only resolved the crisis: "Joining the army will force the young man to meditate a little bit about life and how each of us ought to live."[62]

What is important to note from this and the preceding accounts is the potential that local leaders have to reach nonviolent solutions to local problems, even in the absence of any formal authority or training to intervene in such matters, and with no formal legal system to support them. In doing so, men like don Fulgencio and don Miguel do not implement some sort of formal procedure or process, nor do they rely on an established alternative legal order—traditional, ordinary, or otherwise—to guide their decisions. Instead, in their words and actions they subtly reference a rural authority that they themselves lack, and a system of making justice that does not actually exist in the urban setting. Such references lend credibility to their interventions and momentarily authorize them to mediate situations that otherwise might take a different, more violent turn. This authority is critical, as community justice in the barrios is a more-or-less spontaneous series of decisions that have to be taken and upheld in a context of tremendous ambiguity. This is clear from the cases described in different barrios of Uspha Uspha, including the near-lynching in Monte Rancho. Rather than the unfolding of a set juridical process, that event looked more like a case of improvisation, as different actors—the woman who called don Miguel for help, Miguel himself, and the mother of the accused—searched for ways to avoid violence through creatively suggesting alternatives. In the process, different practices were implemented that resonated with local expectations of what justice should look like, and what would need to be done to guarantee security.

It is also important to recall the context of insecurity and uncertainty within which these events unfold. Evident from Miguel and Senobia's recounting of the event in Monte Rancho was the profound uncertainty that characterized people's behavior, and their indecision about the use of violence as a response to insecurity in the marginal barrios. As the previous chapter explored, and contrary to what government, media, and academic commentators say about lynching, the event in Monte Rancho was characterized less by the rage of a crazed mob bent on vengeance than by a sense of confusion and the lack of a clear avenue to resolve the conflict. Though some in the crowd were certainly angry, the story clearly indicates that the so-called mob did not proceed immediately to a lynching of the supposed criminal. Rather people chose to wait, uncertain of what to do, until finally the woman had the idea to call in don Miguel to settle the matter. The sources of this uncertainty, as described in the preceding chapters, are many, and they include the lack of an established legal system or predictable form of social ordering that includes a routinized way of resolving social conflicts. What we see here instead is the local working out of problems based on individual creativity and imagination, a process for which history and culture provide few reference points, except metaphorically: Doña Senobia describes her husband as being kind of like a *corregidor*, the figure in the rural Andean community charged with judging and punishing criminals under a system of community justice (Fernández Osco 2000). But she knows that he is not really a corregidor, and Miguel himself would balk at the title.

Conclusion

If we consider that there are hundreds of barrios like Loma Pampa and Monte Rancho in Cochabamba and other Bolivian cities, all of which face similar problems of crime, an unreliable police or judicial presence, and a lack of traditional structures for the resolution of conflicts, we may begin to recognize that this highly localized form of adjudication is the principal mechanism for making justice in urban indigenous communities today. Different barrios will follow different sets of practices in this process, ranging from less to more violent, with lynching being one option among many for dealing with criminal suspects. Where does "real" community justice lie? This question, which dominates international debate on this matter, is a classic red herring, distracting us from the true issue at hand. From the examples I have provided, it makes just as much sense to call local urban forms of adjudication "community justice" as it does to so label practices found in rural communities like those described earlier in Laco Laconi. Imposing a cash fine on an adulterer is no more customary than lynching, and the existence of various practices points instead to the complex mixture of procedures that these original indigenous communities adopt in confronting their own legal crises. To insist, as many politicians, academics, and human rights promoters do today, in Bolivia and internationally, that "real" community justice is an unadulterated rural phenomenon descended directly from the Incas is to deny those communities the reality of their own history, in which they have long existed within a broader context of colonial and neocolonial domination and resistance. If we as scholars continue to follow the Bolivian state as it attempts to identify and support "real" indigenous justice, we will come no closer to understanding the complex and hybrid techniques that contemporary indigenous people use to resolve conflicts in their communities, especially in urban settings. But if we recognize the rich diversity of existing approaches to problem solving in marginal areas, we can develop a better understanding of how local forms of leadership and authority are mobilized and of the multiple space-time referents invoked in the framing of local realities and the resolution of conflicts and crises.

The discussion presented in this chapter also suggests a movement away from conceptualizing the sociolegal field as being somehow plural in nature—a concept with broad implications in Bolivia and elsewhere. Pluralism is a founding concept of the new Bolivian constitution, according to which the country is no longer a republic but is now a plurinational state—a reframing meant to express the official recognition of the range of peoples, their languages, and their cultures that make up the Bolivian nation. But pluralism implies an essential coherence, a multiplicity of holistic entities existing parallel to one another within the same sociopolitical space. In terms of legal systems, conceptualizing the Bolivian sociolegal field as plural similarly suggests that multiple legal systems, each in their own way a discrete and integrated whole, coexist within a larger legal universe (Santos 1995), each operating according to its own norms within its own jurisdiction—"the law of the oppressed" as an alternative form of legal ordering to that of the state (Santos 1977). This normative approach leads us to dismiss complex sociolegal realities like those I have described above, writing them off as chaotic or completely without law and order, and seeing their lack of a formal legal system—official, traditional, or otherwise—as suggesting a kind of legal vacuum within which random violence and savage retrogression inevitably emerge. But the reality is much more complex. Urban indigenous communities today do not so much operate under one particular legal system or another as they try to make do through the creative intervention of local leaders, who cobble together some form of judicial process—a legal bricolage—based on what they know or imagine to be part of some other existing legal system. In these marginal barrios, as in many rural communities today, what we find are not coherent legal orders that together comprise a plurally legal field, but assemblages based on imagination, memory, and pragmatism in the face of crime, vulnerability, and the threat of violence. Don Miguel, like others who hold the office of barrio president, are legal bricoleurs who cannot rely on the support of existing systems but must fashion a resolution to a given crisis by drawing on whatever resources are at hand. Though at times modeling his authority on that of his imagined rural counterparts, don Miguel, great fan of action movies that he is, sounds more like Sylvester Stallone's Judge Dredd when he declares "I am the law" in Loma Pampa, and the residents of that barrio see no inconsistencies in these claims.[63] The availability of multiple forms from which to select is critical to the success of this effort.

Finally, in spatial terms, these observations should discourage us from drawing a stark division between rural and urban communities, at least on the question of law and justice making. Anthropologists have long observed the many ways in which rural-to-urban migration does not represent a sharp break in the social or economic commitments of migrants, who often define their identities in terms of their places of origin and maintain a variety of ties to those rural communities. These deep and sustained connections between rural and urban individuals and communities point to the artificiality of political or academic projects that continue to locate indigeneity, authenticity, and tradition in the countryside and whiteness, modernity, and spuriousness in the city. Like their rural counterparts, leaders and residents of urban communities must contend with problems of violence, crime, and conflict often without the assistance of an official state legal system, and so must rely on their own creativity, values, and local tool kits to restore peace and punish offenders in ways they deem appropriate. Similarly, we must break with the tendency—exemplified by the MAS approach to community justice critiqued in this chapter—to locate indigenous people solely in the countryside of Bolivia and other Andean nations. There are multiple ways to be indigenous in the Andes today, involving forms of practice and identity not tied to familiar rural stereotypes, to which it would behoove both policymakers and scholars to attend.

6 | Inhuman Rights?

VIOLENCE AT THE NEXUS OF RIGHTS AND SECURITY

In some respects, the unprecedented election to the Bolivian presidency of Evo Morales can be attributed to his command of the transnational discourse of human rights. In the years leading up to Evo's election, Bolivia saw the emergence of powerful social movements demanding greater political inclusion and representation for indigenous peoples (Kohl and Farthing 2006), and protesting the privatization and expropriation of natural resources (particularly water and gas)—all, in various ways, using the transnational language of human rights. As leader of the Bolivian coca-growers' union and head of the MAS party, Evo articulated the protest against state and transnational programs of neoliberal political economy as struggles for human and citizens' rights in a context of centuries of indigenous exclusion and exploitation by foreign powers (Goodale 2008). Violent state repression of civil protest was critiqued in the same idiom. Like other indigenous activists throughout the hemisphere, Evo and other leaders and participants in Bolivian social movements have deployed the language of human rights—elaborating their own takes on what constitute indigenous and cultural rights in the process (see Albro 2006b)—to reframe their struggles for political recognition, social inclusion, and access to land and other natural resources in terms of democratic citizenship and the right to participate in shaping the future of the Bolivian nation (see Brysk 2000; Speed 2007). Evo's notoriety as a pro-

gressive, populist figure defending the rights of Bolivia's poor and marginalized was further underscored by his explicit denunciation of neoliberalism and his pledge to reverse decades of free market economic
policies that have further impoverished South America's poorest nation.
This rhetoric translated to electoral success in December 2005, when he
carried more than 50 percent of the popular vote—a landslide by Bolivian standards—defeating the rightist candidate Jorge "Tuto" Quiroga,
widely regarded as representing the status quo on neoliberal economic
policy and elite domination of national politics. Evo's similarly resound-
ing reelection in 2009 served to further underscore the success of his
message among the historically poor and marginalized classes that comprise the majority of Bolivia's population.

As the Bolivian social movements illustrate, human rights has achieved a
kind of global ascendancy as the discourse of political and moral accountability, in the process becoming "the language of progressive politics in
the Third World" today (Rajagopal 2003, 168). But as the urban security
crisis in Bolivia also reveals, in parts of the same "Third World," human
rights are being demonized, fueling a violent reactionary politics as well.
In some ways this can be linked to the dramatic emergence of "security" as
a global sociopolitical watchword (a process described in chapter 1), as
what might be called "security talk" has come to stand prominently alongside "rights talk" in contemporary geopolitics (see Cowan, Dembour, and
Wilson 2001; Merry 2003). In the barrios of Cochabamba City, these two
transnational discourses find contradictory expression. The intense pre-
occupation with security, documented in the preceding chapters, encounters the question of human rights as some barrio residents—concerned with defending their own rights to security, property, and freedom
from fear—violate the rights of others by arbitrarily depriving them of life
without benefit of due process and by embracing state practices that seem
to promise greater security in exchange for greater police latitude in using
violence to control crime (Tulchin, Frühling, and Golding. 2003).[1] This
emphasis on security serves to introduce a new kind of right into the
global debate over the meaning of human rights—the right to security—
which shifts local understandings of human rights in ways that are potentially violent and at odds with normative transnational human rights ideals.
At the same time, by embracing the discourse of security, barrio residents
find themselves positioned as antagonists of the discourse of human rights.
Even as they claim to be defending their own rights through violence, many

residents view the rights of criminal suspects as forfeit, obstacles to be overcome on the way to achieving security, and regard with suspicion those NGOs and their representatives who espouse the transnational discourse of human rights in defense of the accused.

As Mark Goodale (2007) has pointed out, the practice of human rights in what are typically defined as local contexts is much more complex than international human rights law and its theorists might presume. As with all global cultural phenomena, the meanings of human rights shift and change over time, as local actors redefine them in response to current material conditions and sociopolitical configurations. The consolidation of neoliberal political economy in Bolivia over the last thirty years has created such profound economic and social insecurity for the urban poor that political and civil rights, originally intended to protect the poor from state violence and abuse, are now seen by some of those same people as rights for criminals and hence as challenges to their own security that must be overcome—by violence, if necessary. Human rights, then, in the course of this history, have shifted from a guarantor of protections for the poor and vulnerable to an obstacle to their protection, in the minds of many (though not all) of the poor and vulnerable themselves. In undergoing this transformation, human rights have come to be understood in very narrow terms, far different from the broadly encompassing sets of protections and guarantees that transnational human rights are meant to include. Human rights discourse in urban Bolivia thus represents a transnational normativity that is adapted, rearticulated, challenged, and redeployed—by state actors, NGOs, and poor barrio residents alike—in ways that challenge basic assumptions about the inherent liberatory potential of the discourse. The "vernacularization" of human rights, to use Sally Engle Merry's term (2006, 39; see also Levitt and Merry 2009), unfolds here in ways that global human rights advocates could never have imagined, as it becomes localized in contexts already highly saturated by the global discourse of security. But, in addition to those human rights activists ordinarily identified as vernacularizers—people who translate global rights conceptions to fit with local contexts—such processes are also marked by the appearance of new kinds of vernacularizers, whose goals may be the demonization, rather than the promotion, of the transnational ideals and language of human rights.

Although more robust conceptions of rights do circulate in Bolivia, these often encounter resistance in local contexts of dissemination. Like "security," the term "human rights" contains multiple meanings and possibilities. It is a discourse that can be deployed by different people in different settings, to accomplish diverse political and social ends; and it can be used in ways that might not make sense in other contexts or that might not be consistent with the intentions of those who consider themselves experts in or originators of that discourse. And, as with "security" —which in Bolivia and globally has experienced a clear narrowing of meaning to focus exclusively on protection from crime and other sources of terror (Buzan, Wæver, and Wilde 1998)—the idea of human rights has been narrowed in the context of the marginal barrio in ways that make it appear antagonistic to the interests of security. Despite the state's and the president's embrace of a transnational rights discourse, with broad human rights conceptions finding their way even into the new Bolivian constitution, the realities of poverty and insecurity on the urban margins constrain the wider adoption of these broad concepts, leaving space for other, narrower conceptions of rights to emerge.

In Bolivia, then, as throughout the Americas, "human rights" as an emancipatory transnational discourse encounters a competing ontology of "security," which not only has the power to defeat "rights" in the daily social practice of ordinary Bolivians but also seems able to rework and redefine "rights" itself, to recast it as a foreign idea inappropriately imposed on local reality, while at the same time appropriating it to the struggle for "security." From this perspective, violence becomes an unending normativity in itself, a practice not antagonistic to rights but, bizarrely, a means of securing them; meanwhile, "human rights" and human rights advocates become demonized as enemies of security and well-being for the poor. This resistance to and redefinition of "rights" at the local level threaten to undermine the political and legal gains that the transnational discourse has globally attained, and they must be taken very seriously by those concerned with human rights as a path to empowerment in the new world order.

Insecurity and the Transnational Discourse of Human Rights

There are a number of reasons why Bolivians might distrust the transnational discourse of human rights, even as Bolivian social movements and their spokespeople publicly deploy rights talk in advancing their own programs for democratic inclusion. First, as Rajagopal (2003, 196) points out, human rights law and language, while highly critical of various forms of physical violence, are virtually silent when it comes to economic violence—that is, violence caused by development, market forces, or transnational fiscal and economic policy regimes. The violence brought on by neoliberal economics, felt widely throughout Bolivian society and motivating numerous uprisings and political confrontations within Bolivia, does not fall under the rubric of human rights violations and is not typically addressed as such by international or domestic rights NGOs. This lacuna is recognized by social movements, as they recast the language of rights to characterize their struggles against the market-driven violence of privatization, debt repayment schemes, and the War on Drugs, but rarely by rights NGOs themselves, which in Bolivia have been slow to articulate critiques of neoliberalism in the same terms. Furthermore, it represents a failure to connect with the quotidian reality of poor urban people, who suffer from the daily structural violence of poverty and joblessness, and to recognize these as motivating rising crime and delinquency among young people who perceive few opportunities for themselves in the urban job market.

Second, human rights are highly state-focused, with activists typically defining their work as the defense of society against the excesses of the state, which they identify as the principal source of human rights violations. However, while expressing a profound mistrust of the state, at the same time human rights are predicated on "a total reliance on the moral possibilities of the state" (Rajagopal 2003, 189), incorporating an implicit model of an expansive state as the best and only means of realizing a just society. As a result, while states may be highly resistant to human rights discourse and those who espouse it, some democratic states actually embrace human rights as the sanctioned language of resistance, welcoming the advocacy by human rights discourse for a strong and expanding state, a position that accords well with the desires of the ruling class who historically have controlled it (Rajagopal 2003, 191). In Bolivia, the administration of Evo Morales has actively endorsed human rights. The new constitution gives ample recognition to a broad spectrum of human and indigenous rights, and in 2007 the Bolivian state enacted a National Action Plan on Human Rights, requiring prefectures and municipalities nationwide to respect human rights in all of their official business (Organizaciones de Derechos Humanos para el Foro Permanente para los Pueblos Indígenas 2010). While such moves represent a step forward in state recognition of transnational human rights accords, given the hostility toward and suspicion of what I call the phantom state, its laws, police, and judicial institutions, the association of human rights with state authority gives the discourse a taint that makes it less likely that local people will accept it. In addition, many human rights advocacy groups "have developed collaborative relationships with the state as a means of deflecting the criticism that rights groups are interested only in attacking police and law enforcement authorities, or that they are concerned merely with abuses committed by police, but not by violence perpetrated by ordinary criminals" (International Council on Human Rights Policy 2003, 6). In Bolivia, the creation of state agencies like the Defensoría del Pueblo—the office of the human rights ombudsperson intended to play a watchdog role over state activities and yet remain a political entity of the state—is regarded by many Bolivians as evidence of the collaboration between human rights and the state, and thus a further reason to be skeptical of the discourse.

Third, for many Bolivians, the discourse and ideology of human rights retain an association with the nonlocal sources from which they originated. Having arrived in Bolivia as part of a larger globalizing movement toward democratization and neoliberal political and economic transformation, the latest wave of human rights, like these other projects, is regarded by many as a foreign imposition that reduces national sovereignty and illegitimately shapes local reality. To use Boaventura de Sousa Santos's terms, human rights in Bolivia remains a kind of "globalized localism," a form of "globalization from above" that clearly bears the label of its foreign manufacture (1997, 3). As such, human rights, though powerful as a global discourse of resistance, do not automatically enjoy local legitimacy, nor do they necessarily serve a counterhegemonic function in local struggles. To the contrary, as evidenced by the local condemnation of human rights described below, ordinary Bolivians are more likely to mistrust human rights precisely because of their global character, as though recognizing and rejecting the power relations implicit in the impositions "from above" (see the discussion of the politics of global/local verticality in Goodale 2007). Thus even as they are critical of what they perceive to be the absent state, many Bolivians confronting problems of insecurity also denounce the state's diminution and loss of sovereignty vis-à-vis foreign nations and international economic institutions like the International Monetary Fund and the World Bank. Suspicion of human rights discourse accompanies the mistrust of other transnational interventions into Bolivian national economic and political life, which are perceived as having contributed to the nation's enduring poverty and social insecurity, extending back to the colonial era.

Perhaps the clearest evidence of human rights' transnational orientation can be seen in the debate about community justice. As discussed in chapter 5, the MAS state's recognition and promotion of community justice as a legitimate alternative to ordinary justice has sparked a great deal of controversy both within Bolivian legal circles and internationally, as foreign observers have expressed concerns about human rights protections under a community justice regime. Although the Bolivian constitution explicitly states that community justice must operate under norms that respect human rights guarantees, its simultaneous insistence on the autonomy of indigenous justice systems from state authority raises questions about how these guarantees will be enforced. The conflation of community justice with the violence of lynching further complicates the matter, as some international human rights advocates openly condemn the constitutional support for community justice on the basis that it represents mob rule and the tyranny of the majority while failing to protect the basic rights of accused criminals (Human Rights Foundation 2008). Given the strong support that many Bolivians express for the community justice provisions in the new constitution, these foreign attacks in the name of human rights serve to deepen local hostility to that transnational discourse, which appears to support the rights of criminals over the rights of barrio residents to make their communities secure.

The transnational associations of human rights discourse and institutions also have an impact in the context of barrio insecurity. Though human rights activists worked in Bolivia even during the dark years of military rule, with the arrival of neoliberalism and the turn to democracy, human rights discourse and activism experienced a new flourishing, unfortunately coinciding with the uptick in levels of criminality that social scientists identify as characteristic of the democratic turn worldwide (Ungar 2011). As authoritarian states are replaced by democratic ones, the abusive policies intended to clamp down on the internal enemies of the state and maintain public order are relaxed, with a resulting increase in the levels of ordinary public crime as state security-making practices shift to operating under a rule of law (International Council on Human Rights Policy 2003). Ironically, this often leads to an increase in public tolerance of more heavy-handed authoritarian measures—la mano dura—to control crime (Call 2003; Duce and Pérez Perdomo 2003). Research has shown that in various Latin American cities, people express a willingness to allow police to conduct illegal searches and detain suspects illegally, as well as increasing support for the death penalty, excluded under most Latin American legal regimes (Lagos 2000; Smulovitz 2003). Even in poor barrios like those of Uspha Uspha, where people despise the corrupt police, they contradictorily express a desire for a stronger and more violent police presence in their communities. In tandem with this trend, as crime rises—or is perceived to rise (Dammert and Malone 2003; Elbert 1998; Rotker 2002)[2]— following democratization, human rights groups emerge as active policers of the police, advocating for the rights of the detained and a strict adherence to the laws governing police procedures and judicial behavior. In a context of insecurity such as that described here—in which the police and judicial system are widely regarded as corrupt or absent, and the poor feel that they have no public advocate—those same human rights groups and the discourse they deploy can come to be seen as working on behalf of criminals and of crime itself, and so as antagonistic to local security (see Caldeira 2000). In Bolivia, human rights defenders and activists, long critical of state violence in the country and so historically threatened and persecuted by the state, have come to be demonized by average citizens, who regard activists' defense of the rights of criminal suspects as another kind of antisocial act, something akin to police corruption. For their part, activists working with transnational or domestic rights NGOs are hampered by the language and approach of human rights itself, which once again tends to focus on the behavior of states, their institutions, and representatives, without providing a clear platform from which to denounce ordinary criminal violence or to articulate a defense of crime victims.

In the next section of this chapter, I consider human rights in Bolivia from the perspective of activists who are involved in human rights promotion and defense in Cochabamba, considering their own vernacularizations of the discourse of human rights and their explanations of why people mistrust them and their institutions. This section also provides an analysis of the ways in which the police, oddly enough, deploy the language of human rights, both to lobby for improved working conditions in the police force and to malign the efforts of human rights activists as damaging the security of urban residents. I go on to examine the perspectives on human rights held by residents of the barrios of Uspha Uspha and the southern zone of Cochabamba. Here, the troubling intersection of rights and security demonstrates the ways in which the right to security emerges as a trump that defeats other kinds of rights in the course of daily encounters. It also raises questions about vernacularization itself, suggesting that the process of localizing transnational discourses can be controlled by a range of individuals and groups, some of them in fact antagonistic to the meanings and goals that provide the foundation for a transnational human rights regime.

Vernaculars of Human Rights in Cochabamba

As human rights language and concepts travel from their sources of origin in the global north to their places of reception and dissemination in the global south, they are adapted and reconfigured to fit within local sets of institutions, meanings, and practices. Merry (2006, 39) has called this process "vernacularization," the localization or indigenization of transnational concepts within particular communities. Vernacularization is particularly useful in undoing the notion of globalization as the flow of ideas and meanings from the global to the local—a perspective on globalization that reproduces and reinforces a unilinear, spatialized dichotomy (see the discussion in Goodale 2007). Such conceptualizations of the local-global dichotomy, like those of the rural-urban divide critiqued in chapter 5, are Euclidean and two-dimensional. The coordinates they identify—the local and the global—produce an image of a static, linear universe, one in which more complex kinds of relationships are difficult to imagine; and even when they include other coordinates, such as region and nation, these appear as intermediate points on the same linear trajectory. This two-dimensional model constrains analysis, doing little to capture the lived experience of complex, multiply positioned social actors (Mascia-Lees and Himpele 2006). Here the local may become fixed, ahistorical, and even denigrated: the language of space implies magnitude and importance, with the transnational realm regarded as more advanced in an almost evolutionary sense, while the local is seen as populated by what Jonathan Friedman (2004, 195) calls "redneck homebodies" with no greater vision beyond their own small realities. The problem is again as much temporal as spatial. As Jean Nadel-Klein observes, people identified as "local" are "barred from participating in change because they are defined as incapable of sharing not only the same space but also the same time or epoch as modern society" (1991, 503).

In terms of human rights, such a perspective suggests that rights language and concepts move along this linear trajectory from the global to the local, a gift that the developed north bestows on the undeveloped, benighted south (Merry 2005). Vernacularization instead describes a process of reception and transformation, a dialectic in which transnational conceptions are made meaningful within, or rejected on the basis of, local realities—themselves already conditioned by their broader inclusion within transnational frameworks of economics, politics, and culture. Concepts of the local and the global need not be discarded within such a framework—they remain distinct domains of discourse and practice that may profitably be explored ethnographically and may usefully be reconceptualized as fully coeval, contingent, and relational spaces within a multidimensional and shifting universe. The rearticulation of global human rights concepts within specific localities is of particular anthropological interest, offering a window onto the dynamics of globalization itself, managed by the various parties to the transaction (Goodale and Merry 2007). These include, most evidently, the activists and NGOs who translate human rights language into locally meaningful terms. These translators of human rights are "both powerful and vulnerable"; they command a transnational discourse and have institutional backing, but their loyalties and sincerity may be dubious (Merry 2006, 40). The translation work of human rights activists can be influenced by a number of factors, including lack of knowledge, training, and resources by the translators, a hostile environment promoted by the state and its institutions, and a profound local resistance to human rights doctrine. And though in practice their work reveals the dialectical nature of human rights dissemination, it may also ironically reinscribe the spatial hierarchy that the global-local dichotomy implies: "The larger structure of economic and political power that surrounds human rights activism means that translation is largely a top-down process from the transnational to the local and the powerful to the less powerful" (Merry 2006, 48–49). All of these factors come into play in Cochabamba, where human rights encounters an array of obstacles to its promotion and reception in the marginal barrios.

HUMAN RIGHTS NGOS

But vernacularization remains conceptually limited unless we recognize the variety of ways in which local translation actually occurs, and the multiplicity of actors, all with varying intentions, involved in that translation. The reality in Cochabamba belies the notion of a linear dissemination of human rights from the global to the local, as "the local" itself emerges as divided and conflictual, and the dissemination of human rights ideas and discourse as highly problematic. Attention to the divergent ways in which human rights are locally rendered points to the complexities of vernacularization in context and to the often confounding entanglements that security and human rights experience in that process.

In Cochabamba, professional human rights activists and promoters play a rather limited role in human rights vernacularization. In point of fact, very little active promotion and dissemination of human rights takes place in the barrios, which occasionally receive visits from or courses offered by rights-based NGOs, but which for the most part see very little of these kinds of activists. Organizations involved in promoting human rights in Bolivia are highly constrained by financial limitations, and in general they maintain very few professional staff members able to offer focused human rights trainings. As a result, knowledge of human rights in the barrios usually comes not from professional translators but more often from rumors, gossip, and conversations among barrio residents and leaders. People hear about human rights through conversations and the media; they know about and sometimes patronize state and nongovernmental rights institutions in the city center; they know human rights can have some positive effects for them and possibly serve as tools in local struggles—but in general, they know little about what rights entail and how they operate. Even the basic notion that human rights represent protections against state abuses is not widely recognized in the barrios. This leads to some unusual problems, as barrio residents know that human rights can help them but are unsure exactly how. Given the general lack of any kind of support institutions in the barrios other than the local political leadership, in times of conflict, barrio residents may take their complaints to the downtown offices of one or another human rights office or NGO to appeal for help in resolving their personal issue. This kind of help is usually unsatisfactory, however, as rights organizations are not staffed for such work, nor do they necessarily understand the residents' problems—fights between neighbors, land legalization issues, ordinary crime victimization—in human rights terms. Their offices are nevertheless swamped by such complainants, leaving them little time or resources to do other kinds of human rights work, even as their would-be constituents typically are disappointed by the attention they receive.

Such is the challenge facing the organization that I will call the Congreso de Derechos Humanos de Cochabamba (the Cochabamba Human Rights Congress, or the Congreso).[3] The Congreso is one of the largest human rights NGOs in Bolivia. Its offices collect citizens' complaints of human rights abuses, and its staff members sometimes hold workshops in the barrios to inform citizens about human rights concepts and tolerance. Founded in the 1970s in response to the repression of the dictatorships and funded by a mix of small grants from different European governments and their international missions, the Congreso is also one of the most prominent rights-based NGOs in Bolivia, with offices in the different departments of the country. Although it has long been a leading proponent of human rights in Bolivia, the Congreso lacks the resources to do its work effectively in the context of neoliberal democracy—an irony not lost on its personnel. Rather than working to denounce state violations of human rights, staffers complain that their organization now merely attends to individual cases like those described above—personal conflicts without a clear human rights dimension. It has become, one staffer said, "una institución meramente asistencialista"—an institution devoted entirely to providing a top-down form of customer service, a kind of "welfarism" (*asistencialismo*) that denies people their dignity and promotes a dependency on the services of the institution.[4] In the meantime, Congreso activists complain, the institution does little to promote human rights more broadly, or to campaign against state violations of rights, and few of its personnel are able to advance their own training in rights concepts and diffusion. The staffer put it this way: "It seems to me that the Congreso is—has lost its way since the era of the 1970s or when there were the dictatorships, when the Congreso justified its existence in political or ideological terms. So it seems that since the democratic era began, it has lost its way and abandoned its true role: the defense of human rights."[5]

The Congreso and its personnel thus experience a tension between what they perceive to be their principal function and the way the institution and its members are perceived by people in the barrios, based on different understandings of what rights entail. Staff members understand the role of the Congreso to be to engage the state, particularly around issues of justice, in order to ensure that in carrying out their duties, state institutions like the police do not abuse the rights of the detained and other citizens. For barrio residents who make up the clientele of the Congreso, the institution exists to help them resolve conflicts, particularly with the state and its representatives, but also with local authorities like barrio leaders and with other vecinos. This puts the Congreso into a difficult intermediary position, a kind of double bind like that experienced by other NGOs positioned between the state and the members of vulnerable populations whose rights they ostensibly seek to protect (Fortun 2001; Leve 2007; Mertz and Timmer 2010). In Cochabamba the tension arises particularly around questions of law enforcement and justice making. The Congreso does not intervene in ordinary criminal matters, though barrio residents sometimes seem to expect it to do so. One activist said: "Whenever we see some citizen in the press, whatever problem arises between individuals, immediately they bring up the question of, 'What is the Human Rights [Congreso] doing about this?,' when we know that the theme of human rights is linked fundamentally to what is considered to be the role of the state . . . in the administration of justice."[6] However, Congreso staff do intervene in cases of police or civilian excess, including vigilante lynchings, seeking to ensure the rights and sometimes to protect the lives of the detained. In doing so, however, these activists risk the ire of barrio residents, who perceive them to be acting in defense of the delinquent while refusing to help crime victims (see the discussion of this point below).

In the same vein, human rights workers tend to neglect the barrios of Cochabamba's southern zone because, like many others, they perceive barrios like those of Uspha Uspha to be abandoned by the state. Throughout this ethnography I have endeavored to show that rather than being completely absent, the state is very much present in the marginal barrios, but in ways that are only partially visible to the residents and outside observers of these barrios. This phantom presence of the state is typically overlooked by rights activists, as is clear in the words of one Congreso activist, who asserted: "The state is totally absent from the barrios."[7] Obviously, then, people who perceive themselves as being in business to keep watch on the abuses and excesses of the state are drawn to those places where the state's presence is more visibly robust, its abuses clear and in need of correction. The absence of the state, its refusals, its passive violations of security, are not understood in terms of human rights, which are invoked only in cases of actions publicly committed. In contrast, inaction is not conceptualized as a rights violation, despite its contributions to local insecurity. This situation deepens the double bind of human rights activists, who are called on by barrio residents to help resolve their problems but who view the barrios as devoid of state presence and so as lying outside their real areas of concern.

Despite this double bind and the institutional limitations they confront, most activists in the Congreso understand the work of human rights to be primarily about public education. Under the Evo Morales administration, the Congreso and other rights organizations have sometimes been included in projects focused on judicial reform, invited to ensure that human rights protocols are respected in this process.[8] Though the results of these projects have been minimal, the Congreso activists who participated felt themselves to have made a major contribution, part of their mission of public education on human rights. Similarly, many of these individuals regard public dissemination of rights knowledge in the barrios to be a principal element of their work as activists, though they recognize their limitations and how these can undo their successes. Another activist put it this way: "I believe that the fundamental work of the Congreso should be education. But not like I have done on various occasions, to go and give a workshop, be with 50, 100, 150, or 200 people, explain to them what are human rights. You can have all the will in the world, make the greatest possible effort, you can be the most eloquent speaker possible, the most persuasive in your explanations, but it is going to evaporate, the next week, a month later. We have to have the capacity to conduct a sequential and sustained project of diffusion, education, and reflection on the philosophy of human rights."[9] Instead, the Congreso and other rights NGOs have a minimal physical presence in the marginal barrios of Cochabamba, and the workshops they offer on human rights are intermittent, often oversimplified, and focused on particular problems rather than the broad sweep of human rights and its possibilities. This system of dissemination does little to counter the narrow perception of rights that other forms of human rights education (described below) promote.

Human rights discourse in Bolivia seems especially silent on the question of citizen security, understood by the state and barrio residents as protection against criminal predation and delinquency (see chapter 3). Even as citizen security has come to discursive prominence in national politics and daily barrio life, human rights NGOs have remained largely outside of the conversation. Another Congreso activist described citizen security as nonexistent in the work of that institution in recent years, affirming that the Congreso addresses matters of security only in response to concrete cases that are brought to the organization in its downtown offices. Individual activists, however, while criticizing the silence of their institutions, have to some extent come to frame their own understandings of human rights in terms of security. Perhaps this is because of the nature of citizen security as a discourse on security: in joining citizenship to security, it suggests that security itself is a kind of basic civil right, one part of the package of rights that national citizens are meant to enjoy by virtue of their membership in the polity. This is reflected in the language of human rights activists, who sometimes talk about security in terms of human rights. Juan Vargas, for example, an activist with more than ten years of experience working with the Congreso, said that for him, citizen security is entirely reducible to human rights; it is, in his words, "the most basic theme of human rights" at large in Bolivia today.[10] When asked to define what a human rights activist can contribute to the society in which he lives, Juan responded with one word: "Security." When asked to elaborate, he described his advocacy on behalf of victims of police abuse, explaining that through this work to defend the rights of others, he helps to give them a sense of security. Security for this activist comes from and extends to "security when you represent someone, certainty about what you are doing, knowledge that you produce, your great capacity for analysis and persuasion, and of course the profound respect you have for individuals when you represent them and support them, as well as for those between whom you are mediating [a conflict] . . . the police, the coercive and repressive forces of the state, and the workers."[11]

The same sense that security and rights are fundamentally linked appears in some of the human rights workshops that NGOs sponsor in the barrios of Uspha Uspha and points to the kinds of vernacularization taking place in this context. Despite their lack of consistency and sustainability, rights workshops are not unknown in the barrios, and when they occur, they can be sites for the vernacularization of human rights. Offered by a variety of NGOs at work in the barrios (including the one I helped found and described in chapter 2), these workshops often focus on matters related to crime, insecurity, and the justice system, in an attempt to address the pressing concerns of workshop participants. A frequent subtext of these workshops is discouraging lynching and taking the law into one's own hands, which lead to rights abuses in the name of security. Nevertheless, in some workshops, security and justice are presented as rights, part of the basic portfolio of rights that citizens possess.

And curiously, the boundaries of that portfolio seem to be expanding, in ways that are meant to appeal specifically to barrio residents. One of these areas is community justice: though international rights groups are highly opposed to it, in local events, human rights promoters sometimes recognize community justice as being among the rights of citizens. This was the case in the months leading up to the national Constituent Assembly, which was responsible for drafting the new constitution that was approved in 2009. In one workshop organized by an NGO, Defense of the Child International (Defensa del Niño Internacional), in Uspha Uspha in May 2006, the presenter stated that among their fundamental rights, all people have the right to an administration of ordinary, alternative, and impartial community justice. When asked to explain why community justice should be included among the list of fundamental rights, the presenter replied that it was important to give visibility and legitimacy to such forms of justice making. He also attributed its inclusion to a recognition of Bolivian culture, which consists of concepts like community justice that must be reconciled with ideas of human rights.

A similar broadening of what rights might include came in a discussion of the right to petition, which was presented in this workshop as the citizen's right to formulate individual or collective complaints to state or "communal" authorities. Here again the notion of rights can be seen to expand, in this case to include community leaders like barrio dirigentes or rural authorities in addition to the state authorities whom human rights more typically address. When asked about this, the presenter explained that the principles of human rights could be enlarged to include any form of power, and given this understanding, the expanded right of petition made perfect sense. More important than transnational generalities about human rights, the vernacularization that occurred in this particular workshop revealed the influence of both local and national concerns. It indicated an effort on the part of Cochabamba-based activists to adapt human rights to local reality, in which the communal authorities (dirigentes and members of the barrio executive committee) have the most power and influence over local life. It also reflected the emerging national concern with autonomy and decentralization, in which both community justice and the legitimacy of indigenous jurisdictions and local leaders were subsequently enshrined in the new constitution. In recognition of this growing trend in Bolivia, the activists running this workshop offered a reframing of certain basic rights so as to resonate with their own understanding of current and emerging Bolivian political and legal reality.

A POLICE VERNACULAR OF HUMAN RIGHTS

As mentioned above, however, workshops of this sort are infrequent events in the marginal barrios, leaving open the possibility for other kinds of vernacularization to occur. In the space left unfilled by human rights advocates and NGOs concerned with the valorization and promotion of human rights, other voices emerge that also vernacularize human rights, but in ways less appropriate for the traditional goals of human rights and their advocates. Among these vernacularizers, surprisingly, are the police. Commandants and officers of the Bolivian national police force are very aware of human rights considerations, something pressed on them by the Morales administration. Particularly in their confrontations with large-scale demonstrations, the police must be somewhat circumspect in their responses—it is not a good idea, for example, to violently repress a protest march by coca growers when the president of the country is the leader of the coca growers' movement. In addition, the human rights values encoded in and the limitations placed on police practice by new legal protocols (including El Nuevo Código de Procedimiento Penal, the New Penal Procedural Code described below) have required some modifications in how the police conduct investigations and handle the accused. While such reforms have had only limited impacts in Bolivia, they have nevertheless required a certain level of recognition among police personnel, who have come to understand human rights as something that they must consider in transacting their daily business. It is interesting to note, then, that in their own discourse some police officials use the language of human rights to defend their personal interests and to criticize the institution of the police, and in the process have become experts in and vernacularizers of human rights.

Sergeant Froilan Mamani, mentioned in chapter 3, is one of these vernacularizers. As a leader of the police union, Sergeant Mamani, like the group he represents, is charged with "defending the rights" (as he puts it) of subordinate police officers and street cops, usually against the police institution itself, which pays them poorly and treats them badly.[12] He frequently leads workshops and teaches courses on human rights to his colleagues on the force—not so that they can reform their policing practices, but so that they can better defend themselves against abuse by their superior officers. Police officers frequently refer to their basic right to a decent salary, good equipment, personal dignity, and respect, so that they can live a good life and carry out their duties adequately. Curiously, some superior officers also use the language of rights to protest the problems their institution faces due to lack of funding and support from the federal government. Even as he complained of the restrictions that human rights imposes on his unit's ability to deal with crowds and protestors, Coronel Enrique Lopez, the commandant of the police department's Organismo Operativo de Orden y Seguridad (the Operative Organization for Order and Security) used rights language to object to public critiques of police inefficacy. They don't give us resources to run our units, he griped, noting that people demand much of the police and are quick to accuse them of the smallest infraction, but do not want to invest in improving their working conditions. "To demand that someone lives up to their obligations," he said, "first you should guarantee him the exercise of certain rights."[13]

At the same time as they use rights language in their own defense, the police are also quick to interpret "human rights" as the cause of the rise of crime in Bolivia. In their vernacularizations, the police offer a narrow, stripped-down conception of human rights, one that ignores human rights' broader implications to focus public attention entirely on questions of crime and delinquency. This is a move similar to that surrounding the discourse of citizen security (described in chapter 3), in which broader understandings of security (such as those contained in the concept of "human security") are eschewed in favor of a conception of security that relates only to freedom from crime and fear of crime, and that can be delivered only by public authorities. In the case of human rights, police officers at all levels frequently complain in the news media that laws limiting the arbitrary detention of suspects and requiring evidence of guilt to incarcerate people are detrimental to citizen security, imposing unreasonable burdens on the police's ability to investigate crimes and control delinquency. Much as they blame judges and prosecutors for their leniency in dealing with criminals and their apparent willingness to set suspects free for the slightest reason (see chapter 3), so do the police charge that representatives of groups like the Congreso interfere in police business and hinder their ability to create security. One judge defended laws like the New Penal Procedural Code that provide for judicial transparency, the presumption of innocence, and the right to a defense, saying that the police blame such laws and the fundamental rights tenets that underlie them for their own investigative ineptitude, and he accused the police of being "poorly trained in human rights."[14] But the police counter that such laws respecting human rights are not suited to Bolivian reality, where the police require greater latitude in dealing with crime. The police also condemn the actions of human rights activists, who attempt to hold them accountable to these laws, and blame activists for the police's inability to detain criminal suspects. Said the human rights activist Juan Vargas:

> Even now if you see an event involving the police authorities, they always mention that the Congreso defends the delinquents, making a big stink about the New Penal Procedural Code, the prosecutors, and the judges. I think that the police opted for that easy discourse because they had the power to detain the suspect twenty-four, up to seventy-two hours under the former Penal Code, and the New Penal Code limits them to eight hours as the most they can detain someone at the precinct. . . . The Congreso doesn't have the power to set people free! . . . I think that that is a stigma that the police have dumped on top of us, because I think the Congreso is fulfilling the role it should fulfill: to ensure that the human rights, the fundamental rights, of every citizen, no matter his condition, are respected.[15]

This discussion of human rights activists and their relationship with the police demonstrates how important recognizing the role of human rights vernacularization is in understanding the deployment of rights in local contexts of reception. As the consideration of activists' work in Cochabamba reveals, although rights-promoting institutions are relatively impoverished and maintain only a minimal presence in the marginal barrios, through their workshops and daily encounters with citizens at their downtown offices, rights activists work to make the transnational discourse intelligible in terms of local reality. But the discussion also shows that activists, hampered by limited resources and their own transnational conceptions, are not the only translators of human rights in Cochabamba. In their simultaneous use and condemnation of rights ideals and discourse, the Bolivian police demonstrate themselves to be active vernacularizers of human rights, deploying the transnational concepts in defense of their own conditions while portraying human rights as an obstacle to security in the city. In this, the police are very effective at demonizing human rights and the individuals and institutions promoting them, casting human rights as antagonistic to security and hostile to those forces that would try to create it. This translation, deployed in the insecure spaces of the marginal barrios, resonates with local experience and finds fertile ground in which to flourish. Though a very different understanding of human rights than the one usually broadcast by rights promoters, it can nevertheless be understood as a kind of vernacularization, in which portrayals of the dark side of human rights unfortunately connect more forcefully with local people's experience than do the more progressive visions of rights. For their part, as the next section of this chapter shows, barrio residents pick up on these multiple conceptions of human rights circulating inside and outside their communities and reveal themselves to be active vernacularizers as well.

Security versus Rights in Uspha Uspha

As the preceding discussion suggests, a concern with rights is an integral part of the discourses and practices of Cochabamba-based activists and legal professionals, providing a language for speaking about social violence in ways that some would regard as progressive and productive. And to some extent, this notion of rights finds its way into local barrio discourse about rights, citizenship, and justice in Bolivia, though usually in the language of the more educated or politically engaged. Some barrio leaders, like don Miguel, use the language of rights as a way to explain their political activism as dirigentes leading their people, criticizing the authorities for their neglect of barrio needs. As mentioned in chapter 4, Miguel is not affiliated with any political party and does not rely on party support to make demands on the authorities. Instead, he relies on a faith in the abstract rights of the citizen to advance his barrio and bring benefits to the community, making him rather unique among barrio leaders: "I don't want to belong to a party, so therefore, as a dirigente, or *a Bolivian citizen with rights under the law*, I demand that the authority fulfill [its obligations] to our barrios, as they do with those places that have more benefits than us, no? Or more influence. Without any other influence [being brought to bear] I would like them to attend to us. . . . That is the fundamental core of what I believe."[16] Silvio Huanca, the District 8 representative, attributed his motivation for embarking on a political career to his support of human rights: "When I came [to Uspha Uspha], when I saw the needs, I became excited: 'I will do something for society, for the people who live here, who have lived without realizing that we have rights to make demands of the authorities.' In that way I began my work as a barrio leader."[17] Similarly, don Silvio understands lynching to be a violation of human rights and criticizes dirigentes who don't work to protect the rights of lynching victims: "We dirigentes have the obligation to control the *bases* [the people] so that they respect the rights of the human being. . . . They have to understand that everyone has rights, be they delinquents or religious people. I believe that we all have rights, but also have to be sanctioned for our crimes." More colloquially, one woman in Juan Pablo II, asked if she had ever heard about human rights, responded, "Yes, we have the right to complain, don't we?"[18]

While some barrio leaders and residents speak fluently in a broad transnational rights language, using it to criticize their own marginality and make demands on the state, others in the barrios of Uspha Uspha seem oblivious to the entire notion of human rights. Many residents, like doña Casilda and doña Cata of Loma Pampa, profess a complete ignorance of human rights.[19] When asked directly if they have heard talk of human rights, what they might entail, or how they as individuals or families might benefit from human rights protections, barrio residents frequently respond with blank looks, shakes of the head, or frank denials that they have any knowledge of what they are being asked about. Their expression of ignorance about human rights may be a product of the interview process, in which informants seek to distance themselves from a stigmatizing topic; but in the context of an otherwise friendly and open conversation, their denials seem to be fairly honest expressions of their lack of knowledge on the subject. Even in Loma Pampa, where don Miguel created the position of secretary of conflict and human rights specifically to try and prevent lynchings, the man who held that office, don Feliciano, seemed completely unaware of what human rights entails:

> *Do you have an idea, more or less, about the meaning of human rights?*
> FELICIANO: Let's see. About that—I'm not—maybe [pause].
> *You have a portfolio of human rights.*
> FELICIANO: Oh.[20]

This unfamiliarity with basic human rights doctrine could also be the result of the spotty dissemination of human rights discourse by NGOs and government agencies or part of the ghostly nature of state (and, in this case, nonstate) entities in the barrios. Even in cases where people have had some exposure to human rights concepts, their knowledge remains partial and unintegrated into their lived experience. In describing human rights, these people seem to struggle for words to explain what they have been told, demonstrating a lack of deep connection with the ideas. As in the case of the Centro's human rights workshops described in chapter 2, people's participation in these information sessions is often in response to solicitation, with the promise of other benefits (knitting lessons, in the case of the Centro; a free toothbrush from the NGO in Mineros San Juan; and so on) being the principal attraction. But the utility of such trainings is dubious. For example, doña Birgith, a patient, earnest woman with five children, participated in a human rights training session that a Bolivian NGO organized at the school in Uspha Uspha Central. From this experience, she understands human rights to be about using state institutions to resolve local problems:

> *Tell me, doña Birgith, have you ever heard talk of human rights?*
> BIRGITH: Yes, down below [in a neighboring barrio] they explained them to us. They come to the schoolhouse every year when there are meetings.
>
> *And what did they say there?*
> BIRGITH: They said that we shouldn't fight, and if your husband hits you a lot you have to go to the family protection [Brigada de Protección a la Familia, a unit of the national police force], like that.
>
> *Oh, really?*
> BIRGITH: You have to go there, they told us.
>
> *Ah.*
> BIRGITH: Drunks shouldn't fight either, they told us.
>
> *Yes. Tell me, did they say that delinquents have human rights, did they tell you that?*
> BIRGITH: No one should order them to be killed, only the police.[21]

One can imagine from this conversation that the content of these human rights trainings often turns to the problem of lynching, as activists try to discourage barrio residents from taking the law into their own hands. With lynching being quite common in the barrios of the southern zone, many human rights groups see themselves as obligated to try to intervene to stop lynching violence, encouraging barrio residents to use state institutions like the police, the courts, and the Defensoría del Pueblo to resolve their conflicts. Given the profound mistrust that many barrio residents have of these institutions and the law in general, however, the suggestion that they rely on them for support makes residents very skeptical of those who make such recommendations. Instead, "human rights" comes to be understood as yet another bogus instrument intended to pacify the people of the margins without doing anything substantial to resolve their complaints about insecurity. Indeed, the fact that so much of the discussion around human rights in Cochabamba now focuses on lynching and its prevention means that the concept of human rights is raised predominantly in reference to the behavior of local people. People who lynch are viewed as violators of others' human rights, in a way that puts barrio residents—even the innocent bystanders and the critics of lynching—on the defensive against the outsiders who clearly fail to appreciate the difficulties of local reality. As doña Birgith's comments suggest, the notion of human rights also calls into question the authority of the paterfamilias, challenging male supremacy in the home by condemning domestic violence and promoting the intervention of the police to resolve such matters. This is extremely risky terrain, and activists who venture onto it tend to push both men and women into a defense of male dominance and the appropriateness of physical punishment to control the behavior of wives and children.

Coupled with public denunciations of human rights by the police like those described above, such instances promote a suspicion of human rights, which many barrio residents regard as antagonistic to their interests and goals. Much of their animosity is directed against the Congreso de Derechos Humanos de Cochabamba, which is known locally as simply Derechos Humanos (Human Rights). Perhaps because of this colloquialism, many people mentally conflate the transnational discourse of rights with this individual organization, and in local conversation it is often difficult to distinguish criticism of the institution (Derechos Humanos) from criticism of human rights more generally (derechos humanos). For example, doña Irma said: "Yes, I've heard of human rights. Human rights when it is convenient for them, but when it's not convenient, Derechos Humanos/derechos humanos becomes deaf, no?"[22] In a similar way, the concept of derechos is very much associated with the state, further contributing to vecinos' wariness of the whole idea of rights. In Spanish, the word "derecho" means "right" but is also used to mean "law," the latter being the object of extreme mistrust in the out-lawed barrios of Cocha-bamba.[23] This linguistic mixture again produces a conflation in which derechos are something that properly belongs to the state or its corrupt functionaries, rather than to individual citizens or human beings. For example, the government office that processes all paperwork for the land-legalization trámites is called the Department of Property Rights, or De-rechos Reales for short. And the office of Derechos Reales is a total chaos— until the late 2000s most of the records were not even computerized, and bored, surly bureaucrats would have to sort through piles of papers to man-ually handle individual claims. Even the *subalcalde* himself—the municipal official in charge of the entire urban district of which Uspha Uspha is a part—described Derechos Reales to me as "*terrible*,"[24] an evaluation echoed by any barrio resident who has had the misfortune of having to deal with it. The idea of "derechos" itself, unfortunately, acquires a taint from this asso-ciation, emblematic of both the state-imposed burdens that local people regularly confront and the state's own apparent lack of interest in helping people to respond to these burdens—out-lawing in the double sense in which I earlier defined it.

Given this range of associations, many barrio residents condemn De-rechos Humanos, the rights-promoting entity, which is made to stand for all the problems that human rights apparently allow in questions of se-curity. Derechos Humanos (i.e., the Congreso), like other institutions, is understood as having abandoned the people of the barrios while defend-ing the rights of the criminals: "Derechos Humanos, these institutions," said a resident of Concordia, "they do nothing for the poor family, for the distant barrios."[25] Similarly, the Defensoría del Pueblo does not offer sup-port to barrio residents: "It's the other way around, they are in favor of the maleantes."[26] Many barrio residents regard representatives of Derechos Humanos in the same way that they regard the police: as accomplices of thieves, who protect the rights of individuals facing incarceration and punishment. Some people appreciate the irony of this situation:

FIRST WOMAN: Last week a señor, my neighbor, took his car out of the garage to wash it. He left it out for five minutes, and it was stolen. And this señor worked for Derechos Humanos, those who defend the delinquents! They robbed him, in five minutes they robbed him.

SECOND WOMAN: He deserved it, no?[27]

Others describe human rights and social service NGOs, even those devoted to serving the poor, as creating social imbalances that favor the criminal class. Such evaluations rely on a Manichaean moral calculus—a familiar staple of the security paradigm—which divides the world into good and evil, the deserving and the undeserving, and arranges these categories in an oppositional and exclusionary relationship to one another. According to a resident of Concordia, "Derechos Humanos is very disconnected, there is no usable system. [They are] for the delinquents, their systems are completely for them, not for the citizen who supports his family and works hard. It is not for the honest citizen. For him who gets locked up, for the delinquent, who sometimes they let out after eight hours. So what guarantee is there for the honest, hardworking, humble citizen?"[28] Similarly, in the interview cited below, the "antisocials" referred to are *cleferitos*, glue-sniffing street children who live by petty crime, often robbing market vendors in the Cancha, and who are frequently the targets of police and resident reprisals. Though they are often beaten, harassed, and sometimes executed in extrajudicial killings (either by vigilantes or in covert police actions), the cleferitos are characterized in this informant's testimony as constituting a privileged class, who are rewarded by human rights defenders for their delinquency. This privileging of the bad over the good, the man said, "is one thing that has to change. A clear example: The antisociales that are in the street, there is an NGO . . . where they provide these antisociales with food, they provide them with clothing, health care, they provide them with everything. Turns out that this NGO, to have thirty or forty cleferitos, they go to the Cancha and recruit them. 'Come on, I'm going to rehabilitate you.' . . . There has to be a total change. These kids who want to reform have to make their living by the sweat of their brow. If you want to eat, you have to work."[29]

Barrio leaders and intellectuals, articulating more sophisticated political ideologies, point to the evident link between human rights NGOs and the system of global capitalism to call into question the goals of Derechos Humanos and similar organizations. In the town of Vinto, a short distance outside of Cochabamba City, a group of local leaders and MAS party members explained that while Derechos Humanos activists do advocate for the rights of working people in Bolivia, ultimately they must be seen as "accomplices of capitalism."[30] One leader's testimony echoed the critique of institutional welfarism offered by some of the Congreso activists themselves:

> Derechos Humanos also is part of the system—that is, they try to humanize the capitalist system but they don't try to destroy it. . . . Take the Communist Party as an ideal, as an example, no? The Communist Party tried to educate or raise the consciousness of the people so that they could take power. Has Derechos Humanos, as defender of human rights, ever thought of doing that? . . . Or have they stuck only with providing welfare services? Because what Derechos Humanos does is welfarism. . . . And the Defensoría del Pueblo, what is that? It is a state institution that precisely tries to "humanize capitalism," in quotes. And what does that mean? To be an accomplice.[31]

This speaker points to the Defensoría del Pueblo as evidence that human rights law and language, intended to protect citizens from the state, have been effectively incorporated into the state itself. It is interesting to note in this testimony—by populist party members and activists in Bolivian social movements—the condemnation of transnational human rights discourse, regarded here as a collaborator with the state and transnational capital, even as these individuals are liable to use human rights language in their protests against neoliberalism and state policy on natural resources.

The Violence of Human Rights

In January 2003, the body of Jerry Rodríguez, also known as El Ruso (the Russian), was found lying in a gutter on the outskirts of Cochabamba. El Ruso had been shot seven times, in a manner that police would describe as "execution style."[32] In the preceding months, El Ruso had become somewhat infamous in Cochabamba as a poster boy for the supposed failure of Bolivia's New Penal Procedural Code, enacted in 2001. The New Code was intended to replace the former inquisitorial system—which, due to basic deficiencies in its operation, accorded to police the liberty to (among other things) arrest and detain criminal suspects indefinitely and without leveling formal charges. The procedural guarantees of the New Code mandated greater police attention to the presumption of innocence and severely restricted the measures that police formerly used to extract confessions from detainees, typically including actual or threatened torture or other violence. Given the national police force's low budget, lack of training, and widespread corruption, as well as the relatively small number of police officers on the streets in Cochabamba, the requirements for detention imposed under the New Code are difficult to satisfy, and criminal suspects are frequently released (many people say) for lack of evidence. According to the daily newspaper *Los Tiempos*, El Ruso was "one of the delinquents who benefited most from the New Penal Procedural Code (just this [past] year he was in and out of jail on more than ten occasions)."[33] A few hours after the discovery of El Ruso's corpse, a *Los Tiempos* reporter received an anonymous phone call from someone claiming responsibility for the murder. The caller was a representative of Triple C (Ciudadanos Contra el Crimen, or Citizens against Crime), a group of urban residents willing to take the law into their own hands to clean up the streets of Cochabamba. For this vigilante group, the motivation was not only to protect themselves against crime, but also to protest the so-called rights of delinquents supposedly protected by the New Code. "We are fed up," the caller told the journalist, "with the robberies of our vehicles going unsolved, and we decided to undertake a cleansing (*limpieza*) against those delinquents who obtain their freedom after being detained."[34]

As this case illustrates, individuals and groups around Cochabamba exhibit a high level of intolerance for the rights of accused criminals, and they sometimes express in violence their frustration with what they consider to be the leniency of criminal laws. The New Code (first introduced in 1999 by the Banzer administration, in an effort to bring Bolivian law more in line with international, rights-based standards) is a particular target of local criticism. In many ways a landmark effort in the country, the New Code was the first real attempt at judicial reform in the democratic era. Based on fundamental values of transparency, equity, and enforcement of constitutional guarantees, the New Code tries to bring the operations of the judicial system under a rule of law founded on respect for basic human rights; it provides for habeas corpus, prohibits preventive detention of accused criminals, and requires that a complaint (*denuncia*) be filed before the suspect can be judicially processed. Not surprisingly, the incomplete adoption of the New Code in the context of Bolivia's profound social and economic problems has not resulted in comprehensive judicial reform. However, the New Code itself has become a scapegoat for all manner of social ills. It is the target of much official and popular criticism in Cochabamba, and the rights it guarantees to accused criminals are widely regarded as obstacles to security in the marginal barrios. For example, asked to identify when the incidence of crime in Cochabamba began to worsen, one informant replied: "Since they began to implement the New Penal Procedural Code, it began to grow. Why? One, you can't detain him [the suspect] for very long. Two, we don't have definitive proof [of guilt]. So it is on this basis that delinquency is growing and growing with greater intensity."[35]

In particular, many regard the New Code's elimination of preventive detention from Bolivian law as a serious obstacle to keeping delinquents off the streets. The New Code has come under particular fire from the police, who claim that without preventive detention it is impossible for them to do their jobs and that they are forced to release detainees back onto the streets in the absence of evidence, which the underresourced police claim they are unable to provide. In this way, the police encourage the perception that requiring proof of culpability limits their effectiveness and compromises citizen security. This critique is also expressed by some barrio residents who, despite their hatred and mistrust of the police, find themselves echoing the self-exculpatory line of the police. A resident of Juan Pablo II, for example, stated that when they catch a thief, "the police arrive and take him away, and as there is no denuncia made, what is going to happen? They will take him [to the station] to process him, the citizen with all these rights, he can be detained only for eight hours investigating what kind of crime he has committed. Then with this proof, the denuncia, he can be judged, but if not [without the denuncia], nothing happens and they let him go. But you all know that that right he has, of being detained only eight hours and being freed if there is no denuncia, that is what is happening."[36] Another resident of the same barrio added: "Human rights support the delinquent. Even when he is caught red-handed, he has his rights; they give him a guarantee, and the delinquent is out. Meanwhile they investigate, it being a flagrant case, and if there is no denunciation then nothing happens." Many barrio residents complain (as in the case of El Ruso) that even if they turn a criminal suspect over to the police for prosecution, all too often these individuals are quickly back on the street, owing either to police corruption (that is, an officer accepts a bribe to free the prisoner) or to the law itself, which requires the presentation of evidence to continue to detain a suspect.

Human rights defenders like the staff members of the Congreso are particularly demonized by both state officials and ordinary citizens for their efforts to ensure that suspected criminals are prosecuted according to the dictates of the Bolivian legal code. Human rights activists in Cochabamba have been forceful campaigners for the New Code, and they often take it upon themselves to ensure that police respect the eight-hour limit on detention, after which time they must file charges or release the suspect. Though only one small part of what human rights is meant to include, this advocacy for the rights of detainees has led to suspicion of and contempt for all human rights, and human rights promoters in general. As suggested in the previous section of this chapter, in the barrios of Cochabamba, human rights advocates are widely perceived to defend the delinquents, leading residents to view the advocates as enemies of law-abiding citizens. Some, like Silvio Lopez, the dirigente of District 8, point to a sort of conspiracy of local institutions as the cause of barrio insecurity, suggesting that human rights give criminals unfair advantages, while affording no protection to innocent victims. From his perspective, the thieves always return to rob again "because there is no authority that defends the citizen. Many times the police, the justice,[37] defend the delinquent. Who knows how many times they [the delinquents] have mistreated [people], robbing—who knows, maybe even killing. But who does anything for the vecino? But when the delinquents are mistreated, everybody reacts: Derechos Humanos, the police, the justice. He can only be detained for eight hours; the next day he is free."[38]

Another negative interpretation of rights is that they permit certain liberties that are inappropriate to Bolivian reality, another way of framing crime and social deviance. Barrio residents sometimes blame rights and basic legal protections for the escalation of crime and delinquency in Bolivia, owing to the leniency with which children are supposedly treated nowadays. In some people's understanding (reflecting the temporal ideology discussed in chapter 5 in reference to community justice), rights today allow children to misbehave, disrespect their elders, and basically disregard local standards of decency as they pursue malicious mischief and crime. In the same way that modern law and the ordinary justice system are seen as representing a decline from the traditional justice of the countryside that people envision as part of an older community justice system, so the idea of rights is believed to have undermined traditional forms of parenting and the values once espoused, thus creating a generation of unmanageable, delinquent children. A dirigente from Uspha Uspha Central put it this way:

> Sometimes I think that the laws are not well planned, and children are not being well raised. The laws say you have to respect the child, you can't touch him. On the bus, too, you can't sit down before them. They do anything they want, you can't touch them, so they are becoming more rebellious, more protected. If one wants to call attention to this or to how in the old days they would use a whip, "No, I'm going to go complain [to the authorities]." So in this way the children are growing up poorly, spoiled; they can do whatever they want; they have no fear. Before, we [as children] were very afraid, they [our parents] would beat us with a whip, but there was fear, more discipline. . . . [The law] clearly defends the child, the adolescent, he can't be touched, he can only be verbally corrected. So it is because of that, I believe, that the delinquency is mounting.[39]

Such ideas are not uncommon in the barrios, where people view poor parenting and the expansion of rights as culpable in the rise of delinquency in Bolivia.[40] Even don Miguel, a strong believer in the importance of human rights, shares this view and the temporal ideology it implies. In the past, he said, "they were much stricter than they are now, no? Because now there is so much liberty. But before, in my epoch, children didn't have the rights that they have now."[41]

As these comments imply, some barrio residents advocate for the state taking a mano dura approach to crime control so as to make the barrios secure. These individuals understand the laws to be overly protective of the delinquent and too weak to deter repeat offenders. One man, said: "It would be better if the rules of the police were stronger to scare off the rateros, to give us confidence in the police."[42] Another man echoed this sentiment, expressing the desire to "reform the laws," code words for allowing for greater police latitude in the use of violence against criminal suspects: "I believe that we have to reform our laws. . . . I don't know if Derechos Humanos—who they want to defend, but . . . there are more advantages for the delinquent than there are for the citizen. Everybody knows it, they know how it is. That's especially the case in the periurban barrios. Now we are impotent."[43] Another vecino put it this way: "Why do [things happen] like this? Because [the delinquents] know there is no law. If there was law, at least they would respect it. Where is it, in India? They put a rapist in the plaza, and they cut off his balls with an axe."[44] One barrio resident, himself a police officer, condemned the New Code for limiting the investigative powers of the police and hence jeopardizing the security of the populace. At the same time, he reiterated the belief that delinquents receive more services and protections than do ordinary citizens, in this case in terms of their rights to legal counsel:

> The policeman is a common citizen like us, the only difference being that he wears a uniform and complies with what the law says, nothing more. Because beyond that he can do no more, because he doesn't have power like before. Before at least with a stick, or with kicks, the policeman could make the delinquent talk, and later he recovered. But now, no, even the worst delinquent—we can't touch a hair on his head, so says the law. These are exactly the reasons given by Derechos Humanos, the Defensor del Pueblo, Defensa Pública [the public defender's office]. For the delinquent, I tell you honestly, I think they bring four or five professionals, but for the common citizen they don't provide a single professional. So there are circumstances in which the citizen has to be prepared, he has to know the law.[45]

Again, both the discourse and the institution of human rights are seen as antagonists, obstacles to justice that not only contribute to delinquency but, remarkably, are described as driving extrajudicial violence. For example, one young barrio resident attributed the violence of lynching to the actions of human rights defenders: "The police are always on the side of the thief. And so is Derechos Humanos. Derechos Humanos is always involved. When a thief is caught, we lock him up. In less than eight hours, there is Derechos Humanos. Derechos Humanos arrives, they investigate: for what, for what reason is he there? If there is no plaintiff, then no one can accuse him. They take him out, and right away the offender is back on the street. So for that reason I believe, more than anything else I say, we poor people, we want to make justice with our own hands."[46]

In these commentaries, local discourse reveals itself to be a hybrid (Merry 2006, 46), a complex interweaving of both positive and negative valuations of the transnational discourse of human rights. Though often restricting human rights in its totality to a narrow focus on the rights of the detained, local understandings also can demonstrate a broader conceptualization of rights, one more frequently promoted by transnational and national rights advocates. Below, the testimony of another barrio resident reveals the hybrid nature of the rights discourse in this context. On the one hand, the very idea of "rights" is stigmatized, an avowal of the commonly held belief that human rights equal rights for criminals. While this belief is clearly operative here, on the other hand, the speaker simultaneously reveals the penetration and local appropriation of the positive, progressive rights discourse, deployed here to characterize the difficulties facing poor rural and urban Bolivians, who are neglected and abandoned by the neoliberal state and its allies, the transnational and domestic NGOs. When asked to explain who is responsible for this state of affairs, this speaker points to the international NGOs at work in Bolivia, invoking a rights discourse to argue, in a backhanded way, against certain basic human rights assumptions:

> In some respects it's the NGOs [that are at fault]. For example, the Defensor del Pueblo, or rather the officers of DNI [Defensa del Niño Internacional], for example—it's an NGO, isn't it? It isn't administered by the state. It happens that some cleferito is mistreated, and the DNI automatically is called, right? . . . Yes, the defensor, DNI, for example, always protects the rights of the cleferito. And the children of peasants who are without food, don't they have the same rights as the cleferito? *We all have the same rights.* The DNI, for example, if they want to protect the rights of the child, they have to protect all children equally, not only those who sniff glue, who do harm to the population. . . . In other words, there is not a fair administration of justice in this respect, it is more on the side of the wrongdoer in this case.[47]

This perspective on rights is shared by a range of barrio residents, many of whom appreciate the importance of the rights that they themselves are denied, even as they complain of the unfair enforcement of rights for detained criminals. Here, residents reveal themselves to have a much fuller understanding of the meaning and potential of rights than they previously admitted to having, and they emerge as active vernacularizers themselves, translating rights into the local context of insecurity with which they must daily contend. Within this context, barrio residents engage in a moral calculus to determine who is worthy of rights, measured by the quality of their character and their motivations in committing various acts. Rights, then, become articulated locally as properly belonging to some people but not others—a departure from the universalizing norms of transnational conceptions of human rights. Some people believe that delinquents should not have any rights, that they have forfeited their rights as a result of their delinquency. Josias, for example, stated: "I think—it seems to me that here at least, [the delinquent] shouldn't have any rights. But those who have money rule, they even control the police, the cop is submissive to the thief, because the thief has money."[48] Implicit here is the suggestion that rights are for sale, available to the thief who has money and can purchase them, but not to poor barrio residents. Others agree, though they can draw subtle and sometimes contradictory distinctions in their evaluations. For example, one woman expressed the view that delinquents, like barrio residents, are human beings, and so naturally enjoy a certain basic right to life. Nevertheless, when asked if delinquents should have rights, she responded: "I don't think so. They shouldn't have them, they make people cry. I don't know—I am very cruel to say that."[49] Doña Pacífica said: "But what right should they have? The right to rob? Of course not. Obviously they should have the right to live, they shouldn't be killed, [but] should they be punished? You punish them, but they don't seem to learn."[50] Here, doña Pacífica denies the delinquent his legal rights while sparing his life, drawing the line at lynching as a response to insecurity. Other people are even less severe and take the motives of the delinquent into consideration. They distinguish between the thief who robs as a way of life from the one who robs out of necessity, to feed himself or his family. Some believe that in the latter case, the thief deserves to have rights, perhaps because his evident poverty evokes some sense of shared humanity. But in most cases, even when denouncing rights as protections for criminals, people still recognize rights as a powerful discourse of which they, too, wish to partake. Said doña Dora: "And what—don't we have rights? Just as they [delinquents] have rights, we too have rights. That's why I say that the judge should be—should respect our rights."[51]

The hybrid discourse that joins security and rights, often in contradictory ways, combines with the insecurity of life on the margins to create strong contradictions for barrio residents (compare Burrell 2010). This is particularly evident in regard to lynching, whose violence is interpreted through the optics of both security and rights. Lynching obviously represents an assault on the rights of individuals living in a supposedly free and democratic society—a point not lost on many barrio residents. For many, the fact that lynching and harsh police practice disproportionately affect the poor is cause for them to mistrust the state, the police, even their neighbors and acquaintances. But while they reproduce the security discourse in interviews and private conversations, many barrio residents also express strong reservations about the ends to which security practice seems to be leading, and the means that people (themselves included) are willing to employ. Indeed, as explored in chapters 4 and 5, many people express grave misgivings about lynching violence, even as they sympathize with the conditions and the mind-set that produce it, precisely because of the human rights violations that it obviously entails. Although rights may be to blame for lynchings in the opinion of some barrio residents, for others, rights are precisely what make lynching inhumane. This contradiction is part of the hybrid nature of human rights in the marginal barrio, a vernacular form that can at once both sanction violence and limit its most extreme expressions. Said a barrio resident, reflecting on this conundrum:

> So whom can you trust? Not the police, not private security, I don't know . . . I don't know whom I can trust. . . . I think that this then leads to something else, to lynching, for example. That to me seems like a crime but—that is to say . . . I don't know if it is justified or not, but more or less it has a basis. Everybody is fed up, sick and tired of seeing their things taken that they have earned with so much effort. Then the only thing that they can do is try to make justice with their own hands. But that also is a crime, and a grave one, too, because we are violating the rights of another person.[52]

Conclusion

In a world that prefers security to justice, there is loud applause whenever justice is sacrificed on the altar of security. The rite takes place on the streets. Every time a criminal falls in a hail of bullets, society feels some relief from the disease that makes it tremble. The death of each lowlife has a pharmaceutical effect on those living the high life. The word "pharmacy" comes from *pharmakos*, the Greek name for humans sacrificed to the gods in times of crises.

—EDUARDO GALEANO, QUOTED IN NANDINI SUNDAR, "TOWARD AN ANTHROPOLOGY OF CULPABILITY"

My analysis in this chapter puts a finer point on Galeano's poignant observation. As I have shown, it is not only those "living the high life" but also the poor and marginalized—those who typically find themselves on the receiving end of state violence—who support state programs (formal and unofficial) of la mano dura, which seek to justify expanded violence, surveillance, and control. The familiar dichotomies break down in the climate of pervasive fear and insecurity that characterizes barrio life, described in detail in the chapters of this ethnography. The poor line up with the rich to administer violence to the poor, or to advocate for its administration; men and women alike are capable of brutal force and acts of extreme vengeance; civil society does not restrain the state or protect against its abuses, but spurs the state on to greater acts of violence, undermining the very limits put in place to moderate state excess. Meanwhile human rights, the transnational discourse of Third World resistance, becomes demonized as antagonistic to the well-being of the citizenry, its very transnationality being a further source of its delegitimation in the minds of those skeptical of perceived threats to national sovereignty.

As I stated at the beginning of this chapter, a powerful irony inherent in this situation is that even as some kinds of rights are demonized, the discourse of rights itself continues to provide Bolivian social movements with a powerful platform from which to articulate demands on the state and to garner international attention and support, and for the state itself to defend its stance on such matters as indigenous autonomy and public investment. Struggles over control of natural resources, access to land, political representation, self-determination for indigenous communities, production of coca—all are framed within a discourse of human rights that is both transnational and deeply local, deployed on the ground in ways that are very specific to Bolivia. But on issues of crime and social violence, as this chapter has suggested, it is the right to security that is paramount and that justifies the suspension of other kinds of rights, especially the rights of detained criminals. It is as though there were two categories of rights: one set that social movements embrace and that promise to transform society through the promotion of justice and equality; and another set of rights—the rights of the accused—that are antagonistic to the first set, harmful to the realization of justice and thus potentially disposable. Imagined as oppositional rather than part and parcel of a single human rights regime, these two sets of rights confront one another in the struggle for security, justifying a stronger and more repressive state to foster their realization. Even the social movements are complicit in this: the MAS party's electoral platform in the 2005 presidential campaign articulated the vision of citizen security that is today so prominent in Bolivia, promising to "modify the penal laws, to guarantee the effective sanction of delinquents," "to install [police] control posts in the barrios," to increase the police presence in the nation's principal cities, and "to utilize new technologies to combat crime" (MAS 2005).

For scholars of human rights in transnational perspective, what is perhaps most significant about the predicament of violence and insecurity described in this chapter is the way in which the discourses of security and rights are not merely oppositional but are being reworked in the barrios of Cochabamba into a single hybrid discourse that accounts for and perpetuates violent practice. Many parties have a hand in shaping this discourse, suggesting the need to look beyond activists to other groups in society who also play a translator role, taking the global discourse of human rights into new arenas where it is reworked and redeployed in ways that can run counter to the best intentions of domestic and international activists and NGOs. The consequences of this process for human rights as a language of liberation bear watching, in Bolivia and elsewhere, as the global security crisis continues to unfold.

7 | An Uncertain Anthropology

In the chapters of this book I have cast an ethnographic eye on the questions of security and insecurity, and their meanings and manifestations, in the context of the marginal barrios of Cochabamba's far southern zone. I began by framing security as a problem that is both global and local in scope, examining some of the diverse and shifting meanings of "security" at the national and international levels. I also explored the changing nature of "security" in the context of neoliberalism with particular attention to Latin America—where, over the last thirty years, security has undergone a change in emphasis from state security and public order under the dictatorships to a concern with citizen security and the effort to bring peace and stability to the national population in the democratic era. But these efforts have been fragmentary and incomplete, compromised by ineffective systems of law, policing, and judicial administration and the general inability or unwillingness of the state to commit fully to its official concern with citizen security. In the marginal barrios of Cochabamba, a sense of insecurity predominates: insecurity is the frame through which people experience their daily reality, and the object they attempt to transform through the various measures that they adopt and employ in their localities. Insecurity was also the object of my own interventions (chapter 2), as I explored the possibilities of an engaged anthropology to make life more stable and secure for the people with whom I worked and collaborated on this project.

In chapters 3 and 4, I provided a "thick" description of insecurity in the barrios of Uspha Uspha. Chapter 3 explored the many effects that insecurity has on the lives of barrio residents. In particular, I focused on the ways in which the state at once produces insecurity for residents while subjecting them to various forms of ordering and legalization, in an attempt to make the barrios and their populations more legible to state authorities and institutions. But it is through these very techniques of ordering—the legalization of land claims, for example, and the formalization of identities through the carnet—that what I call the phantom state generates insecurity, a process of out-lawing that gives this book its title. People left outside the law's protections are also problematically positioned as illegal; they are excluded from the security that a rule of law can and should provide, while recognized by state law only as outlaws who have failed to conform to state prescriptions for ordering their property and identities. Barrio residents are out-lawed, a situation that they interpret as abandonment. The state, they claim, has left them to fend for themselves in facing problems of crime and violence, so they must seek alternative ways to solve their problems. Chapter 4 documented these responses to insecurity, identifying three principal techniques or instruments that people deploy: alert watchfulness, reliance on local leadership, and lynching violence. In my analysis of these three approaches, I tried to show that while the lynching is the most obviously "spectacular" response to insecurity, it is but one technique among several that barrio residents adopt. People in the barrios are deeply ambivalent about violence as a method for producing security, and rather than the stereotypical lynch mob, what one finds on closer examination is a group of people divided over the appropriateness and effectiveness of lynching violence, sometimes desperately in search of alternative approaches that would allow them to avoid violent acts.

It is in this that the role of the barrio president, or dirigente, is so critical, as I showed in chapter 5. In a context in which community justice has emerged as a controversial political issue, lynching violence is sometimes explained as an urban manifestation of rural traditions for making justice, appearing in the marginal barrios in the absence of state law. This claim, sometimes offered up by barrio residents attempting to understand their own behavior in light of this national political movement, is rejected by state officials, in part because urban forms of justice making do not conform with the official, romanticized vision of community justice as it supposedly exists in the indigenous communities of the Bolivian countryside. But, as chapter 5 showed, even rural indigenous people and their techniques of justice making fail to conform with the official vision. Instead, in both rural and urban forms of what might be called "community justice," people rely on spontaneity and creativity to respond to the legal problems that arise in their communities. This is particularly the case in the urban barrio, where neither a formal state nor a traditional indigenous legal system can be said to exist, and where people rely on the leadership of their local dirigentes to resolve conflicts and crises. In such a setting, I argued, the ability of the dirigente to provide creative, pragmatic solutions to problems that arise—his skill in assembling a legal bricolage—is more critical to the resolution of local conflicts than the implementation of some coherent legal system within a broader, legally plural society. This claim runs counter to understandings of barrio justice as constituting some kind of separate legality, parallel to or nested within a more formal system of state justice. Instead, I contend that what we see here are actually hybrids, locally manufactured solutions to emerging problems constructed from the remembered, imagined, and partially understood fragments of what might be or once have been systems, but that in the present are legal assemblages whose purpose answers to the demands of the moment.

The importance of creativity is a central theme that runs through the chapters of this book. Local creativity and imagination are vital to the resolution of legal problems and the deployment of techniques for making justice, and creativity also figures prominently in the ways in which people understand and respond to matters of human rights in the barrios. Chapter 6 examined the conflict that emerges as the transnational discourses of security and human rights collide in the space of the marginal barrio. Here the efforts of various sets of human rights translators play a key role, as they vernacularize the transnational language and meanings of human rights by fitting them to local understandings, each trying to advance his or her political or practical objectives through the promotion or, alternatively, demonization of human rights. The outcomes of this vernacularization are sometimes in direct opposition to the goals of the transnational human rights regime: human rights can appear to be an obstacle to security rather than a key to its realization, and people sometimes authorize violence, surprisingly, as a way of defending their right to security. Nevertheless, the ways in which transnational human rights language and ideas are locally vernacularized points to the creative use that differently positioned actors make of them, and the consequences that these different vernacularizations have for social justice and human rights at the moment of lived daily experience. This chapter also expands our understanding of the kinds of groups that might be considered to be human rights vernacularizers, showing that these may include not only the human rights activists and NGOs familiar from other ethnographic work on human rights localization, but also public institutions and individuals like the police, and even ordinary citizens.

The ethnography contained in these chapters enables us to identify what I call the absent presence of the state and state law on the margins of its domain. In contrast to the claims of many—including scholars, media observers, NGOs, and barrio residents themselves—this ethnography reveals that far from being completely absent, the state is in fact significantly present in the barrios of the urban periphery. In its many requirements and restrictions on land legalization, individual citizenship, and the disposal of dead bodies, for example, the state is continually present in the lives of barrio residents, creating forms of ordering that render people more legible to the state's gaze but that do little to enhance their lived sense of stability and safety. The state and state law thus do not contribute to the security of local life; in fact, they foster a pervasive sense of insecurity, which animates a host of dispositions and responses.

Another key thread that weaves together the chapters of this ethnography is the question of uncertainty. In a fundamental way, insecurity is about uncertainty, the sense that the world is unpredictable and out of control, and that danger haunts one's every step. Recognizing the existence of that uncertainty is key to understanding the state and its relationship to security, another important theme that has run throughout the preceding chapters.

The Meanings of Security and the Governmental State

One slow afternoon during my fieldwork, I visited the *hemeroteca*, the municipal newspaper archive on the corner of avenues Heroinas and 25 de mayo in downtown Cochabamba, to peruse back issues of one of the local papers, *Opinión*. Just out of curiosity, I began noting usages of the word *seguridad* (security or safety) in the headlines of articles between the years 1998 and 2001. Although in no way systematic, the survey was revealing. I found more than forty different contexts in which the term "security" was used, to characterize an enormous variety of issues. These included economic security (January 5, 1998), highway security (January 18, 1998), aviation security (October 18, 1998), flood security (October 27, 1998), bank security (January 21, 1999), vehicular security (May 4, 1999), student security (May 5, 1999), security of the streets (May 15, 1999), juridical security (May 22, 1999), security of domestic workers (August 12, 1999), security of wells (September 27,1999), church security (September 27, 1999), security in new construction sites (March 16, 2000), blood security (April 3, 2000), food security (May 18, 2000), labor security (May 29, 2000), social security (October 27, 2000), health security (November 16, 2000), biosecurity (December 8, 2000), and carnival security (February 19, 2001). Most of these usages occurred in reference to the Bolivian state's efforts to contend with problems in these fields so as to manage, stabilize, and establish order for the Bolivian people. *Seguridad de sangre* (blood security or safety), for example, was about state efforts to protect the blood supply from HIV and other possible diseases, while *seguridad carnavalesca* (carnival security) was about maintaining order in the streets during the national *carnaval de Oruro*.

This vast array of references points to the proliferation of security as a frame for understanding a wide variety of social experiences, bracketed in terms of an avoidance of risk and a desire to maximize the well-being of the population. Security is both spatially and temporally oriented, addressing what might happen in any given setting or location. It pertains to "a series of possible events; it refers to the temporal and the uncertain, which have to be inserted within a given space" (Foucault 2007, 20). The apparatuses of security pattern the social milieus in which life unfolds, targeting not only individual bodies and selves but whole groups, even the "population"—which is itself the subject of state projects of governmentality. For Michel Foucault, governmentality refers to (among other things less relevant to the present discussion) "the rationalities and mentalities of governance and the range of tactics and strategies that produce social order. It focuses on the 'how' of governance (its arts and techniques) rather than the 'why' (its goals and values). Techniques of governmentality are applied to the art of governing the self as well as that of governing society" (Merry 2001, 18). Foucauldian approaches suggest the immanence of power, at once everywhere and nowhere, embedded in state forms like the law but also, less visibly, extant in the body politic. Power (state and otherwise) penetrates bodies and stimulates our own self-regulation. Government—"the conduct of conduct" for Foucault (quoted in C. Gordon 1991, 2) is about governance of self and others; it inculcates within individuals certain dispositions, ways of being in the world that are invisibly or imperceptibly shaped by power, that lead to the "responsibilization" of individual citizens so critical to the maintenance of a neoliberal social order (Rose 1996, 328). A key rubric here is security: the object of governmentality—theorists seem unable to resist the "why" of government—is "to ensure good and avert ill" (Rose 1996, 328), the creation of an order in which all can be safe and secure, defined in the broadest possible terms. Thus, Jonathan Inda notes that "political and other authorities have come to understand the work of governing as requiring them to act upon the particulars of human conduct so as to enhance the security, longevity, health, prosperity, and happiness of populations. All told, then, governmentality draws attention to all those strategies, tactics, and authorities—state and nonstate alike—that seek to mold conduct individually and collectively in order to safeguard the welfare of each and of all" (2005, 6).

Making security, then, is the work of the state in the "society of security" (Foucault 2007, 11), not just in Bolivia but worldwide. Globally, security has become a way of thinking about potential threats—to "our" community, economy, nation, beliefs, way of life—as well as a means of neutralizing them, subsuming under the single rubric of security (that is, securitizing) the vast and sundry domains of social, political, and economic life. Through the institutions and apparatuses of security, states can offer promises of safety and order to their populations in a range of areas. But never full guarantees: the security frame always maintains an element of possibility, a lingering doubt, so that the security quest is never fulfilled, and the state must be perpetually vigilant against new threats as they arise. Individuals and communities play a vital role in this securitization of society, particularly in a context of neoliberal governmentality, in which the state assigns responsibility for security to local actors. While the state polices society, society also polices itself: as in the famous model of the panopticon, we are never sure if we are being watched by external forces, and thus we become the monitors of our own selves (Foucault 1977). We order our lives according to dictates both imagined and imposed, and we live according to their injunctions.

In some ways, the Bolivian government's promotion of citizen security as a cornerstone of its contemporary politics can be understood as an effort to establish governmentality, to manage its population so as to produce order and safety for all. As discussed in chapter 1 and again in chapter 3, citizen security is generally understood across Latin America to refer to establishing the conditions within which national populations can live full and happy lives under a democratic rule of law, free from corruption and criminality and able to enjoy the full exercise of their citizenship rights. Others have defined it even more broadly to mean "a concern for quality of life and human dignity in terms of liberty, access to the market, and social opportunities" (Arriagada and Godoy 1999, 9). In terms of policing, the goal of citizen security has been described as being "to eliminate or at least reduce the possibilities of conflict or violence that produce victims and to offer the people broader assurances of moral and physical security that guarantee their lives and property" (Molina Viaña 2001, 6; see also Mollericona, Tinini, and Paredes 2007). In addition, citizen security is based on the principal that, in a democratic society, citizen participation is a crucial element in establishing security. Under this model, individual citizens and communities are charged with a shared responsibility for creating the conditions of their own security (Cardona Álvarez 2005). From a governmentality perspective, citizen security is about inculcating in subjects a willingness to subscribe to state forms of social ordering and to engage as participants in the project of policing of oneself and others to promote the common good. Individuals are encouraged to be watchful, adopting a vigilant disposition in the face of any and all possible threats that might emerge.

The discourse of citizen security has been central to the ongoing work of state formation in the society of security (Joseph and Nugent 1994). The state, in Bolivia as elsewhere in Latin America, has managed to define the security crisis as being entirely about crime and delinquency without engaging any of the broader problems that confront the population. Though supposedly pertaining to a range of protections intended to guarantee the population's safety and freedom, citizen security is in fact about policing and crime control (Ungar 2011). With rising crime rates in the country since the 1990s,[1] the Bolivian state has equated citizen security with protection from delinquency and has adopted this language to frame its efforts in this regard. Through five successive presidential administrations, neoliberal and postneoliberal alike, the state passed laws and issued decrees, creating new institutions and manage-

FIG. 9 A publicity photo distributed by the national police as part of a campaign promoting citizen security in Bolivia, n.d.

ment plans intended to strengthen policing and better fight the forces of delinquency in the country (see fig. 9). These plans typically included promises to increase the police presence on the streets of Bolivia's cities, to provide more resources for policing, and to encourage popular participation in the work of increasing security through such things as community policing, an idea imported from the United States via Argentina.

These promises, however, have not been realized in daily practice. Although "security is the work of all of us" remains a popular political mantra, few attempts have been made to involve citizens and communities directly in the work of policing, raising doubts about the governmentalization of security work and the extent to which citizens have been effectively responsibilized in this regard. The lack of a strong political and institutional commitment by the state to advance police reforms has meant that citizen security remains a talking point rather than a real national priority (Mollericona, Tinini, and Paredes 2007). Despite the changes in institutions and administration, little has changed in the way police do their work, maintaining pronounced tendencies toward centralization, bureaucracy, racism, corruption, and the use of violence as a technique of policing. Indeed, the use of force—what is often called la mano dura, the heavy hand of the state—remains part of the work of crime control, and it has become more widely accepted by a frightened population (Burrell 2008; Godoy 2006; Goldstein, Achá, Hinojosa, and Roncken 2007). The idea that citizen security should be about more than just crime control has not been seriously contemplated by the police or other state institutions; instead, "the repressive organs [of the government] have monopolized the 'securitization' of society by coopting the units, departments and bureaus of citizen security in the prefectures and municipalities."[2] And where the state lacks the resources and the will to police its population and extend access to the instruments of justice administration, it has simply withdrawn, allowing individuals and collectivities to fill the gap by providing their own forms of policing and justice making in their communities.

But such conditions are not confined to Bolivia, or even to Latin America. As I have discussed elsewhere (Goldstein 2005a), the incitement to adopt a "flexible" disposition vis-à-vis security—a willingness to take on the responsibilities of policing and resolving conflicts that otherwise might be the duty of the state—can be understood as part of the neoliberal transformation of society, in which the tasks of creating security devolve from institutions to individuals, willingly or unwillingly responsibilized to assume those duties. For residents of Cochabamba's marginal barrios, as the ethnography of chapter 4 details, this has become part of daily life, as they struggle to find ways to cope with the insecurity that they regularly confront. In doing so, the residents of Uspha Uspha's barrios show themselves to be fully incorporated into and representative of what is, in effect, a global culture of security and securitization, part of a global securityscape that includes a range of nation-states and national citizens. Rather than serving as exemplars of anomie and marginality or demonstrating their deviance from broader social norms, the fear, hypervigilance, and willingness to use violence that barrio residents express and practice instead suggest their conformity, as they fully embody the paranoid disposition of the neoliberal citizen, cultivated by states and civil societies worldwide. Just as riders of the New York City transit system and shoppers in a world of Walmarts are encouraged to "see something, say something" (United States Department of Homeland Security, Office of the Press Secretary 2010), residents of the marginal barrios are poised and alert, sounding an alarm when they see someone suspicious, doing their part to create "hometown security" in their OTBS (United States Department of Homeland Security, Office of Public Affairs 2011). And given the extent to which Bolivians, like citizens of other neoliberal democracies, have been exhorted to become responsible for their own social welfare, it makes perfect sense that barrio residents have taken on the duty of policing their own neighborhoods against crime (Goldstein 2005a; Harvey 2001). Far from making them deviants, the willingness of some barrio residents to pursue and punish rateros—the latest iteration of the spectral enemy within national society—demonstrates their cultural orthodoxy, as they embrace the call for a hard line and a heavy hand in dealing with malefactors and the disseminators of terror and aggression. The appalled reactions of so many commentators, both in Bolivia and abroad, to the excesses of lynching may in fact be motivated by their recognition, not of the alterity of these supposedly brutal and irrational actors, but of the uncomfortable similarity between their actions and the dominant ethos of the contemporary security society.

The discourse of citizen security, then, can be seen as contributing to the demonization of human and civil rights, as explored in chapter 6. Since the mid-1990s, the Bolivian state has issued numerous proclamations and decrees, creating a host of programs and initiatives intended to improve citizen security in Bolivia, without producing any discernible changes in the daily lives of most Bolivians. This could be interpreted as an example of state failure, an inability of the state to live up to its claims and responsibilities. But the closer one looks (and contrary to what governmentality theorists seem to suggest), the clearer it becomes that the state's principal objective is not the betterment and well-being of the population, but its own self-defense and self-perpetuation, and the establishment of a certain kind of order that limits state responsibility and preserves state authority. The Bolivian state does not operate to make the people of the marginal barrios feel more secure; instead, it functions to maintain a set of rather arbitrary laws and statutes with which residents must comply if they hope to achieve legal status and, ultimately, the rights of citizens. Rights in this context, then, can be seen to extend not from the basic guarantees of democratic society, but through compliance with state regulations and participation in the rituals of rule that are meant to establish public order and shape individual identities, part of the daily routines of state formation through which the moral regulation of society is, tentatively and temporarily, achieved (Corrigan and Sayer 1985). Rather than making citizens more secure, citizen security is about producing citizens as subjects of the security state, in which rights are protections unfairly given to antisocial elements who threaten the well-being of everyone.

From that perspective, the hostility to human rights that some barrio residents express (see chapter 6) is consistent with global security culture more generally. In the months following the 9/11 terrorist attacks in the United States and the ramping up of the Bush administration's Global War on Terror, social scientists found that Americans were very willing to surrender civil liberties in exchange for a heightened sense of security (D. Davis and Silver 2004). This willingness was encouraged through the establishment of military tribunals and the Guantánamo penitentiary and encoded in laws like the USA Patriot Act, which provided for the suspension of rights in times of security crisis, a state of exception justified as protecting the security and safety of the American public (Agamben 2005). This sense that rights are "too extravagant to endure" (Glasser and Siegel 1997) in times of insecurity is a fundamental aspect of security culture, one that is clearly at play in the perceptions of many barrio residents, who have come to understand rights and security as being inherently oppositional.[3] In the never-ending quest for security, in both local and global contexts, it would seem that rights must be perpetually postponed in the interests of keeping all of us safe.

Reassessing Security and Rights

Even as official discourses and practices of citizen security continue to define security in terms of protection from crime and delinquency, the broader inflections of citizen security offer the possibility of radical transformation. As it labors to establish the terms by which subjects construct identities and experience social reality through processes of moral regulation and quotidian administration (Nugent and Alonso 1994), the state continually offers the terms under which this same rule can be contested. This potential is clearly present in the case of citizen security, which—as we have seen—is originally and fundamentally about more than just policing. Throughout much of this ethnography, I have illustrated the ways in which barrio residents frame their experience in terms of the security paradigm, using the language of security to characterize their experiences and deploying the practices of watchfulness and even violence to extirpate the enemy within. But woven throughout this discourse are hints of transgression, implicit or explicit challenges to the conception of security that puts it in opposition to rights.

Given all the talk about security in Bolivia, it is not surprising that barrio residents' ideas and sentiments on the topic are, at times, contradictory. Having heard so much about security—in the news media, from government representatives and institutions, at public meetings, and the like—residents are well aware that citizen security is officially about crime control, and many of them share this perspective. But such a perspective also can clash with their own lived experience, which suggests that much more is needed to make them feel secure than just the elimination of delinquency. One man from Juan Pablo II was quite certain in offering this more expansive understanding: "Seguridad ciudadana means that we need everything in every respect. For example, in the area of nutrition, of our children, of robberies—it consists of all of these."[4] Other people talk about education, health care, and jobs using the language of citizen security as well. Even as don Fulgencio identifies criminality as the most significant source of local insecurity, for example, and equates security with crime control, he suggests that security might apply to other areas of local experience as well: "There is so much insecurity, insecurity in the area of health, physical insecurity, the security of our children, the security of our homes, the security of our families . . . but the security that we most lack is physical security, citizen security."[5] Fulgencio's statement is somewhat muddled, suggesting an uncertainty about what security might mean. This kind of murkiness about what security entails came through frequently in conversations with residents of the barrios of Uspha Uspha. As another resident of Juan Pablo II put it to us directly, in a manner that was both poignant and provocative: "In our case we want to know what security is. . . . For one thing it is health, for another robbery, the police— but you have to clarify for us what security is. You come here and we hear 'security,' but we don't know which security: health, robbery, the police."[6]

Don Fulgencio's statement, though retaining the state's reductive conception of citizen security as physical security, nevertheless points to an awareness that "security" means more than just crime control. With its references to health, children, and family, his statement reflects broader discourses of citizen security that also circulate in Bolivia and elsewhere in Latin America, though with less hegemonic potency than that of the state's "citizen security as crime control" discourse. Other people, including some local human rights promoters, work with a much broader understanding of what citizen security can mean; and though their presence in the barrios is highly problematic (a point discussed in chapter 6), these activists offer a distinct perspective on security that resonates strongly with barrio experience. Citizen-security-as-crime-control restricts to the bare minimum the range of rights that security is supposed to provide, a point that one activist of the Cochabamba Human Rights Congress observed: "We should not understand citizen security as just the protection of the right to life, or the right to private property, as it is understood by the police. Rather, it is something much more complete (*integral*). I think we should push so that the state permits, [so] that every citizen can have the possibility of fully realizing our fundamental rights. This means a decent wage, a job, a home—that you can walk freely in the street, that is, the full exercise of our fundamental rights in their entirety. From this perspective, that is what I understand citizen security to be."[7]

This more encompassing understanding of citizen security poses a direct challenge to the state in its efforts to restrict the meaning of security (and hence to limit the range of its interventions and responsibilities) to crime control. It suggests that security includes a much broader set of rights than the narrow conception entailed by the state's citizen security paradigm, and it challenges the postneoliberal state to take up its responsibility for ensuring those rights. The state's conception of citizen security, like the broader global security discourse of which it is part, inherently opposes security to rights, suggesting that in an insecure and uncertain world, rights are luxuries that society just cannot afford. In the society of security, rights must be postponed until such time as security can finally and reliably be established for the population. In contrast, the broader understanding of citizen security articulated above suggests that rights and security are not antithetical but complementary, even isomorphic. Without the fundamental rights of work, health, education, access to resources, and dignity, people like those in the barrios of Uspha Uspha cannot be secure. The state's job, this discourse suggests, is not just to control crime, but to guarantee to its subjects the full range of rights that can allow them to be truly secure in every aspect of their daily lives.

Uncertainty

At its root, security is about certainty. This is clear enough from the Spanish usage of the term "seguridad": it means both security in the conventional English sense of safety and certainty, as someone might offer a guarantee *con toda seguridad* (with absolute certainty). Security is also about order and hence predictability: seguridad can mean stability, firmness (as in a secure foothold or investment). When people in the barrios describe themselves and their spaces as insecure, they mean more than that there is a lot of crime there, with no reliable police or judicial presence to protect them from harm. The sense of vulnerability is compounded by the sense of risk that they constantly face by exposing themselves to the unknown or the unknowable, the dangerous presence that may or may not be waiting in the shadows (Moodie 2010).[8] The source of this danger is not just the maleficent semipresence, the spectrality, of the ratero, with his scarred face and hands perhaps waiting just outside one's door. Its source is in fact the whole social fabric of disorder that barrio residents perceive as characteristic of their lives on the urban periphery, which the state does not resolve but rather exacerbates. When they complain of the lack of police and, more than that, the lack of law and the absence of the state in their communities, what they are decrying is the absence of a force capable of providing order, rationality, stability, and predictability in their physical and social environments. Their efforts to embrace community justice, for example, can be understood in these terms as an attempt to establish some kind of order, a predictable, sanctioned response to insecurity, even if it is the imagined order of tradition, whose parameters they don't fully understand and that sometimes includes lethal violence. This violence, interpreted by outside observers as an indication of the chaos that characterizes these barrios, can in fact be better understood as an attempt to control chaos, a kind of order striving to be born amid the disorder that otherwise exists in local conditions of insecurity.

Anthropology, too, is about order. In our analyses of observed cultural realities, presented in the books and articles we produce from our fieldwork, we strive to impose our own kind of order on the chaos of daily life. The ethnography—neatly laid out in sections and chapters, each with its own synthetic headline—provides a structure through which we can comprehend the story the ethnographer tells, grasping the narrative that imposes a pattern over the messy sprawl of actually experienced life. Ethnographers, like states, understand ordering—turning chaos into legibility—to be a critical aspect of their function. In the stories we tell in our ethnographies, we as anthropologists provide coherence, an ordering of the inherently disorganized experience that is part of life's unfolding, and so render the world meaningful. This pertains not only to writing but to theorizing as well. We use concepts to make sense of the things we witness, to subordinate them to the ordering of our analysis. Again, this need not be understood as an act of violence, at least on the ethnographer's part; it is instead the necessary, if at times arbitrary, process of social analysis, a way in which reality is created through rendering it comprehensible. In this, too, ethnographers have much in common with states and social actors who similarly must impose meaning on experience, bringing into being that which, prior to our description of it, exists only in imagination. This is particularly so for legal anthropology, and for matters of the law. As Susan Coutin and Barbara Yngvesson have noted, "legal and ethnographic accounts retroactively instantiate realities that potentially existed all along. By narrating versions of reality that were there all along but that, without official recognition, remained potentialities, ethnographers and legal actors perform the act of measurement or assessment that enables social or legal reality to resolve itself into a single outcome. Thus, the 'fictions' that make fieldwork possible—the moments of substitution, for instance, in which field notes come to stand in for events and quotations come to stand in for field notes—enhance rather than undermine ethnography's capacity to convey social truths" (2008, 63).

This is not to say that ethnography invents reality—there *are* rateros out there, and at least some of them *do* have scars on their faces. It is rather to suggest the intolerable nature of uncertainty, which can be counteracted only through ordering. Life lived with uncertainty is stressful and debilitating—without firm knowledge of our own futures and a sense of confidence in our ability to control them, we are exposed and unprotected, and find that fear and anxiety are our constant companions. The poor and marginalized are, of course, most vulnerable to these fears, as their poverty and lack of access to official forms of social and legal ordering leave them without the resources that others enjoy to make their lives predictable and controllable. Uncertainty is thus a basic condition of poverty, one of the critical elements that underlie the vulnerability of the poor, and one of the most difficult to eradicate.

As ethnographers of uncertain situations, we need to be circumspect in our conceptual impositions, as the ways in which we order our data—much like the state's attempts at ordering social life—can obscure, marginalize, and unfairly privilege some things over others. This can be particularly problematic when what we are analyzing is in itself better understood through the lens of uncertainty than order. In chapter 5, for example, I critiqued the notion of legal pluralism, rejecting the idea that the Bolivian legal sphere can be understood as populated by discrete, coherent, and parallel legal orders. What I have argued for instead is an understanding of the creativity and invention required to produce practical solutions to problems in the absence of any clear set of ordering principles—an embrace of individual and collective imagination to produce ad hoc orderings, and people's willingness to accept such orderings amid the daily insecurity of life in Loma Pampa. Such acts are the offspring of disorder and uncertainty: they emerge from the state's refusal to provide a formal legal ordering, prompting state subjects to intervene, taking matters, as the lynchers say, into their own hands. The solutions that they invent draw on a host of sources and are assembled into a pastiche that may not have any generalizable features, nor set anything resembling a legal precedent, yet nevertheless serve in that moment to address a locally defined need. Such interventions are therefore often transient: they may suit the needs of the present moment, but may have no particular staying power, and do not constitute cultural patterns, systems, structures, or institutions that persist or have relevance for other moments of crisis. Nevertheless, they are worthy objects of ethnographic attention, representing the vital, if fleeting, attempts of local people to resolve crises creatively in a context of profound uncertainty. Disorder, then, rather than representing a destructive force that only undermines social life, can here be seen as the fertile ground from which sprout new examples of human creativity and imagination.

To recognize that process requires the ethnographer to surrender the commitment to systems, set in particular spaces and times, and to accept the fact of uncertainty that comes with life on the margins of the state. As the chapters of this ethnography have shown, in the marginal places of the world we are liable to encounter not clear, functional systems—legal, juridical, or otherwise—but the simultaneous expression of contradictory fragments, assembled by people into momentary wholes. To understand such phenomena, anthropologists must be willing to live with the ambiguity of multiple and overlapping possibilities that are shifting, temporary, and uncertain. This kind of uncertain anthropology, I think, is what is required to appreciate the richness and productivity of local people, set amid the poverty and disorder of the urban margins.

Notes

1. SECURITY, RIGHTS, AND THE LAW

1. The actual percentage of the Bolivian population that counts itself as indigenous is difficult to measure. According to national census figures, the self-identifying indigenous population in Bolivia is about 60 percent. Other estimates place it even higher. Bolivia is commonly referred to in the international press as being the "most indigenous" country in Latin America, making Evo's election seem like something of a foregone conclusion.

2. The media luna region of Bolivia (so-called for its crescent shape) consists of the departments of Beni, Pando, Santa Cruz, and Tarija, with Chuquisaca sometimes included as well. The region's principal characteristic is that its population is publicly identified as majority nonindigenous.

3. Simon Romero, "Bolivians Ratify New Constitution," *New York Times*, January 25, 2009.

4. Evo has maintained a strong and publicly close relationship with President Hugo Chávez of Venezuela, whose government has been a principal provider of economic aid to Bolivia. This relationship has been the source of some resentment (and much humor) in Bolivia, with some regarding the ties between the two presidents as detrimental to Bolivia's sovereignty.

5. One of the problems that legislators wrestled with following the approval of the new constitution was how to legally implement many of its community justice provisions. The issue of jurisdiction was a particularly thorny issue. Would nonindigenous people be subjected to indigenous law, if they were accused of a crime in an indigenous jurisdiction? What about members of other indigenous groups? These and many other issues were still unresolved at the time of this writing, but similar issues have plagued community justice efforts in other Andean countries (for example, see Vintimilla Saldaña, Almeida Mariño, and Saldaña Abad 2007).

6. According to Ledo García (2002), 60 percent of Cochabamba's residents survive on one dollar per day or less. On this basis, Mike Davis (2006) identifies Cochabamba as one of the four poorest cities in the world; the other three are all in Africa (Luanda, Maputo, and Kinshasa).

7. When this manuscript was already in production, I encountered another use of the "outlawed" concept similar to my own, though in a very different context; see Peutz 2007.

8. Lynching, the mob execution of the criminally accused, may involve a variety of different techniques, including burning, hanging, and beating of the suspect. Although the lynching event in Cochabamba does not always result in the death of the accused (and hence should better be considered an attempted lynching), I follow local usage by referring to all such events as lynchings (*linchamientos*).

9. In much of Latin America, the philosophy and practice of neoliberal capitalism and democracy is under explicit assault. Although it may be premature to declare Latin America to be postneoliberal (see Leiva 2008), at the time of writing much of the region appears to be in transition to a new historical period. However, as later chapters of this ethnography demonstrate, even in Bolivia elements of neoliberal governing philosophy remain in effect, despite Evo's explicit rejection of *neoliberalismo*.

10. In the United States, for example, such issues as public health and epidemiology (Heymann 2003; Lakoff 2008), energy policy (Helm 2002), and the environment (Khagram, Clark, and Firas Raad 2003; Matthew 2000) have recently come to be framed within a discourse of national or collective security.

11. For more on Marx's comments on the security of states, see Der Derian 2009.

12. For a more detailed, albeit partial, history of the security concept, see Goldstein 2010b.

13. Indeed, much recent anthropological debate about security has focused on the collaboration of anthropologists with military strategists, especially in the formulation of what has been called a human terrain system, to better enable the military to understand the decision-making processes and other aspects of local culture that might arise to threaten combat or military occupations (McFate 2005; Renzi 2006; see also Albro 2007; Albro, Marcus, McNamara, and Schoch-Spana 2011; Goldstein 2010a).

14. For important contributions to this body of work, see Collier 2008; Gusterson and Besteman 2009; Lakoff 2007, 2008; and R. Wilson 2005. Also of note here is work by anthropologists and scholars in related disciplines on the production of "cultures of insecurity" (Weldes, Laffey, Gusterson, and Duvall 1999), in contexts ranging from US military complexes (for example, Lutz 2001) to the nuclear public sphere (Masco 2006), biosecurity (Collier, Lakoff, and Rabinow 2004; Lakoff and Collier 2008), and cybersecurity (Du-

bartell 2006; Kelty 2005; Nelson 1996). Other anthropologists and anthropologically minded social scientists are at work in various locations around the world, studying, for example, the criminalization of supposedly dangerous populations (Caldeira 2000; M. Davis 1992; Low 1997 and 2003; Valverde and Cirak 2002); the production of public fear (Skidmore 2003); and topics in psychiatry, illness, and medical risk (Metzl 2010; Owczarzak 2009), among other issues, all of which make clear and significant contributions to understanding security in specific contexts.

15. In discussing "neoliberalism" here, I refer to it both as a political and economic philosophy with a set of accompanying policy prescriptions—such as favoring open markets and free trade as opposed to a Keynesian welfarism (Larner 2000)—and as a rationality of governance whose characteristics include extending market values to social institutions (Brown 2003). See the discussion in Schwegler 2008.

16. The rise to power in Bolivia of Evo Morales and the MAS was part of a wider shift away from neoliberal policies, which has seen the democratic election of a number of explicitly left-leaning regimes in countries throughout the region. Though Morales himself played a relatively minor role in the two "wars" described here, his evolution as a national political figure can reasonably be traced to these events and the climate of change that they signaled in the country.

17. Although violence may have become normalized or routinized as part of everyday social existence for the urban poor, as many observers claim (for example, Scheper-Hughes 1993), I do not mean to imply an acceptance by the poor of this condition, in the classic sense of false consciousness.

18. The privatization of justice (Caldeira and Holston 1999) that this implies also motivates the lynch mob, the perfect expression of neoliberal logic (see Goldstein 2005a)..

19. According to this model, the presence of one broken window in a building communicates neglect to other would-be vandals, encouraging further vandalism that leads to crimes of greater magnitude. Broken windows literally and symbolically identify high-crime urban areas (J. Wilson and Kelling 1982).

20. Bolivia is often mentioned as having the second-highest frequency of lynchings worldwide, after only postwar Guatemala. However, given the lack of any reliable statistical data on lynching, it is difficult to know how this claim was derived.

21. Despite assertions of its socialist leanings, the MAS state has not been progressive on the question of security, relying on punitive rhetoric and unflinching support of the police and military in its proposals on security. The language of "citizen security," developed under previous neoliberal administrations, continues to find full expression in the Morales regime.

22. The UN secretary general acknowledged this "right to security" more explicitly in a statement on his approach to development, security, and human rights, commenting that "all people have the right to security and development" (Annan 2005, 5). He also noted: "It would be a mistake to treat human rights as though there were a trade-off to be made between human rights and such goals as security or development. We only weaken our hand in fighting the horrors of extreme poverty or terrorism if, in our efforts to do so, we deny the very human rights that these scourges take away from citizens" (37).

23. For example, in 2004 USAID pledged grants of nearly US$50,000,000 for strengthening democratic institutions and improving "access to justice" in Bolivia (United States Agency for International Development 2004).

24. Inter-American Development Bank, "Citizen Security: New Challenges for the Region," July 10, 2003, http://www.iadb.org.

25. The full reemergence of the old authoritarian national security paradigm is limited by the progressive politics of social movements in Bolivia today, even as many Bolivians share the goal of greater security from crime. Thus the state's effort to recast the Gas War of 2003 as a threat to national security was firmly rejected by people across Bolivian civil society, who denounced state killings of protestors as a violation of their human rights. The Bolivian state's audience for this claim was more likely the international community (particularly the United States) rather than its own citizens.

26. The concept of "bricolage" was introduced into anthropology by Claude Lévi-Strauss, understood as a process in which the worker (the *bricoleur*) puts something together—art, perhaps, or myth—using "whatever is at hand" to complete the task. Although in Lévi-Strauss's usage the bricolage was somewhat less than a fully creative expression—the work of assemblage at times seems to require nothing more than borrowing that which already exists without producing anything particularly new—in my adoption of the term, I mean it to refer to a creative process in which old pieces can be assembled into something previously unseen, often spontaneous, and temporally fleeting.

27. Although in some ways reflective of the norms and procedures of state legal cultures, the sociolegal realities that emerge in outlawed communities existing "in the shadow of the law" (Comaroff and Comaroff 2006, 34) represent complex creations only partially contingent on broader legal domains. The work of Jean and John Comaroff, like that of Carolyn Nordstrom (2007), points to the unstable line that divides the legal from the illegal, the acceptable from the illegitimate, in the contemporary field of global political economy.

28. In most instances I have used pseudonyms to disguise the identities of people mentioned in this book; in some cases, following individuals' requests, I have used people's real names. I have used the actual names of

places mentioned in the book, including Loma Pampa and Uspha Uspha, again at the request of local residents and leaders.

2. GETTING ENGAGED

In February 2010 my colleague Dorothy Hodgson and I organized an event titled "Reflections on Engaged Anthropology," a symposium sponsored by the Rutgers University Department of Anthropology. We invited four keynote participants: Kamari Clarke, Charles Hale, Cindi Katz, and Stuart Kirsch. The symposium, meant to be a broad exploration of the field of engaged anthropology, was organized into three segments, during which the four participants were asked to comment on three key questions: Drawing on examples from your own research, writing, and practice, how do you define and practice engaged anthropology? Based on your work, what do you think the possibilities or contributions of engaged anthropology are to the discipline, the people we study, and others? Based on your work, what do you think are the limits and challenges of practicing engaged anthropology? These presentations were followed by questions and comments from the audience. It is from this event that I derived some of the insights presented in this chapter.

1. Singer (2010) makes a similar point in his commentary on Low and Merry (2010), though from his perspective, cultural critique is the single most important variety of anthropological engagement.

2. Although Hale (2008b) discounts the prospect of a conservative engaged anthropology, I think he is overly sanguine about the possibility of engagement's being hijacked by less progressive forces within the discipline.

3. Some have characterized forms of cultural critique as a kind of "luxury" knowledge production (Gilmore 1993, 72) and engaged anthropology a way for cultural critics to feel good about themselves without producing anything meaningful or valuable to the people about whom they write. This seems to me an overly harsh assessment, but an important caution nevertheless.

4. In terms of methodology and its basic orientation toward collaboration and participation, the current trends in activist and engaged anthropology are indebted to earlier disciplinary iterations that expressed similar goals. Sol Tax was a pioneer of what he identified as "action anthropology" (1975), an approach dedicated to working to solve problems through anthropology. In this regard, action anthropology was a forerunner of applied anthropology, some of whose practitioners were dedicated to the development of participatory research methodologies (see Stull and Schensul 1987). In the field of public health, approaches like community-based participatory research represent appropriations of ethnographic methodology, applied collaboratively by the practitioners of other disciplines.

5. For more discussion of this research methodology, see the chapters in Hale 2008a.

6. Even an institution as venerable as the Wenner-Gren Foundation can lay claim to engaged anthropology, when it is defined broadly enough (see Aiello 2010).

7. Certainly, it is difficult to claim that the American Anthropological Association, representative of the discipline of anthropology in North America, is an engaged organization. Its history is marked by resistance to engagement, including the censuring of Franz Boas for his more public political statements and the marginalization of Margaret Mead, whose cultural critiques "were not necessarily received positively within the academy" (Low and Merry 2010, S205).

8. I am often taken aback by conversations with undergraduates and others outside the academy, who sometimes assume that "objectivity" in the classic sense is necessary for good fieldwork; some of them even cite the "prime directive" of the Star Trek franchise as evidence.

9. These perspectives challenge classic notions of objectivity, which themselves have been used to mask other—sometimes illicit—behaviors, including spying for the US government under cover of supposedly doing fieldwork (Price 2005; Speed 2008).

10. For each interview quoted in this ethnography, I have provided references to the date and location of the interview and the member or members of the research team who conducted it: me (DG); Rose Marie Achá (RMA); Eric Hinojosa (EH); Ruth Ordoñez (RO); and Theo Roncken (TR). Rose Marie was primarily responsible for interviews with police, judges, and human rights activists; Ruth conducted many of the interviews with barrio women, often with Eric; and I conducted most of the group interviews, many of the interviews with men, and nearly all of the interviews with local politicians and barrio leaders, often accompanied by Eric. Eric did many individual and group interviews as well, and all of the team members wrote fieldnotes and recorded minutes of meetings, which were shared among the group.

11. The words "don" and "doña" are terms of respect equivalent to Mr. and Mrs. or sir and madam, typically used in reference to people older than oneself.

12. I have chosen to use pseudonyms for both the Center, as I call it here, and the CAJ project. Although I am no longer affiliated with either project, at the time of writing they continue to be active in Cochabamba, and I have no desire to discredit their work or undermine their accomplishments. However, I believe that a critique of their practice is both necessary and instructive.

13. Rutgers University Study Abroad, "International Service Learning," http://studyabroad.rutgers.edu/.

14. See Volunteer Bolivia's website at http://volunteerbolivia.org/.

15. My goal here is not to criticize applied anthropology or the idea of develop-

ment more generally—this critique has already been ably presented by many within the discipline (for example, Edelman and Haugerud 2005). And I appreciate the complaint by some applied anthropologists (for example, Singer 2000) that their work long anticipated the current trend toward public or engaged anthropology. However, I think the notion of applied anthropology is too limiting a characterization for the projects I have described in this chapter, which have political and epistemological groundings that seem to differ fundamentally from the applied approach.

3. THE PHANTOM STATE

1. For example, in 1997 Bolivia ratified the International Labour Organization's Minimum Age Convention, which requires ratifying states to work to abolish child labor and to increasingly push for higher age limits for child workers (Henne and Moseley 2005). Under Bolivian law, children can legally work at the age of fourteen.

2. Interview with doña Delina, February 15, 2007, Loma Pampa (EH, RO).

3. In the years since the conclusion of my fieldwork in Villa Pagador, that barrio has grown and changed tremendously. Today it has its own *sub-alcaldía*, an administrative branch of the municipal government that gives its residents a direct line of communication to city authorities. The barrio has also received some of the infrastructural improvements—including paved streets and running water—that residents struggled for during my time there. However, problems of security remain a major issue in Villa Pagador, which continues to be the site of lynchings.

4. Fulbito is soccer played by six-person teams on a basketball court. It is the most commonly played sport in urban barrios, which often lack the space for full soccer fields.

5. Selling items illegally in the marketplace is a common form of employment for residents of marginal barrios. Without official permission to set up a stall, vendors roam the streets in and around the market, selling any manner of small wares. Concurrent with my research in Uspha Uspha, I conducted an extensive ethnographic research project among legal and illegal market vendors in la Cancha. The results of this study are the subject of a forthcoming ethnography.

6. The process of urbanization and the municipality's attempts to control it are documented in my previous work on this subject (Goldstein 2004).

7. As I discussed in my previous work (Goldstein 2004), the áreas verdes were a particularly intractable obstacle to land legalization in the marginal barrios. Required by law to cede a certain percentage of barrio acreage to the state for public use, barrios were often unable to receive legal recognition because the land intended to be set aside as áreas verdes had already been subdivided and sold by loteadores for settlement. Barrio residents, then, were required

to pool their resources to purchase another lot at a distant location, to be given to the state as compensation for the lack of an área verde in their community.

8. My colleague Angelique Haugerud (1993) has written about land titling and questions of land legalization in Kenya, in ways that present interesting parallels with the Bolivian situation.

9. Interview with don Segundo, November 8, 2006, Loma Pampa (RO).

10. Interview with don Casto, November 27, 2006, Loma Pampa (EH).

11. Interview with don Reynaldo, April 22, 2007, Mineros San Juan (DG, EH).

12. Interview with don Reynaldo, April 5, 2007, Mineros San Juan (DG, EH).

13. Group interview, May 3, 2007, Uspha Uspha Central (RO).

14. Interview with don Miguel, March 18, 2007, Loma Pampa (DG, EH).

15. Interview with Josias, March 25, 2007, Loma Pampa (DG).

16. Interview with doña Dora, January 20, 2006, Tiquipaya (EH).

17. Group interview, June 21, 2007, Mineros San Juan (DG, RO).

18. Interview with Jorge Rojas, June 7, 2007, Cochabamba (DG).

19. Group interview, July 29, 2003, Cochabamba (DG).

20. Ibid.

21. Group interview, June 20, 2007, Concordia (DG, EH).

22. Interview with doña Irma, January 15, 2006, Colcapirhua (EH).

23. Group interview, May 13, 2007, Mineros San Juan (DG, EH, RO).

24. Group interview, July 5, 2007, Concordia (DG, EH).

25. Ibid.

26. Ibid.

27. Voters are required to register with an electoral notary prior to an election. Failure to register to vote is also considered an abdication of civic responsibility and, like failure to vote, may be subject to state sanction. Of course, since an identity card of some sort is required to register to vote, those who lack formal papers will encounter problems registering, further compounding their difficulties. People over seventy are not required to participate, and the mentally ill, convicts, and military conscripts are considered ineligible to vote.

28. Interview with don Angel, August 30, 2007, Loma Pampa (EH, RO).

29. Interview with Josias, March 25, 2007, Loma Pampa (DG).

30. Group interview, April 15, 2007, Juan Pablo II (DG, EH).

31. Ibid.

32. Interview with don Baltazar, April 5, 2007, Loma Pampa (EH).

33. Interview with doña Elena, June 1, 2007, Loma Pampa (RO).

34. Interview with doña Dora, January 20, 2006, Tiquipaya (EH).

35. Interview with don Armando, November 4, 2006, Loma Pampa (EH, RO).

36. Group interview, June 3, 2007, Uspha Uspha Central (DG, RO).

37. Group interview, June 28, 2007, Juan Pablo II (DG, RO).

38. Group interview, June 20, 2007, Concordia (DG, EH).

39. Group interview, May 25, 2007, Juan Pablo II (DG, EH).

40. Ibid.

41. Ibid.

42. Interview with Josias, March 25, 2007, Loma Pampa (DG).

43. Ibid.

44. Although direct correlations are difficult to establish, Bailey and Dammert have shown that the introduction of neoliberal economic reform in Latin America brought increased unemployment in the formal sector, a tremendous expansion of the informal sector, and widening gaps in income inequality, at the same time as these nations were increasingly incorporated into a global consumerist economy: "That is, men and women lost jobs or endured income losses at the same time that they were bombarded with advertising and images of the good life from advanced post-industrial societies" (2006, 6). In addition, already weak state capacity was further undermined by structural adjustment, with police, courts, prisons, and social rehabilitation agencies left unable to handle the upsurge in crime and violence that coincided with the neoliberal turn.

45. Juan Yhonny Mollericona, "Políticas de seguridad ciudadana en Bolivia," *Proyecto Communidad Prevención* (blog), http://www.comunidadypreven cion.org/opinion_13.html.

46. These were Hugo Banzer Suarez (1997–2001); Jorge "Tuto" Quiroga (2001–2); Gonzalo Sanchez de Lozada (2002–3); Carlos Mesa Gisbert (2003–5); Eduardo Rodríguez Veltzé (2005–6); and Evo Morales Ayma (2006–present).

47. See the discussion in Mollericona, "Políticas de seguridad ciudadana en Bolivia."

48. Ibid. Though the mid-1990s marked the rise to prominence of seguridad ciudadana as a public discourse of security in Latin America, this was not the first time the term had been used. During the era of the dictatorships, citizen security was sometimes cited by progressives as a counter to the public security models of authoritarian states, a way to emphasize the needs of citizens over the security requirements of the state (a point made in chapter 1). That Hugo Banzer—a former dictator democratically elected president of Bolivia in 1997—should be one of the first major proponents of seguridad ciudadana in Bolivia is an especially ironic touch. His 1997 Plan de Seguridad y Protección Ciudadana was one of the first formal efforts in Bolivia to establish a program of citizen security for the country.

49. Under the Plan Ciudad Segura, the armed forces participated in the work of policing, conducting patrols and detaining suspects in the cities of Santa Cruz, El Alto, and Yacuiba. As a result of this and other similar initiatives, many observers feel that the police institution lost political ground under the government of Evo Morales, whose efforts to court the military by

encouraging it to take a role in everyday police work deepened the historical divide between the police and military, with the former perceiving itself as being assigned a more marginal role in the area of citizen security.

50. Community policing is a model of policing based on the philosophy that police and citizens should work in close collaboration, with citizens themselves taking on some of the burden of monitoring and policing their own communities. Successfully adopted in parts of the United States and Argentina, community policing has been less well received in Bolivia, where lack of resources, local hostility to the police, and a weak institutional commitment to decentralization have hampered the adoption of the model.

51. These entities, specifically dedicated to the work of citizen security, work alongside other police units, including the Fuerza Especial en la Lucha Contra el Crimen (the Special Force for the Fight Against Crime) and the PTJ, the investigative arm of the police.

52. In January 2007, members of the coca growers syndicate and their supporters marched on Cochabamba's main plaza to protest government policy limiting the acreage that could legally be planted with coca, and set fire to the offices of the Prefectura, causing significant structural damage to that historic building. The police commandant claimed in an interview (March 12, 2007, Cochabamba [RMA]) that the police were left "with hands tied," unable to stop the violence, because the federal government had instructed them not to take action against the coca growers, an important source of political support for Evo Morales. The commandant described that day as a complete "absence of the state," when laws were not enforced and everyone could—and did—do as they pleased.

53. Some efforts to establish community policing in Bolivia have been undertaken, principally in La Paz, where the British Embassy has been an active promoter and supporter of community policing projects.

54. Interview with Elvio Sanchez, March 12, 2007, Cochabamba (RMA).

55. The selection of informants in this discussion is limited to those few individuals willing to speak to us. Police officials and municipal functionaries are extremely reluctant to submit to interviews, and highly circumspect in their comments. Our work here was facilitated by the contacts that one member of our team (Rose Marie Achá) had in certain offices of the national police, contacts who helped to set up the interviews we were able to conduct.

56. Interview with Froilan Mamani, July 27, 2007, Cochabamba (RMA).

57. Interview with Alejandro Bravo, June 18, 2007, Cochabamba (RMA).

58. Interview with Mario Huanca, June 19, 2007, Cochabamba (RMA).

59. It was incidents like this, including the physical abuse of subordinates by officers, that led to the formation of the Asociación Nacional de Suboficiales, Clases y Policías de Cochabamba, the policeman's union. According to several representatives of the organization, conditions have improved

since its founding, with physical battery of officers by their superiors becoming less common.

60. Interview with Mario Huanca, June 19, 2007, Cochabamba (RMA).

61. Interview with Manuel Palacios, June 16, 2007, Cochabamba (RMA).

62. Ibid.

63. Group interview, April 14, 2007, Uspha Uspha Central (DG, EH, RO). This suspicion of the law as a foreign imposition is similar to the perception that some barrio residents have of human rights, a subject that I take up in chapter 6.

64. Quoted in "Plan de Seguridad 'Ciudad Segura' se amplía a El Alto y Yacuiba," *Los Tiempos*, March 22, 2010, http://www.lostiempos.com/diario/actualidad/nacional/20100322/plan-de-seguridad-ciudad-segura-se-amplia-a-el-alto-y_62712_113640.html.

65. Interview with Felipe Antezana, March 16, 2007, Cochabamba (RMA).

66. Ibid.

67. Although experiments with jury trials were initiated toward the end of the 2000s in Bolivia, most trials are heard by a panel of judges, which renders a verdict and passes sentence.

68. Interview with Felipe Antezana, March 16, 2007, Cochabamba (RMA).

4. EXORCISING GHOSTS

1. Interview with don Silvio Lopez, June 30, 2007, Cochabamba (DG).

2. Though clearly a cognate with the English "lynching," I have been unable to identify when or how the word "linchamiento" came into use in Spanish. The English usage is probably derived from the name of a Virginia magistrate, Charles Lynch, whose court punished Loyalist supporters of the British during the American Revolution (Waldrep 2002).

3. Elsewhere (Goldstein, Achá, Hinojosa, and Roncken 2007) I have argued that the lynching is a form of violent civil society, an observation not contradicted by the claim that it is also a very diverse, deeply fragmented set of phenomena.

4. Interview with don Omar, December 17, 2006, Colcapirhua (EH).

5. For Marx, history itself was a ghostly presence, in which "the tradition of all the dead generations weighs like a nightmare on the brain of the living" (Marx 1963 [1852], 15). Specters of the past haunt Marxian thought, the absent presence of the past shaping the way people make history in their daily lives.

6. Ghosts, witches, and other spectral characters are not unknown in anthropological writings on modernity and capitalism. For the relevance of zombies in the context of neoliberal "occult economies," see Comaroff and Comaroff 2002; for the modernity of witchcraft and the occult, see Geschiere 1997. In international relations theory, zombies have recently been invoked

as a useful trope for thinking about politics in the international arena (Drezner 2011).

7. Group interview, May 24, 2007, Mineros San Juan (DG, RO).
8. Interview with doña Birgith, April 3, 2007, Loma Pampa (RO).
9. Interview with doña Casilda, January 22, 2007, Loma Pampa (EH, RO).
10. Interview with Josias, March 25, 2007, Loma Pampa (DG).
11. Group interview, July 5, 2007, Concordia (DG, RO).
12. Interview with doña Delina, February 15, 2007, Loma Pampa (EH, RO).
13. Group interview, April 15, 2007, Mineros San Juan (DG, EH).
14. Interview with don Segundo, November 8, 2006, Loma Pampa (RO).
15. Interview with doña Elena, June 1, 2007, Loma Pampa (RO).
16. Interview with doña Eva, December 18, 2006, Loma Pampa (RO).
17. Interview with Josias, March 25, 2007, Loma Pampa (DG).
18. Interview with doña Dora, January 20, 2006, Tiquipaya (EH).
19. Group interview, May 24, 2007, Mineros San Juan (DG, RO).
20. An anthropologist friend who has worked for many years in Guatemala could not comprehend, after visiting La Paz, how security could be a concern in Bolivia, given how much more dangerous a place like Guatemala City feels. This may be so, but a tourist in the better parts of town is unable to perceive the signs that provoke fear and anxiety in barrio residents when they travel away from their own places of residence.
21. Interview with doña Eva, December 18, 2006, Loma Pampa (RO).
22. Interview with Josias, March 25, 2007, Loma Pampa (DG).
23. Group interview, July 5, 2007, Concordia (DG, EH).
24. Group interview, June 29, 2007, Mineros San Juan (RO).
25. Interview with Froilan Mamani, July 27, 2007, Cochabamba (RMA).
26. Group interview, July 5, 2007, Concordia (DG, EH).
27. Interview with doña Casilda, January 22, 2007, Loma Pampa (EH, RO).
28. Don Miguel had called for a public work group, and we assembled on a Sunday morning atop the Loma Pampa hill to defend the área verde, which was under threat of invasion by some unspecified neighbors. For several hours I helped move rocks and shovel dirt to create visible boundary lines marking out the territory of Loma Pampa's área verde. Unsure of what to expect from me, the people with whom I worked, including don Miguel, were surprised and impressed that a gringo would get his hands dirty in such an endeavor, working alongside barrio residents to secure their public land. From the outset, then, I situated myself on the right side of the security question, in the eyes of many barrio residents.
29. Forms of kidnapping familiar in other Latin American countries (the infamous *secuestro express*, in which people are briefly abducted and forced to withdraw their own ransom money from an ATM, as happens frequently in Venezuela and elsewhere) have recently become more common in Bolivia,

especially in wealthier neighborhoods (until poor people start carrying ATM cards, the phenomenon may remain confined to those parts of town). When kidnappings do happen in Bolivia, Peruvians are often publicly implicated.

30. Interview with doña Dora, January 20, 2006, Tiquipaya (EH).
31. Group interview, May 25, 2007, Juan Pablo II (DG, EH).
32. Group interview, May 24, 2007, Mineros San Juan (DG, RO).
33. Interview with doña Licia, March 8, 2007, Loma Pampa (RO, EH).
34. Interview with doña Altamira, August 12, 2007, Loma Pampa (RO).
35. Interview with doña Licia, March 8, 2007, Loma Pampa (RO, EH).
36. Interview with doña Casilda, January 22, 2007, Loma Pampa (EH, RO).
37. Interview with Josias, March 25, 2007, Loma Pampa (DG).
38. Group interview, June 20, 2007, Concordia (DG, EH).
39. Interview with doña Tadea, November 7, 2006, Loma Pampa (EH, RO).
40. Group interview, April 12, 2007, Loma Pampa (DG, RO).
41. Ayni and mink'a are systems of reciprocal labor exchange common in rural Andean communities (*ayllus*), in which villagers join together to help a family to build a house or perform seasonal agricultural tasks, or to do work in service of the community as a whole. For more details, see Rockefeller 2010.
42. Interview with doña Licia, March 8, 2007, Loma Pampa (RO, EH). Doña Licia's use of the word "vecinos" to refer to her immediate next-door neighbors clearly illustrates the use of this term as a geographical reference to proximity, without a larger sociopolitical meaning—as I suggested above.
43. Interview with doña Delina, February 15, 2007, Loma Pampa (EH, RO).
44. Ibid.
45. Interview with don Miguel, March 18, 2007, Loma Pampa (DG, EH).
46. Interview with doña Irda, February 6, 2006, Loma Pampa (EH, RO).
47. Group interview, May 10, 2007, Uspha Uspha Central (DG, EH).
48. Interview with don Omar, December 17, 2006, Colcapirhua (EH).
49. The Ley de Participación Popular also provided for the reorganization of indigenous and peasant communities along similar lines, with the same financial incentives (see Medeiros 2001). The strategy of state decentralization was a critical pillar of neoliberal structural reforms promoted worldwide by institutions like the World Bank as a strategy for fiscal strengthening—an approach that has been the subject of much criticism (see, for example, Harriss 2002).
50. Interview with don Miguel, March 18, 2007, Loma Pampa (DG, EH).
51. By 2010, the price of land in Loma Pampa had doubled, selling for about eight to ten bolivianos per square meter. For those who settled in the area early, land in Uspha Uspha turned out to be a sound investment.
52. When it was privatized in 1994, ELFEC had been purchased by the New York–based power company PPL, but PPL sold its controlling interest to a

group of ELFEC managers and employees. Subsequently, in 2008, COMTECO, the regional telecommunications firm, purchased a 52 percent stake in the electric utility. In 2010, Evo Morales issued Supreme Decree 494, which allowed for the nationalization of electricity in the country, and the government assumed ownership and control of ELFEC.

53. The privatization of public utilities that occurred during the neoliberal era in Bolivia has resulted in situations like this, where utility companies will only invest in services where there is hope of turning a profit. In barrios like Loma Pampa, individual residents must bear the costs of establishing the infrastructure needed to provide local services. With the nationalization of electricity in 2010, it remains to be seen what changes will result for marginal barrios and their residents.

54. Interview with don Miguel, March 18, 2007, Loma Pampa (DG, EH).

55. All barrio residents pay 2 Bs (about $0.30) each month as a general maintenance fee to the barrio. In addition, those who miss meetings or other public events are usually assessed a fine ranging from 10 to 50 Bs—sometimes more—which also goes into the public coffers. The directorio, and especially the treasurer, also must account for the use of the POA, the money given directly to the barrio by the federal government to support local initiatives. In Loma Pampa, the annual operating budget is about 900 Bs (just over US$1,000) per year.

56. Interview with don Angel, August 30, 2007, Loma Pampa (EH, RO).

57. Interview with doña Delina, February 15, 2007, Loma Pampa (EH, RO).

58. Interview with don Miguel, March 18, 2007, Loma Pampa (DG, EH).

59. Group interview, May 25, 2007, Juan Pablo II (DG, EH).

60. Interview with don Fulgencio, August 26, 2007, Loma Pampa (EH, RO).

61. Gustavo Sierra, "Pacto de silencio por el linchamiento de un alcalde," *Clarín*, June 20, 2004. Don Victor explained the tacit agreement among vecinos to protect a popular dirigente from police investigation: "When the police look for the dirigente we don't tell them who the dirigente is. Everyone agrees. In that case we say, 'We are all dirigentes,' and we don't say who is the original dirigente, no?" (Interview with don Victor, June 20, 2006, Loma Pampa [EH, RO]). This statement seems to suggest a kind of community ethos in the barrio, though as in other situations people may choose to cooperate with one another out of fear or other motives not related to collective sentiment.

62. Interview with Josias, March 25, 2007, Loma Pampa (DG).

63. Interview with doña Tadea, November 7, 2006, Loma Pampa (EH, RO).

64. Interview with don Casto, November 27, 2006, Loma Pampa (EH).

65. Interview with doña Irda, February 6, 2006, Loma Pampa (EH, RO).

66. Rose Marie Achá, Eric Hinojosa, and Ruth Ordoñez all provided fieldnotes, from which I draw the quotes in these paragraphs.

67. The next day, don Miguel accompanied the woman who had accused the man

of entering her home and threatening her family to the police station to file a report. This had to be done, as the police had already been to the barrio to retrieve the detained man and so required those who had been involved in the incident to follow up. At the police station, the woman changed her story— the accused had not actually entered her home but had looked at it menacingly from outside. It also turned out that the accused was mentally disabled, a fact confirmed by his family a few days later, when they visited Loma Pampa in the aftermath of the incident to thank don Miguel and to apologize for the problems that their relative (who had wandered away from his home in a nearby barrio and gotten lost) had caused in the neighborhood.

68. Group interview, May 25, 2007, Juan Pablo II (DG, EH).
69. Ibid.
70. Ibid.
71. Group interview, April 15, 2007, Mineros San Juan (DG, EH).
72. Though effigies are not commonly seen in the barrios of Uspha Uspha, they are familiar sights in other neighborhoods of Cochabamba and elsewhere in Bolivia, particularly in the highland city of El Alto. Such effigies can be ways of reclaiming public space (among other things; see Risør 2010), providing physical warnings to potential rateros to avoid that particular community.
73. Interview with Josias, March 25, 2007, Loma Pampa (DG).
74. Group interview, 15 April 2007, Juan Pablo II (DG, EH).
75. Katiuska Vásquez, "Linchamiento: Miedo, amenazas y silencio," *Los Tiempos*, June 14, 2007.
76. See, for example, "Linchar: Señal de Barbarie," *Los Tiempos*, April 13, 2001; "Lincharían por histeria y estrés," *Los Tiempos*, March 29, 2001; Mabel Azcui, "La brutal justicia que atemoriza Bolivia," *El País*, June 11, 2010.
77. See, for example, Derechos Humanos de Bolivia, "Linchamiento en Bolivia cronologia del 2006 a 2009," June 7, 2010, http://derechoshumanosbolivia.blogspot.com/2010/06/linchamiento-en-bolivia-cronologia-del.html.
78. Despite efforts to document the outcomes of lynchings, it is impossible to measure the frequency with which the lynching concludes with the killing of the accused. Records are spotty and incomplete, with the press providing a better source of lynching accounts than police records. Anecdotally and from press accounts, it does seem that more often than not the police arrive in time to rescue the accused, though it is unclear if the person would have been killed had the police not shown up.
79. Interview with doña Irma, January 15, 2006, Colcapirhua (EH).
80. Interview with doña Tadea, November 7, 2006, Loma Pampa (EH, RO).
81. Interview with don Angel, August 30, 2007, Loma Pampa (EH, RO).
82. Interview with Josias, March 25, 2007, Loma Pampa (DG).
83. Group interview, May 24, 2007, Mineros San Juan (DG, RO).
84. Interview with doña Birgith, April 3, 2007, Loma Pampa (RO).

85. Group interview, April 22, 2007, Mineros San Juan, (DG, EH).

86. Group interview, May 25, 2007, Juan Pablo II (DG, EH).

87. Ibid.

88. Ibid.

89. Interview with doña Irma, January 15, 2006, Colcapirhua (EH).

90. Interview with don Omar, December 17, 2006, Colcapirhua (EH).

91. Interview with doña Pacífica, March 12, 2007, Loma Pampa (RO).

92. Group interview, June 21, 2007, Mineros San Juan (RO).

93. Female market vendors in particular are seen to embody the elements of toughness and the ability to defend themselves. See Seligmann 1989, 2004; Weismantel 2001.

94. Interview with doña Casilda, January 22, 2007, Loma Pampa (EH, RO).

95. Interview with doña Birgith, April 3, 2007, Loma Pampa (RO).

96. Interview with doña Casilda, January 22, 2007, Loma Pampa (EH, RO).

97. Interview with doña Irma, January 15, 2006, Colcapirhua (EH).

98. Group interview, June 3, 2007, Uspha Uspha Central (DG, RO).

99. Group interview, June 21, 2007, Mineros San Juan (RO).

100. Ibid.

101. Interview with doña Isabel, December 13, 2006, Loma Pampa (RO).

102. Interview with doña Casilda, January 22, 2007, Loma Pampa (EH, RO).

103. Group interview, April 15, 2007, Mineros San Juan (DG, EH).

104. Interview with don Angel, August 30, 2007, Loma Pampa (EH, RO).

105. Interview with don Armando, November 4, 2006, Loma Pampa (EH, RO).

106. Interview with doña Eva, December 18, 2006, Loma Pampa (RO).

107. Interview with doña Fausta, February 25, 2007, Loma Pampa (EH, RO).

108. Group interview, June 21, 2007, Mineros San Juan (DG, RO).

109. Ibid.

110. Group interview, April 22, 2007, Mineros San Juan (DG, EH).

111. In a forthcoming work, I explore questions of insecurity in the places where these people work, particularly in the context of the urban marketplace, la Cancha.

5. COMMUNITY JUSTICE AND IMAGINATION

1. I use the terms "security making" and "justice making" interchangeably in this discussion, reflecting local usage. Concepts of security and justice are often conflated in barrio discourse, with both referring to safety, stability, and the sense that people—good and bad alike—should get what's coming to them.

2. Although the constitutional recognition of community justice was a powerful political statement, it was not unprecedented in Bolivian law. The much-maligned New Penal Procedural Code, adopted in 1999, also contains a general recognition of indigenous justice, as did the so-called Ley Blattman (1997) that preceded it.

3. The 2001 census reported that 63 percent of Bolivians identified themselves as indigenous, with a full 50 percent of those so identifying living in urban areas (Instituto Nacional de Estadísticas de Bolivia 2003). After more than a decade, that figure has probably increased significantly, as the ravages of neoliberalism continued to destabilize rural livelihoods, propelling thousands more people from the countryside into the cities of Bolivia. Rivera Cusicanqui (2010) describes the deeply problematic reading of census data by the Bolivian state, which further diminishes the urban indigenous presence by neglecting the extent to which many indigenous people straddle the rural and urban worlds, maintaining a foot in each.

4. In Newtonian physics, everything in the universe has a definite position, path, and momentum; time is taken to be a constant in the universe, part of the natural order of things, stable and unchanging (Gray 1989, 177). Newtonian space, therefore, is "'absolute,' fixed, a God-given framework upon which to lay the coordinates of Descartes" (Mlodinow 2001, 155). A Newtonian approach that flattens space in this way poses problems for understanding multidimensional social relationships.

5. On the use of "blood" as a metaphor joining race and nation, see Williams 1991.

6. In Bolivia and the Andes, "indigenous" is a category of racial identification, having replaced the more derogatory category of "indio" in official and public discourse. In other contexts, including East Africa (for example, see Hodgson 2011), the concept of "indigenous" may be less bound to racial conceptions. See de la Cadena 2000; Weismantel 2001; Poole 1997.

7. Carlos R. Colanzi Z., "La justicia comunitaria," *El Deber* (Santa Cruz, Bolivia), February 17, 2009, http://www.eldeber.com.bo/2008/imprimir.php?id=080312202710.

8. BBC UK, "Morales Inaugural Speech: Excerpts," January 26, 2006, http://news.bbc.co.uk/2/hi/americas/4638030.stm.

9. As Canessa (2006) has observed, the earlier indigenismo differs from the new indigenism in that the former was a project emphasizing the imaginative construction of a mestizo nation, whereas the latter is almost the reverse, an expansive project that casts a broad net of inclusive indigeneity. See also Mayorga 2006.

10. Albro observes that the new constitution has been characterized as "Aymara-centric" (2010a, 72) and the MAS conception of indigenous culture as highland-based or "colla-centric" (Albro 2006a, 411).

11. That the Aymara enjoy a particularly prominent presence in the MAS project is consonant with their national reputation in Bolivia as tough, indomitable, and independent. I have been told by Aymara-speaking people in Cochabamba that the Aymara were the only people of the Andes never to be conquered by the Inca—a claim that locates the Aymara in a separate historical lineage from that of other Bolivians. Quechua people, on the other hand,

are commonly regarded as more "humble" than Aymara people and are characterized as having downcast eyes and a poorer sense of social cohesion and solidarity (Albro 2010b). If the Aymara are seen as active, the Quechua are passive, less capable of concerted action. It is not surprising, then, that an Aymara identity, albeit unmarked, should lie at the center of an aspiring national character.

12. The location of this indomitable Aymara persona is most typically the altiplano, especially the city of El Alto (Lazar 2008). A satellite of the capital city of La Paz founded by altiplano migrants and growing to become Bolivia's third largest city over the course of the last twenty or thirty years, El Alto is a base of MAS support, often characterized by both state officials and academic observers as the key location in Bolivia's recent history of anti-neoliberal and indigenous uprisings (Albro 2010a; Hylton and Thomson 2007). The Aymara presence in El Alto is characterized as a kind of transplant, the relocation of a rural Aymara culture to the urban space of the peripheral city, where the traditional practices and beliefs of the ayllu have been moved and sustained (Webber 2007). Meanwhile, despite being the site of the famous Water War and the locus of much subsequent popular mobilization, as well as an important site of indigenous protest during the 1952 national revolution, Cochabamba has a much less prominent position in the national imaginary. Historically a market town with its roots in mercantile capitalism and Quechua language and culture (Larson 1988; Larson and Harris 1995), Cochabamba today is regarded as less fitting a site than El Alto for the emergence of a new indigenist national project.

13. Amy Goodman, "Bolivian President Evo Morales on Climate Debt, Capitalism, Why He Wants a Tribunal for Climate Justice and Much More," Democracy Now!, December 17, 2009, http://www.democracynow.org/2009/12/17/bolivian_president_evo_morales_on_climate (emphasis added).

14. The constitution clearly distinguishes indigenous rural areas from unmarked or mixed urban areas. Chapter 2, section 1, for example, which discusses the role of the Defensoría del Pueblo in the promotion and defense of human rights, defines two of its distinct areas of operation to include *las naciones y pueblos indígena originario campesinos* and *las comunidades urbanas e interculturales.*

15. Indigenous autonomy is not to be confused with the predominantly right-wing autonomy movement of the lowland departments of Bolivia, whose leadership has agitated for greater autonomy (some say including complete secession) from the Bolivian nation and the MAS-led state.

16. The autonomy project of the MAS state represents the next generation of administrative reinvention of rural and urban communities, shifting from the model of the OTB created by the first Sanchez de Lozada administration as part of the Law of Popular Participation in 1994 (Kohl 2004).

17. The Ley de Deslinde Jurisdiccional, passed by the Bolivian legislature in December 2010, was an attempt to define the jurisdictional reach of indigenous justice, establishing some limits to the offenses that could be subject to indigenous law. Under the law, indigenous justice can consider matters of family and civic law, but not major criminal cases that include rape and murder. Critics of the law have denounced it as a neocolonial attempt to subordinate indigenous justice to ordinary state law by severely circumscribing its areas of implementation (for example, Yrigoyen Fajardo 2011). It would appear that through this related legislation, the state is already backing away from some of the promises of reform contained in the constitution.

18. In a famous essay, Starn (1991) offers a critique of classical ethnography of the Andes, portraying it as essentializing and romantic in its search for the archetypal and deeply Andean. Elements of this romantic essentialism can be found in the contemporary Bolivian state's imaginings of indigenous Andeans.

19. Quoted in Laura Carpineta, "La justicia comunitaria es mucho más transparente que la ordinaria," El Mundo, July 9, 2006, http://www.pagina12.com.ar/diario/elmundo/.

20. Ideas and programs of community justice have emerged widely in the United States as well, also based on ideas of consensus, community, and egalitarian cooperation, which pose an interesting point of comparison with Bolivian conceptions. See Karp and Clear 2002.

21. Canessa (2012) mentions burial alive as a form of justice killing in Larecaja, though this is reserved for severe crimes like murder and incest.

22. Jorge Machicado, "Justicia comunitaria," Apuentos Jurdicos (blog), 2009, http://jorgemachicado.blogspot.com/2009/01/justicia-comunitaria.html.

23. Plurinationalism has its roots in the projects of multiculturalism, which have been influential in the reshaping of national configurations across the Americas. See Gustafson 2002; Hale 2002; Postero 2006.

24. Gisela Alcócer Caero, "Justicia comunitaria hace frente a sus primeros desafíos," Los Tiempos, January 3, 2010.

25. Ibid.

26. Ibid.

27. Luis Eduardo Siles Pérez, "Bolivia: Justicia comunitaria," Perro Negro (blog), October 2, 2008, http://nuestroperronegro.blogspot.com/2008/10/bolivia-justicia-comunitaria-la.html.

28. Colanzi Z., "La justicia comunitaria."

29. In response to the Human Rights Foundation's conflation of lynching with community justice, I wrote a public response, distributed through the Andean Information Network (Goldstein 2008). The foundation responded to my criticisms through a posting on its website (Thor Halvorssen, "Letter to Spero News in Response to Daniel M. Goldstein," March 14, 2008, http://www.humanrightsfoundation.org/LettertoSperoNews.html).

30. "Vecinos quemaron vivos a tres supuestos delincuentes," *La Prensa*, December 15, 2009.

31. Ibid.

32. Ibid.

33. Interview with don Silvio, June 30, 2007, Cochabamba (DG).

34. Interview with don Miguel, March 18, 2007, Loma Pampa (DG, EH).

35. Group interview, April 15, 2007, Juan Pablo II (DG, EH).

36. Interview with doña Casilda, January 22, 2007, Loma Pampa (EH, RO).

37. Group interview, April 15, 2007, Mineros San Juan (DG, EH).

38. Group interview, April 15, 2007, Juan Pablo II (DG, EH).

39. Group interview, May 3, 2007, Uspha Uspha Central (DG, RO, EH).

40. Group interview, May 25, 2007, Juan Pablo II (DG, EH).

41. Interview with don Reynaldo, March 18, 2007, Mineros San Juan (DG, EH).

42. One of these cases was the killing of the mayor of the town of Ayo Ayo, following a dispute about political corruption and involving a power struggle within the community, in the aftermath of which people close to the scene identified it as a case of "community justice." In another case, four policemen were lynched in a pueblo of Uncia, Potosí, over charges of corruption and dealing in illegal automobiles, in an act described in similar terms ("Ayllus admiten linchamiento de cuatro policías y permitirán ingreso de autos chutos," Jornadanet.com, May 27, 2010, http://www.jornadanet.com/n.php?a=48200−1).

43. Interview with don Armando, November 4, 2006, Loma Pampa (EH, RO).

44. Group interview, April 12, 2007, Concordia (DG, RO).

45. Group interview, May 24, 2007, Mineros San Juan (DG, RO).

46. Group interview, July 5, 2007, Concordia (DG, EH).

47. Ibid.

48. Interview with don Casto, November 27, 2006, Loma Pampa (EH).

49. Interview with don Segundo, November 8, 2006, Loma Pampa (RO).

50. Interview with don Miguel, March 18, 2007, Loma Pampa (DG, EH).

51. Ibid.

52. Ibid.

53. Miguel's religiosity, while not a requirement for barrio leadership, gives him a degree of righteousness in the eyes of many of his vecinos, which helps to reinforce his authority. Like rural dirigentes whose authority stems from both their political and spiritual responsibilities, Miguel has a foot in both the material and supernatural worlds, and this aids him in executing his leadership functions.

54. Interview with don Miguel, March 18, 2007, Loma Pampa (DG, EH).

55. Ibid.

56. Interview with don Fulgencio, August 26, 2007, Loma Pampa (EH, RO).

57. The presentation of various kinds of written documents during legal pro-

ceedings is an important element of rural Quechua justice, which Orellana Halkyer (2005) attributes to local recognition of the seriousness of the written word, sometimes lending it the character of truth itself.

58. Group interview, May 3, 2007, Uspha Uspha Central (DG, EH, RO).

59. Interview with don Miguel, March 18, 2007, Loma Pampa (DG, EH).

60. Interview with don Fulgencio, August 26, 2007, Loma Pampa (EH, RO).

61. Ibid.

62. Ibid.

63. Judge Joseph Dredd is a lawman who patrols a post-apocalyptic American landscape in a British comic book, later turned into a feature film starring Sylvester Stallone in the title role. Under the bleak and lawless conditions of the wasteland, the judge's duties include those of policeman, jury, and executioner (Rennie, Bishop, Jowett, and Evans 2006).

6. INHUMAN RIGHTS?

1. The electoral success of Otto Pérez Molina, a former army general, in Guatemala in 2011, campaigning for president largely on a promise of using la mano dura to combat crime in that country, is evidence of the widespread and enduring appeal of this rights-for-security transaction.

2. As some scholars have shown, the perception of rising crime may not coincide with the reality of crime's incidence; fear of crime may be a response to other social anxieties that do not correspond to actual levels of criminality in society (for example, Elbert 1998). However, given the highly incomplete nature of police records and the low level of reporting of crime to the police in most Latin American countries, it is extremely difficult to verify these levels or to correlate them with public perceptions.

3. I have no wish to criticize the well-intentioned work of my colleagues in Bolivian human rights NGOs, though I believe the analysis presented here is an important one. I therefore use a pseudonym for the organization here referred to as the Congreso.

4. Interview with Esteban Luna, December 10, 2005, Cochabamba (RMA).

5. Ibid.

6. Interview with Juan Vargas, January 3, 2006, Cochabamba (RMA).

7. Interview with Juan Vargas, December 8, 2006, Cochabamba (RMA).

8. The Bolivian state has recognized human rights and incorporated them into the fabric of the state in different ways. The government includes a Ministry of Justice and Human Rights, with a vice minister of human rights who oversees the operations of justice in the country to ensure that human rights are observed and protected. The state also has a Defensoría del Pueblo, the office of the human rights ombudsperson described in previous chapters, which is meant to serve as an independent watchdog over the behavior of the state and its functionaries.

9. Interview with Bernardo Chavez, November 16, 2005, Cochabamba (TR).

10. Interview with Juan Vargas, December 8, 2006, Cochabamba (RMA).

11. Ibid.

12. Interview with Froilan Mamani, July 27, 2007, Cochabamba (RMA).

13. Interview with Enrique Lopez, March 12, 2007, Cochabamba (RMA).

14. Interview with Felipe Antezana, May 16, 2007, Cochabamba (RMA).

15. Interview with Juan Vargas, January 3, 2006, Cochabamba, Cochabamba (RMA).

16. Interview with don Miguel, March 18, 2007, Loma Pampa (DG, EH), emphasis added.

17. Interview with Silvio Lopez, June 30, 2007, Cochabamba (DG).

18. Group interview, June 28, 2007, Juan Pablo II (DG, RO).

19. Interview with doña Casilda, November 27, 2006, Loma Pampa (EH, RO); and interview with doña Cata, April 10, 2007, Loma Pampa (RO).

20. Interview with don Feliciano, February 8, 2006, Loma Pampa (EH).

21. Interview with doña Birgith, April 3, 2007, Loma Pampa (RO).

22. Interview with doña Irma, January 15, 2006, Colcapirhua (EH).

23. The word "leyes" is more frequently used in reference to the laws of the Bolivian nation, though lawyers—widely despised in Bolivia—study "derecho." These two words thus distinguish law as a specific form of legal ordering (*la ley*) from law in the abstract or as a discipline (derecho). A derecho can also be a tax, another deeply stigmatizing association, though this term is used less frequently in Bolivia than *impuesto*.

24. Interview with Dr. Angel Navia, June 20, 2007, Cochabamba (DG).

25. Group interview, July 5, 2007, Concordia (DG, EH).

26. Ibid.

27. Group interview, July 29, 2003, Cochabamba (DG).

28. Group interview, July 5, 2007, Concordia (DG, EH).

29. Group interview, July 20, 2003, Villa Sebastián Pagador (DG).

30. Group interview, October 12, 2003, Vinto (DG).

31. Ibid.

32. "Un anónimo se atribuye asesinato de 'El Ruso,'" *Los Tiempos*, January 5, 2003, A4.

33. Ibid.

34. Quoted in ibid. Some speculate that Triple C was actually a front for elements within the police force hostile to the New Code, posing as a group of outraged citizens. Whether or not the Triple C was an unofficial arm of the police, if the vigilantes were responsible, their target was clearly the New Code as much as it was El Ruso and his band of thieves. Others believe that a rival criminal group was responsible for El Ruso's murder.

35. Group interview, July 20, 2003, Villa Sebastián Pagador (DG).

36. Group interview, July 5, 2007, Juan Pablo II (DG, EH).

37. Just as "derechos humanos" is shorthand for the institution known as the Congreso de Derechos Humanos, so "justice" is used, here and elsewhere, as an abbreviation for the entire dysfunctional Bolivian justice system.
38. Interview with Silvio Lopez, June 30, 2007, Cochabamba (DG).
39. Group interview, April 14, 2007, Uspha Uspha Central (DG, EH, RO).
40. It is perhaps not surprising that many barrio residents often use corporal punishment to discipline their children, and that teachers in many schools are allowed to use physical means to control unruly students.
41. Interview with don Miguel, March 18, 2007, Loma Pampa (DG, EH).
42. Group interview, April 15, 2007, Juan Pablo II (DG, EH).
43. Group interview, July 20, 2003, Villa Sebastián Pagador (DG).
44. Ibid.
45. Ibid.
46. Ibid.
47. Ibid.
48. Interview with Josias, March 25, 2007, Loma Pampa (DG).
49. Group interview, June 3, 2007, Uspha Uspha Central (DG, RO).
50. Interview with doña Pacífica, March 12, 2007, Loma Pampa (RO).
51. Interview with doña Dora, January 20, 2006, Tiquipaya (EH).
52. Group interview, July 20, 2003, Villa Sebastián Pagador (DG).

7. AN UNCERTAIN ANTHROPOLOGY

1. In Bolivia, statistics show an increase in crime of 360 percent from 1990 to 2001 (Juan Yhonny Mollericona, "Políticas de seguridad ciudadana en Bo-livia," *Proyecto Communidad Prevención* [blog], http://www.comunidadyp revencion.org/opinion_13.html). Although current data are hard to come by, based on anecdotal evidence it is reasonable to assume that this trend continued during the first decade of the twenty-first century.
2. Mollericona, "Políticas de seguridad ciudadana en Bolivia."
3. The so-called War on Drugs provides another example of rights suspensions justified in the name of safety and security—in this case, keeping our streets safe from the scourge of illegal narcotics. See Glasser and Siegel 1997.
4. Group interview, April 15, 2007, Juan Pablo II (DG, EH).
5. Interview with don Fulgencio, August 26, 2007, Loma Pampa (EH, RO).
6. Group interview, April 15, 2007, Juan Pablo II (DG, EH).
7. Interview with Juan Vargas, January 3, 2006, Cochabamba (RMA).
8. My discussion of the ratero resonates in interesting ways with Moodie's (2010, 172–73) analysis of crime, "not-knowing," and "unknowing" in post-war El Salvador.

References

Abrams, Philip. 1988 [1977]. "Notes on the Difficulty of Studying the State." *Journal of Historical Sociology* 1 (1): 58–89.

Acevedo V., Eduardo. 2004. "La justicia comunitaria en Bolivia." *Cipca Notes* 71 (November 1), http://www.cipca.org.bo/.

Achá, Rose Marie. 2003. *Huellas de fuego: crónica de un linchamiento.* Cochabamba: Acción Andina.

Adams, Richard N., and Delmos J. Jones. 1971. "Responsibilities of the Foreign Scholar to the Local Scholarly Community." *Current Anthropology* 12 (3): 335–56.

Agamben, Giorgio. 2002. "Security and Terror." *Theory and Event* 5 (4): 5–6.

———. 2005. *State of Exception.* Translated by Kevin Attell. Chicago: University of Chicago Press.

Aggarwal, Neil Krishan. 2010. "The Uses of Psychiatry in the War on Terror." *Political and Legal Anthropology Review* 33 (1): 81–98.

Aiello, Leslie C. 2010. "Engaged Anthropology: Diversity and Dilemmas." *Current Anthropology* 51 (Wenner-Gren Symposium Supplement 2): s201–2.

Albert, Bruce. 1997. "'Ethnographic Situation' and Ethnic Movements: Notes on Post-Malinowskian Fieldwork." *Critique of Anthropology* 17 (1): 53–65.

Alberti, Giorgia, and Enrique Mayer, eds. 1974. *Reciprocidad e intercambio en los Andes peruanos.* Lima: Instituto de Estudios Peruanos.

Albro, Robert. 2000. "The Populist Chola: Cultural Mediation and the Political Imagination in Quillacollo, Bolivia." *Journal of Latin American Anthropology* 5 (2): 30–88.

———. 2005. "'The Water Is Ours, Carajo!' Deep Citizenship in Bolivia's Water War." In *Social Movements: An Anthropological Reader*, edited by June Nash, 249–71. Oxford: Blackwell.

———. 2006a. "Bolivia's 'Evo Phenomenon': From Identity to What?" *Journal of Latin American Anthropology* 11 (2): 408–28.

———. 2006b. "The Culture of Democracy and Bolivia's Indigenous Movements." *Critique of Anthropology* 26 (4): 387–410.

———. 2007. "Anthropology's Terms of Engagement with Security." *Anthropology News* 48 (1): 20–21.

———. 2010a. "Confounding Cultural Citizenship and Constitutional Reform in Bolivia." *Latin American Perspectives* 37 (3): 71–90.

———. 2010b. *Roosters at Midnight: Indigenous Signs and Stigma in Local Bolivian Politics*. Santa Fe, NM: School of American Research Press.

Albro, Robert, George Marcus, Laura A. McNamara, and Monica Schoch-Spana. 2011. *Anthropologists in the SecurityScape: Ethics, Practice, and Professional Identity*. Walnut Creek, CA: Left Coast Press.

Alonso, Ana María. 1994. "The Politics of Space, Time and Substance: State Formation, Nationalism, and Ethnicity." *Annual Review of Anthropology* 23: 379–405.

American Anthropological Association. 2007. AAA *Commission on the Engagement of Anthropology with the US Security and Intelligence Communities: Final Report*. Washington, DC: American Anthropological Association.

Anderson, Sarah, Phyllis Bennis, and John Cavanagh. 2003. *Coalition of the Willing or Coalition of the Coerced? How the Bush Administration Influences Allies in Its War on Iraq*. Washington, DC: Institute for Policy Studies.

Annan, Kofi. 2005. In Larger Freedom: Towards Development, Security and Human Rights for All: Report of the Secretary-General. New York: United Nations Publications.

Appadurai, Arjun. 2002. "Deep Democracy: Urban Governmentality and the Horizon of Politics." *Public Culture* 14 (1): 21–47.

Ardila Amaya, Edgar. 2010. "Justicia comunitaria y sociedad nacional." *Cuarto Intermedio* 93–94 (April): 80–103.

Ardito, Wilfredo. 1997. "The Right to Self-Regulation: Legal Pluralism and Human Rights in Peru." *Journal of Legal Pluralism and Unofficial Law* 39: 1–42.

Arias, Enrique Desmond, and Daniel M. Goldstein, eds. 2010. *Violent Democracies in Latin America*. Durham: Duke University Press.

Arriagada, Irma. 2001. "Seguridad ciudadana y violencia en América Latina." Paper presented at the annual meeting of the Latin American Studies Association, Washington, DC, September 6–8.

Arriagada, Irma, and Lorena Godoy. 1999. *Seguridad ciudadana y violencia en América Latina: diagnóstico y politicas en los años 90*. Santiago, Chile: CEPAL.

Austin, J. L. 1962. *How to Do Things with Words*. Oxford: Oxford University Press.

Bailey, John, and Lucía Dammert. 2006. "Public Security and Police Reform in the Americas." In *Public Security and Police Reform in the Americas*, edited by John Bailey and Lucía Dammert, 1–23. Pittsburgh: University of Pittsburgh Press.

Beck, Ulrich. 1992. *Risk Society: Towards a New Modernity*. London: Sage.

Bernstein, Anya, and Elizabeth Mertz. 2011. "Introduction: Bureaucracy; Ethnography of the State in Everyday Life." In "Bureaucracy: Ethnography of the State in Everyday Life," symposium, *Political and Legal Anthropology Review* 34 (1): 6–10.

Berreman, Gerald D. 1968. "Is Anthropology Alive? Social Responsibility in Social Anthropology." *Current Anthropology* 9 (5): 391–96.

Besteman, Catherine. 2005. "Why I Disagree with Robert Kaplan." In *Why America's Top Pundits Are Wrong: Anthropologists Talk Back*, edited by Catherine Besteman and Hugh Gusterson, 83–101. Berkeley: University of California Press.

Bickham Mendez, Jennifer. 2008. "Globalizing Scholar Activism: Opportunities and Dilemmas through a Feminist Lens." In *Engaging Contradictions: Theory, Politics, and Methods of Activist Scholarship*, edited by Charles R. Hale, 136–63. Berkeley: University of California Press.

Bigo, Didier. 2002. "Security and Immigration: Toward a Critique of the Governmentality of Unease." *Alternatives* 27 (January–March): 63–92.

Binford, Leigh, and Nancy Churchill. 2009. "Lynching and States of Fear in Urban Mexico." *Anthropologica* 51 (2): 1–12.

Bobea, Lilian, ed. 2003. *Entre el crimen y el castigo: seguridad ciudadana y control democrático en América Latina y el Caribe*. Caracas: Editorial Nueva Sociedad.

Bolton, Ralph. 1995. "Rethinking Anthropology: The Study of AIDS." In *Culture and Sexual Risk: Anthropological Perspectives on AIDS*, edited by Han ten Brummelhuis and Gilbert Herdt, 285–314. Amsterdam: Gordon and Breach.

Bonilla, Víctor Daniel. 1982. "Algunas experiencias del proyecto 'Mapas parlantes.'" In *Alfabetización y educación de adultos en la región andina*, edited by Juan Eduardo García Huidobro, 145–61. Pátzcuaro, Mexico: UNESCO.

Boyarin, Jonathan. 1994. "Space, Time and the Politics of Memory." In *Remapping Memory: The Politics of TimeSpace*, edited by Jonathan Boyarin, 1–37. Minneapolis: University of Minnesota Press.

Braithwaite, John, Valerie Braithwaite, Michael Cookson, and Leah Dunn. 2011. *Anomie and Violence: Non-Truth and Reconciliation in Indonesian Peacebuilding*. Canberra: Australian National University E Press.

Bratich, Jack. 2006. "Public Secrecy and Immanent Security: A Strategic Analysis." *Cultural Studies* 20 (4–5): 493–511.

Briceño-Leon, Roberto, and Verónica Zubilaga. 2002. "Violence and Globalization in Latin America." *Current Sociology* 50 (1): 19–37.

Brown, Wendy. 2003. "Neoliberalism and the End of Liberal Democracy." *Theory and Event* 7 (1), http://muse.jhu.edu/journals/theory_and_event/v007/7.1brown.html.

Brysk, Alison. 2000. *From Tribal Village to Global Village: Indian Rights and International Relations in Latin America*. Stanford: Stanford University Press.

Burrell, Jennifer. 2008. "Lynching and Post-War Complexities in Guatemala." In *Global Vigilantism*, edited by David Pratten and Atryee Sen, 362–89. New York: Columbia University Press.

———. 2010. "In and Out of Rights: Security, Migration, and Human Rights Talk in Postwar Guatemala." *Journal of Latin American and Caribbean Anthropology* 15 (1): 90–115.

Buzan, Barry, Ole Wæver, and Jaap de Wilde. 1998. *Security: A New Framework for Analysis*. Boulder, CO: Lynne Reiner.

Cable, Vincent. 1995. "What Is International Economic Security?" *International Affairs* 71 (2): 305–24.

Caldeira, Teresa P. R. 2000. *City of Walls: Crime, Segregation, and Citizenship in São Paulo*. Berkeley: University of California Press.

Caldeira, Teresa P. R., and James Holston. 1999. "Democracy and Violence in Brazil." *Comparative Studies in Society and History* 41 (4): 691–729.

Call, Charles T. 2003. "Democratisation, War and State-Building: Constructing the Rule of Law in El Salvador." *Journal of Latin American Studies* 35 (4): 827–63.

Canessa, Andrew. 2000. "Fear and Loathing on the *Kharisiri* Trail: Alterity and Identity in the Andes." *Journal of the Royal Anthropological Institute* 6 (4): 705–20.

———. 2004. "Reproducing Racism: Schooling and Race in Highland Bolivia." *Race, Ethnicity and Education* 7 (2): 185–204.

———. 2006. "Todos somos indígenas: Towards a New Language of National Political Identity." *Bulletin of Latin American Research* 25 (2): 241–63.

———. 2012. *Intimate Indigeneities: Race, Sex, and History in the Small Spaces of Andean Life*. Durham: Duke University Press.

Cardona Álvarez, Germán Rómulo. 2005. "La concepción actual de la seguridad ciudadana y el sistema penal en el mundo," http://www.monografias.com/trabajos21/seguridad-ciudadana/seguridad-ciudadana.shtml?monosearch.

Carranza, Elias. 2004. "Políticas públicas en materia de seguridad de los habitantes ante el delito en América Latina." *Nueva Sociedad* 191 (May/June): 52–64.

Castillo Claudett, Eduardo. 2000. "La justicia en tiempos de la ira: linchamientos populares urbanos en América Latina." *Ecuador debate* 51: 207–26.

Centro de Estudios de la Realidad Económica y Social, Ministerio de Justicia y Derechos Humanos, and Banco Mundial. 1999. *Los quechuas de Tapacari, provincia Tapacari del departamento de Cochabamba. Justicia comunitaria: derecho consuetudinario*, vol. 3. La Paz: Centro de Estudios de la Realidad Económica y Social.

Centro de Estudios Jurídicos e Investigación Social, Ministerio de Justicia y Derechos Humanos, and Banco Mundial. 1999. *Los Guaranies del Izozog (provincia Cordillera—Santa Cruz). Justicia comunitaria: derecho con-*

suetudinario, vol. 2. La Paz: Centro de Estudios Jurídicos e Investigación Social.

Centro de Servicios Integrados para el Desarrollo Urbano, Ministerio de Justicia y Derechos Humanos, and Banco Mundial. 1999. *Los aymara de Machaca (provincia Ingavi—canton Jesus de Machaca, comunidades Sullcatiti-Khonkho. Justicia comunitaria: derecho consuetudinario*, vol. 1. La Paz: Centro de Servicios Integrados para el Desarrollo Urbano.

Chipman, John. 1992. "The Future of Strategic Studies: Beyond Grand Strategy." *Survival* 34 (1): 109–31.

Chisholm, Linda. 2000. *Charting a Hero's Journey*. Portland, OR: International Partnership for Service-Learning.

Chivi Vargas, Idón Moisés. 2010. "Hacia la descolonización de la justicia." *Cuarto Intermedio* 93–94 (April): 6–21.

Christiansen, Steen. 2011. "Hauntologies: Spectral Mechanisms." Unpublished manuscript, http://www.scribd.com/doc/48695187/Hauntologies-Spectral-Mechanisms.

Clarke, Kamari. 2010. Comments at the symposium "Reflections on Engaged Anthropology," sponsored by the Department of Anthropology, Rutgers University, New Brunswick, NJ, February 12.

Clifford, James, and George Marcus, eds. 1986. *Writing Culture: The Poetics and Politics of Ethnography*. Berkeley: University of California Press.

Cohen, Stanley. 2002. *Folk Devils and Moral Panics*. 3rd ed. London: Routledge.

Collier, Stephen J. 2008. "Enacting Catastrophe: Preparedness, Insurance, Budgetary Rationalization." *Economy and Society* 37 (2): 224–50.

Collier, Stephen J., Andrew Lakoff, and Paul Rabinow. 2004. "Biosecurity: Towards an Anthropology of the Contemporary." *Anthropology Today* 20 (5): 3–7.

Colloredo-Mansfeld, Rudi. 2002. "'Don't Be Lazy, Don't Lie, Don't Steal': Community Justice in the Neoliberal Andes." *American Ethnologist* 29 (3): 637–62.

———. 2009. *Fighting like a Community: Andean Civil Society in an Era of Indian Uprisings*. Chicago: University of Chicago Press.

Comaroff, Jean, and John L. Comaroff. 2002. "Alien-Nation: Zombies, Immigrants, and Millennial Capitalism." *South Atlantic Quarterly* 101 (4): 779–805.

———. 2006. "Law and Disorder in the Postcolony: An Introduction." In *Law and Disorder in the Postcolony*, edited by Jean Comaroff and John L. Comaroff, 1–56. Chicago: University of Chicago Press.

Comisión Andina de Juristas. 1999. *Seguridad ciudadana: Cambios necesarios*. Lima: Comisión Andina de Juristas.

Congreso Nacional. 2008. *Nueva constitución política del estado*. La Paz: República de Bolivia.

Corrigan, Phillip, and Derek Sayer. 1985. *The Great Arch: English State Formation as Cultural Revolution*. Oxford: Basil Blackwell.

Coutin, Susan Bibler. 2000. *Legalizing Moves: Salvadoran Immigrants' Struggle for U.S. Residency*. Ann Arbor: University of Michigan Press.

———. 2007. *Nations of Emigrants: Shifting Boundaries of Citizenship in El Salvador and the United States*. Ithaca: Cornell University Press.

Coutin, Susan Bibler, and Barbara Yngvesson. 2008. "Schrodinger's Cat and the Ethnography of Law." *Political and Legal Anthropology Review* 31 (1): 61–78.

Cowan, Jane K., Marie-Bénédicte Dembour, and Richard A. Wilson, eds. 2001. *Culture and Rights: Anthropological Perspectives*. Cambridge: Cambridge University Press.

Curbet, Jaume. 2006. *La glocalización de la (in)seguridad*. La Paz: Plural Editores.

Dammert, Lucia, and Mary Fran T. Malone. 2003. "Fear of Crime or Fear of Life? Public Insecurities in Chile." *Bulletin of Latin American Research* 22 (1): 79–101.

Das, Veena, and Deborah Poole. 2004. "State and Its Margins: Comparative Ethnographies." In *Anthropology in the Margins of the State*, edited by Veena Das and Deborah Poole, 3–33. Santa Fe, NM: School of American Research Press.

Davis, Colin. 2005. "Hauntology, Spectres and Phantoms." *French Studies* 59 (3): 373–79.

Davis, Darren W., and Brian D. Silver. 2004. "Civil Liberties vs. Security: Public Opinion in the Context of the Terrorist Attacks on America." *American Journal of Political Science* 48 (1): 28–46.

Davis, Mike. 1992. *City of Quartz: Excavating the Future in Los Angeles*. London: Vintage.

———. 2006. *Planet of Slums*. London: Verso.

De Genova, Nicholas. 2002. "Migrant 'Illegality' and Deportability in Everyday Life." *Annual Review of Anthropology* 31: 419–47.

De Genova, Nicholas, and Nathalie Peutz, eds. 2010. *The Deportation Regime: Sovereignty, Space, and the Freedom of Movement*. Durham: Duke University Press.

De la Cadena, Marisol. 1995. "'Women Are More Indian': Ethnicity and Gender in a Community Near Cuzco." In *Ethnicity, Markets, and Migration in the Andes*, edited by Brooke Larson and Olivia Harris, 329–48. Durham: Duke University Press.

———. 2000. *Indigenous Mestizos: The Politics of Race and Culture in Cuzco, Peru, 1919–1991*. Durham: Duke University Press.

Delgado Aguado, Julian, and J. Guardia Maduell. 1994. *Seguridad ciudadana y función policial: Una aproximación al análisis de entornos concretos*. Barcelona: Unión de Ciudades Capitales Iberoamericanas.

Del Olmo, Rosa. 2000. "Ciudades duras y violencia urbana." *Nueva Sociedad* 167: 74–86.

De Munter, Koen, and Ton Salman. 2009. "Extending Political Participation and

Citizenship: Pluricultural Civil Practices in Contemporary Bolivia." *Journal of Latin American and Caribbean Anthropology* 14 (2): 432–56.

Der Derian, James. 2009. *Critical Practices in International Theory: Selected Essays*. London: Routledge.

Derrida, Jacques. 1994. *Specters of Marx: The State of the Debt, the Work of Mourning and the New International*. Translated by Peggy Kamuf. London: Routledge.

Domingo, Pilar, and Rachel Seider. 2001. *Rule of Law in Latin America: The International Promotion of Judicial Reform*. London: Institute of Latin American Studies.

Drezner, Daniel W. 2011. *Theories of International Politics and Zombies*. Princeton: Princeton University Press.

Dubartell, Deborah. 2006. "Computer-Mediated Communication: Human-to-Human Communication across the Internet." *Journal of Linguistic Anthropology* 16 (2): 284–85.

Duce, Mauricio, and Rogelio Pérez Perdomo. 2003. "Citizen Security and Reform of the Criminal Justice System in Latin America." In *Crime and Violence in Latin America: Citizen Security, Democracy, and the State*, edited by Joseph S. Tulchin, Hugo Frühling, and Heather A. Golding, 69–92. Washington: Woodrow Wilson Center.

Durkheim, Emile. 1951 [1897]. *Suicide: A Study in Sociology*. Translated by John A. Spaulding and George Simpson. Glencoe, IL: Free Press.

Edelman, Marc, and Angelique Haugerud, eds. 2005. *The Anthropology of Development and Globalization: From Classical Political Economy to Contemporary Neoliberalism*. Oxford: Blackwell.

Elbert, Carlos Alberto. 1998. "Ideología, corrupción y excesos policiales." *Pena y Estado* 3 (3): 63–80.

Elmer, Greg, and Andy Opel. 2006. "Surviving the Inevitable Future." *Cultural Studies* 20 (4): 477–92.

Escobar, Santiago, et al. 2004. *La seguridad ciudadana como política de estado*. Santiago, Chile: Prosur.

Fals-Borda, Orlando. 1991. "Some Basic Ingredients." In *Action and Knowledge: Breaking the Monopoly with Participatory-Action Research*, edited by Orlando Fals-Borda and Mohammad Anisur Rahman, 3–12. New York: Apex.

Ferguson, James. 2006. *Global Shadows: Africa in the Neoliberal World Order*. Durham: Duke University Press.

Fernández Osco, Marcelo. 2000. *La ley del ayllu: práctica de jach'a justicia y jisk'a justicia en comunidades aymaras*. La Paz: PIEB.

———. 2001. "La ley del ayllu: justicia de acuerdos." *Tinkazos* 9: 11–28.

Forman, Shepard. 1993. *Diagnosing America: Anthropology and Public Engagement*. Ann Arbor: University of Michigan Press.

Forman, Shepard, and Joyce Riegelhaupt. 1979. "The Political Economy of

Patron-Clientship: Brazil and Portugal Compared." In *Brazil: Anthropological Perspectives*, edited by Maxine L. Margolis, 379–400. New York: Columbia University Press.

Forsyth, Miranda. 2007. "A Typology of Relationships between State and Non-State Justice Systems." *Journal of Legal Pluralism* 56: 67–112.

Fortun, Kim. 2001. *Advocacy after Bhopal: Environmentalism, Disaster, New Global Orders*. Chicago: University of Chicago Press.

Foucault, Michel. 1977. *Discipline and Punish: The Birth of the Prison*. Translated by Alan Sheridan. New York: Vintage.

———. 1991. "Governmentality." In *The Foucault Effect: Studies in Governmentality*, edited by Graham Burchell, Colin Gordon, and Peter Miller, 87–104. Chicago: University of Chicago Press.

———. 2007. *Security, Territory, Population: Lectures at the Collège de France, 1977–1978*. Edited by Michel Senellart, François Ewald, Alessandro Fontana, and Arnold I. Davidson. Translated by Graham Burchell. New York: Palgrave Macmillan.

Friedman, Jonathan. 2004. "Globalization." In *A Companion to the Anthropology of Politics*, edited by David Nugent and Joan Vincent, 179–97. Malden, MA: Blackwell.

Fuentes Díaz, Antonio, and Leigh Binford. 2001. "Linchamientos en Mexico: una respuesta a Carlos Vilas." *Bajo el volcán* 2 (3): 143–56.

Fukuyama, Francis. 2004. *State Building: Governance and World Order in the Twenty-First Century*. London: Profile.

Fundación de Apoyo al Parlamento y a la Participación Ciudadana. 2007. *Justicia de los pueblos indígenas y originarios: estudios de caso*. La Paz: FUNDAPPAC.

Gabaldón, Luis Gerardo. 2004. *Análisis y propuestas: el observatorio de Nueva Sociedad: seguridad ciudadana y control del delito en América Latina*. Caracas: Nueva Sociedad.

Garland, David. 2001. *The Culture of Control: Crime and Social Order in Contemporary Society*. Chicago: University of Chicago Press.

Geschiere, Peter. 1997. *The Modernity of Witchcraft: Politics and the Occult in Postcolonial Africa*. Charlottesville: University of Virginia Press.

Giddens, Anthony. 1990. *The Consequences of Modernity*. Oxford: Polity.

———. 1999. "Risk and Responsibility." *Modern Law Review* 62 (1): 1–10.

Gilmore, Ruth Wilson. 1993. "Public Enemies and Private Intellectuals: Apartheid USA." *Race and Class* 35 (1): 71–78.

———. 2008. "Forgotten Places and the Seeds of Grassroots Planning." In *Engaging Contradictions: Theory, Politics, and Methods of Activist Scholarship*, edited by Charles R. Hale, 31–61. Berkeley: University of California Press.

Gjessing, Gutorm. 1968. "The Social Responsibility of the Social Scientist." *Current Anthropology* 9 (5): 397–402.

Glasser, Ira, and Loren Siegel. 1997. "'When Constitutional Rights Seem Too

Extravagant to Endure': The Crack Scare's Impact on Civil Rights and Liberties."
In *Crack in America: Demon Drugs and Social Justice,* edited by Craig Reinerman
and Harry G. Levine, 229–48. Berkeley: University of California Press.

Gledhill, John. 2004. "Neoliberalism." In *A Companion to the Anthropology of
Politics,* edited by David Nugent and Joan Vincent, 332–48. Malden, MA:
Blackwell.

Godoy, Angelina Snodgrass. 2006. *Popular Injustice: Violence, Community, and
Law in Latin America.* Stanford: Stanford University Press.

Goldstein, Daniel M. 2003. "'In Our Own Hands': Lynching, Justice and the Law
in Bolivia." *American Ethnologist* 30 (1): 22–43.

———. 2004. *The Spectacular City: Violence and Performance in Urban Bolivia.*
Durham: Duke University Press.

———. 2005a. "Flexible Justice: Neoliberal Violence and Self-Help Security in
Bolivia." *Critique of Anthropology* 25 (4): 389–411.

———. 2005b. "Orphans of the State: Conceptualizing Citizenship, Space, and
Kinship in Bolivian Municipal Politics." *Cultural Dynamics* 17 (1): 5–31.

———. 2008. "Response to the Human Rights Foundation: Don't Mistake Lynching and Other Forms of Vigilant Violence for Community Justice." Andean
Information Network, January 28, http://ain-bolivia.org/2008/01/on-
community-justice/.

———. 2010a. "Security and the Culture Expert: Dilemmas of an Engaged Anthropology." *Political and Legal Anthropology Review* 33 (1): 126–42.

———. 2010b. "Toward a Critical Anthropology of Security." *Current Anthropology* 51 (4): 487–517.

Goldstein, Daniel M., Gloria Achá, Eric Hinojosa, and Theo Roncken. 2007. "La
Mano Dura and the Violence of Civil Society in Bolivia." *Social Analysis* 51 (2):
43–63.

Goldstein, Daniel M., and Fatimah Williams Castro. 2006. "Creative Violence:
How Marginal People Make News in Bolivia." *Journal of Latin American
Anthropology* 11 (2): 380–407.

Goodale, Mark. 2007. "Introduction: Locating Rights, Envisioning Law between
the Global and the Local." In *The Practice of Human Rights: Tracking Law
between the Global and the Local,* edited by Mark Goodale and Sally Engle
Merry, 1–38. Cambridge: Cambridge University Press.

———. 2008. *Dilemmas of Modernity: Bolivian Encounters with Law and Liberalism.* Stanford: Stanford University Press.

———. 2009. "Personhood and Radical Social Change: Notes from a 21st Century
Revolution." Paper presented at the Center for Latin American Studies,
Rutgers University, October 17.

Goodale, Mark, and Sally Engle Merry, eds. 2007. *The Practice of Human Rights:
Tracking Law between the Global and the Local.* Cambridge: Cambridge University Press.

Gordon, Avery F. 1997. *Ghostly Matters: Haunting and the Sociological Imagination*. Minneapolis: University of Minnesota Press.

Gordon, Colin. 1991. "Governmental Rationality: An Introduction." In *The Foucault Effect: Studies in Governmentality*, edited by Graham Burchell, Colin Gordon, and Peter Miller, 1–51. Chicago: University of Chicago Press.

Graeber, David. 2009. *Direct Action: An Ethnography*. Oakland, CA: AK Press.

Gramsci, Antonio. 1971. *Selections from the Prison Notebooks*. Edited by Q. Hoare and G. N. Smith. London: Lawrence and Wishart.

Grandin, Greg. 2006. *Empire's Workshop: Latin America, the United States, and the Rise of the New Imperialism*. New York: Henry Holt.

Gray, Jeremy. 1989. *Ideas of Space: Euclidean, Non-Euclidean, and Relativistic*. Oxford: Clarendon Press of Oxford University Press.

Gribbin, John. 1996. *Schrödinger's Kittens and the Search for Reality: Solving the Quantum Mysteries*. Boston: Little, Brown.

Guerrero, Andrés. 2001. "Los linchamientos en las comunidades indígenas: ¿la política perversa de una modernidad marginal?" *Ecuador debate* 53: 197–226.

Gustafson, Bret. 2002. "Paradoxes of Liberal Indigenism: Indigenous Movements, State Processes, and Intercultural Reform in Bolivia." In *The Politics of Ethnicity: Indigenous Peoples in Latin American States*, edited by David Maybury-Lewis, 267–306. Cambridge: Harvard University Press.

Gusterson, Hugh. 2004. *People of the Bomb: Portraits of America's Nuclear Complex*. Minneapolis: University of Minnesota Press.

Gusterson, Hugh, and Catherine Besteman, eds. 2009. *The Insecure American: How We Got Here and What We Should Do about It*. Berkeley: University of California Press.

Gutiérrez Pérez, Vladimir. 2009. *Justicia comunitaria y pluralismo jurídico*. Sucre, Bolivia: Universidad Mayor Real y Pontificia de San Francisco Xavier.

Gwaltney, John Langston, ed. 1993. *Drylongo: A Self-Portrait of Black America*. New York: New Press.

Hale, Charles R. 2002. "Does Multiculturalism Menace? Governance, Cultural Rights and the Politics of Identity in Guatemala." *Journal of Latin American Studies* 34 (3): 485–524.

———. 2006. "Activist Research vs. Cultural Critique: Indigenous Land Rights and the Contradictions of Politically Engaged Anthropology." *Cultural Anthropology* 21: 96–120.

———, ed. 2008a. *Engaging Contradictions: Theory, Politics, and Methods of Activist Scholarship*. Berkeley: University of California Press.

———. 2008b. Introduction to *Engaging Contradictions: Theory, Politics, and Methods of Activist Scholarship*, edited by Charles R. Hale, 1–28. Berkeley: University of California Press.

———. 2010. Comments at the symposium "Reflections on Engaged Anthropology," sponsored by the Department of Anthropology, Rutgers University, New Brunswick, NJ, February 12.

Hall, Peter. 2004. "Creativity, Culture, Knowledge and the City." *Built Environment* 30 (3): 256–58.

Hall, Stuart, et al. 1978. *Policing the Crisis: Mugging, the State and Law and Order*. London: Palgrave Macmillan.

Hansen, Lene. 2000. "The Little Mermaid's Silent Security Dilemma and the Absence of Gender in the Copenhagen School." *Millennium* 29 (2): 289–306.

Haraway, Donna. 1988. "Situated Knowledges: The Science Question in Feminism and the Privilege of Partial Perspective." *Feminist Studies* 14 (3): 575–99.

Harriss, John. 2002. *Depoliticizing Development: The World Bank and Social Capital*. London: Anthem.

Harvey, David. 1989. *The Condition of Postmodernity: An Enquiry into the Origins of Cultural Change*. Oxford: Blackwell.

——. 1991. "Flexibility: Threat or Opportunity?" *Socialist Review* 21 (1): 65–77.

——. 2001. *Spaces of Capital: Towards a Critical Geography*. Edinburgh: Edinburgh University Press.

Haugerud, Angelique. 1993. *The Culture of Politics in Modern Kenya*. Cambridge: Cambridge University Press.

Hay, James, and Mark Andrejevic. 2006. "Introduction: Toward an Analytic of Governmental Experiments in These Times: Homeland Security as the New Social Security." *Cultural Studies* 20 (4–5): 331–48.

Helm, Dieter. 2002. "Energy Policy: Security of Supply, Sustainability and Competition." *Energy Policy* 30 (3): 173–84.

Henne, Kurt, and David Moseley. 2005. "Combating the Worst Forms of Child Labor in Bolivia." *Human Rights* 32 (1), http://www.americanbar.org/publications/human_rights_magazine_home/irr_hr_winter05_bolivia.html.

Herzfeld, Michael. 1993. *The Social Production of Indifference: Exploring the Symbolic Roots of Western Bureaucracy*. Chicago: University of Chicago Press.

Heymann, David L. 2003. The Evolving Infectious Disease Threat: Implications for National and Global Security." *Journal of Human Development* 4 (2): 191–207.

Hinojosa, Fares. 2007. *Delimitación de las áreas urbanas del Municipio Cercado*. Cochabamba: Oficialia Mayor de Planificación y Medio Ambiente, Dirección de Planeamiento.

Hobbes, Thomas. 1985 [1651]. *The Leviathan*. Bristol, England: Thoemmes Continuum.

Hodgson, Dorothy. 1999. "Critical Interventions: Dilemmas of Accountability in Contemporary Ethnographic Research." *Identities* 6 (2–3): 201–24.

——. 2011. *Being Maasai, Becoming Indigenous: Postcolonial Politics in a Neoliberal World*. Bloomington: Indiana University Press.

Human Rights Foundation. 2008. *Country Report: Bolivia 2007*. New York: HRF.

Hylton, Forrest, and Sinclair Thomson. 2007. *Revolutionary Horizons: Past and Present in Bolivian Politics*. London: Verso.

Hymes, Dell. 1969. *Reinventing Anthropology*. New York: Pantheon.

Inda, Jonathan Xavier. 2000. "A Flexible World: Capitalism, Citizenship, and Postnational Zones." *Political and Legal Anthropology Review* 23 (1): 86–102.

———. 2005. "Analytics of the Modern: An Introduction." In *Anthropologies of Modernity: Foucault, Governmentality, and Life Politics*, edited by Jonathan Xavier Inda, 1–20. Oxford: Blackwell.

Instituto Nacional de Estadísticas de Bolivia. 2001. *Censo nacional de población y vivienda*. Cochabamba: Instituto Nacional de Estadísticas de Bolivia.

———. 2003. *Bolivia: Características socio-demográficas de la población*. La Paz: Instituto Nacional de Estadísticas de Bolivia.

International Council on Human Rights Policy. 2003. *Crime, Public Order and Human Rights*. Versoix, Switzerland: International Council on Human Rights Policy.

Jackson, Jean. 1999. "The Politics of Ethnographic Practice in the Colombian Vaupes." *Identities* 6 (2–3): 281–317.

Jimeno, Myriam. 2008. "Colombia: Citizens and Anthropologists." In *Companion to Latin American Anthropology*, edited by Deborah Poole, 72–89. Oxford: Blackwell.

Johnston, Barbara Rose. 2010. "Social Responsibility and the Anthropological Citizen." *Current Anthropology* 51 (Supplement 2): S235–47.

Joseph, Gilbert M., and Daniel Nugent, eds. 1994. *Everyday Forms of State Formation: Revolution and the Negotiation of Rule in Modern Mexico*. Durham: Duke University Press.

Kaplan, Robert D. 1994. "The Coming Anarchy." *Atlantic*, February 2, 44–77.

Karp, David R., and Todd R. Clear, eds. 2002. *What Is Community Justice? Case Studies of Restorative Justice and Community Supervision*. Thousand Oaks, CA: Sage.

Kelty, Christopher. 2005. "Geeks, Social Imaginaries, and Recursive Publics." *Cultural Anthropology* 20 (2): 185–214.

Khagram, Sanjeev, William Clark, and Dana Firas Raad. 2003. "From the Environment and Human Security to Sustainable Security and Development." *Journal of Human Development* 4 (2): 289–314.

Kirsch, Stuart. 1996. "Anthropologists and Global Alliances." *Anthropology Today* 12 (4): 14–16.

———. 2002. "Anthropology and Advocacy: A Case Study of the Campaign against Ok Tedi Mine." *Critique of Anthropology* 22 (2): 175–200.

———. 2010. Comments at the symposium "Reflections on Engaged Anthropology," sponsored by the Department of Anthropology, Rutgers University, New Brunswick, NJ, February 12.

Kohl, Benjamin H. 2004. "Privatization and Regulation, A Cautionary Tale from Bolivia." *International Journal of Urban and Regional Research* 28 (4): 893–908.

Kohl, Benjamin H., and Linda C. Farthing. 2006. *Impasse in Bolivia: Neoliberal Hegemony and Popular Resistance*. London: Zed.

Krasner, Stephen D., and Carlos Pascual. 2005. "Addressing State Failure." *Foreign Affairs* 84 (4): 153–63.

Kupchan, Charles A., and Clifford A. Kupchan. 1995. "The Promise of Collective Security." *International Security* 20 (1): 52–61.

Lagos, María. 2000. "Between Stability and Crisis in Latin America." *Journal of Democracy* 12 (1): 137–45.

Lakoff, Andrew. 2007. "Preparing for the Next Emergency." *Public Culture* 19 (2): 247–71.

———. 2008. "The Generic Biothreat, or, How We Became Unprepared." *Cultural Anthropology* 23 (3): 399–428.

Lakoff, Andrew, and Stephen J. Collier, eds. 2008. *Biosecurity Interventions: Global Health and Security in Question*. New York: Columbia University Press.

Larner, Wendy. 2000. "Neo-Liberalism: Policy, Ideology, Governmentality." *Studies in Political Economy* 63: 5–25.

Larson, Brooke. 1988. *Colonialism and Agrarian Transformation in Bolivia: Cochabamba, 1550–1900*. Princeton: Princeton University Press.

Larson, Brooke, and Olivia Harris, eds. 1995. *Ethnicity, Markets, and Migration in the Andes*. Durham: Duke University Press.

Lassiter, Luke Eric. 2005. "Collaborative Ethnography and Public Anthropology." *Current Anthropology* 46 (1): 83–106.

Latour, Bruno. 2005. *Reassembling the Social: An Introduction to Actor-Network-Theory*. Oxford: Oxford University Press.

Lazar, Sian. 2008. *El Alto, Rebel City: Self and Citizenship in Andean Bolivia*. Durham: Duke University Press.

Leal Buitrago, Francisco. 2003. "La doctrina de seguridad nacional: Materialización de la Guerra Fría en América del Sur." *Revista de Estudios Sociales* 15: 74–87.

Ledo García, Carmen. 2002. *Urbanisation and Poverty in the Cities of the National Economic Corridor in Bolivia: Case Study, Cochabamba*. Delft, the Netherlands: DUP Science.

Leiva, Fernando Ignacio. 2008. *Latin American Neostructuralism: The Contradictions of Post-Neoliberal Development*. Minneapolis: University of Minnesota Press.

Leve, Lauren. 2007. "'Secularism Is a Human Right!': Double-Binds of Buddhism, Democracy, and Identity in Nepal." In *The Practice of Human Rights: Tracking Law between the Local and the Global*, edited by Mark Goodale and Sally Engle Merry, 78–114. Cambridge: Cambridge University Press.

Lévi-Strauss, Claude. 1966. *The Savage Mind*. Chicago: University of Chicago Press.

Levitt, Peggy, and Sally Merry. 2009. "Vernacularization on the Ground: Local Uses of Global Women's Rights in Peru, China, India and the United States." *Global Networks* 9 (4): 441–61.

Llewellyn, Karl Nickerson, and Edward Adamson Hoebel. 1941. *The Cheyenne Way: Conflict and Case Law in Primitive Jurisprudence.* Norman: University of Oklahoma Press.

Low, Setha M. 1997. "Urban Fear: Building the Fortress City." *City and Society* 9 (1): 53–71.

———. 2003. *Behind the Gates: Life, Security, and the Pursuit of Happiness in Fortress America.* New York: Routledge.

———. 2011. "Claiming Space for an Engaged Anthropology: Spatial Inequality and Social Exclusion." *American Anthropologist* 113 (3): 389–407.

Low, Setha M., and Sally Engle Merry. 2010. "Engaged Anthropology: Diversity and Dilemmas." *Current Anthropology* 51 (Supplement 2): s203–26.

Lutkehaus, Nancy C. 2008. *Margaret Mead: The Making of an American Icon.* Princeton: Princeton University Press.

Lutz, Catherine. 2001. *Homefront: A Military City and the American Twentieth Century.* Boston: Beacon.

Machillanda, José. 2005. "La remilitarización de la seguridad en América Latina." *Nueva Sociedad* 198: 130–44.

Mansilla, H. C. F. 2003. *La policía boliviana: entre los códigos informales y los intentos de modernización.* La Paz: Plural Editores.

Marcus, George. 2005. "The Passion of Anthropology in the US, Circa 2004." *Anthropological Quarterly* 78 (3): 673–95.

Marcus, George, and Michael M. J. Fischer. 1986. *Anthropology as Cultural Critique: An Experimental Moment in the Human Sciences.* Chicago: University of Chicago Press.

Mares, David R. 2008. "The National Security State." In *A Companion to Latin American History*, edited by Thomas H. Holloway, 386–405. Oxford: Blackwell.

Martínez, Samuel. 2008. "Making Violence Visible: An Activist Anthropological Approach to Women's Rights Investigation." In *Engaging Contradictions: Theory, Politics, and Methods of Activist Scholarship*, edited by Charles R. Hale, 183–209. Berkeley: University of California Press.

Marx, Karl. 1967. "On the Jewish Question." In *Writings of the Young Marx on Philosophy and Society*, translated and edited by Lloyd D. Easton and Kurt H. Guddat, 216–48. Garden City, NY: Doubleday.

———. 1963 [1852]. *The 18th Brumaire of Louis Bonaparte.* Translated by C. P. Dutt. New York: International Publishers.

MAS. 2005. *Ayuda memoria MAS: Diez medidas para cambiar Bolivia.* La Paz: Comisión de Planificación y Estrategias, MAS.

Mascia-Lees, Frances E., and Jeff Himpele. 2006. "Reimagining Globality: Toward an Anthropological Physics." *Anthropology News* 47 (5): 10–11.

——. 2007. "Temporalities of the Present: Rethinking Anthropology's Spatial Geophysics." Lecture delivered at the Rutgers University Center for Historical Analysis, New Brunswick, NJ, April 8.

Masco, Joseph. 2006. *The Nuclear Borderlands: The Manhattan Project in Post–Cold War New Mexico.* Princeton: Princeton University Press.

——. 2008. "'Survival Is Your Business': Engineering Ruins and Affect in Nuclear America." *Cultural Anthropology* 23 (2): 361–98.

Matthew, Richard Anthony. 2000. "The Environment as a National Security Issue." *Journal of Political History* 12 (1): 101–22.

Maybury-Lewis, David. 1985. "A Special Sort of Pleading: Anthropology at the Service of Ethnic Groups." In *Advocacy and Anthropology: First Encounters,* edited by Robert Paine, 130–48. St. John's, Newfoundland: Memorial University of Newfoundland.

Mayer, Enrique. 1991. "Peru in Deep Trouble: Mario Vargas Llosa's 'Inquest in the Andes' Reexamined." *Cultural Anthropology* 6 (4): 466–504.

Mayorga, Fernando. 2006. "El gobierno de Evo Morales: entre nacionalismo e indigenismo." *Nueva Sociedad* 26 (November–December): 4–13.

McFate, Montgomery. 2005. "Anthropology and Counterinsurgency: The Strange Story of their Curious Relationship." *Military Review* (March–April): 24–38.

——. 2007. "Building Bridges or Burning Heretics?" *Anthropology Today* 23 (3): 21.

Medeiros, Carmen. 2001. "Civilizing the Popular? The Law of Popular Participation and the Design of a New Civil Society in 1990's Bolivia." *Critique of Anthropology* 21 (4): 401–25.

Menjívar, Cecilia. 2006. "Liminal Legality: Salvadoran and Guatemalan Immigrants' Lives in the United States." *American Journal of Sociology* 111 (4): 999–1037.

Merry, Sally Engle. 1988. "Legal Pluralism." *Law and Society Review* 22 (5): 869–95.

——. 2001. "Spatial Governmentality and the New Urban Social Order: Controlling Gender Violence through Law." *American Anthropologist* 103 (1): 16–29.

——. 2003. "Rights Talk and the Experience of Law: Implementing Women's Human Rights to Protection from Violence." *Human Rights Quarterly* 25 (2): 343–81.

——. 2005. *Human Rights and Gender Violence: Translating International Law into Local Justice.* Chicago: University of Chicago Press.

——. 2006. "Transnational Human Rights and Local Activism: Mapping the Middle." *American Anthropologist* 108 (1): 38–51.

Merton, Robert K. 1938. "Social Structure and Anomie." *American Sociological Review* 3 (5): 672–82.

Mertz, Elizabeth, and Andria Timmer. 2010. "Introduction: Getting It Done:

Ethnographic Perspectives on NGOS." In "Ethnographic Perspectives on NGOS," symposium, *Political and Legal Anthropology Review* 33 (2): 171–77.

Metzl, Jonathan M. 2010. *The Protest Psychosis: How Schizophrenia Became a Black Disease*. Boston: Beacon.

Mier Cueto, Enrique. 2005. "Las prácticas jurídicas aymaras desde una perspectiva cultural." In *Justicia comunitaria en los pueblos originarios de Bolivia*, edited by Vladimir Gutiérrez Pérez, 61–83. Sucre, Bolivia: Instituto de la Judicatura de Bolivia.

Mlodinow, Leonard. 2001. *Euclid's Window: The Story of Geometry from Parallel Lines to Hyperspace*. New York: Free Press.

Molina, Fernando. 2010. "Los límites de la justicia comunitaria." Infolatam, June 10, http://www.infolatam.com/2010/06/11/los-limites-de-la-justicia-comunitaria.

Molina Viaña, Oscar. 2001. *Seguridad ciudadana: consejos prácticos*. La Paz: Creativa.

Mollericona, Juan Yhonny, Ninoska Tinini, and Adriana Paredes. 2007. *La seguridad ciudadana en la ciudad de El Alto: fronteras entre el miedo y la acción vecinal*. La Paz: PIEB.

Moodie, Ellen. 2010. *El Salvador in the Aftermath of Peace: Crime, Uncertainty, and the Transition to Democracy*. Philadelphia: University of Pennsylvania Press.

Morales, Waltraud Q. 2010. *A Brief History of Bolivia*. 2nd ed. New York: Lexington.

———. 2011. "From Revolution to Revolution: Bolivia's National Revolution and the 'Refounding' Revolution of Evo Morales." *The Latin Americanist* 55 (1): 131–44.

Moser, Caroline, Ailsa Winton, and Annalise Moser. 2005. "Violence, Fear, and Insecurity among the Urban Poor in Latin America." In *The Urban Poor in Latin America*, edited by Marianne Fay, 125–78. Washington, DC: The World Bank.

Müller, Katharina. 2008. "Contested Universalism: From Bonosol to Renta Dignidad in Bolivia." *International Journal of Social Welfare* 18 (2): 163–72.

Munn, Nancy D. 1992. "The Cultural Anthropology of Time: A Critical Essay." *Annual Review of Anthropology* 21: 93–123.

Nadel-Klein, Jean. 1991. "Reweaving the Fringe: Localism, Tradition and Representation in British Ethnography." *American Ethnologist* 18 (3): 500–517.

Nader, Laura. 1990. *Harmony Ideology: Justice and Control in a Zapotec Mountain Village*. Stanford: Stanford University Press.

Neild, Rachel. 2002. "The New Face of Impunity." *Human Rights Dialogue* 2 (8): 1–2.

Nelson, Diane M. 1996. "Maya Hackers and the Cyberspatialized Nation-State: Modernity, Ethnostalgia, and a Lizard Queen in Guatemala." *Cultural Anthropology* 11 (3): 287–308.

Nicolas, Vincent, Marcelo Fernández, and Elba Flores, eds. 2007. *Modos originarios de resolución de conflictos en pueblos indígenas de Bolivia*. La Paz: Fundación UNIR.

Niezen, Ronald. 2003. *The Origins of Indigenism: Human Rights and the Politics of Identity*. Berkeley: University of California Press.

Nolasco Armas, Margarita. 1984. "La antropología aplicada en México y su destino final el indigenismo." In *Los Indios y la antropología en América Latina*, edited by Carmen Junqueira and Edgard de A. Carvalho, 125–50. Buenos Aires: Búsqueda-Yuchan.

Nordstrom, Carolyn. 2004. *Shadows of War: Violence, Power, and International Profiteering in the Twenty-First Century*. Berkeley: University of California Press.

———. 2007. *Global Outlaws: Crime, Money, and Power in the Contemporary World*. Berkeley: University of California Press.

Nueva Constitución Política del Estado. 2008. La Paz: Congreso Nacional.

Nugent, Daniel, and Ana María Alonso. 1994. "Multiple Selective Traditions in Agrarian Reform and Agrarian Struggle: Popular Culture and State Formation in the *Ejido* of Namiquipa, Chihuahua." In *Everyday Forms of State Formation: Revolution and the Negotiation of Rule in Modern Mexico*, edited by Gilbert M. Joseph and Daniel Nugent, 209–46. Durham: Duke University Press.

Nye, Joseph S. 1974. "Collective Economic Security." *International Affairs* 50 (4): 584–98.

Olivero, Eduardo Raúl. n.d. "Artes marciales, ética del cuidado y derechos humanos." Unpublished manuscript.

O'Malley, Pat. 1996. "Risk and Responsibility." In *Foucault and Political Reason: Liberalism, NeoLiberalism, and Rationalities of Government*, edited by Andrew Barry, Thomas Osborne, and Nikolas Rose, 189–208. Chicago: University of Chicago Press.

Ong, Aihwa. 1999. *Flexible Citizenship: The Cultural Logics of Transnationality*. Durham: Duke University Press.

———. 2006. *Neoliberalism as Exception: Mutations in Citizenship and Sovereignty*. Durham: Duke University Press.

Orcutt, James D. 1983. *Analyzing Deviance*. Homewood, IL: Dorsey.

Orellana Halkyer, René. 2005. "Prácticas judiciales en comunidades indígenas quechuas." In *Justicia comunitaria en los pueblos originarios de Bolivia*, edited by Vladimir Gutiérrez Pérez, 11–39. Sucre: Instituto de la Judicatura de Bolivia.

Organizaciones de Derechos Humanos para el Foro Permanente para los Pueblos Indígenas. 2010. *Situación de los Derechos Humanos de los Pueblos Indígenas en Bolivia 2010*. La Paz, Bolivia.

Owczarzak, Jill. 2009. "Defining HIV Risk and Determining Responsibility in Postsocialist Poland." *Medical Anthropology Quarterly* 23 (4): 417–35.

Painter, Michael. 1991. "Re-Creating Peasant Economy in Southern Peru." In *Golden Ages, Dark Ages: Imagining the Past in Anthropology and History*, edited by Jay O'Brien and William Roseberry, 81–106. Berkeley: University of California Press.

Park, Robert E. 1928. "Human Migration and the Marginal Man." *American Journal of Sociology* 33 (6): 881–98.

Pearce, Adrian. 2011. *Evo Morales and the Movimiento al Socialismo in Bolivia: The First Term in Context, 2005–2009*. London: Institute for the Study of the Americas.

Peattie, Lisa. 1958. "Interventionism and Applied Science in Anthropology." *Human Organization* 17 (1): 4–9.

———. 1974. "'The Concept of Marginality' as Applied to Squatter Settlements." In *Anthropological Perspectives on Latin American Urbanization*, edited by Wayne A. Cornelius and Felicity M. Trueblood, 101–109. Beverly Hills, CA: Sage.

Petrella, Laura, and Franz Vanderschueren. 2003. "Ciudad y violencia: seguridad y ciudad." In *La ciudad inclusiva*, edited by Marcelo Balbo, Ricardo Jordan, and Daniela Simioni, 215–35. Santiago, Chile: CEPAL.

Peutz, Nathalie. 2007. "Out-laws: Deportees, Desire, and 'The Law.'" *International Migration* 45 (3): 182–91.

Pierre, Jemima. 2008. "Activist Groundings or Groundings for Activism? The Study of Racialization as a Site of Political Engagement." In *Engaging Contradictions: Theory, Politics, and Methods of Activist Scholarship*, edited by Charles R. Hale, 115–35. Berkeley: University of California Press.

Poole, Deborah. 1997. *Vision, Race, and Modernity: A Visual Economy of the Andean Image World*. Princeton: Princeton University Press.

Postero, Nancy. 2006. *Now We Are Citizens: Indigenous Politics in Postmulticultural Bolivia*. Stanford: Stanford University Press.

———. 2010. "The Struggle to Create a Radical Democracy in Bolivia." In "Actually Existing Democracies," special issue, *Latin American Research Review* 45: 59–78.

Price, David. 1998. "Cold War Anthropology: Collaborators and Victims of the National Security State." *Identities* 4 (3–4): 389–430.

———. 2005. "America the Ambivalent: Quietly Selling Anthropology to the CIA." *Anthropology Today* 21 (5): 1–2.

Prillaman, William C. 2000. *The Judiciary and Democratic Decay in Latin America: Declining Confidence in the Rule of Law*. Westport, CT: Praeger.

———. 2003. "Crime, Democracy, and Development in Latin America." *Papers on the Americas* 14 (6): 1–30.

Pulido, Laura. 2008. "FAQs: Frequently (Un)asked Questions about Being a Scholar Activist." In *Engaging Contradictions: Theory, Politics, and Methods of Activist Scholarship*, edited by Charles R. Hale, 341–65. Berkeley: University of California Press.

Quintana, Juan Ramón, et al. 2003. *Policia y democracia en Bolivia: una politica institucional pendiente*. La Paz: PIEB.

Rabinow, Paul. 1977. *Reflections on Fieldwork in Morocco*. Berkeley: University of California Press.

Radcliffe, Sarah A., and Sallie Westwood. 1996. *Remaking the Nation: Place, Identity, and Politics in Latin America*. London: Routledge.

Rajagopal, Balakrishnan. 2003. *International Law from Below: Development, Social Movements and Third World Resistance*. Cambridge: Cambridge University Press.

Ramos, Alcida Rita. 1999. "Anthropologist as Political Actor." *Journal of Latin American and Caribbean Anthropology* 4 (2): 172–89.

Rappaport, Joanne. 2008. "Beyond Participant Observation: Collaborative Ethnography as Theoretical Innovation." *Collaborative Anthropologies* 1: 1–31.

Redfield, Robert. 1941. *The Folk Culture of Yucatan*. Chicago: University of Chicago Press.

Rennie, Gordon, David Bishop, Simon Jowett, and Peter Evans. 2006. *I Am the Law: The Judge Dredd Omnibus*. Nottingham, UK: Games Workshop.

Renzi, Lt. Col. Fred. 2006. "Networks: Terra Incognita and the Case for Ethnographic Intelligence." *Military Review*, September–October, 16–22.

Riaño-Alcalá, Pilar. 2006. *Dwellers of Memory: Youth and Violence in Medellín, Colombia*. New Brunswick, NJ: Transaction.

Ribeiro, Gustavo Lins. 2006. "World Anthropologies: Cosmopolitics for a New Global Scenario in Anthropology." *Critique of Anthropology* 26 (4): 363–86.

Risør, Helene. 2010. "Twenty Hanging Dolls and a Lynching: Defacing Dangerousness and Enacting Citizenship in El Alto, Bolivia." *Public Culture* 22 (3): 465–85.

Rivera Cusicanqui, Silvia, ed. 1996. *Ser mujer indígena, chola or birlocha en la Bolivia postcolonial del los años 90*. La Paz: Ministerio de Desarrollo Humano.

———. 2010. "The Notion of 'Rights' and the Paradox of Postcolonial Modernity: Indigenous People and Women in Bolivia." *Qui Parle* 18 (2): 29–54.

Roberts, Simon. 1998. "Against Legal Pluralism: Some Reflections on the Contemporary Enlargement of the Legal Domain." *Journal of Legal Pluralism and Unofficial Law* 42: 95–106.

Robin, Corey. 2004. *Fear: The History of a Political Idea*. Oxford: Oxford University Press.

Rocabado Rodríguez, Mary, and Rolando Caballero Romano. 2005. *Delincuencia y seguridad ciudadana en Bolivia*. La Paz: Fondo Editorial de los Diputados.

Rockefeller, Stuart Alexander. 2010. *Starting from Quirpini: The Travels and Places of a Bolivian People*. Bloomington: Indiana University Press.

Rose, Nikolas. 1996. "The Death of the Social? Re-Figuring the Territory of Government." *Economy and Society* 25 (3): 327–56.

Rotker, Susana, ed. 2002. *Citizens of Fear: Urban Violence in Latin America*. New Brunswick, NJ: Rutgers University Press.

Rylko-Bauer, Barbara, Merrill Singer, and John van Willigen. 2006. "Reclaiming Applied Anthropology: Its Past, Present, and Future." *American Anthropologist* 108 (1): 178–90.

Salcedo Fidalgo, Andrés. 1998. "Imaginarios de justicia en contextos barriales." *Colombia Controversia* 172 (July): 119–32.

Sanford, Victoria, and Asale Angel-Ajani, eds. 2008. *Engaged Observer: Anthropology, Advocacy, and Activism*. New Brunswick, NJ: Rutgers University Press.

Santos, Boaventura de Sousa. 1977. "The Law of the Oppressed: The Construction and Reproduction of Legality in Pasargada Law." *Law and Society Review* 12: 5–126.

———. 1995. *Toward a New Common Sense: Law, Science and Politics in the Paradigmatic Transition*. New York: Routledge.

———. 1997. "Toward a Multicultural Conception of Human Rights." *Zeitschrift Für Rechtssoziologie* 18 (1): 2–16.

Sawyer, Suzana. 2004. *Crude Chronicles: Indigenous Politics, Multinational Oil, and Neoliberalism in Ecuador*. Durham: Duke University Press.

Scheper-Hughes, Nancy. 1993. *Death without Weeping: The Violence of Everyday Life in Brazil*. Berkeley: University of California Press.

———. 2004. "Bodies, Death, and Silence." In *Violence in War and Peace: An Anthology*, edited by Nancy Scheper-Hughes and Philippe Bourgois, 175–85. Oxford: Blackwell.

Schultz, Jim. 2000. "Bolivians Win Anti-Privatization Battle." *NACLA Report on the Americas* 33 (6): 44–46.

Schumacher, E. F. 1973. *Small Is Beautiful: Economics as If People Mattered*. New York: Harper and Row.

Schwegler, Tara A. 2008. "Take It from the Top (Down)? Rethinking Neoliberalism and Political Hierarchy in Mexico." *American Ethnologist* 35 (4): 682–700.

Sconce, Jeffrey. 2000. *Haunted Media: Electronic Presence from Telegraphy to Television*. Durham: Duke University Press.

Scott, James C. 1998. *Seeing Like a State: How Certain Schemes to Improve the Human Condition Have Failed*. New Haven: Yale University Press.

Seligmann, Linda. 1989. "To Be in Between: The *Cholas* as Market Women." *Comparative Studies in Society and History* 31 (4): 694–721.

———. 2004. *Peruvian Street Lives: Culture, Power, and Economy among Market Women of Cuzco*. Urbana: University of Illinois Press.

Selmeski, Brian R. 2007. "Who Are the Security Anthropologists?" *Anthropology News* 48 (5): 11–12.

Sierra, María Teresa. 2005. "The Revival of Indigenous Justice in Mexico: Challenges for Human Rights and the State." *Political and Legal Anthropology Review* 28 (1): 52–72.

Silverman, Sydel. 2007. "American Anthropology in the Middle Decades: A View from Hollywood." *American Anthropologist* 109 (3): 519–28.

Singer, Merrill. 1990. "Another Perspective on Advocacy." *Current Anthropology* 31 (5): 548–49.

———. 2000. "Why I Am Not a Public Anthropologist." *Anthropology Newsletter* 11 (2): 12–13.

———. 2010. "Comment on Low and Merry." *Current Anthropology* 51 (Supplement 2): S220–21.

Sivak, Martín. 2010. *Evo Morales: The Extraordinary Rise of the First Indigenous President of Bolivia*. New York: Palgrave Macmillan.

Skidmore, Monique. 2003. "Darker than Midnight: Fear, Vulnerability, and Terror Making in Urban Burma." *American Ethnologist* 30 (1): 5–21.

———. 2008. "Scholarship, Advocacy, and the Politics of Engagement in Burma (Myanmar)." In *Engaged Observer: Anthropology, Advocacy, and Activism*, edited by Victoria Sanford and Asale Angel-Ajani, 42–59. New Brunswick, NJ: Rutgers University Press.

Sluka, Jeffrey A. 2010. "Curiouser and Curiouser: Montgomery McFate's Strange Interpretation of the Relationship between Anthropology and Counterinsurgency." *Political and Legal Anthropology Review* 33 (1): 99–115.

Smulovitz, Claudia. 2003. "Citizen Insecurity and Fear: Public and Private Responses in Argentina." In *Crime and Violence in Latin America: Citizen Security, Democracy, and the State*, edited by Joseph S. Tulchin, Hugo Frühling, and Heather A. Golding, 125–52. Washington: Woodrow Wilson Center.

Solares Serrano, Humberto. 1990. *Historia, espacio, y sociedad: Cochabamba 1550–1950; formación, crisis y desarrollo de su proceso urbano*. Cochabamba: CIDRE.

Speed, Shannon. 2006. "At the Crossroads of Human Rights and Anthropology: Toward a Critically Engaged Activist Research." *American Anthropologist* 108 (1): 66–76.

———. 2007. *Rights in Rebellion: Indigenous Struggle and Human Rights in Chiapas*. Stanford: Stanford University Press.

———. 2008. "Forged in Dialogue: Toward a Critically Engaged Activist Research." In *Engaging Contradictions: Theory, Politics, and Methods of Activist Scholarship*, edited by Charles R. Hale, 213–36. Berkeley: University of California Press.

Starn, Orin. 1991. "Missing the Revolution: Anthropologists and the War in Peru." *Cultural Anthropology* 6 (1): 63–91.

———. 1999. *Nightwatch: The Politics of Protest in the Andes*. Durham: Duke University Press.

Stavenhagen, Rodolfo, and Diego Iturralde, eds. 1990. *Entre la ley y la costumbre: el derecho consuetudinario indígena en América Latina*. Mexico City: Instituto Indigenista Interamericano.

Stonequist, Everett V. 1935. "The Problem of the Marginal Man." *American Journal of Sociology* 41 (1): 1–12.

Stull, Donald, and Jean J. Schensul. 1987. *Collaborative Research and Social Change: Applied Anthropology in Action.* Boulder, CO: Westview.

Susser, Ida. 2010. "The Anthropologist as Social Critic: Working toward a More Engaged Anthropology." *Current Anthropology* 51 (Supplement 2): S227–33.

Tate, Winifred. Forthcoming. "Local Governance, Claims of Jurisdiction and the Aspirational State in Putumayo." In *Off-Centered States*, edited by David Nugent and Christopher Krupa.

Taussig, Michael. 1984. "Culture of Terror—Space of Death: Roger Casement's Putumayo Report and the Explanation of Torture." *Comparative Studies in Society and History* 26 (3): 467–97.

———. 2003. *Law in a Lawless Land: Diary of a Limpieza in Colombia.* New York: New Press.

Tax, Sol. 1975. "Action Anthropology." *Current Anthropology* 16 (4): 514–17.

Taylor, Diana. 1997. *Disappearing Acts: Spectacles of Gender and Nationalism in Argentina's "Dirty War."* Durham: Duke University Press.

Tórrez, Yuri. 2005. "¿Por quién doblan las campanas? Los linchamientos una bomba de tiempo." *Cuarto Intermedio* 76 (August): 32–43.

Trouillot, Michel-Rolph. 2001. "The Anthropology of the State in the Age of Globalization: Close Encounters of the Deceptive Kind." *Current Anthropology* 42 (1): 125–38.

Tulchin, Joseph S., Hugo Frühling, and Heather A. Golding, eds. 2003. *Crime and Violence in Latin America: Citizen Security, Democracy, and the State.* Washington: Woodrow Wilson Center.

Ungar, Mark. 2003. "Contested Battlefields: Policing in Caracas and La Paz." *NACLA Report on the Americas* 37 (2): 30–36.

———. 2011. *Policing Democracy: Overcoming Obstacles to Citizen Security in Latin America.* Baltimore: Johns Hopkins University Press.

United Nations Development Programme. 1994. *Human Development Report 1994.* Oxford: Oxford University Press.

United Nations Human Settlements Programme. 2003. *The Challenge of Slums: Global Report on Human Settlements 2003.* London: Earthscan.

United States Agency for International Development. 2004. "Budget: Bolivia." Washington: United States Agency for International Development, http://www.usaid.gov/policy/budget/cbj2005/lac/bo.html.

———. 2005. *USAID Promotes the Rule of Law in Latin America and Caribbean Democracies.* Washington: United States Agency for International Development.

United States Department of Homeland Security, Office of Public Affairs. 2011. "DHS 8th Anniversary: Homeland Security Starts with Hometown Security." Washington: Department of Homeland Security.

United States Department of Homeland Security, Office of the Press Secretary. 2010. "Secretary Napolitano Announces Expansion of 'If You See Something,

Say Something' Campaign to Walmart Stores across the Nation." Washington, DC: Department of Homeland Security, December 6.

Urquidi Zambrana, Jorge. 1967. *La urbanización de la ciudad de Cochabamba: Síntesis del estudio.* Vol. 1: *Antecedentes.* Cochabamba: Editorial Universitaria.

———. 1986. *La urbanización de la ciudad de Cochabamba y el desarrollo regional y urbano.* Vol. 2: *Examen crítico.* Cochabamba: Colegio de arquitectos de Bolivia, Filial Cochabamba.

———. 1995. *Evolución urbana de la ciudad de Cochabamba: A través de ordenanzas y reglamentos municipales 1786–1982.* Cochabamba: Genial S.R.L.

Valverde, Mariana, and Miomir Cirak. 2002. "Governing Bodies, Creating Gay Spaces: Security in 'Gay' Downtown Toronto." *British Journal of Criminology* 43 (1): 102–21.

Vilas, Carlos M. 2001. "(In)justicia por mano propia: linchamientos en el México contemporáneo." *Revista Mexicana de sociología* 63 (1): 131–60.

———. 2008. "Lynchings and Political Conflict in the Andes." *Latin American Perspectives* 35 (5): 103–18.

Vintimilla Saldaña, Jaime, Milena Almeida Mariño, and Remigia Saldaña Abad. 2007. *Derecho indígena, conflicto y justicia comunitaria en comunidades Kichwas del Ecuador.* Lima, Peru: Instituto de Defensa Legal.

Wæver, Ole, Barry Buzan, Morten Kelstrup, and Pierre Lemaitre. 1993. *Identity, Migration and the New Security Order in Europe.* London: Pinter.

Waldrep, Christopher. 2002. *The Many Faces of Judge Lynch: Extralegal Violence and Punishment in America.* New York: Palgrave MacMillan.

Walters, William. 2002. "Deportation, Expulsion, and the International Police of Aliens." *Citizenship Studies* 6 (3): 265–92.

———. 2004. "Secure Borders, Safe Haven, Domopolitics." *Citizenship Studies* 8 (3): 237–60.

Webber, Jeffery R. 2007. "Bolivian Horizons: An Interview with Historian Sinclair Thomson." Upside Down World, November 13, http://upsidedownworld.org/main/bolivia-archives-31/997-bolivian-horizons-an-interview-with-historian-sinclair-thomson.

———. 2011. *From Rebellion to Reform in Bolivia: Class Struggle, Indigenous Liberation, and the Politics of Evo Morales.* Chicago: Haymarket.

Weber, Max. 1946. "Politics as a Vocation." In *From Max Weber: Essays in Sociology,* edited and translated by H. H. Gerth and C. Wright Mills, 77–128. New York: Oxford University Press.

Weismantel, Mary. 2001. *Cholas and Pishtacos: Stories of Race and Sex in the Andes.* Chicago: University of Chicago Press.

Weldes, Jutta, Mark Laffey, Hugh Gusterson, and Raymond Duvall, eds. 1999. *Cultures of Insecurity: States, Communities, and the Production of Danger.* Minneapolis: University of Minnesota Press.

Williams, Brackette F. 1991. *Stains on My Name, War in My Veins: Guyana and the Politics of Cultural Struggle*. Durham: Duke University Press.

Williams, Raymond. 1977. *The Country and the City*. New York: Oxford University Press.

Wilson, James Q., and George L. Kelling. 1982. "Broken Windows: The Police and Neighborhood Safety." *Atlantic Monthly*. http://www.manhattan-institute.org/pdf/_atlantic_monthly-broken_windows.pdf.

Wilson, Richard Ashby, ed. 2005. *Human Rights in the "War on Terror."* Cambridge: Cambridge University Press.

Wolf, Eric R. 1964. *Anthropology*. Upper Saddle River, NJ: Prentice Hall.

——. 1966. "Kinship, Friendship, and Patron-Client Relations in Complex Societies." In *The Social Anthropology of Complex Societies*, edited by Michael Banton, 1–22. New York: Praeger.

World Health Organization. 2002. *World Report on Violence and Health*. Geneva: World Health Organization.

Yrigoyen Fajardo, Raquel. 2011. "Legal Pluralism and Indigenous Jurisdiction in the Latin American Pluralist Constitutionalism." Paper presented at the Legal Pluralism in Latin America: Challenges and Comparative Perspectives conference, University of San Diego Center for Iberian and Latin American Studies, and California Western Law School, May 5–6, San Diego, CA.

Zilberg, Elana. 2011. *Space of Detention: The Making of a Transnational Gang Crisis between Los Angeles and San Salvador*. Durham: Duke University Press.

Index

Note: Page numbers in italics indicate figures.

AAA (American Anthropological Association), 262n7

abajeños, 90, 136

Abrams, Philip, 83

Access to Justice Houses (Casas de Acceso a la Justicia, CAJs): assistance available at, 59–60; budget and funding issues for, 60–61; goals for, 57–58; other projects compared with, 58–59; pseudonyms for, 262n12; reflections on, 62–63, 73–75

Achá, Rose Marie, 262n10, 266n55

activist (engaged) anthropology: collaboration and teamwork in, 47–51; community services provided by, 51–53; concept of, 35–37, 72–73; earlier forms of, 261n4; engagement vs. activism in, 38–42; institutionalization issues for, 55–63; international service learning linked to, 64–68; locals' expectations of, 53–55; location of research as key to, 45–46; positioned objectivity and transparency in, 44–45; potential conservative political use of, 261n2;

as process of discovery, 46–47; reflections on, 31–32, 62–63, 73–75; symposium on, 261; warnings about, 43–44. *See also* reciprocity tradition; uncertain anthropology

Albarracín, Waldo, 186

Albro, Robert, 174, 273n10

alcohol and alcoholism, 117, 150–51, 162

Altamira (pseud.), 136

Amazonians, 18–19

American Anthropological Association (AAA), 262n7

Amnesty International, 179

Andean code, 179–80

Andean Information Network, 275n29

Andean region: crime statistics of, 20; critique of ethnographic interpretations of, 275n18; generic gestures toward, 179–80; reciprocity tradition in, 50–51, 54–55; space-time project in, 170–71

Andrejevic, Mark, 13–14

Angel (pseud.), 103, 155

Annan, Kofi, 260n22

anthropology: academic type of, 36;

anthropology (*cont.*)
antiquated notions of, 44–46;
applied type of, 39, 72, 262–63n15;
basic concerns of, 38; community
justice theorized in, 181–82; critical
type of, 15–16; cultural critique discourse in, 40; human terrain system
and, 258n13; legal type of, 253;
objectivist stance in, 43–46,
262nn8–9; order in, 252–53; "original indigenous peasant community"
in, 177; regional and national differences in, 43; uncertainty in, 10, 34,
253–55. *See also* activist (engaged)
anthropology; ethnographers
antiquity and ancestors, 184, 191, 194.
See also authoritarian past; rural
areas
"antisocials." *See rateros*
áreas verdes (green areas), 92, 131–32,
263–64n7, 268n28
Argentina: community policing in,
266n50
Armando (pseud.), 105, 190
armed forces. *See* military; police force
arribeños, 90, 136
Asociación Nacional de Suboficiales,
Clases y Policías de Cochabamba,
111, 219, 266–67n59
authoritarian past: invoked in community justice, 197–99; tracings in
security agenda, 12, 25–26
automobiles: aftermath of accident
with, 104; humor about driving, 99–
100; insurance required for, 79–80,
81, 98. *See also taxi-trufi*
autonomy. *See* indigenous autonomy
project
autonomy movement (lowland
departments), 274n15
Aymara language, 95
Aymara people: characteristics and

values of, 175, 176, 273–74n11;
legal practices of, 181; local leaders
of, 180; Morales's identification
with, 173–74; privileged in cultural
politics, 273n10; spatialized persona
of, 274n12; stereotype of, 136
Ayo Ayo (Bolivia): mayor killed in,
276n42

Bailey, John, 265n44
baking classes, 59–60, 67
Baltazar (pseud.), 104
Banzer Suarez, Hugo, 21, 109, 265n46,
265n48
barrio president. *See* leadership, local
barrios. *See* marginal barrios; outlawed communities; *and specific
barrios*
bars (*chicherías*), 130, 150–51
Basic Police School (Escuela Básica
Policial), 113
Bechtel corporation, 17
bill of sale (*minuta*), 92–93, 98
Birgith (pseud.), 156, 159, 224, 225
blog entries: community center, 68–
72; Wilmer's death, 77–78, 116–17
Boas, Franz, 42, 262n7
Bolivia: Andean code as mantra of,
179–80; Center's institutional
structure and, 61–62; crisis of legitimacy in, 17–19; economic aid for,
257n4; map, *87*; plurinationalism of,
168, 176–77, 201, 275n23; population of, 83–84, 169, 257n1, 273n3;
presidents listed (most recent),
265n46; "refounding of," 1, 3–4; revolution of (1952), 91. *See also* citizen security; Cochabamba; community justice; indigenous peoples;
New Political Constitution of the
State; race-space-time; security;
state

Bolivian Episcopal Conference, 185
Bolivian National Police. *See* police
  force
booby traps (*casabobos*), 94
Bratton, William, 21–22
Bravo, Alejandro, 111–12
bricolage. *See* legal bricolage
Brigade for the Protection of the Family, 60, 110
bureaucratic procedures (*trámites*):
  length of time to complete, 97–98;
  offices and personnel for, 95–96;
  proof of voting needed in, 103,
  264n27. *See also* land legalization
bureaucratic procedures (*trámites*),
  specific: bill of sale (*minuta*), 92–
  93, 98; birth certificates, 96–97; car
  ownership and license plates, 98;
  driver's license, 98–99; identity
  cards, 96–97, 127, 264n27; military
  service proof, 97; OTB organization,
  138; resident's card and visa, 99
Bush administration, 13–14, 249
bus transportation, 89. *See also*
  automobiles

CAJs. *See* Access to Justice Houses
Caldeira, Teresa P. R., 132
Cancha, la (Cochabamba's outdoor
  market): access to, 22; Barrio Chino
  (resale section) of, 125; as danger
  zone, 130–31, 272n111; market
  vendor federation and, 140–41;
  vendors in, 89, 159, 272n93
Canessa, Andrew, 174, 273n9
carnets (identity cards), 96–97, 127,
  264n27
casabobos (booby traps), 94
Casas de Acceso a la Justicia. *See*
  Access to Justice Houses
Casilda (pseud.): on la Cancha, 130; on
  community justice and lynching,

159, 160, 188; on *rateros*, 126, 131;
  response to question about rights,
  223; Samuelia's assistance and, 135;
  watchfulness of, 133–34; women
  stereotypes of, 158–59
Casto (pseud.), 147, 191
Cata (pseud.), 223
census data problems, 273n3. *See also*
  Bolivia: population of
Center for Justice and Rights (El Centro para Justicia y Derechos,
  pseud.): CAJ program of (*see* Access
  to Justice Houses); founding and
  goals of, 56–57; funding for, 57;
  human rights workshops of, 60–61,
  224; institutional structure of, 61–
  62; international service learning
  program linked to, 66–68; reflections on, 62–63, 73–75
Cercado province: belonging to, 96;
  Uspha Uspha and Loma Pampa in,
  88
Chaco War (1932–35), 91
Chambi, María, 183–84
Chávez, Hugo, 2, 257n4
chicherías (bars), 130, 150–51
children: antisocial type of, 227; danger zones for, 130–35, 272n111;
  family's responsibility for behavior
  of, 158, 195–96; fears for safety of,
  23, 95, 159; labor laws on, 78, 263n1;
  martial arts classes for, 53, 57, 59–
  60, 67, 149, 151; punishment for,
  156, 157–58, 279n40; rights discourse linked to misbehavior of,
  231–32; school for, 86, 89
Chisholm, Linda, 64
Christianity, 143, 185, 276n53
chuto. See illegal
Citizens against Crime (Triple C, or
  Ciudadanos Contra el Crimen), 229,
  278n34

citizen security (*seguridad ciuda-dana*): absence of path to, 168; alertness, unity, and beliefs about, 152–54, 163; costs of, 101–2; as crime control, 26, 33, 245–47, *246*, 249–52; definitions of, 108–10, 206, 220, 249–52; elusiveness of, 113–16; history of, 265n48; human rights in context of, 23–27, 216–17, 222–28, 260n22; justice in context of, 59, 172, 236–38, 272n1; paradox of violence as path to, 7–8, 147–63; phantom nature of, 83–84, 117–18; privatization of, 21, *21*; responsibilization linked to, 247–48; state rhetoric of, 108–9, 244–49; transnational corporations' security vs., 18–19, 24–25. *See also* community justice; insecurity; lynching; security; state; vigilantism

Citizen Security Headquarters (Jefatura de Seguridad Ciudadana), 109–10

Citizen Security Unit (Unidad de Seguridad Ciudadana), 109

Ciudadanos Contra el Crimen (Triple C, or Citizens against Crime), 229, 278n34

Ciudad Segura (Secure City) plan, 109

civil society. *See* collective social life, local

Clarke, Kamari, 261

class: hierarchies of, 112–13; role in distancing of law from barrios, 104

cleansing (*limpieza*), 229. *See also* vigilantism

cleferitos, 227

club de madres (mothers club), 52

coca growers, 22, 110, 203, 219, 266n52

Cochabamba: cemeteries of, 80–81; citizen security units of, 109–10; climate of, 88; coca growers' protest in, 110, 219, 266n52; community justice and lynching debated in, 187–89; conditions in, 22–23, 258n6; danger zones in, 130–35, 272n111; economy of, 54, 207; history of, 90–95; in-migration to, 85–86; Jesus Christ statue in, 99; judo tournament in, 59–60; map, *87*; privatized security in, 21, *21*; spatial and racialized legal frontier of, 27–31; urban district of, 88–89; Water War in, 17–18, 67, 143. *See also* bureaucratic procedures; Cancha, la; citizen security; insecurity; municipal governance; phantom state; police force; Uspha Uspha; *and specific barrios*

Cochabamba Human Rights Congress (Congreso de Derechos Humanos de Cochabamba, pseud.): barrios ignored by, 215–16; citizen security and, 216–17, 251; function and challenges of, 214–15; police view of, 220, 221; residents' hostility toward, 225–28, 231–33

Cold War. *See* communism

collaboration, local: concern about research with, 43; encouragement of, 42; ethnographer's obligations due to, 36–37, 72–73; expectations based on, 53–55; funding issues in, 63; ISL students' projects with, 67–68; limitations on, 41; reciprocity tradition and, 50–51, 54–55; team work and, 47–55; theoretical insights possible in, 45–46. *See also* activist (engaged) anthropology; ethnographers; Loma Pampa community center; reciprocity tradition

collective social life, local: absence of, 55–56, 146–47; diversity of opinion masked by, 148; divisions preventing, 135–37; fear and, 4–5, 11, 20, 23, 106–8, 134–35, 149–51, 236–38 (*see also* insecurity); lack of unity in, 146–47, 152–54, 163; "pact of silence" and, 145, 190, 270n61. *See also* citizen security; community justice; Loma Pampa community center; neighbors; watchfulness

Colombia, engaged anthropologists of, 43

colonialism: Cochabamba's founding and, 90–91; denunciation of, 175; indigenous peoples' place in, 27–28, 200, 276–77; legal legacy of, 182; rural community systems impacted by, 184; urban space defined in, 172

Comaroff, Jean and John, 260n27

Comité de Vigilancia (Vigilance Committee), 138

Comité Impulsor, 139, 144–45

communism: delinquents likened to communists, 25; educational intent of, 228; West's fear of, 11–12, 13

community. *See* collective social life, local; marginal barrios; outlawed communities; *and specific barrios*

community centers. *See* Access to Justice Houses; Loma Pampa community center

community justice (*justicia comunitaria*): abstract concept of, 182–83; ambiguities and confusions about, 179–80, 183–85; approach to, 33, 119, 172–73, 241; assumed locale of, 178–79; constitutional recognition of, 2–3, 8–9, 168, 183; debates about, 185–91; diversity and flexibility of, 180–82, 200; documents used in, 196, 276–77n57; human rights in context of, 8, 209, 218; interrogation of accused in, 150, 151, 160–61, 196; jurisdictional

issues in, 179, 183–84, 257n5, 275n17; lynching conflated with, 185–86, 188–89, 275n29; lynching distinguished from, 180, 181, 186–88, 194; race-space-time framework for, 171–72; rationale for, 124, 169; rural authority channeled in, 169, 171–72, 189–91, 197–99; as security-making practice, 192–99; spatialization of, 169–70; state law both coexisting and conflicting with, 2–3, 29–31; testimony of witnesses in, 149, 167, 196–97. *See also* citizen security; conflict resolution; indigenous autonomy project; leadership, local; lynching; vigilantism

community policing concept, 109–10, 266n50, 266n53

COMTECO, 270n52

Concordia: área verde of, 131–32; community justice and lynching as understood in, 191; police linked to delinquents in, 102; proposed barricading of, 132

conflict resolution: complexity of systems of, 181; creativity in, 195–96; local leaders' efforts in, 144–46, 197–98; in lynching situations, 150–52, 167–68, 193–95, 197–99, 270–71n67; rural authority channeled in, 197–99. *See also* community justice; leadership, local

Congreso. *See* Cochabamba Human Rights Congress

Consejo Distrital (District Council), 139

Consejo Municipal (Municipal Council), 139

Consejo Nacional de Seguridad y Orden Público (National Council of Citizen Security and Public Order), 109

Consejo Zonal (Zonal Council), 138–39
constitution. *See* New Political Constitution of the State
Copenhagen School of security studies, 14
corruption (real and perceived): in bureaucratic procedures, 95–100; of dirigentes, 142; of lawyers, 104–5; mutual fingerpointing in, 113–14; in party politics, 141; of police force, 20–21, 100–102, 111–12, 155, 188–89
Coutin, Susan, 253
creativity: approach to, 5–6, 33, 241, 254; community center mural as example, *68*, 71–72; of dirigentes in conflict resolution, 195–96; of dirigentes in lynching interventions, 167–68, 193–95; legal bricolage as, 30–31, 33, 201, 241, 260n26; margins characterized by, 28; of security-making practices, 192–99
Cridland, Lee, 66–67
crimes and criminality: "broken windows" philosophy of, 22, 259n19; citizen security as control of, 26, 33, 245–47, *246*, 249–52; fear of, 4–5, 11, 20, 23, 106–8, 134–35, 149–51, 236–38; "get tough on crime" talk about, 21–22, 204–5, 209–10, 232–33, 246–48; human rights activists blamed for increase in, 220–21, 229–32; increases (perceived and real), 19–20, 108–9, 210, 230, 277n2, 279n1; law viewed as favoring, 7, 155, 209, 210, 215, 220–21, 226–27, 229–33 (*see also* human rights); *la mana dura* (heavy-hand approach to crime control) and, 21, 26, 209, 232, 237, 247, 277n1; unreported, 100–102; zero-tolerance approach to, 21–22. *See also* community justice; corruption; delinquents; gangs; insecurity; land speculators; lynching; police force; *rateros*
criminal law. *See* law; New Penal Procedural Code
cultural critique: activist research vs., 40–41; availability to local peoples, 42; dismissal of, 261n3
culture, local: anthropologists' and military strategists' strategy of understanding, 258n13; authority of paterfamilias in, 225; rights discourse and perceived decline of, 231–32. *See also* cultural critique
culture of terror, 5. *See also* insecurity

Dammert, Lucía, 265n44
Das, Veena, 28
Davis, Mike, 258n6
Declaration of Independence (US), 176
Defense of the Child International (Defensa del Niño Internacional), 218
Defensoría del Pueblo: community justice and lynching debates and, 187–88; function of, 274n14, 277n8; mother's case and, 183–84; residents' distrust of, 208, 225, 226, 228, 233
Delina (pseud.), 135–36, 143
delinquents (*delincuentes*): burning used to punish, 156; as embodiment of unease, 25; human rights blamed for, 231–32; insecurity due to, 122; in local rights discourse, 235; mothers blamed for, 158, 195; origins of, 131–32; police linked to, 102, 155; watchfulness of, 129, 133. *See also* crimes and criminality; insecurity; *rateros*

Delta Group, 110
democratization: citizen security and,
245–47, *246*; citizens' expectations
in, 17; human rights enforcers in,
210; USAID funds for strengthening,
260n23
Departmental Police (Cochabamba),
109–10
Department of Property Rights
(Derechos Reales), 226
derecho: use of term, 225–26, 278n23.
See also human rights
Derechos Humanos. *See* Cochabamba
Human Rights Congress
Derrida, Jacques, 81
Dirección Departmental de Seguridad
Ciudadana (State Department of
Citizen Security), 109
Dirección General de Seguridad
Ciudadana (General Department of
Citizen Security), 109
dirigentes. See leadership, local
District Council (Consejo Distrital),
139
División de Policía de Tránsito, 79, 100
Dora (pseud.), 101, 105, 132–33, 235
due process, 7, 21, 204. *See also* New
Penal Procedural Code
Durkheim, Emile, 163

Ecuador: indigenous rights vs. global
capital security in, 18
education and training: Center's
classes offered, 52–54, 57, 59–60,
67, 149, 151; Center's institutional
structure and, 61–62; corporal
punishment in schools, 279n40; on
human rights, 60–61, 216, 217–19,
224; for police, 112–13; state laws
on, 78. *See also* international service
learning; languages
effigies, *153*, 153–54, 271n72

El Alto (Bolivia): Aymara persona of,
274n12; effigies in, 271n72; Gas
War in, 18, 143, 260n25; military
forces for policing in, 265–66n49;
USAID projects in, 58
elections: required voting in, 103,
264n27
electricity, 142–43, 269–70nn52–53
Elena (pseud.), 104
Empresa de Luz y Fuerza Eléctrica
Cochabamba (ELFEC), 142–43,
269–70n52
engaged anthropology. *See* activist
(engaged) anthropology
engagement: definitions of, 72–73; of
postcolonial anthropology, 42–43.
See also activist (engaged)
anthropology
Escuela Básica Policial (Basic Police
School), 113
ethnographers: authorial techniques
of, 43; ethical responsibilities of,
35–37, 72–73; location of research,
45–46; questions about obligations
of, 38; reciprocity tradition and, 50–
51, 54–55, 72–75; as spies under
cover of fieldwork, 262n9; surren-
dering commitment to systems and
certainty, 252–55. *See also* activist
(engaged) anthropology; anthropology; methodology
Eva (pseud.), 130–31

false consciousness, 259n17
family: authority of paterfamilias in, 225;
called on, in lynching intervention,
167–68, 193–94, 195; corporal
punishment of children in, 156, 157–
58, 279n40; as responsible for children's behavior, 158, 195–96; rights
discourse and perceived decline of,
231–32. *See also* neighbors

Hobbes, Thomas, 11
Hodgson, Dorothy, 261
housing: example in Loma Pampa, *129*; fear of leaving unattended, 22, 23, 128, 134–35; materials of, 86–87; outer wall to protect, 87, 128–29
Huanca, Mario, 112, 113
Huanca, Silvio, 222–23
human rights: citizen security in context of, 23–27, 216–17, 222–28, 260n22; community justice and, 8, 178–79, 209, 218; to land ownership, 93–94; multiple meanings of, 205–6, 241–42; to petition, 218; public willingness to circumvent, in favor of security, 21–22, 204–5; reassessment of, 249–52; residents' distrust and blaming of, 7, 155, 206–11, 215, 220–21, 223–28, 229–37, 249; security and justice as, 24, 26, 59, 217–18, 260n22; state's ability to suspend, 15; violence of, 228–36; workshops on, 60–61, 216, 217–19, 224. *See also* citizen security; human rights vernacularization; indigenous peoples: rights of; New Penal Procedural Code
human rights and security nexus: context of, 203–6; distrust and insecurity in context of, 206–11; division between, in Uspha Uspha, 222–28; oppositional discourses in, 236–38; violence and, 228–36
human rights discourse (Bolivia): compliance-based rights in, 249; discourse on citizen security and, 23–27; diverse goals in, 206; as force of illegality and chaos, 7; hybrid nature of, 233–38; indigenism in, 175–76; local definitions and practices of, 118–19, 205, 212–

19, 234–36; neoliberal state's need to limit, 14; police voice in, 219–22; questions about, 9; silent on citizen security, 216–17; transnational discourse adapted in, 34, 205, 211–22. *See also* Defensoría del Pueblo; human rights vernacularization; indigenous autonomy project; politics
human rights discourse (transnational): approach to, 33–34; global ascendancy of, 204–6; Morales's use of, 8, 203–4, 207–8; residents' distrust and blaming of, 206–11, 225–28, 231–32, 234–37, 249. *See also* nongovernmental organizations
Human Rights Foundation, 185–86, 275n29
human rights vernacularization: concept of, 205, 211–12; police use of, 219–22; process of, 34; process of local adaptation in, 212–19, 234–36; summary of, 241–42
human security: definition of, 13. *See also* citizen security
human terrain system concept, 258n13

identity: exclusions in national, 28–29; interrogation of accused to determine, 150, 151, 160–61, 196; uncertainty about, 127. *See also* family; indigeneity
identity cards (*carnets*), 96–97, 127, 264n27
illegal (*chuto*): automobiles as, 79–80; dangers of living as, 99–100; people as, 98, 118–19. *See also* outlawed communities
ILO (International Labour Organization), 263n1
Inda, Jonathan, 244

indigeneity: as category and concept, 273n6; community justice in context of, 171–72, 192–99; lived experiences vs. official concept, 184–85

indigenism: generic conceptualization of, 3–4, 33, 169, 172, 173–77; site for, 274n12. *See also* indigenous autonomy project

indigenismo movement (1920s and 1930s), 174, 273n9

indigenous autonomy project: community justice in context of, 185–92; constitutional mandate for, 177–78; language of community justice and, 177–85; legal pluralism as foundation of, 183. *See also* human rights discourse (Bolivia); politics; *pueblos indígena originario campesinos*

indigenous legal tradition. *See* community justice; family; rural areas

indigenous peoples: assumed locale of, 178–79; citizenship claims and, 17–19; implications of new constitution for, 1–3, 176–78; Morales's identification as, 173–74; move from margins to center, 3–4; as percentage of population, 257n1; rights of, 1–2, 16–19, 173, 176; stereotypes of, 171–72; traditions valorized in national ideology, 3. *See also* community justice; Morales Ayma, Evo; rural-to-urban migration

individualization: effects of, 146–47; of human rights complaints, 214–15; insecurity as fostering, 123, 135–37; neoliberal strategies of, 13–14, 16, 243–44, 247–48

infrastructure and services: electricity, 142–43, 269–70nn52–53; insecurity due to lack of, 128; telephone service, 128, 161, 168, 194; water

resources, 17–18, 67–68, 136. *See also* municipal governance; natural resources

inquilinos (renters), 91, 132–33

INRA (Instituto Nacional de Reforma Agraria), 94

insecurity (*inseguridad*): approach to, 32, 239–40; danger zones in, 130–35, 272n111; distrust of human rights discourse due to, 7, 155, 206–11, 215, 220–21, 223–28, 229–37, 249; fear of criminals in, 4–5, 11, 20, 23, 106–8, 134–35, 149–51, 236–38; fostered in perceptions of law, 6–7, 20, 83–84, 103–5, 106–8, 117–18, 121–22; hauntology of vecinos and criminals, 125–30; ignored by NGOs and agencies, 48–49; loneliness and isolation of, 135–37; lynching violence as perpetrating, 162–63; lynching violence as response to, 155–56; personal and social phenomena due to, 4–6; phantom state and law linked to, 83–84, 117–18, 121–22; police and judicial system blamed for, 101–2, 113–16; sources of, 122, 252; spatialization of, 27–31; tactics for dealing with, 7–9, 163–65, 192, 240; of workers in the Cancha, 272n111. *See also* citizen security; creativity; judicial system; land legalization; law; leadership, local; lynching; phantom state; police force; uncertainty and "not-knowing"; vigilantism; watchfulness

inseguridad domicilaria, 134–35

institutionalization: issues for activist anthropology, 55–63; small projects that avoid, 74–75

Instituto Nacional de Reforma Agraria (INRA), 94

Inter-American Development Bank, 25

International Labour Organization (ILO), 263n1

International Monetary Fund, 12, 208

international service learning (ISL): blog entries about project, 68–72; goals of, 64–65; projects of, 65, 67–68, 68, 71; proposal for, 66–67; reflections component of, 70; success of, 74

Interpol, 99

Irda (pseud.), 147

Irma (pseud.), 102, 132, 155, 157

Isabel (pseud.), 159–60

ISL. See international service learning

Ivirgarzama (Bolivia): lynchings in, 186–87

Jefatura de Seguridad Ciudadana (Citizen Security Headquarters), 109–10

Josias (pseud.): on dangers for taxi drivers, 131; on driving, 99, 100; on falsely accused man, 107–8; on human rights, 235; on law, 103–4; on lynching, 154, 155; on *rateros*, 127; on unity in barrio, 146; on watchfulness, 134

Juan Pablo II: community justice and lynching as understood in, 187–89; conflict resolution in, 144; fear of accusing criminals in, 106–7; illegal land sales in, 106; organizing for security in, 152–53; police and law inaccessible in, 104, 105–6; proposed barricading of, 132

judicial system: absence of, 7; fear of using, 106–8; human rights discourse and, 114–15, 220–21; humor about, 99–100; inaccessibility of, 20–21, 23, 104, 105–

6, 144–46; insecurity blamed on, 113–16; residents' encounters with, 103–5; trial process in, 267n67. *See also* bureaucratic procedures; New Penal Procedural Code

Junta Escolar, 139

juntas vecinales (neighborhood organizations), 138–39. *See also* neighbors

justice: citizen security in context of, 59, 172, 236–38, 272n1; as human right, 217–18; privatization of, 20–21, 259n18; problems in state's administration of, 183–84; rehabilitation-focused, 180; residents' use of term, 231, 279n37

justicia comunitaria. See community justice

Justicia comunitaria (collection), 181–82

Kaplan, Robert, 164

Katz, Cindi, 261

kidnapping, 268–69n29

Kirsch, Stuart, 37, 75, 261

knitting classes, 52–54, 57, 59–60, 67

labor organizing, 140–41

land: hopes for purchasing, 91–93; price of, 141–42, 269n51

land legalization: absence of, 29; advice on, 51; insecurity due to, 6–7, 93–96, 128–29; lack of *áreas verdes* as obstacle to, 92, 263–64n7; monetary losses and, 141–42; process of, 95, 226; requirements for amnesty in, 92–95. *See also* green areas; housing

land owners (*propietarios*), 91–94

land speculators (*loteadores*), 92–94, 122

languages: Aymara, 95; bureaucratic

languages (*cont.*)

issues in, 95–96; classes in, 66, 69; constitutional recognition of, 176; divisions based on, 90, 136; issues for research team, 47–48; lynching (linchamiento) in, 267n2; role in distancing of law from barrios, 104; Quechua, 47–48, 95; Spanish, 47–48

La Paz (Bolivia): community policing in, 266n53; tourist impressions of, 268n20. *See also* El Alto

Latin America: citizen security concept in, 24–25, 245–46; crime statistics of, 19–20; engaged anthropologists of, 43; kidnapping in, 268–69n29; neoliberalism's effects on, 12–13, 207, 265n44; postneoliberal societies in, 9–10; security and neoliberalism in, 16–23. *See also specific cities and countries*

Latour, Bruno, 170

law (state): community justice both coexisting and conflicting with, 2–3, 29–31; criminals favored over victims in, 7, 155, 209, 210, 215, 220–21, 226–27, 229–33; *esquivar* (dodging the law) encouraged in effect, 98–99; insecurity fostered by, 6–7, 20, 83–84, 103–5, 106–8, 117–18, 121–22; jurisdictional issues of, 179, 183–84, 257n5, 275n17; lack of enforcement, 78, 108, 188–89; preventive detention eliminated in, 230, 231; security as superseding, 15; use of term *la ley*, 278n23. *See also* bureaucratic procedures; legal pluralism approach; New Penal Procedural Code; New Political Constitution of the State; outlawed communities; state

law (state), specific subjects: automobile insurance, 79–80, 81–82;

barrio governance, 138, 269n49, 274n16; child labor, 78, 263n1; citizen security, 19, 109; death certificates, 80–81; land distribution, 94–95; voting in elections, 103, 264n27

Law of Citizen Security (2003), 19, 109

Law of Popular Participation, 138, 269n49, 274n16

lawyers, 104–6

leadership, local: approach to, 32–33, 119, 240–41; barrio operating budget and, 270n55; constitution on, 178–79; fines collected by, 183–84, 196; insecurity problems managed by, 123, 163; interventions in attempted lynchings, 150–52, 167–68, 193–95, 197–99, 270–71n67; lack of unity among residents and, 146–47; NGOs distrusted by, 227–28; personal qualities needed in, 140–44; political organization and governance of, 137–40; rights language of, 222–23; rural authority channeled through, 197–99; social behavior regulated by, 180–81. *See also* community justice; conflict resolution; legal bricolage; Miguel; municipal governance

League of Nations, 11

legal bricolage: concept of, 30–31, 33, 260n26; creativity of, 201, 241. *See also* creativity; leadership, local

legal pluralism approach: Bolivian state influenced by, 2–3, 182–83; community justice and state law in context of, 29–30; shortcomings of, 30–31, 200–201, 254

legibility concept, 83–84

Lévi-Strauss, Claude, 260n26

ley. See law (state)

Ley de Deslinde Jurisdiccional (2010), 179, 275n17

Licia (pseud.), 133, 269n42
limpieza (cleansing), 229. *See also* vigilantism
linchamiento. See lynching
lived experiences: absent presence of law in, 81–84, 103–5 (*see also* phantom state); ambiguities around community justice and, 183–84; ignorance about law in, 105–6; indigeneity definitions vs., 184–85; insecurity in, summarized, 4–10; of law as scarcely legal, 7; race-space-time project vs., 170–71; rights vs. security contradictions in, 26–27; security as frame for understanding, 243–44. *See also* bureaucratic procedures; creativity; crimes and criminality; insecurity; leadership, local; uncertainty and "not-knowing"
Llave Mayu: land disputes of, 94, 131–32
Llorenti, Sacha, 114
Loma Pampa: administrative governance of, 88–89; área verde of, 132, 268n28; barrio operating budget of, 270n55; choice as research site, 49; collective fusion of people in, 152–53; community justice and lynching as understood in, 187; differences among residents in, 89–90; electricity brought to, 142–43; funding and day-to-day struggles in, 63; housing example in, *129*; lack of unity of residents in, 146–47; languages in, 184–85; legal recognition of, 138; Quechua-Aymara division in, 136–37; research in, described, 31–32; research office in, 49–50; settlement and conditions of, 88, 91, 141–42; tactics for alerting residents, 149, 152; view of, *90*; watchfulness as official policy in, 134–35

Loma Pampa community center: anniversary celebration of, 71–72; construction of, 67–70; exterior and patio of, *68*, *71*; funding for, 68; international service learning project of, 64–68, *65*; reflections on, 70; Wilmer Vargas as participant at, 77–78
Lopez, Enrique, 220
Lopez, Silvio, 121, 231
loteadores (land speculators), 92–94, 122. *See also* land; land legalization
Low, Setha, 38–39, 42, 43–44
lynching (*linchamiento*): ambivalence and uncertainty about, 8–9, 148–52, 155, 156–63, 168, 199, 236; approach to, 32–33, 147–48; collective fusion in crowd for, 152–53; community justice conflated with, 185–86, 188–89, 275n29; community justice distinguished from, 180, 181, 186–88, 194; context of, 7–8; description of attempted, 148–52; dirigente's interventions in, 150–52, 167–68, 193–95, 197–99, 270–71n67; dirigentes sometimes blamed for, 145, 194; as diverse set of practices, 8–9, 23, 30, 148, 154–55, 258n8; documentation of, 271n78; etymologies of, 267n2; as form of violent civil society, 267n3; frequency of, 259n20; in human rights discourse, 224–25; insecurity as prompting, 124; insecurity fostered by, 162–63; interrogation of accused before, 150, 151, 160–61, 196; neoliberal logic of, 259n18; "pact of silence" surrounding, 145, 190, 270n61; persistence of, 263n3; of police and public official, 276n42; as security-making practice, 192; as traditional justice practice, 169,

National Council of Citizen Security and Public Order (Consejo Nacional de Seguridad y Orden Público), 109

National Science Foundation, 47, 52

National Strategy for Homeland Security (US), 13–14

nation-state. *See* state

native peoples (American West), 42. *See also* indigenous peoples

natural gas reserves: conflict over control of, 18–19, 143, 260n25; implications of new constitution for control of, 1–2; tax revenues for social reforms, 109

natural resources: collective rights to, 17–19; exploitation protested, 203–4; water, 17–18, 67–68, 136. *See also* land; natural gas reserves; water resources

neighborhood organizations (*juntas vecinales*), 138–39

neighbors (*vecinos*): advocacy for police presence, 21–22, 204–5; barrio maintenance fee of, 270n55; community awareness among, 164–65; conditions faced by, 22–23; funds raised for electricity, 142–43, 269–70n52; human rights understanding among, 8, 213, 223–27, 234–36; identification and recognition of, 133–35; isolation of, 135–37; lack of unity among, 146–47, 152–54, 163–64; land ownership difficulties for, 6–7; meanings of, 123; "pact of silence" among, 145, 190, 270n61; on *rateros*' appearance, 126–27; rural community justice invoked by, 189–91; security's meaning for, 19–20; store robbery and, 125; tactics for alerting, 149, 152; as torn between rights and

security, 26–27; uncertainty and ambivalence about lynching, 8–9, 124, 148–52, 155, 156–63; use of term, 269n42; as victims, 105–8; as vulnerable to uncertainty, 253–54. *See also* citizen security; collective social life, local; community justice; family; insecurity; leadership, local; marginal barrios; phantom state; watchfulness

neoliberal democracies: crisis of legitimacy in, 17–19; human rights NGOs in, 214; use of term, 259n15

neoliberalism: Bolivia's break with, 3–4, 84–85, 204, 208–9, 258n9, 259n16; effects on Latin America, 12–13, 207, 265n44; flexibility and, 189; human rights associated with, 205, 227–28; increased crime linked to, 12–13, 108–9; indigenism deployed against, 175–76; migration and relocation due to, 27–28, 91, 273n3; "occult economies" in, 267–68n6; protests of, 203–4; responsibilizing and individualizing strategies of, 13–14, 16, 243–44, 247–48; security in context of, 14–19, 23, 239; state decentralization in, 138, 269n49. *See also* International Monetary Fund; privatization; security; World Bank

New Penal Procedural Code (El Nuevo Código de Procedimiento Penal, 1999): criticisms of, 229–31, 233; human rights values encoded in, 106–7, 219, 229–30, 231; indigenous justice recognized in, 272n2; judicial and police differences over, 114–15, 220–21; ratero as poster boy for failure of, 228–29, 278n34

New Political Constitution of the State (Nueva Constitución Política del

Estado): Andean code in, 179–80; community justice recognized in, 2–3, 8–9, 168, 183; generic indigenous values in, 176–77, 273n10; human rights discourse preceding, 218; human rights recognized in, 207–8, 209; legal jurisdictional issues after passage, 179, 183–84, 257n5, 275n17; passage of, 1–2; plurinationalism of, 176–77, 201, 275n23; race-space-time expressed in, 170–71; radical vision of, 3–4; rural and urban areas distinguished in, 274n14. *See also* indigenous autonomy project

nongovernmental organizations (NGOs): agendas of, 52–53; decision to found, 56; human rights–based concerns, 212–19, 221, 224–25; lacuna in perspective of, 207; reflections on operating as, 74–75; research team mistaken for, 48–49; residents' distrust and blaming of, 225–28, 231–32, 234–37. *See also* Center for Justice and Rights; Cochabamba Human Rights Congress

Nordstrom, Carolyn, 260n27

Nueva Constitución Política del Estado. *See* New Political Constitution of the State

Nuevo Código de Procedimiento Penal, El. *See* New Penal Procedural Code

objectivist stance, 43–46, 262nn8–9

occupations, 89, 97, 107–8

Officers' Academy (police), 112–13

Omar (pseud.), 125, 137, 157

Operative Organization for Order and Security (Organismo Operativo de Orden y Seguridad), 110–11, 220

Opinión (newspaper), 242–43

Ordoñez, Ruth, 262n10

Orellana Halkyer, René, 181, 195, 196, 276–77n57

Organización Territorial de Base (OTB). *See* Territorial Base Organization

outlawed communities: absence of solidarity in, 123; as both excluded and included by state, 28–29, 85, 240; community justice as attempt to overcome status of, 169; concept of, 3; creativity in sociolegal realities of, 5–6, 30–31; doubled effects of, 6–7; human rights distrusted in, 225–28; insecurity and lived reality of, 4–5, 9–10; spatialization of, 27–28; as trapped in illegality, 118–19. *See also* marginal barrios; phantom state

Pachamama (Mother Earth), 175

Pacífica (pseud.), 158, 235

"pact of silence," 145, 190, 270n61

"pain of death" punishment, 181

Palacios, Manuel, 113, 114

Patriot Act (US), 249

patronage state, 16, 138, 141. *See also* welfare state

Pérez Molina, Otto, 277n1

performance: security speech act as, 14–15; of unity among vecinos, 152–54

Peruvians, 132, 268–69n29

phantom state: absence of path to security in, 168; concept of, 10, 32, 77, 81–84, 118–19, 242; human rights discourse linked to, 207–8, 215–16, 226–28; inaccessibility of, 20–21, 23, 144–46; insecurity linked to, 83–84, 117–18, 121–22, 240; judicial system and, 103–8; law

phantom state (*cont.*)
as threat vs. aid and refuge, 79–81;
lynching violence as response to,
155–56; mutual fingerpointing in,
113–16; police as inaccessible and
corrupt in, 20–21, 100–102, 109–
14, 155, 188–89; residents' encounters with, 95–100; Wilmer's death
as illustrating, 77–82. *See also*
bureaucratic procedures; corruption; hauntology; judicial system;
law; outlawed communities; police
force; spectrality concept
Pierre, Jemima, 41
Plan Ciudad Seguridad (Morales), 109,
265–66n49
Plan de Seguridad y Protección
Ciudadana (Banzer), 109, 265n48
Plan Nacional de Empleo de Emergencia (program), 89
pluralistic approach, 41–42, 200–201.
See also legal pluralism approach
police force (*pacos* or cops): attempted
lynching and, 150–52; citizen
security and, 109–10, 245–47, *246*;
conditions and salaries of, 108,
110–13, 266–67n59; corruption of,
20–21, 100–102, 111–12, 155,
188–89; as force of illegality and
chaos, 7; "get tough" approach and,
21–22, 204–5, 209–10, 232–33,
246–48; human rights discourse of,
114–15, 219–22; identity card process overseen by, 97; inaccessibility
of, 104, 105–6, 109–14; insecurity
blamed on, 101–2, 113–16; lynching investigations by, 145, 154;
lynching of, 276n42; *la mana dura*
(heavy-hand approach to crime
control) and, 21, 26, 209, 232, 237,
247, 277n1; reluctance to call, 125;
remilitarization and expansion of,

26–27; traffic force of, 79, 100;
withdrawn from barrio, 121. *See
also* community policing concept
police union (Asociación Nacional de
Suboficiales, Clases y Policías de
Cochabamba), 111, 219, 266–67n59
Policía Técnica Judicial (PTJ), 100–
102, 266n51. *See also* police force
politics: debates about community justice in, 185–91; "get tough on crime"
discourse in, 21–22, 204–5, 209–10,
232–33, 246–48; party affiliation
and, 141; security as superseding, 15.
See also human rights discourse
(Bolivia); indigenous autonomy project; Morales Ayma, Evo; Movement
toward Socialism
Poole, Deborah, 28
PPL (New York utility co.), 269–70n52
privatization: of civil society, 13–14;
of electricity, 269–70nn52–53; of
natural resources, 17–19; of
security forces, 21, *21*, 133, 137; violence of, 207
propietarios (land owners), 91–94. *See
also* land; land legalization
Proyecto Rutgers: community contributions of, 52–54; end of, 56; local
office for, 49–50; organizational
approach of, 51–52, 55, 61. *See also*
Center for Justice and Rights
PTJ (Policía Técnica Judicial), 100–
102, 266n51. *See also* police force
*pueblos indígena originario campesi-
nos*: barrio appropriations of discourse of, 192–99; community justice envisioned in, 178–79;
constitution on, 2, 168–69, 176. *See
also* indigenous autonomy project

Quechua language, 47–48, 95
Quechua people: characteristics and

values of, 176, 273–74n11; legal practices of, 181, 195–96, 276–77n57; Morales's identification with, 173–74; stereotype of, 136

Quiroga, Jorge "Tuto," 204, 265n46

Quiroz, Roberto, 186

Quispe, Felipe, 175

race: essentialized notion of, 174–75; hierarchies of, 112–13; indigenous as category of, 273n6; role in distancing of law from barrios, 104. *See also* indigenous peoples

race-space-time (multidimensionality): in community justice context, 171–72; concept of, 170–71; debates about community justice and, 185–91; in indigenism concept, 174–77; reframing barrio in, 192–99; security meanings in, 243–44

Racicot, Denis, 186–87

racism: in community justice debates, 185–86; isolation fostered by, 136–37

Radio Patrol 110, 110, 112. *See also* police force

Rajagopal, Balakrishnan, 206–7

Rappaport, Joanne, 43

rateros: appearance of, 126–27; approach to, 32–33; concept of, 5; context for, 128; lynching of, 7, 155–57; perceived as outsiders, 131–32, 196; police linked to, 102, 155, 188–89; recognized as human beings, 159; warnings for, *153*, 153–54; watchfulness of, 129, 133; women as, 158. *See also* crimes and criminality; delinquents; insecurity

reciprocity tradition: deployed against neoliberal capitalism, 175–76; in ethnographic context, 50–51, 54–55, 72–75; labor exchanges in (ayni

and mink'a), 269n41. *See also* activist (engaged) anthropology

Redfield, Robert, 169

renters (*inquilinos*), 91, 132–33

responsibilization as neoliberal strategy, 13–14, 16, 243–44, 247–48

Reynaldo (pseud.), 94, 95, 189, 194

rights. *See* human rights

Rivera Cusicanqui, Silvia, 273n3

Roberts, Simon, 30

Rodríguez, Casimira, 180

Rodríguez, Jerry (El Ruso), 228–29, 230, 278n34

Rodríguez Veltzé, Eduardo, 94, 265n46

Roncken, Theo, 262n10

rule of law: citizen security linked to, 24–25, 245–46

rural areas: community justice in, 169–70, 195–96; difficulties of getting birth certificate in, 96–97; goals of self-governance systems in, 180–81; indigenous peoples defined by, 174–78; justice making in, echoed by barrio residents, 169, 171–72, 189–91; local leaders as channeling authority based in, 197–99; mutual assistance in, 135, 269n41; pishtacos or kharisis of, 126; urban areas distinguished from, 274n14. *See also* antiquity and ancestors; indigenous autonomy project; *pueblos indígena originario campesinos*

rural-to-urban migration: area and process described, 85–86, 88–91; attitudes toward human rights and, 208–9; continuum of, 192–93, 201–2; lynching transposed to city via, 169, 171–72; neoliberal policies fostering, 27–28, 91, 273n3. *See also* rural areas; urban areas

Ruso, El (Jerry Rodríguez), 228–29, 230, 278n34

Rutgers University: ISL program of, 64–68, 65, 68. See also Loma Pampa community center; Proyecto Rutgers

Samuelia (pseud.), 135

Sanchez de Lozada, Gonzalo ("Goni"): citizen security policy of, 109; hydrocarbon policy of, 18; popular participation policy of, 138, 269n49, 274n16; security codified under, 19; term of, 265n46

San Juan. See Mineros San Juan

Santos, Boaventura de Sousa, 29–30, 208

Sawyer, Suzana, 18–19

sayings: "an eye for an eye," 156; "The law is like a snake . . . ," 6; versions of Andean code, 179–80

scars, 122, 125, 126, 252–53

security (national and/or collective): approach to, 9, 33–34; citizen security as discourse on, 217; in context of marginal barrios, 29–31; critical anthropology of, 15–16; definitional difficulties, 10–15, 19–20; meaning of *seguridad*, 252; meanings of, 239, 242–49; in neoliberal context, 13–14, 16–17, 18–19; newspaper's use of term, 242–43; paradigm of, 23–27, 204–5, 227; *seguridad carnavalesca*, 243; *seguridad de sangre*, 243; shifting rhetoric of, 108–9. See also citizen security; community justice; judicial system; law; neoliberalism

"security anthropologists," use of term, 40

Segundo (pseud.), 93, 191

seguridad ciudadana. See citizen security

Seguro Obligatorio de Accidentes de Tránsito (SOAT), 79–80, 81, 98

Senobia, 142, 144, 167, 168, 199

Shakespeare, William, *Hamlet*, 72, 73

Siles Pérez, Luis Eduardo, 185

Silvio (pseud.), 187, 223

sindicatos. See workers' guilds

Singer, Merrill, 261n1

Skidmore, Monique, 37

SOAT (Seguro Obligatorio de Accidentes de Tránsito), 79–80, 81, 98

soccer. See *fulbito*

social anomie concept, 163–64

social movements: anthropology linked to, 35–37. See also activist (engaged) anthropology; human rights discourse (transnational)

sources of infection (*focos de infección*), 130

Spanish language, 47–48

spatialization: of community justice, 169–70; of indigenism, 175–77; of insecurity, 27–31; multidimensional vs. Newtonian view of, 170–71, 273n4. See also race-space-time

Special Force for the Fight Against Crime (Fuerza Especial en la Lucha Contra el Crimen), 266n51

spectrality concept, 79–82, 139, 267n5. See also hauntology; phantom state; *rateros*

speech act theory, 14–15

Speed, Shannon, 42

Stallone, Sylvester, 201, 277n63

Starn, Orin, 275n18

state: absence of, 110, 266n52; absent presence of, 32, 77, 81–84, 118–19, 242 (see also phantom state); barrio residents' hopes for, 84–85; citizen security rhetoric of, 108–9, 244–49; human rights activists focused on, 207–8; margins both excluded and included in, 28–29; as "night-watchman," 13; public order defined by, 6, 12, 25–26, 108; as security provider for global capital, 16–19. *See also* bureaucratic procedures; law; Morales Ayma, Evo; Movement toward Socialism; police force; security

State Department of Citizen Security (Dirección Departmental de Seguridad Ciudadana), 109

street vendors, 67, 78, 89, 117, 263n5

surveillance. *See* watchfulness

Tadea (pseud.), 146, 155

Tate, Winifred, 84–85

Taussig, Michael, 5

Tax, Sol, 261n4

taxi-trufi, 77–80, 89, 131. *See also* automobiles

telephone service, 128, 161, 168, 194

temporality. *See* race-space-time

Territorial Base Organization (Organización Territorial de Base, OTB): definition of, 55–56; dirigente's role in, 138, 139–40, 143–46; lack of unity among residents in, 146–47; local terrain and factors in, 122–24; recognition of barrios as, 138–39. *See also* Loma Pampa; marginal barrios

thieves. *See* delinquents; *rateros*

Tiempos, Los (newspaper), 229

Toledo, Francisco de, 90

trámites. See bureaucratic procedures

transnationalism: development activities and, 24–25; nation-states as security providers for corporations, 16–19; zero tolerance of crime, 21–22. *See also* human rights discourse (transnational); security

transportation: bus, 89. *See also* automobiles; *taxi-trufi*

Triple C (Citizens against Crime, or Ciudadanos Contra el Crimen), 229, 278n34

uncertain anthropology, 10, 34, 253–55

uncertainty and "not-knowing": concept of, 31; creativity in overcoming, 192–99; habitus of, 4–5; of identifying *rateros*, 127; key thread of, 242, 252; of local actors in lynching situations, 148–52, 155, 156–63, 168; lynching as reflection of, 8–9; persistence of, 5, 9–10; public security discourse as fostering, 20; vulnerability to, 253–54. *See also* insecurity; lived experiences

Unidad de Seguridad Ciudadana (Citizen Security Unit), 109

United Nations, 11, 13

United Nations Development Programme, 24

United States: action movies and police procedurals of, 197; community justice in, 275n20; community policing in, 266n50; lynching in, 267n2; responsibilization expanded and civil liberties surrendered in, 13–14, 249; Tea Party's impact in, 84–85. *See also* Global War on Terror; neoliberalism; War on Drugs

urban areas: assumptions about, 172; community justice debates and, 185–91; crime statistics of, 19–20; danger zones of, 130–35, 272n111; growth and expansion of, 90–92; majority of indigenous people now living in, 169, 176–77; migrants' hopes for, 88–89; rural areas distinguished from, 274n14; as source of

urban areas (*cont.*)
social decay, 177. *See also* community justice; insecurity; leadership, local; marginal barrios; Territorial Base Organization; Uspha Uspha; *and specific barrios*

urbanizaciones, 138

USAID (US Agency for International Development), 24–25, 58, 260n23

Uspha Uspha: climate of, 88; community justice and lynching as understood in, 187–89; governance structure of, 88–89, 138–39; land disputes in, 94, 131–32; meaning of name, 85; occupations of residents, 89; police absence in, 20–21, 100–102; research in, described, 31–32, 36–37; security-making context in, 168–73; security vs. rights in, 222–28; settlement and conditions of, 85–88; size of, 49; state's abandonment perceived in, 121–22. *See also* Access to Justice Houses; activist (engaged) anthropology; Center for Justice and Rights; Loma Pampa; methodology; phantom state

utilities. *See* infrastructure and services

Vargas, Juan, 217, 221

Vargas, Wilmer: death of, 77–78, 88, 89, 118; funeral of, 116–17; roadside memorial to, *116*; spectral state in aftermath of death, 79–82, 139

vecinos. See neighbors

Venezuela, Bolivian links to, 2, 257n4

vernacularization process. *See* human rights vernacularization

Victor (pseud.), 270n61

Vigilance Committee (Comité de Vigilancia), 138

vigilantism ("self-help" practices):

approach to, 32–33; conditions leading to, 3, 7–8, 22–23, 119; justification for, 26; murder of El Ruso and, 228–29, 278n34. *See also* citizen security; community justice; leadership, local; lynching; watchfulness

Villa Sebastián Pagador: recent improvements in, 263n3; settlement and growth of, 86

violence: citizen security perceptions and, 147–63; conditions leading to, 3, 7–8, 22–23, 119; as crime control, 8–9; domestic, 146–47, 157–58; economic form of, 207; in Gas War, 18; of human rights, 228–36; income inequalities correlated with, 20; lynching as contributing to rather than reducing, 124; reduced during CAJs' presence, 63; requirement for investigating, 101–2; social anomie linked to, 163–64. *See also* community justice; crimes and criminality; lynching; military; police force; vigilantism

Volunteer Bolivia, 66–67

War on Drugs, 207, 279n3

Washington Consensus, 16. *See also* neoliberalism

watchfulness: approach to, 32–33, 119; concept of, 122–23; function of, 132–35, 163; individualization of, 137; responsibilization linked to, 247–48

water resources, 17–18, 67–68, 136

Water War (1999), 17–18, 67, 143

Weber, Max, 11

welfare state, 13–14, 16. *See also* patronage state

Wenner-Gren Foundation, 262n6

Wolf, Eric, 38

Daniel M. Goldstein is an associate professor in the Department of Anthropology at Rutgers University.

Library of Congress Cataloging-in-Publication Data
Goldstein, Daniel M., 1965 –
Outlawed : between security and rights in a Bolivian city /
Daniel M. Goldstein.
p. cm.—(A John Hope Franklin Center book)
(The cultures and practice of violence)
Includes bibliographical references and index.
ISBN 978-0-8223-5297-6 (cloth : alk. paper)
ISBN 978-0-8223-5311-9 (pbk. : alk. paper)
1. Violence—Bolivia—Cochabamba. 2. Crime prevention—Bolivia—
Cochabamba. 3. Human rights—Bolivia—Cochabamba. I. Title.
HN280.Z9V545 2012
303.60984'23—dc23   2011053297